Cambridge studie.

Edited by WALTER ULLMANN, LITT.D, F.B.A.
Professor of Medieval History in the University of Cambridge

Third series, vol. 13

THE DIPLOMAS OF
KING ÆTHELRED 'THE UNREADY'
978–1016

CAMBRIDGE STUDIES IN
MEDIEVAL LIFE AND THOUGHT

THIRD SERIES

THE DIPLOMAS OF
KING ÆTHELRED 'THE UNREADY'
978–1016

A STUDY IN THEIR USE
AS HISTORICAL EVIDENCE

SIMON KEYNES

*Fellow of Trinity College and
Assistant Lecturer in Anglo-Saxon History
in the University of Cambridge*

CAMBRIDGE UNIVERSITY PRESS

CAMBRIDGE

LONDON   NEW YORK   NEW ROCHELLE

MELBOURNE   SYDNEY

CAMBRIDGE UNIVERSITY PRESS
Cambridge, New York, Melbourne, Madrid, Cape Town, Singapore, São Paulo

Cambridge University Press
The Edinburgh Building, Cambridge CB2 2RU, UK

Published in the United States of America by Cambridge University Press, New York

www.cambridge.org
Information on this title: www.cambridge.org/9780521227186

First published 1980
This digitally printed first paperback version 2005

A catalogue record for this publication is available from the British Library

Library of Congress Cataloguing in Publication data
Keynes, Simon.
The diplomas of King Æthelred 'the Unready' 978–1016
(Cambridge studies in medieval life and thought; 3d ser., v. 13)
Bibliography: p.
Includes indexes.
1. Great Britain – History – Ethelred II, 979–1016 – Sources.
2. England – Charters, grants, privileges.
I. Title. II. Series.
DA154.7.K49   942.01'74   79–7651

ISBN-13 978-0-521-22718-6 hardback
ISBN-10 0-521-22718-6 hardback

ISBN-13 978-0-521-02308-5 paperback
ISBN-10 0-521-02308-4 paperback

TO MY MOTHER AND FATHER

NOTE TO THE PAPERBACK REPRINT (2005)

When this book was first published, in 1980, it incorporated a pocket inside the back cover which itself contained a set of eight folded tables, representing attestations of the different categories of witnesses in the charters of King Æthelred the Unready: athelings, 993–1015; archbishops and bishops, 979–90 and 993–1016; abbots, 979–90 and 993–1016; ealdormen, 979–1016; and *ministri*, or thegns, 979–90 and 993–1016. The tables were an essential part of the book, and were published with the aid of special grants from the Frederic William Maitland Memorial Fund (University of Cambridge) and Trinity College, Cambridge.

It would have been impracticable for various reasons to include these tables in this reprint, and they have accordingly been omitted. Revised and updated versions of all of the tables are to be found in the following publication: Simon Keynes, *An Atlas of Attestations in Anglo-Saxon Charters, c, 670–1066,* I: *Tables,* ASNC Guides, Texts, and Studies 5 (Cambridge, 2002), Tables LIX–LXIV. Copies of the *Atlas of Attestations* are available from the Department of Anglo-Saxon, Norse, and Celtic, Faculty of English, 9 West Road, Cambridge CB3 9DP; further details are given on the Department's website (www.asnc.cam.ac.uk).

The book in its present form is otherwise a reprint of the original edition, without correction or revision.

CONTENTS

Contents

FIGURES

TABLES

(IN POCKET INSIDE BACK COVER)

PREFACE

It has long been customary amongst students of the Anglo-Saxon
period to regret the lack of a satisfactory edition of one of the
principal classes of source material available to them: the series of
royal diplomas recording grants of land and privileges made by
successive kings to individuals and to religious foundations, extending from the second half of the seventh century to the second half
of the eleventh, and comprising approximately one thousand texts.
John Mitchell Kemble's *Codex Diplomaticus Aevi Saxonici*, published
in six volumes between 1839 and 1848, must for the comprehensive-
ness of its coverage be rated one of the most formidable achievements of nineteenth-century scholarship, and Walter de Gray
Birch's *Cartularium Saxonicum*, published in three volumes between
1885 and 1893, was no less remarkable for the further advance it
represented in editorial method carried out on so large a scale,
though Birch was never able to realize his intention of continuing
his work beyond the reign of King Edgar. While both of these
collections have remained of inestimable value to this day, it was
only two years after the publication of Birch's third volume that
A. S. Napier and W. H. Stevenson produced an edition of a small
group of pre-Conquest documents from the Crawford collection
in the Bodleian Library, setting new standards for the editing of
diplomatic records and at the same time demonstrating to great
effect what depth of analysis and discussion the individual records
both required and could sustain; in this way their own work
provided ample justification for their oft-repeated pronouncement,
'it cannot be said that the O.E. charters have yet been edited'. The
importance of the diplomas as historical evidence has been fully
appreciated ever since Kemble first deployed them in his two-volume
study of *The Saxons in England* (1849), and they naturally lie at the
heart of the more recent contributions to the subject, notably by

Sir Frank Stenton and Professor Dorothy Whitelock; but as years pass, historians and other scholars in related disciplines, in seeking to build on work already completed, make fresh demands on the material, so that the need for a new edition of the diplomas is now more keenly and more widely felt than ever before.

The need will gradually be met as the constituent volumes of the projected edition of all Anglo-Saxon documentary records, sponsored by the British Academy, appear from the press: the first volume, Professor Campbell's *Charters of Rochester*, was published in 1973; the second, Professor Sawyer's *Charters of Burton Abbey*, in January 1979; and the next volumes promised for publication include an edition of charters from south-western houses by Dr Pierre Chaplais, and an edition of the charters of Christ Church Canterbury by Dr Nicholas Brooks. The organization of the new edition – of necessity by distributing the labour involved amongst several editors, each responsible for a particular archive or group of archives – has certain important advantages: the editors are in an excellent position to apply a full understanding of the make-up of their respective archives and of the endowment of the religious houses concerned to the establishment and criticism of the individual texts; they are well placed also to ascertain whether there are any continuous and significant diplomatic threads linking the diplomas together, and so whether the diplomas were at times drawn up under the auspices of the community; moreover, the texts themselves will be accorded uniform treatment following the high standards laid down by the Academy, and interpreted with the specialist assistance, which only a corporate venture can guarantee, of scholars competent in the various disciplines that may need to be brought into service. The organization of the new edition does, however, have certain inherent and unavoidable disadvantages: the attention of an editor may be focussed to such an extent on the documents preserved in the archive for which he is responsible that documents preserved elsewhere are not brought sufficiently to bear on the problems of editing, criticism and interpretation; and the documents of a given type, relating to estates in a particular area, and issued in the name of any one king or during any one period, will be scattered throughout the many different volumes of the series, rendering it difficult (albeit in varying degrees) to judge a text in its appropriate contexts or against its proper diplomatic background, and thus obscuring the connections which often exist between documents preserved in different archives. But however awkward the new edition may be to handle, there can be no doubt that, when it is complete, students of the Anglo-Saxon period will have at their disposal a tool of such intrinsic interest and value that important revelations about diplomatic, historical, topographical, literary and linguistic aspects of the material are bound to follow; for the time being we can only look forward to the day when we shall be able to exploit it fully ourselves.

It may seem a rash venture to produce a study of Anglo-Saxon royal diplomas at the outset of the new edition, when the texts collectively are still in the process of being securely established and properly criticized for the first time. On the other hand, it could be argued that it is precisely at such a stage that the importance of looking beyond the diplomas preserved in a single archive should be emphasized, and that one should seek to demonstrate what advantages accrue from consideration of them from a chronological point of view and, in particular, from consideration in some detail of all those issued in the name of a selected king. No attempt shall be made, however, to provide the much-needed manual of Anglo-Saxon diplomatic, not least because it would assuredly be premature to do so. Ideally, a comprehensive manual should contain each of the following elements: an account of the various forms in which diplomas have been preserved, of the compilation and composition of cartularies and of the differences between the many archives in the range of documents which they contained and in their relationship to the endowments of the religious houses concerned; a discussion of the available principles and techniques for the criticism of the texts, including an investigation of the various circumstances under which diplomas were forged or interpolated both before and after the Norman Conquest; a discussion from a palaeographical point of view of those diplomas preserved on single sheets, establishing by what criteria originals can be distinguished from contemporary or near-contemporary copies, and whether individual scribes can be identified in other contexts or associated with particular scriptoria; an examination of the nature of bookland against the background of the system of land tenure in Anglo-Saxon England,

and the place of the different types of diplomatic instrument (in Latin and the vernacular) within this system, and their relationship to one another; an account of the considerations that might be involved in the drawing up of a diploma, both from the beneficiary's and from the king's point of view, coupled with an investigation of the circumstances under which and the stages by which this was accomplished; a discussion of the development of the diploma in form and substance from its origins to its demise, in which due attention is paid to each of the constituent elements (pictorial and verbal invocations, proem, superscription, dispositive section, immunity and reservation clauses, blessing and sanction, boundary and dating clauses, witness list, and endorsement), explaining how they were brought together and estimating where possible how they reflect on the training and identity of the draftsmen; and finally, a discussion of the status and value of the diplomas from a historical point of view, as records of royal action. The work would have to proceed from familiarity with the entire corpus of Anglo-Saxon documentary records (including the vernacular writs, wills and charters, as well as the Latin leases and diplomas), for it is to be expected that situations might vary from one region to another at all times, though perhaps in differing degrees from one century to the next. Moreover, since there were so many opportunities between the seventh and eleventh centuries for the transmission of ideas and practices across the frontiers of the areas controlled by the Anglo-Saxon kings, it would also be necessary to study the characteristics of insular diplomatic practice in the context of practices obtaining amongst their continental and Celtic neighbours. The task of producing such a manual is indeed a daunting one, demanding knowledge at once so wide and deep that its essayer would not only desire but also require access to all the volumes of the new edition for guidance on whatever aspects of the material were unfamiliar to him.

In setting down some account of the diplomas of the tenth and eleventh centuries, several of these matters are touched upon directly or indirectly and in more or less detail. But I have chosen to concentrate on investigating the historical value of royal diplomas, particularly those issued in the name of King Æthelred the Unready, and so on the matters that affect their use as historical evidence. The full potential of the material can only be realized after much preparatory groundwork. It has been well said that records 'only speak when they are spoken to, and they will not talk to strangers':[1] we may on occasion ask them questions which they are not competent to answer, and there may even be subjects on which they would willingly yield information if only we knew what questions to ask, but we cannot approach the diplomas with the necessary positive attitude at all until we have developed a clear understanding of the circumstances of their preservation and production, and until we have become well acquainted with their form and know what role each of the constituent elements has to play. Only then is one in a position to appreciate the significance (or otherwise) of particular features when they arise, and thus to attempt a proper historical evaluation of the material. The problem of identifying the circumstances under which royal diplomas were produced in the tenth and eleventh centuries is so vital a part of this groundwork that it is considered here at some length. If it could be shown that the documents were invariably drawn up in ecclesiastical scriptoria, acting for themselves or on behalf of other beneficiaries, they would have to be regarded as only 'literary accounts of royal action',[2] and would reflect directly on the work of the different religious houses that produced them; such an arrangement would itself indicate that the executive role in one of the king's important activities was delegated to others, and the witness lists would seem in consequence to represent unofficial or even idealized statements of those present at meetings of the king and his *witan*.[3] If, on the other hand, it could be shown that most of the diplomas emanated from a central writing office acting for different beneficiaries on the occasion of the *witenagemot* which ratified the transactions, they would truly constitute royal acts and would reflect directly on the operation of royal government. The problem is approached in the first instance by the examination of the diplomas issued in the names of the Anglo-Saxon kings from Æthelstan to Edgar, since an understanding of the arrangements that existed for the production of diplomas during Æthelred's reign must turn to a considerable extent on knowledge of the arrangements that existed in the period leading

---

[1] Cheney, *Medieval Texts*, p. 8.

[2] Barlow, *Edward the Confessor*, p. xxv; see also *idem*, *English Church*, p. 127 n. 2.

[3] *Ibid.* p. 46 n. 2 and p. 154 (where the remarks are applied specifically to the diplomas of Edward the Confessor).

up to his accession; however, the historical implications and applications of the proposed explanation of the problem are explored only for the reign of Æthelred himself.

The principal literary sources available for the reign of King Æthelred, notably the *Anglo-Saxon Chronicle* and Archbishop Wulfstan's *Sermo ad Anglos*, arose from the conditions prevailing in the closing years of the reign and are accordingly preoccupied with the sorry tale of treachery and military disaster that led to the Danish conquest of the Anglo-Saxon kingdom; yet it is these sources that have done most, from the twelfth century onwards, to shape the prejudices of some historians and to inform the judgement of others concerning the conduct of affairs during the reign. The present study of the royal diplomas issued in the name of King Æthelred is intended to make some progress towards a reassessment of the period, primarily by suggesting what factors should be considered in any balanced survey, besides the alleged incompetence of the king and the ineptitude of his military advisers. The texts of over one hundred diplomas have been preserved, though not more than eleven of them in a form that could be claimed as original; a few of the remainder survive on single sheets of a slightly later date than that given in the document itself, but most only as copies entered in later medieval monastic cartularies and charter rolls, or in transcripts made by antiquaries working in the aftermath of the Reformation. They have been exploited individually in the past to supplement the literary sources. Several of them incorporate a discursive section in which the recent history of the estate concerned or the general circumstances of the transaction are described, and in such contexts information is sometimes found which illuminates events mentioned in independent records. The fact that a particular person was the recipient of an estate in a given area at a given time may itself be of historical significance, though one could never be sure that this significance would rest unchanged in the context of other transactions of which no record has survived, or indeed that the beneficiary had not himself solicited and financed the 'grant'. However, since the literary sources remain the basis of a connected account of the reign, the use of diplomas in these ways has not greatly affected its overall interpretation. The value of the diplomas is raised to an altogether different level when they are examined collectively. In the first place, it will be seen that they have an important contribution to make to the administrative and institutional history of the reign, and thus serve to complement the valuable evidence for these areas of royal activity derived from, for example, Æthelred's legislation and coinage. In the second place, the witness lists attached to the diplomas can be shown to provide reliable information on attendance at meetings of the king's council, enabling one to identify and then to characterize those men who were frequently in the king's presence and who may therefore have exercised the strongest influence over him. As it turns out, they afford a unique opportunity to watch how the composition of the council was modified from year to year, and in this way to perceive political developments within the kingdom which are barely hinted at in the literary sources. These developments serve as the basis of the framework for King Æthelred's reign provided in the last chapter, and itself intended to restore a sense of perspective to our understanding of a long and complex period by suggesting how the influence of the king's advisers affected his policies at different stages of his career. This aspect of Æthelred's reign might be considered of especial interest, since he has entered the historical tradition as a king who was grievously misled by his ill-chosen councillors.

This book is essentially a modified version of my Ph.D. thesis, which was itself distilled from my Fellowship dissertation for Trinity College, and I should like therefore to thank those who guided my thoughts and criticized my work during five years of research and revision. Above all, my supervisor, Professor Dorothy Whitelock, gave very generously both of her time and of her advice in reading successive drafts and in discussing them with me; with her prodigious knowledge of the period she has constantly been a source of helpful information and criticism, and I have derived particular advantage from her experience and judgement in the handling of Anglo-Saxon royal diplomas. My colleagues in the Department of Anglo-Saxon, Norse and Celtic, especially Mr Peter Kitson of Emmanuel College (now of Birmingham University) and Dr David Dumville of Girton College, have been patient listeners, acute critics and helpful advisers, as well as good friends, and long may they remain so. I am most grateful also to Dr Nicholas Brooks, Dr Pierre Chaplais, Dr Cyril Hart, Mr Eric John, Professor Peter Sawyer and Dr

Pauline Stafford for their comments on my work as it was presented in my Ph.D. thesis, and no less for the benefit I have derived by perusal of their own writings, whether on diplomas in general or on Æthelred in particular. It will be as obvious to any reader as it is inevitable in Anglo-Saxon studies that there are areas where our respective interpretations of the evidence may differ, and in expressing my obligations to these scholars I must therefore hasten to add that I alone should be held responsible for the statements here given and the opinions here expressed. For eight years now Trinity College has sheltered me in its buildings, and sustained me with both the food of its tables and the friendship of its members, so I have accumulated a debt to it which I cannot acknowledge adequately here. But I should like to record my particular gratitude to Professor Walter Ullmann for his support within the college and for his encouragement as editor of the series in which this book appears; I should like also to record my gratitude to the staff of the College Library for their unfailing kindness and help, and especially to Miss Rosemary Graham not only for typing substantial amounts of my work with exemplary care and skill, but also for showing such interest in it over a long period.

Having passed five years with Æthelred the Unready never far from mind, I naturally wondered from time to time whether he deserved the censure he received from posterity for manifold weaknesses of his character; but far from experiencing a deepening awareness of his personal qualities as work progressed, I experienced only a deepening frustration that one has hardly the faintest idea of what he was really like. In thanking others for their guidance in connection with my research I feel that it would nevertheless be invidious not to express my indebtedness to the unknown quantity of Æthelred himself, at least for presenting such an interesting and rewarding historical problem; and it was certainly with particular satisfaction that I was able to proceed to the degree which was the object of my research on 18 March 1978, being – to the day – the one thousandth anniversary of his accession.

Trinity College   S.D.K.
Cambridge
4 May 1979

NOTE ON SYSTEM OF REFERENCE

Royal diplomas (and the miscellaneous vernacular documents) are cited by their number in P. H. Sawyer, *Anglo-Saxon Charters. An Annotated List and Bibliography* (London, 1968), abbreviated as S; the separate entries in this catalogue indicate in which manuscript or manuscripts the records have been preserved and supply references to such facsimiles, printed texts, translations and discussions as are available. Where there is a choice, quotations follow the printed text which has been judged to represent the original most faithfully, though it must be admitted that these texts vary considerably in their quality, since the different editors adopted different practices and achieved different standards of accuracy in transcription, and were more or less concerned to collate their main manuscript with any others known to them. The many discrepancies observed between text and manuscript generally involve relatively minor details of orthography, punctuation and capitalization, but in direct quotations the readings of the manuscript are naturally preferred if the discrepancies involve diplomatic and historical matters of particular moment.

The *Anglo-Saxon Chronicle*, abbreviated as *ASC* in footnotes, is cited by manuscript (following the conventional *sigla*) and annal number. Where it is deemed advisable to record the exact wording of the original, it is quoted from whichever edition provides the best text of the manuscript in question; where it seems adequate for the purposes of the argument to provide a translation only, it is quoted from *The Anglo-Saxon Chronicle. A Revised Translation*, ed. Dorothy Whitelock, David C. Douglas and Susie I. Tucker (London, 1961). Other primary sources are similarly cited in text or translation as appropriate, from the most readily accessible editions (if adequate). In references to manuscripts, B.L. = London, British Library.

Books and articles are cited on first and subsequent occasions by abbreviated titles; full titles and references are supplied on pp. 274–84.

Chapter 1

THE PRESERVATION AND CRITICISM OF ANGLO-SAXON ROYAL DIPLOMAS

THE PRESERVATION OF ROYAL DIPLOMAS

At and for some time after the time of its production an Anglo-Saxon royal diploma was valued as evidence of title to a particular estate, for its owner, whether or not the person named as the beneficiary, had a claim to the estate simply by virtue of possessing the document. But for the diploma to have had any chance of survival in the long term, it first had to find its way into the archives of a religious community, and this normally meant that the estate to which it referred had to come into the community's possession. By the close of the Anglo-Saxon period, an archive might contain a series of royal diplomas in favour of laymen, comprising the title-deeds transferred when the estates concerned were acquired by the community, whether from the king, from the beneficiary of the diploma or from one of his heirs. In addition it might contain a number of royal diplomas directly in favour of the community itself, and perhaps some that had been entrusted to the community by laymen for safe-keeping in times of disturbance and that for one reason or another had never been recovered. Besides the diplomas, a considerable number of miscellaneous documents may have entered the archive in connection with the process of the community's endowment: for example, records of agreements, wills and royal writs, and perhaps a series of documents recording leases of the community's property to local landowners. During the course of the Middle Ages the value of the diplomas as title-deeds diminished, as their condition deteriorated, as they were made redundant by later forms of documentary evidence, and as the often bizarre language in which they were cast made them less well suited to the immediate needs of the community. Some diplomas were preserved because they came to be venerated as ancient muniments and were treated accordingly; others, especially those relating to lands never or no longer held by the community, were allowed to perish. At the time of the Dissolution, when the endowments of the suppressed monasteries were broken up, the royal commissioners were instructed to secure the documents pertaining to the lands and to preserve them carefully. Though one imagines that many documents were in fact destroyed or lost in the process, some did pass to the Keeper of Records of the Court of Augmentations, and when the monastic estates were redistributed amongst the king's subjects the appropriate documents were often transferred to the new owners. In this way, some Anglo-Saxon diplomas returned to private hands; certainly very few remained amongst the Exchequer records, now in the Public Record Office. While hundreds of manuscripts dispersed from monastic libraries at the same time were gathered and preserved by acquisitive antiquaries, it appears that royal diplomas were initially less eagerly sought after. Many must have perished through negligence or have been wilfully destroyed,[1] and they were already rare in the first half of the seventeenth century when the major collections were formed.[2] Those that had returned to secular possession would always have been subject to the vicissitudes of a private life and thus vulnerable to loss and destruction. The consequence is that most Anglo-Saxon archives are now represented by mere handfuls of original documents, if indeed any at all have survived in their contemporary form;[3] only from Christ Church Canterbury do they survive in a quantity that may do justice to the former contents of the archive.

We are therefore largely dependent upon the copies of purportedly pre-Conquest documents entered in those monastic

---

[1] It is salutary to read John Aubrey's description (Britton, *Aubrey*, pp. 78–9) of the various uses to which the manuscripts of Malmesbury Abbey were put: in his grandfather's time 'the manuscripts flew about like butterflies', and in his own time they were used for covering books, wrapping up gloves, scouring fire-arms and stopping the bung-holes in barrels of ale. No wonder that he remarks: 'Before the late warres a world of rare manuscripts perished hereabouts.'

[2] Sir Henry Spelman claimed that in his day Anglo-Saxon charters were so rare, 'as though I have seen diverse, yet could I never obtein one Originall' (Gibson, *Reliquiæ*, p. 236).

[3] This is true not only of monastic archives, but also of the archives of episcopal churches: for though they may have survived the sixteenth century, they were often seriously depleted in the following centuries. Thus John Chase describes the devastation of the archives at the Old Minster Winchester when soldiers of Cromwell's army broke into the Chapter House in 1646: '. . . divers of the Writings and charters burnt, divers throwen into the River, divers large parchments being made kytes withall to flie in the aire . . .' (Stephens and Madge, *Documents*, p. 57).

cartularies which themselves survived the disturbances of the sixteenth century. The motives and interests of the compilers of these
cartularies varied as much as the date of their compilations, and
determined the criteria of selection that were applied to the original
documents available to them. Most cartularists were primarily
concerned to supply the documentary evidence of title for the
landed property of their community, whether by incorporating all
the pre-Conquest documents in the archives (and in so doing
covering some estates that had since been alienated or lost), by
selecting only those documents that related to the endowment as it
stood at the end of the Anglo-Saxon period, or by selecting only
those that related to the endowment as it stood at the time of
compilation. Their collections might be organized chronologically,
to represent the process of the accumulation of estates during the
reigns of successive kings, or geographically, by grouping together
all documents that concerned the same estate without regard to their
purported date. The cartularists might choose to restrict themselves
to royal diplomas directly in favour of the community, or they
might incorporate all documents (miscellaneous vernacular charters
as well as royal diplomas) which explicitly concerned the community
and its endowment, with or without the diplomas for laymen
relating to estates that had become part of the endowment. A few
cartularists admitted a larger range of documents into their collections, including several that seem not to bear any relation to the
endowment, though still they might restrict themselves to royal
diplomas.

Thus the extant cartularies display such diversity of character
that some pre-Conquest archives are now much better represented
than others. One has to emphasize, therefore, that the chances of
survival for royal diplomas were far from being equal across the
country: the differing criteria of selection applied by the compilers
of the various cartularies have served to distort the distribution of
the surviving evidence, and since each archive naturally tends to
contain diplomas for the estates in the vicinity of the religious house
where they were preserved, the distortion means that certain areas
are better covered by diplomas than others. This accident obviously
affects the use that can be made of the diplomas for historical
purposes. Moreover, the distortion extends to the treatment accorded

by the cartularists to the individual diplomas. Every element of a diploma, including the endorsement, form of pictorial invocation and witness list, as well as the text itself, is of some potential significance, and yet unfortunately different cartularists adopted different standards in the reproduction of these features: very few bothered to record the endorsement or pictorial invocation, several abbreviated the witness lists, and some even took substantial liberties with the texts. Indeed, the distinctive stamp of a given copyist can create the impression that a group of diplomas preserved in one cartulary can be distinguished in form from a group preserved in another, though in fact the originals behind both groups may have been of much the same general appearance. It is essential, therefore, that each cartulary should be the subject of a separate study, both to judge how representative it might be of the archive concerned and to ascertain how the compiler's standards of transcription affected his treatment of the documents.

THE CRITICISM OF ROYAL DIPLOMAS

It has been truly said that 'no religious house nor any other religious institution turned without good reason to the forgery of legal instruments',[4] and indeed the motives behind the concoction of royal diplomas in particular are often not hard to find. Some spurious diplomas were evidently intended to represent a stage in the purported history of an estate that would not otherwise have been covered by documentary evidence; others served to assert that a religious house was entitled to certain privileges, whether, for example, freedom from interference by the bishop of the diocese, the right to elect an abbot from amongst the community, or exemption from the burdens attendant on the tenure of land. A proportion of such forgeries would obviously have been produced in contentious circumstances, specifically for use in litigation; but a considerable number would perhaps have been no more than harmless flights of fancy, the products of wishful thinking on the part of monks eager to pander to the self-esteem of their communities, and not directed against any other parties. Nevertheless, it would be mistaken to imply that the *absence* of a known motive for

[4] Stenton, *Latin Charters*, p. 19.

forgery can always be construed as a point in favour of the authenticity of a diploma. There must be some instances of diplomas manufactured for use in disputes of which no record has survived. And since a substantial proportion of the estates that formed part of a community's endowment would have been covered in its archives only by diplomas in favour of laymen, it might under some circumstances have been to the community's advantage to manufacture more direct and explicit evidence of title to the land, especially after the Conquest, when the mere possession of any diploma for an estate might not have guaranteed the security of tenure that it had offered previously when the diploma was a current form. Thus, for example, the enquiries of the Domesday commissioners in 1086 may have encouraged some communities to ensure that their property was adequately protected by title-deeds directly in their own favour, or at least in favour of the founder or some other known benefactor. Again, the compilation of a cartulary to represent the endowment of a community may have involved the concoction of diplomas for estates that were either not covered at all in the archives, or that were covered only by documents felt by the compiler to be inadequate for his particular purposes. In such cases there might be no apparent motive for forgery, for the diplomas only claimed what was anyway the rightful property of the community.

The quality of the forgeries varied immensely, whether they were produced before or after the Conquest, whether they were intended for use in litigation or only to substantiate, augment and improve a community's history. Some can be exposed by the most elementary (and yet conclusive) of historical, topographical and diplomatic tests: the witness list might contain an impossible selection of names, incompatible within itself and with the purported date; the details of the transaction might contradict more reliable independent information on the history of the estate; or the diploma might be cast in formulae that can be shown to be anachronistic when compared with the usages of contemporary texts. Some diplomas parade themselves as forgeries by the concession of excessive privileges which the Anglo-Saxon kings would not have countenanced; others have to be judged by more subtle standards, since the forged element might be confined to the interpolation of a clause into an otherwise authentic text. But one should never underestimate the ability of a member of a religious community to fabricate a diploma that satisfies all the available tests of authenticity. A diploma is essentially a combination of various discrete elements, and it would not have been difficult to concoct one by borrowing these elements, suitably adapted, from genuine texts available in the community's archives: therefore the presence of demonstrably pre-Conquest formulae, a set of bounds that clearly derives from an Anglo-Saxon original, and an acceptable dating clause with witness list, does not automatically weigh in favour of a text's authenticity. If the document survives on a single sheet, it may be possible to establish palaeographically whether it is contemporary with the purported date or an apograph, and if the latter one could infer that it was produced in an ecclesiastical scriptorium and perhaps for use in litigation. If, on the other hand, the document survives only in a cartulary copy, it would now be indistinguishable from the genuine texts preserved with it.

The examination of a diploma in the context of the archive or cartulary in which it was preserved furnishes an invaluable approach towards its criticism where the other approaches fail. It is always necessary, and sometimes useful, to ask why a particular diploma was preserved, and to discover what role, if any, it had to play in relation to the endowment of the religious house concerned: in some instances a positive argument for or against the authenticity of a text can be adduced simply by this means. The approach depends on some general propositions. Many cartularies were apparently intended to cover the endowment of a house as it stood at the end of the Anglo-Saxon period, and as it was recorded in *Domesday Book*;[5] thus they show how, when and from whom the component estates were held to have been acquired. Compiled in this way as collections, the cartularies have to be criticized as collections. It may be possible to judge the credibility of a given cartulary in terms of the overall impression of the process of endowment which the

---

[5] Several cartularies incorporate the relevant extracts from *Domesday Book* (or from surveys that went into its making) in connection with the transcriptions of Anglo-Saxon documents: e.g. B.L. Cotton Claudius C ix (Abingdon), B.L. Loans 30 (Burton), Cambridge, Corpus Christi College MS iii (Bath), B.L. Lansdowne 417 (Malmesbury), the *Textus Roffensis* (Rochester), B.L. Lansdowne 442 (Romsey), B.L. Add. 46487 (Sherborne) and B.L. Cotton Tiberius A xiii (Worcester). In the case of B.L. Cotton Vespasian B xxiv (Evesham), the Domesday record of the endowment seems actually to have determined the arrangement and to some extent the contents of the documents.

collection affords. For it is arguable that the general circumstances of endowment of religious houses would not vary widely from place to place, given at least some tolerance for special local conditions. Certain houses would naturally receive especially lavish gifts at certain times, and the foundations which had enjoyed close historical connections with the Anglo-Saxon monarchy might well receive a greater share of direct royal benefactions over a longer period than was accorded to the foundations with more restricted horizons. And there would be communities with particularly able or energetic leaders who could manage the resources of the community and secure gifts from the king and from local landowners with greater success than their predecessors or successors. But overall the various communities would accumulate their endowments in broadly similar circumstances and against a common historical background.

One should emphasize in the first instance that the process of endowment could never be a long and uninterrupted tale of acquisition and subsequent retention of estates, given the known vicissitudes to which lands of monastic foundations and episcopal sees were subjected throughout the Anglo-Saxon period, until the situation as recorded in *Domesday Book* was achieved. Indeed, we should generally expect the late eleventh-century endowment of a religious house to have been accumulated in the 150 years before the Conquest, with slight additions perhaps made during the reign of William I. The general decline of organized monastic life during the ninth century would seem to disqualify the claims of some monastic foundations to hold substantial parts of their endowment by pre-Alfredian title-deeds, though of course there are instances of estates once held by an abbey which were restored during the tenth and eleventh centuries; even the endowments of some of the episcopal sees which had enjoyed a continuous existence throughout the period were more the creation of the reform and post-reform years than a survival from earlier centuries. Owing to the distinctive nature of the histories of the houses, we are particularly well informed about the endowing of Ely and Ramsey. As one might expect, it emerges that the years immediately following the re-foundation saw the greatest amount of activity, with significant contributions by the founders themselves (acting with royal support),

7

by the early leaders of the communities, and by particular lay patrons. Thereafter, much depended on the generosity of local landowners, whose bequests continued spasmodically throughout the late tenth and first half of the eleventh centuries; a lesser proportion of the endowment was owed to contributions made directly by the successive kings.[6] The century before the Conquest may also have seen some rationalization of the early endowment, as outlying estates were exchanged for more conveniently-placed ones. Nevertheless, there were several factors that operated after the heyday of the reform movement to interrupt the continuity of endowment. The resentment harboured by some laymen towards the accretion of landed wealth by ecclesiastical foundations during the tenth century received active expression as soon as King Edgar died, and apparently persisted well into the reign of King Æthelred. It is known that an Ealdorman Ælfric appropriated land from Glastonbury in the late tenth or early eleventh century, and it is clear that during the 980s King Æthelred himself, under the influence of a group of his thegns, appropriated a considerable amount of ecclesiastical property and redistributed it to members of this group.[7] Some at least of the land appropriated by the king was restored to the churches and monasteries in the 990s, but other estates may never have been recovered. The Danish raids of the late tenth and early eleventh centuries would again have had a disruptive effect on ecclesiastical endowments, and we know, for example, that land was sometimes sold in order to raise money to buy off the attackers.

Returning – against this background – to the individual cartularies, one can ask three questions. First, what proportion of the estates known from *Domesday Book* to have belonged to the religious house concerned was credited directly to the generosity of kings? Secondly, what proportion was credited to the generosity of local landowners (or represented only by diplomas in favour of laymen)? And thirdly, to what period (if to any) was the acquisition of the property held at the end of the Anglo-Saxon period assigned? The answers to these questions vary far more from cartulary to cartulary

---

[6] For detailed accounts of the endowing of Ely and Ramsey, see Miller, *Abbey of Ely*, pp. 16–25, and Raftis, *Estates of Ramsey*, pp. 6–19. These may be compared with accounts of the endowing of other East Anglian monasteries in Raban, *Estates of Thorney and Crowland*, pp. 8–20, and King, *Peterborough Abbey*, pp. 6–11.

[7] See further below, pp. 176–86.

than one would expect, were one to imagine that each cartulary accurately reflects the process of endowment, and in this variation lies the essence of the archival approach towards the criticism of diplomas. Some collections emerge in a favourable light. The Wilton cartulary, for example, provides a reliable series of tenth-century royal diplomas, most of which are in favour of laymen and yet refer to land held by the community in 1066; only a small proportion of its property was credited to direct royal benefactions. A comparable predominance of tenth-century diplomas for laymen can be observed amongst the documents in the lost *Liber Terrarum* from Glastonbury.[8] The collections from some lesser houses, such as Thorney, Horton and Abbotsbury,[9] similarly show that many estates were represented only by diplomas for laymen, often issued several generations before the foundation of the house in question. Of course, the dependence on indirect title-deeds means that one now has little idea of the chronology of the endowment of these houses, but one may assume that the diplomas were transferred to the respective communities during the tenth and eleventh centuries, largely in connection with bequests by local landowners. Certain cartularies, however, seem to convey an improbable impression of the process of endowment, and their overall authority seems thus to be suspect. Particularly blatant examples are the Malmesbury and Sherborne cartularies. There are about thirty purportedly pre-Conquest documents in the former (Oxford, Bodleian Library, Wood empt. 5), and all but one of them either directly concern Malmesbury itself or are privileges to the Church in general.[10] Over half are assigned to the pre-Alfredian period; of these, and of the diplomas for the abbey assigned to the later tenth and eleventh centuries, very few can be accepted (as they stand) as authentic instruments. Yet together the diplomas account for the greater part of the Domesday endowment. Thus we are invited to believe that

---

[8] The *Liber Terrarum* has generally been regarded as a late tenth-century compilation (Robinson, *Essays*, pp. 29 and 45; Finberg, *Lucerna*, p. 97), but in 'Studies' I, 164–86, I argue that it was probably compiled in the late eleventh or early twelfth century.

[9] For the Thorney charters see Hart, *Charters of Eastern England*, pp. 146–209; the Horton collection is incorporated into the Sherborne cartulary (B.L. Add. 46487); the Abbotsbury cartulary disappeared during the Civil War, but its contents can be partially reconstructed from references to it made by antiquaries working in the first half of the seventeenth century (Keynes, 'Studies' I, 57–68).

[10] The exception is S 862, on which see below, pp. 94–5.

Malmesbury not only received almost all of its land directly from kings, but had also retained quite a large amount of it acquired between the seventh and ninth centuries. The Sherborne cartulary (B.L. Add. 46487) is no less suspicious, for analogous reasons. The contents of the Bath cartulary (Cambridge, Corpus Christi College MS 111) might be counted acceptable from the chronological point of view, since most of the documents belong to the tenth century, but there seem to be rather too many royal diplomas directly in favour of the abbey, accounting for too great a proportion of the Domesday endowment. Even the high reputation of the Rochester cartulary (the *Textus Roffensis*) must be tarnished, when one appreciates how many estates were allegedly held by virtue of eighth- and ninth-century diplomas directly in favour of that church, and especially when one remembers that the property of Rochester was the subject of much devastation and litigation in the later tenth century.[11]

The two Abingdon chronicle–cartularies (B.L. Cotton Claudius C ix and Cotton Claudius B vi[12]) respond particularly well to archival criticism. A striking feature of the documents preserved from the Abingdon archives, regardless of the question of their authenticity, is that the vast majority date from the tenth and eleventh centuries, an encouraging sign that in spite of the antiquity of the house the monks did not pretend to hold many estates by virtue of correspondingly ancient title-deeds. By comparing the contents of the two collections with each other and with the abbey's endowment as recorded in *Domesday Book*, it is possible to distinguish three series amongst the documents. The first series comprises those documents contained in both collections, amounting to seventy-one texts, all of which relate to estates that were either claimed by the abbey or are known to have formed part of its endowment at the time of the Conquest. The series includes twenty-one diplomas in

---

[11] See below, pp. 178–80.

[12] The collection in Claudius C ix seems originally to have been compiled in the 1130s, though the manuscript itself was probably written in the 1160s. The collection in Claudius B vi is a reworking and expansion of C ix undertaken in the late twelfth or thirteenth century. While C ix may have greater authority as a historical narrative (Stenton, *Early History of Abingdon*, p. 4), it is important to emphasize that B vi is the better cartulary: its compiler was not dependent on C ix in this respect, returning to the documents themselves and giving full transcriptions of the witness lists (abbreviated in C ix).

favour of individuals,[13] which are largely of the mid-tenth century and the great majority of which appear to be authentic title-deeds transferred to the abbey when it acquired or was given the estates in question. The remaining documents in the first series explicitly concern Abingdon, and leaving aside six which illustrate the traditions of the abbey's early history and which are all spurious,[14] they include thirty-seven diplomas ranging in date from 930 to 1054.[15] Many of these purport to be the title-deeds for estates known to have belonged to the abbey at one time, but it is interesting that there is almost no overlap in this respect between them and the diplomas for laymen in the same series. On close inspection it emerges that in terms of their constituent formulae the diplomas for Abingdon are extensively interrelated,[16] and one can hardly doubt that the great majority were drawn up at the abbey. However, there are strong grounds for suspecting that many were produced there not in the years given by the diplomas themselves but rather were concocted subsequently on the basis of a few authentic diplomas in the archives,[17] presumably to serve as direct evidence

---

[13] S 335, 355, 460, 482, 558, 587, 590, 594, 611, 614, 617–18, 622, 639, 665, 713, 761, 769, 901, 927 and 1201.

[14] S 93, 183, 241, 278, 302 and 1179. S 166, 239, 252 and 1603, preserved only in C ix, may be associated with this group.

[15] S 404, 408–10, 567, 583, 605, 607, 658, 663, 673, 682, 688–90, 700, 701, 708, 724, 732–4, 756–60, 829, 876, 896, 918, 937, 964, 993, 1020, 1023 and 1025. S 843 (in B vi, and probably on the leaf now missing from C ix) and Cnut's diplomas for Abingdon relating to Myton, viz. S 967 (in B vi only) and 973 (in C ix only), should be included in this series. The remaining documents in the first series are miscellaneous in character: S 1065–6, 1208, 1216, 1292, 1404 and 1488.

[16] S 408, 410, 682, 732–4, 829, 1020 and 1023 are, *mutatis mutandis*, in identical terms throughout, and, of them, S 732–4 (dated 965) have intimately related witness lists; some of the formulae that characterize these texts occur also in S 607, 689, 708, 967, 993 and 1025 (the last two being almost identical); the proem common to S 708, 993 and 1025 is closely related to that in S 701, the second sanction in S 967 occurs also in S 964, and S 993 and 1025 share various features with S 918. Again, S 409 (with a witness list very similar to that in S 410) and S 757–60 are, *mutatis mutandis*, in identical terms throughout (compare S 896, and see also S 1014, from Peterborough); the sanction common to these texts occurs also in S 688, 690, 700, 701, 708 and 967, with a variant in S 567. Further, there are extensive parallels between S 658, 673 and 876; the sanction common to these texts occurs also in S 756 (dated 958 in C ix, but 968 in B vi, with some alterations to the witness list).

[17] Some of the formulae used in S 409 and 757–60 may have been derived from S 896; a diploma whose witness list was drawn from the same memorandum as that used in S 737 and 738 (dated 966) probably served as the model for the lists in S 757–60 (and 769) and, slightly abbreviated and altered, for the lists in S 756 (and 761), all of which are dated 968; S 876 was probably the model for S 658 and 673 (and 756); S 688 was probably derived

of the abbey's interest in the estates. The second series of Abingdon documents comprises thirty-eight diplomas which occur only in Claudius B vi, but which like those in the first series refer to estates in which Abingdon is known to have had an interest: nearly all of them belong to the period between 940 and 995 and are in favour of laymen.[18] In most cases there are diplomas for the same estates in the first series (normally later in date and often directly in favour of the abbey), which were apparently regarded by the more selective compiler of Claudius C ix as adequate for his purposes. The third series of Abingdon documents comprises thirty-one diplomas preserved only in Claudius B vi, all in favour of individuals and relating to estates with no known connection with the abbey:[19] many of the estates lie in Berkshire and Oxfordshire (though several of these are detached from the cluster around Abingdon itself), but there are also diplomas for land in Gloucestershire, Wiltshire, Surrey, Sussex, Buckinghamshire and Leicestershire. They range in date from the ninth century to the reign of Edward the Confessor, with an emphasis on the central decades of the tenth century. A few of the diplomas may relate to estates that had in fact once been associated with the abbey, and that in the course of time had been appropriated, alienated or exchanged for ones better suited to the needs of the community (though it would not be easy to explain why in the last two cases the diplomas had remained at Abingdon). An alternative explanation for their presence in the archives is that they had been deposited there for safe-keeping by laymen who had perhaps left home for service in the army or whose homes were threatened by Viking invaders, and who had not subsequently been able to resume possession of them.[20] The fact that these diplomas

in its entirety from S 690, which may also have served as the model for the witness list in S 689.

[18] S 225, 268–9, 369, 396, 411, 413, 471, 480, 491, 494, 529, 539, 542, 552, 561, 577, 581, 588, 591, 597, 603, 650, 651, 654, 657, 687, 705, 778, 828, 851, 855, 858, 886, 897, 934, 1022 and 1604. Of these, the spurious S 897 is the only diploma directly in favour of Abingdon: it may have been omitted accidentally from C ix, or it may not have been concocted until after C ix was compiled.

[19] S 202, 448, 461, 496, 500, 525, 559–60, 564, 578, 620–1, 624, 634, 678, 691, 698, 714, 722, 725, 737, 750, 833, 839, 852, 883, 887, 902, 915, 999 and 1271.

[20] The only explicit evidence for the use of ecclesiastical archives as repositories by local landowners comes from the later Middle Ages (see Stenton, *Early History of Abingdon*, p. 43, and Dodwell, *Charters of Norwich*, pp. xi–xii), but one might recall that King Eadred entrusted many title-deeds to Abbot Dunstan at Glastonbury 'to be faithfully kept in the security of his monastery' (see Stubbs, *Memorials*, p. 29). Since it was possession of

in the Abingdon archives bear no relation to the abbey's endowment constitutes presumptive evidence for their authenticity.[21]

An archival approach to the criticism of diplomas can thus help to establish a case for or against the authenticity of certain texts, individually and collectively, sometimes reassuring us that a diploma which satisfies the other available tests is indeed genuine and sometimes exposing apparently genuine texts as fabrications. But it remains to emphasize that the criticism of diplomas is patently not a scientific discipline whose principles can be expressed as a series of canons and whose application leads to firm results. Each diploma presents individual problems that require a particular variety of approaches, though generally much has to be left to delicate and intuitive judgements for which the only qualification is thorough familiarity with all aspects of the extant corpus.[22]

the diploma that guaranteed title to the estate, a landowner's interests would be best served if in more peaceful times he reclaimed his diplomas; moreover, ecclesiastical archives were not entirely secure (see S 1258 and 1457).

[21] Besides the compiler of B vi, the only cartularists prepared to admit a number of apparently 'unrelated' diplomas into their collections were the compilers of National Library of Wales, Peniarth 390, and B.L. Add. 15350, from Burton and the Old Minster Winchester respectively; there are, however, isolated examples of such diplomas preserved from other archives.

[22] The generalizations made in the foregoing pages are based upon the results of a survey of twelve archives (Abbotsbury, Abingdon, Burton, Christ Church Canterbury, Evesham, Glastonbury, Rochester, St Albans, Sherborne, Wilton, New Minster Winchester and Old Minster Winchester), presented in more detail in Keynes, 'Studies' I, 57–260.

Chapter 2

THE PRODUCTION OF ANGLO-SAXON ROYAL DIPLOMAS BEFORE THE REIGN OF KING ÆTHELRED

THE CASE FOR A ROYAL CHANCERY

In its current form, the debate on the arrangements that existed for the production of Anglo-Saxon royal diplomas in the tenth and eleventh centuries was initiated in 1896 by W. H. Stevenson, writing in response to Giry's assertions in the *Manuel de diplomatique* that the Anglo-Saxon kings 'n'avaient pas, semble-t-il, de chancellerie organisée . . . et . . . les documents de cette période n'ont pas servi de modèles à ceux de l'époque suivante'.[1] Stevenson demonstrated quite conclusively that Giry's second assertion was untrue, by assembling a considerable amount of evidence which pointed to the use of pre-Conquest diplomatic forms in the Anglo-Norman chancery, and he interpreted this evidence in terms of the continued employment of members of the 'Old-English royal *scriptorium*' by the Norman chancellors. He did not, however, attempt to establish the existence of this royal scriptorium by the presentation of any detailed evidence; he was content to assert that 'it is only by the supposition of the existence of a trained and organised body of royal clerks corresponding to the chancery of the continent that we can account for the highly technical way in which an Old-English royal charter is drawn up'.[2] In 1898 Stevenson delivered a series of lectures entitled 'The Anglo-Saxon Chancery' to a small audience in Cambridge,[3] but again he assumed the existence of a royal

---

[1] Giry, *Manuel*, p. 795. For the earlier history of the debate, see Drögereit, 'Königskanzlei', pp. 335–41.

[2] Stevenson, 'An Old English Charter', p. 731. The argument also depended on the belief, expressed *ibid.* pp. 733–5, that the chancery of pre-Conquest Normandy was not so highly developed that it could have re-established itself in England. Modern authorities deny the existence of an organized chancery in pre-Conquest Normandy: e.g. Douglas, *William the Conqueror*, pp. 146–8, and Le Patourel, *Norman Empire*, pp. 243–5.

[3] See Fifoot, *Letters of Maitland*, p. 194. The lectures were never published, but the manuscript of them is preserved in the library of St John's College, Oxford.

scriptorium without attempting to justify his position except in the most general terms. He conceived the allegation that the Anglo-Saxons did not possess a chancery as an unwarranted slight on their reputation, and as a further manifestation of the view that 'almost everything that we call civilization was introduced into this country by the Normans'. Accordingly, his argument is virtually confined to an effective demonstration that Anglo-Saxon culture was of a sufficiently high quality to invalidate the assumption that a chancery could not have existed simply because the Anglo-Saxons were not sophisticated enough to have developed one.[4]

In adopting his position, Stevenson dismissed as anachronistic the various references to the office of chancellor in purportedly Anglo-Saxon contexts, maintaining that while the Anglo-Saxon kings had the organization which corresponded to a chancery they did not designate it as such and did not accord to its officials titles that expressed their specialized function.[5] H. W. C. Davis, on the other hand, gave more credence to these references, and in endorsing Stevenson's general conclusions revived an older view that the office of chancellor was known at least from the reign of Edward the Confessor.[6] Though this refinement has remained controversial,[7] Stevenson's position gained its needed weight by the accumulation of more tangible evidence from examination of the extant original diplomas of the tenth century, and in particular from the observation that groups of them were written by single scribes though for different beneficiaries. The credit for drawing attention to this fact seems to belong to Stevenson himself. Some time before 1916 he wrote an important letter to a German scholar:

It is quite clear that after the union of the Kingdom under Aethelstan the royal chancery (if we may use the term) was in possession of fixed formulas and methods of drawing up charters. This favours the view that the actual scribes of the charters would be royal clerks. The invariable use of West Saxon in the charters, even outside Wessex, proves that there was a chancery language and that militates against the theory that the charters were drawn up by the recipients. West Saxon was not only the chancery language but also the literary language, so that the last argument is

---

[4] The lectures otherwise consist of a general survey of the development of the Anglo-Saxon royal diploma, from its origin in the late Roman private deed to its replacement by the writ during the reign of Cnut.

[5] Stevenson, 'An Old English Charter', pp. 731–2 n.

[6] Davis, *Regesta*, pp. xiii–xv.

[7] But see further below, pp. 149–51.

perhaps not a conclusive one. Already in Aethelstan's time we find charters in the hand of one and the same scribe in different parts of England. In this case the inference seems unavoidable that the writer was a royal clerk.[8]

It was left to another German scholar, Richard Drögereit, to marshal the evidence on which Stevenson's final remark was based. In 1935 he published an intimidating but seminal paper under the title 'Gab es eine angelsächsische Königskanzlei?', and was able to give a qualified answer in the affirmative after a palaeographical study of the extant apparent originals dated between 931 and 963, coupled with an investigation of the texts of a slightly larger range of diplomas preserved only in later copies. For the period up to 951, he identified the hands of three scribes in ten diplomas which survive in contemporary form:

S	Date	Details of transaction	Archive
		(i) 'Æthelstan A'	
416	931	King Æthelstan to Wulfgar, his *fidelis minister*: grant of land in Wiltshire	Old Minster Winchester
425	934	King Æthelstan to Ælfwald, his *fidelis minister*: grant of land at *Derantune* (in Sussex or Kent)	Christ Church Canterbury
		(ii) 'Æthelstan C'	
447	939	King Æthelstan to Ealdulf, his *fidelis minister*: grant of land in Kent	Christ Church Canterbury
464	940	King Edmund to Æthelswith, a nun: grant of land in Kent	Christ Church Canterbury
512	943	King Edmund to Ælfstan, his *minister*: grant of land in Kent	Christ Church Canterbury
		(iii) 'Edmund C'	
497	944	King Edmund to Ælfstan, his *minister*: grant of land in Kent	Christ Church Canterbury
510	946	King Edmund to the brothers Ordhelm and Alfwold, his *homines*: grant of land in Kent	Christ Church Canterbury
528	947	King Eadred to Oswig, his *minister*: grant of land in Surrey	Christ Church Canterbury
535	948	King Eadred to Ælfwyn, a religious woman: grant of land in Kent	Christ Church Canterbury
552	949	King Eadred to Wulfric, *fidelis*: grant of land in Berkshire	Abingdon

Drögereit located these scribes in a royal chancery by application of the principle that diplomas issued in favour of different beneficiaries

---

[8] Cited in Drögereit, 'Königskanzlei', p. 340.

yet written by the same hand have the king as common denominator and can therefore be regarded as the work of royal scribes. On the assumption that the scribe and the draftsman of a royal diploma were one and the same, he extended the argument to incorporate details of formulation, identifying further diplomas drafted by the three known scribes and even creating more royal scribes by grouping together other diplomas with related formulation. Thus his scribes 'Æthelstan B', 'Edmund A' and 'Edmund B' are known only from diplomas preserved in cartulary copies. Drögereit argued that the clear picture of the chancery vanishes suddenly in 951, and he associated this phenomenon with the deaths in the same year of Ælfheah, bishop of Winchester, and Theodred, bishop of London,[9] whom he regarded as successive 'chancellors' to the Anglo-Saxon kings. He was able to identify only one scribe at work in the 950s, 'Eadred B', represented by a solitary original diploma dated 957 (S 649); the other texts assigned to the same scribe are extant only in cartulary copies. One of them (S 554) enabled Drögereit to claim that 'Eadred B' began his work shortly before the death of Bishop Ælfheah, but the other diplomas belong to Eadwig's reign. Drögereit saw a breakdown of the chancery and of the central government, beginning in the latter part of Eadred's reign and culminating in Eadwig's reign, but he argued that the chancery was partially restored in a rather different form for a brief period during the reign of King Edgar. Only one recurring scribe, 'Edgar A', was identified amongst the available originals, and Drögereit located him in the Abingdon scriptorium, going so far as to suggest that he might even have been Abbot Æthelwold himself.[10] Drögereit lost sight of a chancery in any form after 963, and inferred that diplomas were drafted thereafter by many different agencies, often the beneficiaries themselves. He regarded this decentralization as reflecting at the same time a decline in royal power and the increasing influence of the monastic reformers, who assumed the responsibilities which had previously been entrusted to the royal secretariat.[11]

The strengths and weaknesses of Drögereit's tract are quite clear. His palaeographical examination of the extant originals can rarely

[9] It is not, in fact, entirely certain that Theodred died in 951: see O'Donovan, 'Episcopal Dates, Pt. II', p. 98.
[10] On this scribe, see further below, pp. 70–9.
[11] Drögereit, 'Königskanzlei', esp. pp. 410–18.

be faulted, and his attributions of the different diplomas to particular scribes have been endorsed by subsequent commentators, though they might not attach the same significance to the evidence. But much of the elaboration which was based solely on the formulation of diplomas preserved only in cartulary copies should be questioned, since Drögereit's assumption that the draftsman and scribe of an Anglo-Saxon royal diploma were necessarily the same person[12] is misleading in the way that it is applied. For he appears not to make allowance for the evident fact that the formulation of a diploma was often, even generally, derived from existing texts, so that the act of drafting might involve the process of selecting formulae from them rather than a more active process of composition; the use of particular formulae was not the prerogative of a particular draftsman, though a draftsman might himself display a personal preference. Therefore the common denominator between texts of different provenance with related formulation cannot always be personified as a common draftsman, especially if the texts were produced over several years, during which the formulae may have gained a wider currency: the similarities could be attributed simply to dependence on an ultimately common model. It remains possible that the functions of drafting and writing were performed by a single scribe, or perhaps that a particular draftsman was consistently assisted by the same scribe; but just as one cannot assume that diplomas with common elements of formulation were necessarily the work of the same scribe (or team), so one cannot expect a single scribe (or team) always to produce closely-related diplomas. Drögereit's interpretation of the evidence in broader historical terms should also be viewed with some scepticism, for few scholars would follow his lead in regarding the progress of the 'chancery' as an index to fluctuations of royal power in the tenth century. Much depends on his contention that the organization which had existed for the production of royal diplomas in the 930s and 940s began to collapse in the 950s, but T. A. M. Bishop's identification of a further 'royal scribe' active in 956 and 957 demonstrates that the organization lasted longer than Drögereit thought it did.[13] Nevertheless, the

---

[12] *Ibid.* p. 413 n. 1. Cf. Bishop, 'A Charter of King Edwy', pp. 370–2, and Chaplais, 'Diplomas of Exeter', p. 27.
[13] Bishop, 'A Charter of King Edwy', pp. 371–2. The scribe was responsible for S 624 and 646.

overall value of Drögereit's tract cannot be gainsaid: some of the diplomatic and historical aspects of the argument may be tenuous, but it has served to provide the vital palaeographical evidence in substantiation of the position adopted by Stevenson on more general grounds.

THE CASE FOR ECCLESIASTICAL SCRIPTORIA

The view that Anglo-Saxon royal diplomas were drawn up on the initiative of the beneficiary in ecclesiastical scriptoria is at least as old as the view that they were the products of a royal chancery. It arises in part from the assumptions that only ecclesiastics would have attached importance to the special protection afforded by written documents and that only religious foundations would have been capable of producing such documents, with the corollary that diplomas in general were intended exclusively to serve the interests of the Church, whence their distinctive ecclesiastical character. These assumptions were expressed as assertions by Hubert Hall, who was then led to declare dogmatically: 'The Old English royal charter is a religious and local product. The handwriting is local, the language is local, the formulas are adapted by local scribes from academic models; the attestation only is official, inasmuch as the court by which it is ratified followed the king into the locality.'[14] Hall's insistence on the 'local' character of the handwriting and the language found little support when the diplomas themselves were subjected to more careful scrutiny, and his opinions have rarely been revived without considerable modification. We have seen that Drögereit, having maintained the existence of a royal chancery in the 930s and 940s, and having argued that it collapsed during the 950s, himself believed that from the time of King Edgar diplomas were drawn up in ecclesiastical scriptoria acting as or for the beneficiaries, and he observed in this connection that the formulation of royal diplomas became more diffuse during the 960s.[15] The point was taken up and developed by Florence Harmer, who drew attention to the evidence that from the reign of King Æthelred onwards the king sometimes entrusted the production of a diploma

---

[14] Hall, *Studies*, p. 177.
[15] Drögereit, 'Königskanzlei', pp. 402 and 417–18.

to an 'interested ecclesiastic', wondering whether this procedure was exceptional or routine, and whether it represented a departure from or a continuation of traditional measures.[16] The concept of the 'interested ecclesiastic' can apparently be applied in different ways according to the circumstances of a given transaction. The ecclesiastic may be equated with the beneficiary, as the representative of the religious house in whose favour a diploma was to be drawn up. A distinction between 'immediate' and 'eventual' beneficiary can be introduced, to accommodate the possibility that some diplomas for laymen were drawn up to empower them to transfer the estates concerned to religious houses; in such cases the original diploma may have been produced by the intended eventual beneficiary. The application of 'interested' can be further extended to accommodate the ecclesiastics (and in particular the bishops) in whose dioceses the lands to be conveyed by diploma were situated. The concept was understood by T. A. M. Bishop to imply 'that charters from the archives of a single monastery were written in a single scriptorium, and this even if they record grants in favour of different and secular persons', presumably on the grounds that preservation in a community's archive presupposes at least an indirect interest of the community in the transaction. He pointed out that the diplomas attributed by Drögereit to 'Æthelstan C' were all from the archives of Christ Church Canterbury, so that in consequence the common denominator was not necessarily the king as grantor: it might have been the Christ Church community, and the diplomas might therefore have been produced in the Christ Church scriptorium on behalf of the beneficiaries.[17] The estates concerned are all in Kent, so the possibility does indeed seem attractive.[18]

A more radical modification of Drögereit's interpretation of the palaeographical evidence arose from incidental remarks made by N. R. Ker. He cited nine original diplomas dated between 939 and 957 as written in a script that resembled that of the annals for 925–55 in the Parker Chronicle, inferring that the script of the annals was 'of the type used in the Winchester scriptorium in the middle of the tenth century'; he also observed that one of them (S 636) was

---

16 Harmer, *Writs*, pp. 34–41.
17 Bishop, 'A Charter of King Edwy', p. 370.
18 But see below, pp. 44–5, for evidence that 'Æthelstan C' was not exclusively concerned with diplomas preserved at Christ Church.

probably written by the scribe who inserted the annal for 951 in the chronicle.[19] The significance of this observation in a diplomatic context was fully exploited by Dr Pierre Chaplais. He argued that the uniformity of script and formulation in diplomas for different beneficiaries need not be attributed to their production in a 'problematic' royal chancery, but could be explained more simply as the result of entrusting the responsibility for drawing up diplomas to a single ecclesiastical scriptorium: for by the beginning of the tenth century, following the decline of learning and monastic life in the ninth, most scriptoria had ceased to exist, so that the king would have had no option but to concentrate the production of diplomas in whatever scriptorium was still available. The Winchester scriptorium had remained active; moreover, the scribe of one mid-tenth-century diploma had been located there, and since the scribes of other contemporary diplomas practised a similar type of script, it followed that they too could be regarded as Winchester scribes.[20] In this way, three of Drögereit's 'royal scribes', 'Æthelstan C', 'Edmund C' and 'Eadred B', together with Bishop's additional 'royal scribe' active in Eadwig's reign, were transformed into members of the Winchester scriptorium, and the substance of the royal chancery vanished. Dr Chaplais more tentatively located the earliest 'royal scribe', 'Æthelstan A', in the same scriptorium, observing that one of the diplomas written by him (S 425) was *perscripta* at Winchester and that his hand resembles one in a manuscript of probable Winchester provenance.[21] According to Dr Chaplais's hypothesis, the Winchester scriptorium may have enjoyed a virtual monopoly of the writing of royal diplomas for as long as it remained the only scriptorium available for the purpose. But during the course of the monastic reformation, and so especially from the reign of King Edgar onwards, new scriptoria were established and were able to serve as additional centres for the production of royal diplomas: thus Glastonbury became active under Dunstan

---

[19] Ker, *Catalogue*, p. lix.

[20] Chaplais, 'Origin and Authenticity', p. 41.

[21] *Ibid.* pp. 41–2. Dr Chaplais's further point, that the hand of Wulfgar's will (S 1533), a document closely associated with the other document written by 'Æthelstan A' (S 416), is similar to another hand in the Parker Chronicle, is not decisive, since it is likely anyway that a document recording a 'private' bequest to the Old Minster would be drawn up by a Winchester scribe, and since it was not necessarily written at the same time or in the same place as the diploma.

in the 950s, diplomas were drawn up at Abingdon (during the abbacy of Æthelwold) in the early 960s,[22] and thereafter the drafting and writing of royal diplomas became progressively decentralized as the new episcopal and monastic scriptoria came into operation. In this connection, Dr Chaplais has drawn attention to the fact that in a few instances the writing of a diploma can indeed be traced to a particular ecclesiastical scriptorium, acting for itself as immediate or eventual beneficiary; in addition, he has drawn attention to the occurrence in a substantial number of tenth- and eleventh-century diplomas of formulae of subscription that appear to suggest that the drafting was controlled by one of the ecclesiastical witnesses – in some cases the bishop in whose diocese the estate concerned was situated and in others an abbot in his capacity as beneficiary.[23] His general conclusions are of great moment: on the one hand, 'there is not a shred of evidence to indicate that at any time between the seventh and the eleventh centuries Anglo-Saxon diplomas were drafted or written in what might be called, even loosely, a central royal secretariat, that is to say in a single organized department staffed with royal scribes who specialized in royal business';[24] on the other hand, the diplomas 'were produced, not in a self-staffed secretariat, but at all times in monastic or episcopal scriptoria',[25] and their drafting and writing 'was a local affair, involving only the beneficiary or a near-by ecclesiastical scriptorium'.[26]

In certain respects, however, the argument behind these conclusions appears susceptible of criticism. It is said, for example, that it was a decline in the number of scriptoria available for the writing of diplomas that led to the centralization of their production at Winchester during the reign of King Æthelstan. The attraction of

[22] Like Drögereit, Chaplais suggests that the scribe known as 'Edgar A', active between 960 and 963, may have been a member of the Abingdon scriptorium: 'Origin and Authenticity', p. 42, and 'Anglo-Saxon Chancery', pp. 48–9.

[23] Chaplais, 'Origin and Authenticity', p. 42 and n. 107.

[24] Chaplais, 'Anglo-Saxon Chancery', p. 49.

[25] *Ibid.* pp. 45–6. See also Chaplais, 'Diplomas on Single Sheets', p. 85.

[26] Chaplais, 'Diplomas of Exeter', p. 33. Dr Chaplais's arguments are restated and in some respects refined in his article 'La chancellerie royale anglaise des origines au règne de Jean sans terre', which he has kindly allowed me to see in advance of publication. See also Brooks, 'Anglo-Saxon Charters', pp. 217–20, and Sawyer, 'Worcester Archive', pp. 84–5. Hart, *Charters of Northern England*, pp. 17–41, attempts to distinguish the work of various ecclesiastical scriptoria as centres for the production of royal diplomas in the tenth and eleventh centuries.

this idea is that it enables one to view the production of diplomas as a process that changed according to a single factor, viz. the number of ecclesiastical scriptoria active at any time. For it is generally accepted that up to the end of the ninth century diplomas were often drawn up in the scriptoria of religious communities, whether acting for themselves or on behalf of secular beneficiaries:[27] so centralization at Winchester in the early tenth century, followed by progressive decentralization as more scriptoria were established, implies a satisfactory continuum, with a return in the last century of the Anglo-Saxon period to the situation that had obtained before the reign of King Alfred. However, the argument clearly depends on the belief that by the beginning of Æthelstan's reign there were very few scriptoria in operation, and indeed that the scriptorium attached to the Old Minster at Winchester was then the only one left – a belief that seems to arise largely from King Alfred's complaints about the state of learning in England at the time of his accession.[28] Perhaps one should not forget that Alfred undertook to rectify the situation: there was extensive production of manuscripts in his reign,[29] presupposing the existence of several scriptoria, and there is no apparent reason why those attached to the important sees should have ceased to function in the early tenth century. It therefore seems dangerous to argue that the drawing up of diplomas was of necessity entrusted to a single scriptorium; yet if diplomas *were* invariably drawn up in ecclesiastical scriptoria, only necessity *could* dictate the evident centralization during the 930s and 940s.

The identification of Winchester as the scriptorium made responsible for the production of the diplomas of Æthelstan and his immediate successors is not, of course, explained merely by a process of elimination. It depends also on the location of one scribe there, and then on the affinities of script that associate the single

---

27 Parsons, 'Scribal Memoranda', pp. 31–2; Chaplais, 'Origin and Authenticity', pp. 36–40, and 'Diplomas on Single Sheets', *passim*; Bruckner, *Ch. L. A.* III, *passim*, and IV, xiii–xxiii.

28 See Chaplais, 'Origin and Authenticity', pp. 40–1, and 'Anglo-Saxon Chancery', p. 47.

29 King Alfred sent the translation of the *Pastoral Care* 'south and north to his scribes', to be copied for distribution to his bishops (Whitelock, *EHD*, p. 890); several copies must have been made, of which only two have survived (Ker, *Catalogue*, nos. 195 and 324). There is reason to suppose that some of the other works available in Alfred's reign, such as the *Chronicle*, the laws, the OE *Martyrology* and the series of vernacular translations, were also copied fairly often; of these copies only the Parker Chronicle and two fragments of the *Martyrology* have survived (*ibid.* nos. 39, 127 and 132).

diploma he is known to have produced with other contemporary diplomas, including those previously attributed to royal scribes. Perhaps those aspects of the diplomas that suggest the connection with Winchester in particular have been emphasized at the expense of other aspects which imply at least some variety of scribal practice in the scriptorium where the diplomas were produced – and thus dilute its 'Winchester' characteristics. For example, the hand of 'Æthelstan A', known from diplomas dated 931 and 934, is not of the distinctive 'Winchester' type of square minuscule,[30] though that the type had been developed by the time he was writing is shown by its occurrence in the early tenth-century annals of the Parker Chronicle.[31] Furthermore, two diplomas (S 449 and 495) whose scribes were not associated with the Winchester scriptorium by either Ker or Chaplais were nevertheless apparently produced in the same scriptorium as the supposed Winchester diplomas, since they display the features of layout characteristic of almost all originals issued between 939 and 957: a small cross to serve as a pictorial invocation (though giving way to a decorated chrismon by 956); the division of the dating clause into separate elements spread out on one line across the width of the membrane; the exclusion of the word *Ego* from witnesses' subscriptions after the first column of names; and the insertion of a small cross above the word *crucis* where it occurs in formulae of attestation.[32] These features first occur in combination on two original diplomas of King Æthelstan issued in 939. One of them, S 447, was written by 'Æthelstan C', one of the scribes who has been assigned to the Winchester scriptorium; the other, S 449, is one of the two diplomas under consideration, and must have been produced at the same time as S 447, by a scribe working from the same memorandum of witnesses' names and adopting an identical layout of the text: so there can be little doubt that he was a colleague of 'Æthelstan C' 's.[33]

[30] Brooks, 'Anglo-Saxon Charters', p. 218.

[31] See Parkes, 'Parker Manuscript', p. 158.

[32] Also, Whitelock, *Bishops of London*, pp. 20–1 n., draws attention to a new diplomatic practice which began *c.* 935: the bishops of Winchester and London were named first amongst the bishops in the witness lists and were identified by the names of their sees.

[33] Note also that the endorsement on S 449 is of the same type as that in S 447. The type in question, distinguished by the opening clause '✠ Þis is [place-name in genitive] land-boc . . .', was current between 937 and 939 (S 438, 441, 446–7 and 449); a variation, with 'boc' for 'landboc', was employed in 940 and 943 (S 463–4, 467–8, 470 and 492).

If the diplomas written by 'Æthelstan A', as well as S 449 and 495, are to be regarded as products of the Winchester scriptorium, then one would have to admit at least some variety in the scripts practised there, thereby weakening the logic of locating a scribe at Winchester in the first place simply on the basis of his script: if the scriptorium did not so clearly determine the script, the script cannot be used to identify the scriptorium of the scribe.

The apparent 'Winchester' associations of the script in many of the original diplomas can perhaps be explained in another way. According to Dr Parkes, the Winchester scriptorium of the tenth century 'seems to have pioneered and propagated new standards and new models of handwriting':[34] in the early part of the century a distinctive scriptorium type of square minuscule was developed there, and was disseminated thence to gain a wider currency. Given the obvious importance of the Winchester scriptorium, many scribes may have been trained there, or trained by someone who had himself worked there for some years during the first three decades of the century; consequently, they may have practised the same type of square minuscule as occurs in Winchester manuscripts and notably in the Parker Chronicle. Again, if the scribe of S 636 did insert the annal for 951 in the Parker Chronicle, he must at one time have been attached to the Winchester scriptorium,[35] but one could not guarantee that he always worked there, that he had not entered the king's service after training at Winchester or before retiring there. Moreover, two diplomas whose scribes have been assigned to the Winchester scriptorium are known to have been produced elsewhere: King Æthelstan's grant of land at Ham in Wiltshire to Wulfgar (S 416) was written at Lifton in Devon, and King Eadwig's grant of land at Ely to Archbishop Oda (S 646) was written at Edington in Wiltshire. It is pertinent to enquire in what capacity the so-called 'Winchester scribes' acted when they wrote these diplomas. For even if they were members of the Winchester scriptorium, it is arguable that once they had left the precincts of the monastery they should cease to be regarded as Winchester scribes, a description which carries the implication that the diplomas were drawn up in

---

[34] Parkes, 'Parker Manuscript', p. 163.
[35] The insertion was probably made after a different scribe had entered annal numbers and annals from 925 to 955: see Ker, *Catalogue*, p. 59.

the Winchester scriptorium. And under what circumstances did these scribes leave the monastery in the first place and then come to write the diplomas? Were they members of the bishop's entourage,[36] or had they been seconded to the king to act in his own service? Perhaps in this connection one should consider the implications of Dr Chaplais's important observation that an inscription recording the gift of a gospel book by King Æthelstan to Christ Church Canterbury was written by the scribe known as 'Edmund C', who appropriately described the king with a style that occurs quite frequently in royal diplomas.[37] The diplomas written by 'Edmund C' are dated 944–9, yet it appears that he was active already during the reign of King Æthelstan; and the fact that he was employed for the king's personal purposes raises the possibility that when he wrote the diplomas he may have been acting not on behalf of the beneficiaries, but rather in the capacity of a royal scribe.

Finally, it is arguable that the styles of subscription that seem to imply some role in the drafting or writing of the text on the part of the witness in question will not always bear the interpretation suggested for them. There are about fifty tenth- and eleventh-century diplomas in which such formulae occur, and they can be divided into four main groups. In the first place, a group comprising those in which the verb *dictavi* (or *condictavi*) is associated with one of the bishops: occurrences are concentrated markedly in the diplomas of King Eadwig issued in 956 and are rare thereafter, in the period when perhaps one might most expect to find them.[38] Secondly, there is a group of diplomas dated between 963 and 1028 in which a more explicit formula, 'Ego .N. episcopus hanc cartulam dictitans rege suisque percipientibus perscribere iussi', occurs in

---

[36] See Brooks, 'Anglo-Saxon Charters', p. 218.

[37] Chaplais, 'Anglo-Saxon Chancery', pp. 46–7. The gospel book in question is B.L. Cotton Tiberius A ii, and the inscription occurs on fo. 15v; see further Robinson, *Times of St Dunstan*, pp. 59–60. It should be noted in this connection that three other manuscripts given by Æthelstan to religious foundations contain apparently contemporary inscriptions: B.L. Cotton Claudius B v, fo. 5r (see *ibid.* p. 61); B.L. Royal 1 A xviii, fo. 3v (*ibid.*); and London, Lambeth Palace MS 1370, fo. 3v (*ibid.* pp. 55–9); there was another inscription in B.L. Cotton Otho B ix (largely destroyed by fire; *ibid.* pp. 52–3). As a group these inscriptions would clearly repay further study, from both diplomatic and palaeographical points of view, for the light they may throw on Æthelstan's writing office.

[38] S 386–7, 455; S 584, 589, 593–4, 597, 614, 616–18, 623, 626, 637 and 661 (all from 956); S 574, 651, 832, 834, 856, 883, 887 and 1034; cf. S 917. Of these, a direct object (e.g. *hanc cartam*) is employed with the verb in S 597, 917 and 1034. For claims that bishops actually wrote diplomas, see S 880, 1028 and 1042.

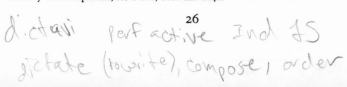

association with one of the bishops.[39] Thirdly, there are several diplomas in which miscellaneous verbs implying a hand in the production of the text (for example, *dictavi* and *composui*) are associated with an abbot, who is generally the beneficiary: most of the diplomas are connected in some way with Abingdon, but many of these, and two of the four that remain, are texts of dubious authenticity.[40] Fourthly, there is a group of diplomas dated between 1018 and 1049 in which the formula *dictando titulavi* is employed for one of the attesting bishops and all of which are associated with the south-west.[41] The different types of formulae should not all be taken together as if thus to acquire a collective force. Some of the instances in which a witness claims to have 'dictated' may not be capable of a literal interpretation, given the obvious falseness of claims to autography (*manu propria*) referring to the act of subscription itself:[42] indeed, one gets the impression that *dictavi* on its own and *dictando titulavi* may be no more than two of the available styles for the act of giving consent to or expressing approval of the transaction, to be used according to the draftsman's inclination and for the sake of varying the styles of attestation.[43] It is noticeable, moreover, that in only a few instances is either style attached to the diocesan bishop.[44] On the other hand, there may be some truth in claims that it was the abbot who drafted a diploma in favour of his own house, especially when the diploma contains references to the traditional history of the house which would not be well known to outsiders; but his participation in the production of the diploma may have been restricted to co-operation with another agency,

[39] S 712, 730, 755, 931, 977 (cf. 957) and 983. Cf. S 736, 774 and 1605.

[40] S 567, 658, 673, 876 (cf. 786 and 788), 896, 902, 918 and 993 are associated with Abingdon, and of these only S 876, 896 and 902 are likely to be authentic. The others are S 509, 546 (on which see Chaplais, 'Anglo-Saxon Chancery', pp. 47-8), 555 and 1038, of which the first and third are probably authentic.

[41] S 953, 962-3, 971, 998 and 1019, of which the first two are suspicious.

[42] Chaplais, 'Anglo-Saxon Chancery', p. 47.

[43] In the case of *dictavi*, this is suggested by its concentration in Eadwig's reign, and by its association in his diplomas with the same group of verbs of attestation, as if it were just one of a particular series (e.g. *favi*, *dictavi*, *subscripsi*) used irrespective of the bishop to whom it was attached. One might also note that it is used for different bishops in diplomas which for other reasons can probably be regarded as the work of a single agency: see below, p. 63 n. 113. In the case of *dictando titulavi*, Chaplais ('Diplomas of Exeter', p. 24) points out that S 963 and 971 (both dated 1031) were written by the same scribe, though the formula occurs in both, attached to different bishops; and again, the formula seems to be one of a set series of styles (cf. S 951) to be used at will.

[44] S 594, ?616, 832, 834, 883, 887, 1019 and 1034.

itself responsible for the writing.[45] The formula which indicates that the diploma was written at the command of one of the bishops is potentially the most interesting. In three or four of its six occurrences it is attached to the diocesan bishop,[46] and it is possible that in each case its use reflects the entrusting by the king to an 'interested ecclesiastic' of responsibility for the production of the diploma. But one should not overlook the fact that the formulation of the diplomas in which it occurs often stands apart from that of other diplomas issued at roughly the same time, suggesting indirectly that the arrangement was adopted only under certain and perhaps special circumstances. In addition, one should remember that the operative formulae, to the effect that someone 'dictated' a diploma or ordered it to be written, are found attached not only to ecclesiastics but also to the king.[47] Thus, while the idea that the production of diplomas might on occasion be entrusted to 'interested ecclesiastics' can be substantiated on the basis of some of these formulae of attestation, it would nevertheless be mistaken to interpret such evidence as proof that diplomas were always drawn up by ecclesiastics, and then transform the argument into one against the existence of a central office capable of producing royal diplomas on the assumption that the two arrangements were mutually exclusive. For it would be surprising if whatever arrangements did exist operated so inflexibly that evidence for one system could be regarded as evidence against another. And it is obvious that any attempt to identify and characterize these arrangements should arise from consideration of all the diplomas now extant, rather than from consideration of just a small proportion of them, and should accommodate all the palaeographical, diplomatic and historical aspects of the material.

THE NATURE OF THE ANGLO-SAXON ROYAL DIPLOMA

The two schools of thought represented by Drögereit on the one hand and by Chaplais on the other share common ground in their recognition that during the 930s and 940s a single scriptorium was

---

[45] See further below, pp. 121–3.
[46] S 755, 931, 977 and ?983; see also Whitelock, *EHD*, p. 378.
[47] See, e.g., S 667, 677, 723–4, 744, 803, 916, 930, 955, 960 and 1042. In S 900 King Æthelred subscribes 'hanc largitatem ita dictavi'; see also the rubric of S 914. In S 891 Æthelred refers to the charters which he 'dictated' in his youth.

employed for the production of royal diplomas in favour of various beneficiaries; the differences of opinion arise only when an attempt is made to decide whether the scriptorium approximated to a department within the royal household or whether it was that of an ecclesiastical community. Since any interpretation of the evidence is bound to be affected and even determined by one's view of the nature of the Anglo-Saxon diploma as an instrument of royal government, it seems advisable to discuss the problem initially in this general context. The case for identifying the agency as the scriptorium of an ecclesiastical community is founded on the belief that the characteristic features of Anglo-Saxon royal diplomas are compatible only with their production by the Church. They have no outward signs of authentication: neither the crosses nor the signatures in the subscriptions are autograph, despite the use of formulae that suggest the contrary if understood literally, and the documents were never sealed. Moreover, notarial subscriptions, which served as marks of secondary authentication in that they reflected the delegation of responsibility for the drawing up of the diploma, were the exception rather than the rule; indeed, the personnel of the continental chanceries have no obvious counterparts in Anglo-Saxon England. Since the distinguishing attribute, even the *raison d'être*, of a chancery was the authentication it lent to the documents produced under its auspices, then *a priori* diplomas not outwardly authenticated were not issued from a royal chancery. In this context, Dr Chaplais introduced an elegant refinement into the argument. In his view, the authenticity of an Anglo-Saxon diploma was 'a purely religious and ecclesiastical one': the penalties imposed on those who contravened it were ecclesiastical, and in this respect the insular documents are to be distinguished from their continental counterparts, which stipulate monetary fines; a diploma might derive *ex post facto* authenticity from being entered in a gospel book, being kept with the king's relics, or being entrusted into the safe-keeping of a monastery; and the responsibility for drawing it up in the first place might be entrusted to ecclesiastics as *authentice persone*, whose status guaranteed the authenticity of the documents issued by them.[48] In short, the authenticity of the Anglo-Saxon royal diploma was ecclesiastical, reflecting the place and

---

[48] See Chaplais, 'Origin and Authenticity', pp. 32–6.

circumstances of its production. Another feature of documents produced in chanceries is the use of a distinctive form of script, such as the diplomatic minuscule found in Carolingian charters. Yet the scribes of Anglo-Saxon royal diplomas always employed normal bookhands, and it is apparent from developments in the scripts used, as well as from the language and content of the documents, that the diplomas were never isolated from the mainstream of monastic culture, and were indeed intimately bound up with it.

All these seem to be compelling reasons for associating the production of diplomas exclusively with ecclesiastical scriptoria. But while the distinctive features of a Frankish diploma when set beside an Anglo-Saxon one can be explained in terms of the production of the former in a royal chancery, it may not necessarily follow that the distinctive features of the Anglo-Saxon diploma reflect its provenance in quite the same way. Perhaps the continental analogy should not be pressed too hard. The Frankish kings consciously modelled several of their institutions on those of the Roman emperors whom they had displaced, and the Merovingian chancery is a case in point. It could not be said that conditions for continuity of this sort existed in England. The incentive for the introduction of written documents to protect title to land and privileges was probably ecclesiastical in origin, and at the moment when churchmen considered it desirable to protect their own interests in this way, the equipment or organization necessary for the production of such documents would presumably not have been available in the king's court. The nature of the instrument introduced by the Church and the manner of its production would have been determined by these circumstances. The model chosen was the late Roman private deed, and the earliest examples were drawn up by the Church on behalf of the king for use in an illiterate society. Hence, it would seem, the presence of a witness list, since the private deeds were required by law to have a certain number of witnesses (unlike the diplomas of the Merovingian kings, which were generally witnessed only by the king and the chancellor). Hence also the absence of any outward sign of authentication such as a seal or autograph subscriptions. Hence, perhaps, the absence of a notarial subscription, since the diploma, though written by the Church, was nevertheless presented as an act of the king, and it would hardly have been appropriate for an officer of the beneficiary to cast himself in the role of an officer of the king and in this way lend authentication to the document. And hence the primarily ecclesiastical nature of the Anglo-Saxon diploma: the proem, which establishes the act as arising from religious considerations, and the sanction, which threatens religious as opposed to worldly penalties, were modifications to the model, and reflected the provenance of the earliest documents as well as the purpose for which they were intended. The essential characteristics of the Anglo-Saxon diploma are displayed from the time that the first originals appear in the last quarter of the seventh century, and thereafter they remain substantially the same. But if they reflect the origins of the instrument, need they at all times reflect its provenance? At least the possibility should be admitted that the form of royal diplomas, established since the seventh century, could have remained unchanged even if the circumstances of their production subsequently underwent some development.

The religious and ecclesiastical associations of royal diplomas should not be allowed to obscure the fact that the documents had a precise role to play in the secular context of Anglo-Saxon land tenure and law. Two texts, one of the early tenth century and the other apparently of the eleventh century, suggest that for the purposes of the law land could be classified as either bookland or folkland.[49] An estate of bookland was held according to the privileges stated or implied in a 'book', or diploma – that is, with immunity from all secular burdens (except the common three of bridge-work, fortress-work and military service) and with full power to bequeath the land to any heir of the owner's choosing; an estate of folkland was subject to the secular burdens from which bookland was exempt, and for as long as it remained folkland it apparently could not be alienated outside the owner's kindred.[50] The landed property of any individual, king and his subjects alike, could comprise holdings in both bookland and folkland, though parts of either might be leased to others in the form of loanland.

---

[49] I Edward 2 (Liebermann, *Gesetze* I, 140) and *Ymb æbricas* (Flower, 'Burghal Hidage', p. 62).

[50] This distinction between bookland and folkland may involve some simplification, but for the system to be workable it would have to have been readily understandable. See further Loyn, *Anglo-Saxon England*, pp. 171–5, and cf. John, *Land Tenure*, pp. 51–3, and *Orbis Britanniae*, pp. 64–127.

The uniform appearance and apparent import of the royal diplomas issued in the tenth century conceal transactions of widely disparate character within this broad tenurial framework. In some cases, the diploma represents no less than the conveyance itself of a privileged estate of bookland by the king to the beneficiary: but the land might have been part of the king's own folkland which he booked for the first time in order to be able to dispose of it at will;[51] or the land might have come from the king's holdings in bookland, whether inherited from his predecessors or acquired in his own reign through the operation of the laws of forfeiture, through confiscation from laymen or appropriation from the Church, or through bequests made to him by his subjects. Whether the land had been folkland or bookland, the effect of the transaction might simply have been to convert an estate that had previously been leased to a tenant into bookland for the same man to hold in perpetuity. A diploma might in other circumstances create the privileges that characterized bookland without representing the conveyance of the land itself by the king to the beneficiary.[52] The owner of folkland might desire to convert his estate into bookland, so that he could enjoy the privilege of immunity from many secular burdens or so that he could alienate the land outside his kindred, perhaps to a religious foundation. Alternatively, a man who already owned an estate as bookland might have lost the diploma which guaranteed his title to it and would in consequence desire to secure a replacement from the king for security's sake.[53] Finally, it is apparent that the form of the diploma, normally reserved for estates of bookland, could be

---

[51] In some instances it appears that the king first booked the land to himself (S 298, 715 and 727, on which see Stenton, *Latin Charters*, pp. 20–2), but normally the diploma must have been drawn up directly in favour of the intended beneficiary.

[52] The common form of the diploma turned such transactions into apparent grants of privileged estates and thus they became indistinguishable from transactions which did involve the conveyance of land as well as privileges. But see S 190, 396 and 397, and note the use in S 929 of two dispositive verbs (*dabo* and *liberabo*), perhaps implying that the giving of the estate and the freeing of it from burdens could be distinct actions.

[53] Several diplomas were explicitly drawn up to replace older ones that for various reasons were not available, whether stolen by pagans (S 222), burnt (S 367, 371 (and see Sawyer, *Charters of Burton*, p. 4 n. 1), 803 and 954), immersed in water so as to be virtually illegible (S 369), consumed by old age (S 1042) or simply mislaid (S 225, 277, 358, 361, 368, 378, 395, 460, 469, 488, 496, 744, 811 and 835). There were doubtless many other diplomas drawn up to replace ones that had been lost, which can no longer be distinguished from genuinely new issues since they were cast in the common form.

adapted for transactions whose effect was the creation of loanland.[54]
It is clear, therefore, that a diploma did not always reflect royal
favour towards the beneficiary, whether altruistic or for some
ulterior motive. One imagines that it was often the beneficiary
who took the initiative in soliciting land or privileges from the king,
and under such circumstances one would expect that he had to
purchase the favour that he was seeking. In many diplomas the
beneficiary is indeed said to have paid for the land, for the privileges
or for the production of the diploma, and since it seems that the
inclusion of a reference to such payment was largely a matter of
preference,[55] it is likely that there were many more examples of
this than we know about. The promulgation of royal diplomas
would thus have provided an important source of revenue for the
king, and as such it would have been an activity over which he
would scarcely be prepared to relinquish control: if he left the
drafting and writing of the documents to agencies acting without
his or his subordinates' supervision, not only would he seriously
compromise his own power to dictate what was conceded to the
beneficiary, but he would also deny himself a fee which presumably
would otherwise have to have been paid to the independent agency
for its trouble.

The existence of facilities for the production of royal diplomas
under royal supervision would have been in the interests of the
beneficiary as well. In the context of Anglo-Saxon land law it was
the possession of the diploma itself that established ownership of
the land to which it referred or right to the privileges which it
created. Thus, when an estate changed hands the diploma was
transferred together with the land to the new owner;[56] indeed, the
act of transferring the diploma could apparently effect the change
of ownership.[57] The preservation of diplomas in favour of laymen
in the archives of the religious foundations which came into possession of the estates concerned reflects the operation of this procedure

[54] E.g. S 430, 467, 513, 526, 565, 693, 901 and 905.
[55] The examples are less evenly distributed over the years than one would expect, had it
been customary to specify payment whenever it was made. In S 535, it looks as if the
statement '✠ duas libras purissimi auri dedit' was inserted as an afterthought.
[56] See, e.g., statements in some diplomas that bequests of the property were to be made
'cum cirographo perpetuo' (S 625, 830, 910 and 1005). Note also the second endorsements
on S 717 and 795.
[57] See, e.g., S 882, 1211 and 1445.

on a large scale; and it is frequently clear that the same diploma
had served as the title-deed for several generations after the date of
its production, before its final transfer to the church.[58] The value
permanently attached to a diploma is suggested also by the several
cases of disputed ownership which turned on the possession of
documents giving title to the estate, even though the documents
would not necessarily have been in favour of either of the litigating
parties:[59] it seems to have been axiomatic that the case of the party
in possession of the documents was inherently stronger than that of
the party without them.[60] Against this background, it becomes clear
that the diploma was not regarded solely as an evidentiary instrument, a supplement to the fragile memory of mortal man. It may
have stood in this relation to the original transaction, but it was
produced for the good reason that the beneficiary required its
support as a title-deed thereafter and it served the same purpose for
subsequent owners of the land. Because the diploma played such an
important role in the transaction, it would arguably have been
unsatisfactory from the beneficiary's point of view if he did not
receive it on the same occasion as the transaction was completed,
especially in those cases when he handed over a sum of money to
the king as a purchase price; if he was left to acquire his diploma by
application to a local religious house, the value of the document
would have been undermined by the freedom with which others
could have been obtained and security of tenure would have been
seriously jeopardized. Of course there may have been circumstances
in which there was a lapse of time between the transaction itself
and the production of a record of it,[61] and circumstances in which
an independent agency was entrusted with the responsibility for
drawing up a diploma, but for the system just described to have

---

58 See, e.g., S 795 (endorsement), 1376 and 1512. Note also that the archives of eleventh-
century foundations, such as Abbotsbury and Horton, contained diplomas dating back
to the mid tenth century.

59 See, e.g., S 1211, 1242, 1258, 1429, 1436, 1442, 1447 and 1456–7.

60 A dispute over title which took place following the death of King Edgar was decided
partly on the ground that 'proprior erat ille, ut terram haberet, qui cyrographum habebat
quam qui non habebat' (Blake, *Liber Eliensis*, p. 99). The position of a certain Brihtwine,
who held an Abingdon estate without the permission of the community, was regarded
as quite strong, 'cum Landboc (id est, telluris descriptæ libellum,) secum haberet. Poterat
enim quis illo fiducialius pro qualibet terra disceptare, in cujus manu hujuscemodi scrip-
tura haberetur' (Stevenson, *Chronicon* I, 475).

61 See, e.g., S 876, 891 and 960.

operated effectively these are more likely to have been the exceptions than the rule.

A similarly presumptive case for the production of the diploma on the same occasion as the completion of the transaction can be made out on other grounds. The transaction itself was represented as arising from the proceedings of a *witenagemot*, strengthened by the witness of the king, the higher ecclesiastics and the prominent laymen: it was their subscriptions that validated the act in the first place, while the religious sanction of the written record extended a more lasting protection to the beneficiary and his successors. In a small proportion of the extant diplomas the draftsman chose to specify where the diploma was drawn up: for example, a formula current between 930 and 935 stated that the document was *perscripta* at a named place, while the assembled company rejoiced;[62] more ambiguous statements that a transaction was *facta* or *acta* at a named place probably carry a similar implication. These formulae demonstrate not only that meetings of the king and his *witan* were held throughout the kingdom, in royal manors, minor towns and boroughs,[63] and more often than not in places without an ecclesiastical scriptorium in the neighbourhood; they also suggest that arrangements could nevertheless be made for the drawing-up of diplomas on such occasions and in such places. But is the statement that a diploma was written at a particular place to be understood literally? If diplomas were generally drawn up on the occasion of the *witenagemot*, we might expect those that survive in their original form to contain some reflection of their use in a ceremony of conveyance. Several diplomas issued before the tenth century and apparently preserved in their original form have been judged to be originals because of the presence of external features which indicate that the preparation of the document was not a continuous process, presumably because it was at one stage required for use in a ceremony of some kind: for example, the dating clause and the witness list were perhaps added in a different ink, by a different hand, or after the document had been folded.[64] However, from the tenth century onwards the preparation of a diploma in distinct stages appears to

---

[62] S 379, 403, 405, 407, 412–13, 416–19, 422–3, 425–6, 428, 434–6, 1604 and 1792.
[63] See Fig. 1 and Appendix 2; see further below, pp. 126–34.
[64] Parsons, 'Scribal Memoranda', *passim*, and Chaplais, 'Diplomas on Single Sheets', *passim*.

1 Meeting places of the king's councillors during the tenth and eleventh centuries.

have been exceptional:[65] the whole text, including bounds, dating clause and witness list, was generally written by a single scribe at one time, and the membrane was then folded and endorsed before delivery to the beneficiary.[66] The documents were thus apparently

[65] The chief exceptions are S 690 (Bishop, *English Caroline Minuscule*, p. 9) and 971 (Hart, *Charters of Northern England*, p. 25 n. 1).

[66] It has been suggested that the endorsement on a royal diploma can be regarded as a form of scribal memorandum, written on an otherwise blank membrane before use in a ceremony of conveyance, and that the membrane was afterwards returned to the beneficiary, 'so that an ecclesiastical scribe may write down the charter at leisure' (Chaplais, 'Diplomas of Exeter', p. 34). But the scribe of the endorsement is invariably the scribe of the text

drawn up when all the details of the transaction were known and when the identity of the witnesses had been established, but it does not necessarily follow that they were drawn up some time after the transaction, on the application of the beneficiary to an ecclesiastical scriptorium. Consideration of the witness lists suggests very strongly that the diplomas were produced by scribes who had access to memoranda which represented actual records of attendance at the meetings of the king and the *witan*: one can often detect in diplomas from different archives a common order of precedency or a consistency of composition which imply that the lists were compiled according to officially established conventions, and details of the careers of identifiable individuals are reflected so neatly in lists otherwise independent of one another that the lists in turn can only reflect reality.[67] It is inconceivable that the lists are idealized or unofficial records drawn up by scribes working in different ecclesiastical scriptoria; and it seems improbable that the beneficiary would be given a memorandum to hand on to an ecclesiastical scriptorium, for if one document could be produced, then why not the finished article? But if we may accept that diplomas were drawn up in full and at one time on the occasion of the *witenagemot*, it remains uncertain whether they were produced shortly before or soon after the ceremony of conveyance: if the former, the lists would represent statements of those whose presence at the ceremony could be anticipated because they were present at the *witenagemot*, and the completed document could be transferred to the beneficiary during the course of the ceremony; if the latter, one would have to imagine either that no document was required for the purposes of whatever ceremony was performed, or that a symbolic substitute of some kind could be used.

It is important finally to emphasize that the Anglo-Saxon royal diploma had become as much a document for use in the secular world as it had always been one for the conveyance of land and privileges to the Church. The number of references in pre-Conquest sources to bookland, to the privileges attendant on possession of

---

as well; moreover, the endorsements were invariably written on one of the panels created by folding the membrane, yet the texts were apparently written before folding.

[67] These assertions should and could be justified for each reign in the tenth and eleventh centuries, but it is hoped that the tables of witness lists for the diplomas of King Æthelred, and the discussions below, pp. 48–61, 118–20, 130–4 and 154–62, will suffice here.

it and to the legal treatment of disputes over it, make it abundantly clear that tenure of land by diploma pervaded Anglo-Saxon England in the tenth and eleventh centuries (though there can be no doubt that bookland was more common in some areas than in others). The diplomas themselves create the impression that they were primarily intended for transactions taking place in an ecclesiastical context, an impression apparently confirmed by the overtly religious element in their formulation and one that provides useful support for the notion that diplomas were often drawn up by 'interested ecclesiastics'; but an awareness of the combination of circumstances that determined the survival of diplomas in favour of laymen suggests that this impression is misleading. The majority were preserved in the first instance only because a religious house acquired an interest in the land, leading to the deposit of the diploma in its archives; their preservation thereafter generally depended on the criteria of selection applied by the compiler of a cartulary or on his treatment of the documents available to him.[68] So diplomas issued in favour of laymen which referred to lands that never formed part of the endowment of a religious house would have had a relatively poor chance of preservation. It follows that the extant corpus can represent only a selection of those diplomas in circulation during the Anglo-Saxon period, and moreover that it is an unrepresentative selection. Accordingly, it is hardly surprising that one can detect an ecclesiastical interest of some kind in many diplomas, but it is a factor of their preservation rather than a factor of their production; the interest is often indirect and has to be expressed as that of an 'eventual bene-ficiary', but in such cases one might wonder whether the interest existed at the moment of the diploma's production, since some time may have elapsed before the land was acquired by or given to the church. On the whole it seems probable that the majority of the royal diplomas issued in the tenth and eleventh centuries were issued in favour of laymen, and represented transactions whose main purpose from the king's point of view was to augment his supplies of ready cash and whose main advantage from the beneficiary's point of view was to enable him to hold land freed from certain customary burdens and restrictions. Each layman would obviously have been dependent on a scriptorium of some description for the

[68] See above, pp. 1–4.

38

writing of his diploma, but since it is unlikely that ecclesiastics would be 'interested' in transactions which took place entirely in a secular context, and since some of these would have involved politically sensitive issues such as the appropriation of ecclesiastical property or the confiscation of estates from other laymen, it would be essentially improbable that the scriptorium would always have been that of a religious house. Improbable, and also intolerable from the king's point of view: the kings of the tenth and eleventh centuries could not have acted in every instance with deference to the views of the higher ecclesiastics,[69] and it would be curious if they nevertheless allowed themselves to be entirely dependent on them and on their scriptoria, especially in such an important matter as the production of diplomas for the conveyance of land and for the creation of worldly privileges.

THE CENTRALIZED PRODUCTION OF DIPLOMAS, *c*. 925–*c*. 975

An understanding of the nature of Anglo-Saxon royal diplomas thus gives rise to five general propositions which must be considered in any account of their production: first, that the prominent religious element of their formulation can be attributed simply to the circumstances under which diplomas were first introduced and drawn up in seventh-century England; secondly, that the ecclesiastical interest detectable in so many diplomas is often indirect and as such is to be regarded as a factor of their preservation and so does not bear on the circumstances of their production; thirdly, that the secular associations of the diplomas should not be underestimated, are indeed pronounced and would not always be compatible with the production of the diplomas in ecclesiastical scriptoria; fourthly, that the production of royal diplomas would have been carefully controlled, in the interests of the king and the beneficiary alike; and fifthly, that they were produced by an agency able to operate on the occasion of the *witenagemot* where the transaction was completed.

[69] One wonders what degree of assent or approval is implied by the lists of ecclesiastical witnesses which occur in diplomas like S 864, by which King Æthelred appropriated land from the see of Rochester. To some extent their assent must have been merely a legal fiction, but of course there may have been some unscrupulous ecclesiastics who were prepared to be party to such transactions. The bishop of Rochester himself was not a witness to S 864 (see below, pp. 178–9), but the bishop of Winchester attested S 861, by which land was appropriated from his see.

These propositions serve in some ways to weaken the view that diplomas were always produced in ecclesiastical scriptoria, and more constructively as the foundation of a case for their production under circumstances that allowed direct royal supervision. For further light on the problem one has to turn to more substantial and specific diplomatic evidence.

It must first be emphasized that one cannot approach the material with one's attention focussed on the diplomas preserved in the archives of a single religious house. Such a process would involve the fallacious assumption that diplomas preserved by a given house had also been produced there, thus judging the question of their production prematurely. For the eventual preservation of a diploma was determined by factors that might come into operation many years after the time of its production and that need not bear any relation to the agency of its production. It might have been transferred to the religious house when the estate to which it referred was acquired, but not perhaps before it had served as the title-deed for several generations in the family of the original beneficiary; alternatively, it might have been deposited by a local landowner for safe-keeping, at a time when the security offered by a religious house was especially desirable. The study of the individual archives will only reflect on the production of diplomas if it is known that a common denominator linked the documents with the religious house at the time of their production: a geographical link between the house which preserved the diploma and the estate to which it referred would not be sufficient, for it is evident that diplomas could be drawn up at a distance from the land concerned. In the case of diplomas in favour of religious houses or episcopal sees one is naturally on different ground, and certainly every attempt should be made to discern whether there are any continuous diplomatic threads linking a series with the same beneficiary. Overall, however, the only way to develop an argument based on the diplomatic evidence is by an examination of the entire corpus, irrespective of archive.

It seems reasonable to expect that the formulation of an Anglo-Saxon royal diploma will in some way reflect the circumstances of its production. If investigation of the extant corpus leads to the identification of several distinct diplomatic traditions, each might be held to represent the output of a different agency, or arguably that of a particular religious house; if, on the other hand, the investigation suggests the existence of a single (or at least a dominant) diplomatic tradition, the homogeneity of the documents would imply that they emanated from a common source.[70] However, it might be dangerous to attach too much significance to a superficial classification of the diplomas on the basis of their formulation. It is conceivable that different types of diploma, seeming to represent distinct diplomatic traditions, might be produced by the same agency, especially once a type had gained some currency and so was available for use as a model for diplomas drawn up by an agency other than its originator. It is also conceivable that an appearance of diplomatic homogeneity could be preserved despite the decentralized production of diplomas, perhaps by the use of common formularies or by the wide dissemination of a particular type of document. In the face of this uncertainty at one level it seems more advisable to approach the evidence of diplomatic in a different way. If we may assume on historical grounds that there would not have been more than a few meetings of the king and his council during the course of a single year, we may expect that some of the witness lists attached to a series of diplomas issued in a given year might emanate from the same gathering of the *witan*. By the analysis and comparison of the lists it may be possible to detect similarities strong enough to suggest that two or more lists represent essentially the same combination of bishops, abbots, ealdormen and *ministri*, and in such cases we might infer that the diplomas were probably issued on the same occasion. However, since only a handful of diplomas are generally available for any single year in the tenth and eleventh centuries, it is difficult to be confident that the procedure would be entirely effective: it is possible that the composition of the king's council did not change noticeably in so short a period, or, conversely, that different memoranda of those present on one occasion were used for separate transactions. Moreover, there exists no group of diplomas which by entirely different methods of approach can be shown to have been produced on the same occasion, so it is not possible to establish an independent control for the procedure.[71] But where the similarities

---

[70] Cf. Chaplais, 'Origin and Authenticity', p. 29.
[71] S 399 and 400 are both dated 16 April 928, and S 418 and 419 are both dated 24 December 932, but unfortunately the copyist of one of the diplomas in each pair drastically abbreviated the witness list.

between lists extend to the order in which the names are recorded, it is reasonable to infer that a single memorandum underlies them, perhaps indicating that the diplomas were drawn up together. And where the similarities between the diplomas concerned extend to details of their formulation, we may further infer that they were produced by the same agency. A careful distinction should be drawn between significant and fortuitous similarities. The person responsible for drawing up an Anglo-Saxon royal diploma assembled his text by combining in an established pattern a series of discrete formulae, each of which served a particular purpose in the document, and for each of which there were several alternatives from which he was required to make a choice, if he was not prepared to compose one himself. There is no reason to believe that a formulary was necessary for this purpose, nor indeed is there any evidence that such a compilation existed in the Anglo-Saxon period.[72] Existing diplomas would have provided sufficient examples of the constituent formulae, and the draftsman probably selected at random from whichever diplomas happened to be available, or reproduced the formulation of one in its entirety. Consequently, when a diploma is examined in its diplomatic context, one expects to find that each of its constituent and separate formulae can be paralleled in earlier and later texts, though perhaps less often in the case of a proem than the other formulae. Therefore the occurrence of the same formula in two or more diplomas is not *by itself* a reason for suggesting that the diplomas were produced by a single agency, if there is already a possibility that they were issued on the same occasion, though arguably more significance can be attached to a common proem than to, for example, a common sanction. On the other hand, if the diplomas share the same *combination* of formulae, there is a strong reason for making such a suggestion, and the same applies if they share a feature of structure or formulation which by comparison with other extant diplomas can be regarded as irregular or unusual.

There are several examples of pairs or groups of diplomas related in this way among those issued during the reign of King Æthelstan. In 926 he booked land in Bedfordshire to his *minister* Ealdred (S 396) and land in Derbyshire to Uhtred (S 397). The diplomas recording these transactions were preserved in the archives of

---

[72] See below, pp. 115–20.

Abingdon and Burton respectively, yet there is no doubt that they were drawn up together: as far as it extends, the abbreviated witness list in S 397 is identical with the list in S 396, and the formulae employed in the two texts are also intimately related.[73] In 928 the same king booked an estate in Wiltshire to his *minister* Brihtferth (S 400) and another estate in Wiltshire to Ælfflæd (S 399); one diploma was preserved in the archives of the Old Minster at Winchester and the other in the archives of Glastonbury. The witness list in the latter was heavily abbreviated by the cartulary copyist, but the two diplomas share the same formulation and both are said to have been drawn up on 16 April at Exeter.[74] Similarly, of two diplomas dated 24 December 932 and drawn up at Amesbury in Wiltshire, one refers to land in Dorset and was preserved in the archives of the beneficiary, Shaftesbury nunnery (S 419), and the other, in favour of the king's *minister* Alfred, refers to land in Hampshire and was preserved in the archives of the New Minster at Winchester (S 418): again the witness list of one was heavily abbreviated, but both have the same formulation.[75] In 939 King Æthelstan booked an estate in Kent to his *minister* Ealdulf (S 447) and an estate in Wiltshire to Wulfswyth, *Christi ancilla* (S 449): both diplomas are extant in their original form, the one from the archives of Christ Church Canterbury and the other from the Old Minster at Winchester, and though they are not apparently written by the same scribe they have extensive elements of their formulation in common and the witness lists were clearly based on the same memorandum; the similarities extend to the layout of the text on the membrane.[76] On a more general level, it is noticeable that a

---

[73] The sanction which occurs in both texts lacks a vital clause and is therefore nonsensical, supporting the common origin of the diplomas: for *sciat se* . . . does not have anything (such as *rationem redditurum*) to govern; moreover, a word like *digna* was omitted before *satisfactione* (*satisfactionem* in S 397).

[74] In several respects S 399 and 400 anticipate features of the diplomas of Æthelstan issued in the following years. Thus the positioning of the dating clause after the superscription in these two texts can be paralleled in S 403 and 405, themselves closely related diplomas from the archives of Chichester and Crediton respectively and both issued in April 930 (though S 405 is not authentic in its received form). A development of the sanction common to S 399 and 400 became the standard sanction used between 930 and 934.

[75] Note that the witness list of S 393 (a spurious diploma from the Old Minster Winchester) is identical with that in S 418.

[76] See above, pp. 24–5. The witness list in S 446 is very similar to that in S 449 (and 447), but the diploma is also from the Old Minster: it seems likely nevertheless that S 446 was not modelled on S 449, since the list contains a few additional names which were probably

substantial proportion of Æthelstan's diplomas issued during the 930s fall into groups clearly defined both chronologically and diplomatically. In the first place, a group characterized by the employment of a proem beginning 'Flebilia fortiter detestanda', and by other shared diplomatic features, accounts for all the authentic diplomas of Æthelstan issued between 23 March 931 and 26 January 933, at various places from Lifton in Devon to Colchester in Essex.[77] Secondly, a group characterized by the employment of a proem beginning 'Fortuna fallentis saeculi' comprises diplomas issued between 28 May 934 and 21 December 935 at places as far apart as Winchester and Nottingham.[78] There are several diplomatic points of contact between these two groups, and it is probably significant that an original of the first group (S 416) was written by the same scribe (designated 'Æthelstan A' by Drögereit) as an original of the second group (S 425); indeed, it is difficult to avoid the conclusion that all these diplomas were the work of this scribe, and that he followed the king on his travels around the kingdom.[79] A third group comprises diplomas issued between 935 and 939,[80] and a fourth comprises diplomas issued in 938 and 939.[81]

A striking instance of the production of several diplomas on the same occasion by a single agency can be detected among those issued at the beginning of the reign of King Edmund. In 940 he booked an estate in Berkshire to his *minister* Ælfsige (S 461), an estate in Somerset to his kinsman and *minister* Ælfheah and to

present in the scribal memorandum and which were perhaps omitted when S 447 and 449 were copied. The list in S 448, from Abingdon, is also very similar.

[77] S 412–13, 416–19 and 422; see also S 379, 421, 423 and perhaps 1604. The proem (or a variation of it), with or without other elements of the same formulation, occurs thereafter in S 692, 777, 781, 822, 928 and 1006.

[78] S 407 and 425–6. Three Malmesbury texts in this group, S 434–6, are all spurious, and though dated 21 December 937 they were probably based on an authentic diploma issued (presumably on the same day) in 935, since the indiction, regnal year, epact and concurrents are all correct for that year. See also the spurious S 1166 (from Malmesbury) and the incomplete S 458 (from Wilton, and related most closely to S 434–5).

[79] For important remarks on the latinity of these diplomas, see John, *Orbis Britanniae*, pp. 49–50, Lapidge, 'Hermeneutic Style', pp. 99–101, and especially Bullough, 'Educational Tradition', pp. 466–78.

[80] S 411, 429–31, 437–8 and 445–6.

[81] S 351 (in the name of King Alfred, but a forgery based on a genuine diploma of King Æthelstan), 441–2 and 449. Note that each of the third and fourth groups could be extended into the opening years of Edmund's reign: S 469 and 470 (cf. group three) and S 466 (cf. group four). The same continuity from reign to reign is personified by 'Æthelstan C' (S 447 and cf. S 468; S 464 and 512) and by 'Edmund C' (above, p. 26); cf. also S 448 and 459.

Ælfswith, Ælfheah's wife (S 462), an estate in Hampshire to his *minister* Æthelgeard (S 463) and an estate in Kent to a nun named Æthelswith (S 464); the diplomas recording these transactions were preserved in the archives of Abingdon, Glastonbury, the Old Minster at Winchester and Christ Church Canterbury respectively. The witness list attached to S 462 was not transcribed by the compiler of the Glastonbury cartulary, in accordance with his usual custom, but the lists attached to the other diplomas can be compared. It is clear that they were based on the same memorandum; the only points of difference in the lists of over thirty names are the relative positions of Eadred (the king's brother) and of Bishop Ælfric, the omission of Bishop Wulfhun from S 461, the inclusion of Siric *minister* in S 463 and the inclusion of Wulfric *minister* in S 461. S 464 has six additional *ministri* after Wulfhelm (the last witness in S 461 and 463), but reference to the extant original version of the diploma reveals that the names were added by a different hand to complete the column: the main scribe (designated 'Æthelstan C' by Drögereit) wrote only the first name in the fifth column, thus ending with Wulfhelm as in S 461 and 463; the same scribe adopted an identical layout in S 512 (dated 943) and had also left space beneath the last witness in S 447 (dated 939). The three diplomas with full witness lists were certainly produced on the same occasion,[82] and there is a strong probability that all three, together with S 462, were drawn up by the same agency: *mutatis mutandis*, S 461, 462 and 463 are in identical terms throughout, and S 464 shares substantial elements of the same formulation, differing chiefly in its superscription and sanction.[83]

Further instances of a similar relationship between diplomas dated to the same year could be cited from the 940s,[84] but the important principle is already well established: that diplomas in favour

[82] S 461 and 463-4 were produced while Æthelwold, Ealhhelm and Æthelmund were still *ministri*; two other diplomas of 940, S 465 and 470, from the Old and New Minsters at Winchester respectively, were issued later in the year when these three had become ealdormen, and contain witness lists certainly based on a common memorandum (see also the lists in S 467 and 469).

[83] The sanction in S 464 was current between 937 and 947: S 438, 447, 449, 460, 464, 468-9, 476, 490, 510, 518, 527, 580 and 1811; cf. S 442 and 663. It recurs in S 831.

[84] Indeed, the diplomas issued during the 940s constitute such a closely related group in terms of their formulation and witness lists that to specify the examples would be to describe the diplomatic tradition of the whole decade. One is left with no doubt that the great majority of them were the work of a single agency.

of various beneficiaries, ecclesiastical as well as lay, referring to estates in different parts of the country and preserved in the archives of different religious houses, could be produced by a single agency, acting on the same occasion and necessarily at a distance from some or all of the estates concerned. We may designate this agency a central secretariat, because it catered for a variety of beneficiaries, and obviously we may exclude the possibility that it was in any way 'interested' in the transactions, since they cut across diocesan boundaries and involve lands which came into the possession of different religious houses. Of course the examples cited so far derive from the period when the production of diplomas in a single scriptorium (or by a single secretariat, to avoid the implication of a fixed geographical location) is firmly established on palaeographical grounds. One has next to discover whether there is further evidence for the centralized production of diplomas in the 950s and 960s, during the period when an increasing number of ecclesiastical scriptoria became active and when it is suggested that the homogeneity of the documents evident in the 930s and 940s gave way to greater diversity, reflecting the decentralization of their production amongst the new scriptoria. Should such evidence be forthcoming, the case for interpreting the centralized production of diplomas in terms of a royal secretariat and not in terms of an ecclesiastical scriptorium with a monopoly would be considerably stronger: for it would emerge that the organization established during the reign of Æthelstan persisted in the heyday of the monastic reform movement.

The years between 950 and 955 present something of a diplomatic puzzle. Fewer diplomas appear to have been issued during this period than during comparable periods in the two preceding decades, and none at all have survived from 954 (see Fig. 2). Moreover, most of those that were produced in the closing years of Eadred's reign are of a distinctive type that sets them apart from earlier diplomas. The diagnostic features are the occurrence of the date at the beginning of the text, the absence of a proem, and characteristic elements of formulation from the superscription to the sentence introducing the list of witnesses; but the most curious feature is the absence of the king's name from the list itself, as if he had not been present when the diploma was drawn up. The type

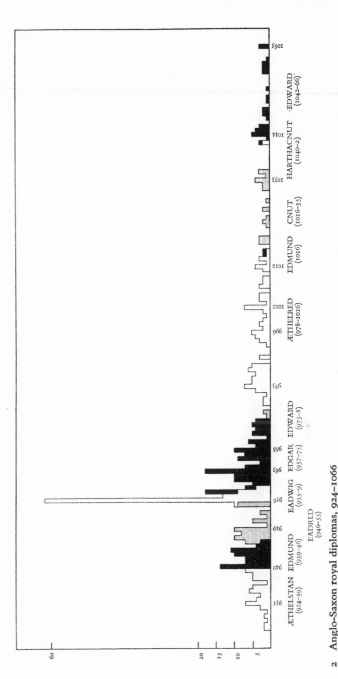

2 Anglo-Saxon royal diplomas, 924–1066

Note. This diagram is intended to convey a general impression only of the relative numbers of diplomas issued from year to year between the reigns of Æthelstan (924–39) and Edward the Confessor (1042–66) inclusive. The figures for each year as plotted represent the number of diplomas now extant (whether as originals or in later copies), including texts judged to be spurious insofar as these appear to have been modelled on authentic exemplars which have not otherwise survived. The shading distinguishes the diplomas of one king from those of his predecessor or successor.

appears for the first time in 953 (S 560–2), and again in 955 (S 563–5, 568).[85] The combination of the king's apparent absence and the distinctive structure and formulation of the diplomas raises the possibility that they were drawn up under abnormal circumstances, and the explanation may lie either in the king's illness or in the turbulent political history of the period:[86] perhaps King Eadred was too ill to attend meetings of his councillors, or if he was not, he was possibly preoccupied with the subjugation of the Northumbrian kingdom, and in either case he may have authorized an agency independent of his own entourage to draw up diplomas on his behalf. There is some slight evidence connecting this type of diploma with Glastonbury Abbey,[87] and it may be significant that Eadred is known to have been on particularly close terms with Abbot Dunstan;[88] the features of formulation characteristic of the type recur in a later series of diplomas distributed more sporadically between 956 and 986 and attested by the king,[89] some of which also have intriguing links with Glastonbury and Dunstan.[90]

The exceptionally large number of diplomas preserved from the reign of King Eadwig (see Fig. 2) affords an excellent opportunity

---

[85] See also S 570 and 579. It was used again for diplomas of King Edgar in 958 (S 676 and 678) and 975 (S 802).

[86] For the former, see Stubbs, *Memorials*, p. 31, and for the latter, see Stenton, *Anglo-Saxon England*, pp. 360–3.

[87] Elements of the formulation are anticipated in S 509 and 555, both preserved at Glastonbury and said to have been written at Dunstan's command; see also Chaplais, 'Anglo-Saxon Chancery', pp. 47–8, where it is suggested that the extant original of S 563 was written at Glastonbury. S 802 is said to have been *acta* in the monastery at Glastonbury.

[88] Stubbs, *Memorials*, pp. 29–31, and see further below, pp. 147–8. The coincidence of King Eadred's entrusting, for a while before his death, his royal treasures and charters to Dunstan at Glastonbury, and the appearance of this distinctive group of diplomas in the closing years of Eadred's reign, is certainly most intriguing.

[89] S 571, 574, 605, 661, 670, 694, 726, 735, 743, 750, 753, 785, 790–1, 803, 854 and 862. Several of these are in favour of Bath Abbey (S 661, 694, 735, 785 and 854), but they may not all be authentic: S 661 and 854 are certainly spurious in their received form, and share an error in the sanction (cf. the formula in S 694) which suggests that they have a common origin.

[90] S 571 is said to have been witnessed by Abbot Dunstan and the Glastonbury community, and S 670 was allegedly issued at the abbey; neither is likely to be authentic in its received form, but the fact that neither was preserved at Glastonbury reassures one that their association with the abbey may derive ultimately from genuine texts. S 753 is in favour of Dunstan as archbishop; S 743 and 791 are in favour of Glastonbury. There is, however, no reason to believe that a diploma belonging to this series was necessarily produced at Glastonbury, for the type could have been imitated by anyone. Hart, *Charters of Northern England*, pp. 19–22, designates the type 'Dunstan B' and assigns the diplomas variously to Glastonbury, Bath, Worcester and Abingdon.

of establishing what arrangements existed for the production of diplomas in the later 950s. For by analysing the witness lists and formulation of the sixty-odd diplomas issued in 956 in particular, one might (for example) be able to identify distinct groups amongst the diplomas, each of which would arguably represent the output of a single agency operating on successive occasions during the year; or one might detect such heterogeneity as most naturally to suggest that the production of diplomas had become decentralized. Some progress towards arranging the diplomas of 956 in a relative chronological order can be made initially by the application of criteria involving the careers of individual witnesses and suggested either by external sources or by the internal evidence of the lists themselves. In the first place, we learn from the earliest *Vita Dunstani* that Dunstan lived in exile during the reign of King Eadwig, having incurred the king's enmity when, at the request of the bishops and leading men of the kingdom, he recalled the lustful king from his diversions to his coronation banquet.[91] Three diplomas of 956 have the subscription of Abbot Dunstan, and if we may assume that he left the country soon after the coronation in January,[92] these may reasonably be assigned to the opening weeks of the year.[93] The author of the *Vita Dunstani* associates Dunstan's kinsman Cynesige, bishop of Lichfield, with him in the attempt to recall the king, and it is interesting that Cynesige also attested only three of the diplomas of 956, two of which were attested by Dunstan;[94] the third is arguably of the same period as the others, since it now appears that Cynesige, like Dunstan, was excluded from the king's court for the greater part of the year, whether by his own or by Eadwig's choice, though he had returned by 9 May 957 (S 636). One of the diplomas attested by both Dunstan and Cynesige happens also to be the only diploma of 956 with the subscription of Wulfstan, archbishop of York (S 605): Wulfstan had attested a diploma (S 582) issued in 955 after the accession of King Eadwig, in late

---

[91] Stubbs, *Memorials*, pp. 32–4.
[92] See Nelson, 'Inauguration Rituals', p. 66 n. 99, for the date of Eadwig's coronation (probably 27 January).
[93] S 597, 605 and 663; see also S 633. One should bear in mind that abbots were not by this time established as regular witnesses to royal diplomas, so Dunstan's absence is certainly no indication that the diploma was issued after he went into exile.
[94] S 597, 605 and 629.

November, and may still have been in the south in the early weeks of 956 and thus available for inclusion in S 605; but his absence from diplomas thereafter suggests perhaps that he became ill or that he returned north and remained there until his death on 16 December.[95] The second criterion arises from the fact that the see of Wells shows a change of bishops during the course of the year: Wulfhelm attested only S 608 in 956, and was succeeded by Brihthelm, perhaps the priest of S 614 and the 'bishop-elect' of S 615.[96] Subscriptions of a bishop called Brihthelm occur in most of the diplomas of 956 and probably belong to Brihthelm, bishop of London; but five or six diplomas were witnessed also by a second Brihthelm and are arguably later as a group than those with only one bishop of the name.[97] Thirdly, there are three ealdormen who appear for the first time in 956, and whose subscriptions enable one considerably to refine the relative order of the diplomas. Ealdorman Ælfhere of Mercia occurs in the majority of them, and the reasonable inference that he was appointed at the beginning of the year is confirmed by his attestation in S 607, dated 13 February.[98] Ealdorman Brihtnoth occurs in only four of the diplomas dated 956 and may therefore have been appointed towards the end of the year: it seems likely on other grounds that he succeeded Brihtferth as ealdorman of Essex, and certainly the two men do not overlap in the witness lists.[99] Ealdorman Æthelwold of East Anglia also appears for the first time in 956, attesting twenty-one diplomas. The subscriptions of a *minister* called Æthelwold occur on fourteen diplomas and never

[95] The date of Wulfstan's death is disputed: see Hart, *Charters of Northern England*, pp. 376–7, and Whitelock, 'Appointment of Dunstan', p. 241. The case for 956 depends on his subscription to S 605, on *ASC* MS 'D' and on the relative sequence of events implied by Florence of Worcester in his annal for the year.

[96] That the Brihthelm 'priest' of S 614 had become a bishop by 957 is shown by S 1292; the Brihthelm 'deacon' of S 582 may be the same man.

[97] S 602, 610–13 and ?630.

[98] He can probably be identified as the 'Ælfhere .ex parentela regis. minister' who attested S 582, and whose brother Ælfheah was prominent amongst the *ministri* during the reign, before being appointed an ealdorman himself. But I cannot agree with Hart, *Charters of Northern England*, p. 260, that the Ælfhere *minister* of S 609 and 622 can be identified as the ealdorman, requiring these diplomas to be dated before 13 February 956. This Ælfhere does attest beside the known Ælfheah, but he is not the same Ælfhere: cf. S 603, with Ælfhere beside Ælfheah and yet also attested by Ealdorman Ælfhere; cf. also S 594 and 608, if (as is most likely) 'Ælfre' can be regarded as a contracted form of 'Ælfhere'.

[99] Brihtnoth is the beneficiary of S 611 (dated 26 November 956) and attests last amongst the ealdormen; he also attests last in S 602, 610 and 616. S 617 is a diploma issued in his favour when he was still a *minister*, referring to land at the same place as S 611.

coincide with the subscriptions of Ealdorman Æthelwold, thus creating a strong presumption that the *minister* was the man who later became the ealdorman.[100]

When these criteria are applied collectively to the diplomas of 956 one is struck by the extent to which they support one another. The group of diplomas witnessed by Ealdorman Brihtferth overlaps substantially with the group witnessed by Æthelwold as *minister*; the subscriptions of Æthelwold *minister*, Abbot Dunstan, Bishop Cynesige, Archbishop Wulfstan and Ealdorman Brihtferth are interlocked, and the subscription of Bishop Wulfhelm occurs on a diploma in favour of Æthelwold *minister*; Ealdorman Brihtferth coincides with Brihthelm as priest and bishop-elect; the subscriptions of Æthelwold as ealdorman are interlocked with those of the two Bishops Brihthelm and do not overlap with those of Ealdorman Brihtferth; a diploma in favour of Brihtnoth *minister* is witnessed by Ealdorman Æthelwold, indicating that he became an ealdorman first, but otherwise Brihtnoth's subscriptions as ealdorman overlap with Æthelwold's as ealdorman and with the two Bishops Brihthelm. It is, then, with some degree of confidence that we can arrange the diplomas of 956 in a rough chronological sequence, and, as it happens, only a few remain untouched by any of the criteria. When this has been done, it becomes much easier to detect general similarities between witness lists in such a large series of diplomas, simply because the possibilities have been considerably reduced. Without making reference at this stage to details of formulation, the following groups emerge:

Group One (Fig. 3)

S	Details of transaction	Archive
589	King Eadwig to Ælfric, his *familiarissimus* and *fidelis*: grant of land in Hampshire	Old Minster Winchester
594	King Eadwig to Ælfwine, his *familiarissimus*: grant of land in Berkshire	Abingdon
597	King Eadwig to Ælric, his *adoptivus parens*: grant of land in Berkshire	Abingdon

[100] The diplomas attested by Æthelwold as *minister* are: S 583, 590, 592, 594, 597–8, 604, 607, 609, 615, 621–2, 624 and 663. The diplomas attested by Æthelwold as ealdorman are: S 581, 584–5, 587, 588, 591, 593, 602, 610–13, 616–19, 623, 634, 638, 659 and 661. An Æthelwold *minister* or *fidelis* was also the beneficiary of S 606 and 608, neither of which has the subscription of Æthelwold as ealdorman or *minister*.

608	King Eadwig to Æthelwold, his *fidelis*: grant of land at *Wudetune* (unidentified)	Old Minster Winchester
614	King Eadwig to the priest Brihthelm, his *fidelis*: grant of land in Berkshire	Abingdon
627	King Eadwig to Hehelm, his *familiarissimus fidelis*: grant of land in Somerset	Bath
629	King Eadwig to Malmesbury Abbey: grant of land in Wiltshire	Malmesbury
631	King Eadwig to Wistan, his *fidelis*: grant of land in Wiltshire	Wilton
637	King Eadwig to Wulfric, his *dilectus fidelis* and *famosissimus venator*: grant of land in Wiltshire	Christchurch (Twynham)
666	King Eadwig to Wiferth, his *fidelis vassallus*: grant of land in Wiltshire	Wilton

The witness lists attached to these diplomas can be grouped together for the following reasons. In the diplomas of 956, the atheling Edgar is generally positioned immediately after the king and before Oda, archbishop of Canterbury. The exceptions are four anomalous diplomas,[101] and S 589, 597, 608, 614, 629, 637 and 666, all of which are in Group One; the criterion cannot be applied to S 594, 627 and 631, because in the first Archbishop Oda does not occur, and in the two others Edgar does not occur. A feature shared by all the diplomas in this group is the appearance of Daniel, bishop of Cornwall, at the end of the lists of bishops.[102] Another important common denominator is that the lists of ealdormen are always headed by Æthelstan, followed in second place by Æthelsige: it is the position of the latter that is significant, since he is usually lower down in the lists. The lists of *ministri* are headed by the brothers Ælfgar and Brihtferth in the two diplomas in which they are included (S 589 and 594), but otherwise the precedence appears to belong to Ælfheah and Ælfsige, who head four (S 597, 608, 614 and 631) and two (S 627 and 666) lists respectively; Ælfheah, Ælfsige, Æthelgeard, Æthelmær and Alfred occur more consistently than any others. The group includes diplomas that have the subscriptions of Abbot Dunstan, Bishop Cynesige, Bishop Wulfhelm and Ealdorman Brihtferth; one is in favour of Brihthelm the priest, and Æthelwold occurs twice as a witness (and possibly once as a

---

[101] S 581, 630, 633 and 659.

[102] It may sometimes have been the procedure to select witnesses' names from a memorandum according to the availability of space on a particular membrane, but to include the last name on the list, as if – by including him – to imply the presence of the rest.

	S										
	605	589	594	597	608	614	627	629	631	637	666
KING EADWIG	1	1	1	1	1	1	1	1	1	1	1
Archbishop ODA	2	1		1	1	1	1	1	1	1	1
„ WULFSTAN	3										
EDGAR	1	2	1	2	2	2		2		2	(2)
Bishops											
ÆLFSIGE	1	1	1	1		1	1	1	1	1	1
OSULF	4	2	4	6	2	2	2	2	2	2	3
WULFSIGE	5	3	2	2	1	3		3	3		2
OSCETEL	9		3	5	3			5		3	
CENWALD	7			4		4		4			
CYNESIGE	6			3				6			
ATHULF	8			7				7			
WULFHELM					4						
ÆLFWOLD	2								5		
BRIHTHELM	3						3		4		
DANIEL		4	5	8	5	5	4	8	6	4	4
Abbot DUNSTAN	1			1							
Ealdormen											
ÆTHELSTAN	1	1	1	1	1	1	1	1	1		1
ÆTHELSIGE	2	2	2	2	2	2	2	2	2		2
ÆLFHERE	3	3	3	3	3	4	5		4		
EDMUND	4	4		4	4	3	3	3	3		3
ÆTHELSTAN	5	5	4	7		7	4	4			
ÆTHELMUND		6	5	6	5	6			5		
BRIHTFERTH			6	5	6	5		6			
Ministri											
ÆLFGAR	1	1	1								
BRIHTFERTH	2	2	2								
ÆLFHEAH		3	5	1	1	1			1		
ÆLFSIGE	5	4	4	2	7	2	1	2	2		1
ÆTHELGEARD	3	6	6	9		3	3	3	4		
ÆTHELMÆR		5	3	8	6	5	2		3		
ALFRED		7	9		10	4	4		5		
ÆLFWINE				12		6		4	6		
WULFRIC	4	10	10		5						
ÆLFRIC		8									
ÆLFSIGE		9		3							
ÆTHELWOLD			7	11							
ÆLF[HE]RE			8		2						
ÆLFHEAH			11								
ÆTHELWEARD			12								
EADRIC				4							
OSWEARD				5							
LEOFWINE				6							
EDMUND				7							
OSWIG				10							
WULLAF					3						
WITGAR					4						
WULFRIC					8						
WULFGAR					9						
ALFRED						7					
ÆTHELSIGE							5				
ÆLFHELM								1			

Notes

S 605, apparently issued at the very beginning of 956, before the diplomas of Group One, is included here for purposes of comparison.

S 666: Edgar is listed after the bishops.

3 The diplomas of King Eadwig issued in 956: Group One

beneficiary) with the status of *minister*. The group therefore belongs to the earlier part of the year, in fact before 13 February (see next group) and conceivably to the occasion of the king's coronation on about 27 January.

Group Two (Fig. 4)

S	Details of transaction	Archive
583	King Eadwig to Abingdon Abbey: grant of land in Berkshire	Abingdon
590	King Eadwig to Ælfric, his *minister*: grant of land in Berkshire	Abingdon
592	King Eadwig to Ælfsige, his *minister*: grant of land in Northamptonshire	Peterborough
596	King Eadwig to Ælfwold, his *fidelis minister*: grant of land in Somerset	Old Minster Winchester
598	King Eadwig to Æthelgeard, his *princeps*: grant of land in Hampshire	Old Minster Winchester
600	King Eadwig to Æthelhild, a *nobilis femina*: grant of land in Hampshire	Old Minster Winchester
601	King Eadwig to Æthelhild, a *nobilis femina*: grant of land in Devon	Sherborne (Horton)
603	King Eadwig to Æthelnoth, his *fidelis minister*: grant of land in Berkshire	Abingdon
604	King Eadwig to Æthelsige, his *fidelis minister*: grant of land in Hampshire	Old Minster Winchester
606	King Eadwig to Æthelwold, his *fidelis minister*: grant of land in Somerset	Old Minster Winchester
607	King Eadwig to Abbot Æthelwold and the monks at Abingdon Abbey: grant of land in Berkshire	Abingdon
609	King Eadwig to Alfred, one of his *optimates*: grant of land in Dorset	Wilton
615	King Eadwig to Brihthelm, bishop-elect, one of his *chari propinqui*: grant of land in Northamptonshire	Abingdon
621	King Eadwig to Eadric, one of his *cari*: grant of land in Surrey	Abingdon
622	King Eadwig to Eadric, his *minister*: grant of land in Berkshire	Abingdon
624	King Eadwig to Edmund, one of his *optimates*: grant of land in Sussex	Abingdon
635	King Eadwig to Wulfric, one of his *proceres*: grant of land in Wiltshire	Old Minster Winchester
636	King Eadwig to Wulfric, one of his *principes*: grant of land in Hampshire	Old Minster Winchester
663	King Eadwig to Abbot Æthelwold and Abingdon Abbey: grant of land in Berkshire	Abingdon
1662	King [Eadwig] to ? : grant of land on the Isle of Wight	Evesham

Category	S	583	590	592	596	598	600	601	603	604	606	607	609	615	621	622	624	635	636	663	1662
	KING EADWIG	1	1	1	1	1	1	1	1	1	1	1	1	1	1	1	1	1	1	1	(1)
	EDGAR	2	2	2	2	2	2	2		2	2	2	2	(2)	2	2	2	2	2	2	2
	Archbishop ODA	1	1	1	1	1	1	1	1	1	1	1	1		1	1	1	1	1	1	1
Bishops	ÆLFSIGE	2	2	2	2	2	2	2	2	2	2	2	2	(2)	2	2	2	2	2	2	2
Bishops	CENWALD	3	3	3	3		3	3	3	3	5	3		1	3	3		3		3	3
Bishops	OSCETEL	4	4	4	4	3	4	4	4	4	6	4	3	2	4	4	3	4	3	4	4
Bishops	OSULF	5	5	5	5	4	5	5	5	5	7	5	4	3	5	5	4	5	4	5	5
Bishops	WULFSIGE	6	6		6	5			6	6	8							6	5		
Bishops	BRIHTHELM	7	7	6	7	6	6	6	7	7	3	6	5	4	6		5	7	6	6	6
Bishops	ÆLFWOLD	8	8	7					8	8	4	7						8			7
Bishops	ATHULF	9	9	8		7			9		9	8	6	5	7			6	9	8	7
Bishops	DANIEL					10					9										
Abbots	DUNSTAN																			1	
Abbots	ÆTHELWOLD									1										2	
Ealdormen	ÆTHELSTAN	1	1	1	1	1	1	1			1	1	1	1	1	1	1	1	1	1	1
Ealdormen	EDMUND	2	2	2	2	2	2	2	2	2	2	2	2	2	2	2		2	2	2	2
Ealdormen	ÆTHELSTAN	3	3	3	3	3	3				3	3	3	3	3	3	3			3	3
Ealdormen	BRIHTFERTH	4	4			4	4	3			3	4	5	4			2	4	3	4	4
Ealdormen	ÆTHELMUND	5	5	6				5	4	3	4	6	7							6	6
Ealdormen	ÆLFHERE	6	6	4	4	5	6	5	1		5	4			5				5	4	5
Ealdormen	ÆTHELSIGE	7	7	5	5		7	6		5	7	6	4	4		4	4	7		7	5
Ministri	ÆLFSIGE	1	1	1	1	1	1	1		1	1	1			1	1	1	1	1	1	1
Ministri	WULFRIC	2	2	3	2	2	2	2	2	2	2	2			2	2	2	2	2	2	2
Ministri	ÆTHELGEARD	3	3	4	3		3	3	3	3	3	3			3	3	3	3	3	3	3
Ministri	ÆLFHEAH	4	4	2	4	3	4	4	8	1	6	4	5		4	5	4	4	4	4	4
Ministri	ÆLFSIGE	5	9	7	5	4				7		7	9		5	6	10				7
Ministri	ÆLFGAR	10	5	8		6	5	5		8	8	7	1	7		5	5	5	8		
Ministri	BRIHTFERTH	8	6	9		7	6	6	4	5	9	9	8		6			6	6	6	9
Ministri	WULFRIC	6	14		8					5											
Ministri	ÆLFHEAH	7	7			8	7		10	4							7				
Ministri	ÆLFWOLD	9	8	5								10		2		9			10		
Ministri	ÆLFRIC	11	10	6	6	9			7	13		6	6	4		7				6	
Ministri	ÆTHELWOLD	12	12	10		10			9			12	10	3	8	9	7				12
Ministri	WULFGAR	13	13	13		10			10			13	11		9	11	8				13
Ministri	ALFRED	14				5				8		5						7		5	5
Ministri	CYNESIGE								12	11		14	12								14
Ministri	ÆLFWIG		11		7																
Ministri	ÆLFSIGE			11							12						8				
Ministri	ÆLFWINE			12																	
Ministri	EADRIC			14								16									
Ministri	ÆLFNOTH					5															
Ministri	ÆLFGARD					6															
Ministri	ÆLFHERE					9	6							4			4				
Ministri	EADRED					11															
Ministri	LEOFRIC									4											
Ministri	ÆTHERED									7											
Ministri	ÆLFRIC											11								11	
Ministri	LEOFWINE											15									
Ministri	ÆTHELFERTH											17									
Ministri	ÆLFSIGE																10				

Notes

S 592: Ealdorman Æthelsige occurs as 'Ælfsige'.
S 600: Bishop Cenwald occurs twice; Æthelgeard *minister* occurs as 'Æðelhearð'.
S 603: Ælfsige *minister* occurs as 'Æþelsie'.
S 604, 607 and 609: the first *minister* occurs as the last ealdorman; in S 604, Ælfheah may however be an error for (Ealdorman) Ælfhere.
S 621: the copyist displaced Edgar and Bishop Ælfsige.
S 1662: King Eadwig occurs as 'Eadred'.

4 The diplomas of King Eadwig issued in 956: Group Two

The principal feature that characterizes the diplomas attributed to this group is the relative order of the bishops, identical in every list with the exception of S 606, in which Brihthelm and Ælfwold are displaced.[103] Any two or three of the bishops might be omitted in a given list, and in distinction from earlier and later groups Daniel occurs only twice, at the end of long lists. The ealdormen are headed by Æthelstan and Edmund, and Æthelsige is generally listed last; the subscriptions of Brihtferth still occur, though they are not found in Groups Three and Four. The *ministri* are dominated consistently by a triumvirate comprising Ælfsige, Wulfric and Æthelgeard,[104] and it is interesting to find the same names among the beneficiaries as well. Ælfheah and a second Ælfsige are also consistent witnesses, and Ælfgar and Brihtferth often occur together, though never in a particularly prominent position; the subscriptions of Æthelwold as *minister* are quite common, but they do not occur in Groups Three and Four; Wulfgar and Ælfric attest several times apiece, the former often in the penultimate or final position. It is the fact that the separate lists of bishops, ealdormen and *ministri*, characterized in this way, occur in combination in so many diplomas that justifies the attribution of the diplomas to the same group. S 607 clearly belongs to the group, and is dated 13 February,[105] suggesting roughly when the other diplomas may have been produced. The subscription of Abbot Dunstan in S 663, and that of Abbot Æthelwold, may be insertions, but given the probable date of the diploma Dunstan's appearance is still acceptable. That this group is later than Group One is suggested by S 615, in favour of Brihthelm as bishop-elect, and by the non-appearance of his predecessor Wulfhelm.

---

[103] In S 615, Archbishop Oda and Bishop Ælfsige are omitted, but the transcriber's note suggests that the condition of his exemplar was poor: 'Multa hic non quivi legere set conjectavi ut potui.' In S 621, the atheling Edgar and Bishop Ælfsige have clearly been displaced by careless transcription. In S 663, Bishop Ælfsige is supplied from B.L. Cotton Claudius C ix.

[104] The exception is S 615: but the transcriber may well have been unable to read the first column of *ministri* on his exemplar (see previous note).

[105] The diploma may be spurious, but the list is genuine and may have been copied from a dated original. Of course, if the date is not accepted, the position is radically altered, and it becomes impossible to date the diplomas of Groups One and Two with any accuracy before the only other dated list, in November (S 611).

Group Three (Fig. 5)

The diplomas here assigned to a third group should be divided into two sections, both of which represent situations transitional between the preceding and following groups but which may or may not themselves represent the same situation.

S	Details of transaction	Archive
584	King Eadwig to Abingdon Abbey: grant of land in Oxfordshire	Abingdon
617	King Eadwig to Brihtnoth, his *minister*: grant of land in Oxfordshire	Abingdon
618	King Eadwig to Brihtric, *minister*: grant of land in Oxfordshire	Abingdon
623	King Eadwig to Eadwig, his *fidelis minister*: grant of land in Northamptonshire	Burton

In a sense we are dealing with only two independent lists in this section, since those in S 617 and 618 are identical, and that in S 584 is attached to a spurious diploma and was probably derived from either S 617 or 618; all three diplomas refer to estates at the same place. The diplomas of this section have curious links with Group One, and yet are later than Group Two. The appearance of Daniel at the end of the lists of bishops, the position of Æthelsige second amongst the ealdormen, the prominence of Ælfgar and Brihtferth and the occurrence of Æthelmær amongst the *ministri*, together suggest the association with Group One; but the position of the atheling Edgar dissociates these diplomas from it, and the appearance of Æthelwold as an ealdorman places them, moreover, after Group Two, while the occurrence of Brihtnoth *minister* as the beneficiary of S 617 places them before Group Four. One may also note the non-appearance of the second Ealdorman Æthelstan and of Ealdorman Brihtferth: the former occurs again in the next group, but Brihtferth does not, and his absence may thus imply the permanent end to his subscriptions and therefore in another way set this section apart from the diplomas of Group Two.

S	Details of transaction	Archive
585	King Eadwig to Ælfheah, his *fidelis minister ac propinquus*: grant of land in Wiltshire	Old Minster Winchester
634	King Eadwig to Wulfric, his *minister*: grant of land in Berkshire	Abingdon
638	King Eadwig to Wynsige, his *fidelis minister*: grant of land in Wiltshire	Old Minster Winchester

	S	584	617	618	623	585	634	638
KING EADWIG		1	1	1	1	1	1	1
EDGAR		2	2	2	2	2	2	2
Archbishop ODA		1	1	1	1	1	1	1
ÆLFSIGE		2	2	2	2	2	2	2
CENWALD						3	3	3
OSCETEL						4	4	4
OSULF		3	3	3	3	5	5	5
BRIHTHELM		4	4	4	4	6	6	6
WULFSIGE		5	5	5		7	8	
ÆLFWOLD						8	7	
ATHULF						9	9	7
DANIEL		6	6	6	5			8
ÆTHELSTAN		1	1	1	1	1	1	1
ÆTHELSIGE		2	2	2	2	5	6	5
ÆLFHERE		3	3	3	4	3	5	4
EDMUND		4	4	4	3	2	2	2
ÆTHELWOLD		5	5	5	5	6	7	6
ÆTHELMUND			6	6	6	4	4	
ÆTHELSTAN							3	3
ÆLFGAR		2	1	1	1	6	4	7
BRIHTFERTH		3	2	2	2	7	5	8
ÆLFHEAH		4	3	3	3?	4		3
ÆTHELGEARD		1	4	4		3	3	2
ALFRED		5	5	5	5	9	6	
ÆTHELMÆR		6	6	6	4			
WULFRIC					6	2	2	
ÆLFSIGE						1	1	1
ÆLFSIGE						5	8	5
ÆLFRIC						8	9	11
ÆLFWOLD						10		
ÆLFRIC						11		
ÆLFSIGE						12		
ÆLFWIG						13		12
EADRIC						14		9
CYNESIGE						15		4
WULFGAR							7	
ÆLFWINE							10	10
ÆLFHEAH								6

Notes

S 584: Æthelgeard *minister* occurs as 'Ælgeard'.
S 585: the first *minister* occurs as the last ealdorman.

5 The diplomas of King Eadwig issued in 956: Group Three

58

The diplomas in this section have quite strong links with the second group: the order of the ealdormen is comparable, and the *ministri* are dominated by Ælfsige, Wulfric, Æthelgeard and Ælfheah, with Ælfgar and Brihtferth together lower down. But again, the appearance of Æthelwold as an ealdorman, and perhaps the non-appearance of Ealdorman Brihtferth, set this section apart from the previous group; yet the prominence of Wulfric among the *ministri*, and the occurrence there also of Ælfgar and Brihtferth, distinguish it from the next. The differences amongst the *ministri* and in the order of the ealdormen prevent one from suggesting that the diplomas of both sections were drawn up on the same occasion using a common memorandum of witnesses' names, but there are sufficient similarities to suggest that the sections represent the same general period: the indications setting them apart from Groups Two and Four, the subscriptions of Ealdorman Æthelwold but not of Ealdorman Brihtferth, and perhaps the same slight variation in the normal order of the bishops, in the relative positions of Brihthelm and Wulfsige.

Group Four (Fig. 6)

S	Details of transaction	Archive
587	King Eadwig to Ælfhere, *comes*: grant of land in Oxfordshire	Abingdon
588	King Eadwig to Ælfhere, *comes*: grant of land in Warwickshire	Abingdon
591	King Eadwig to Ælfsige, his *fidelis*: grant of land in Berkshire	Abingdon
602	King Eadwig to Æthelnoth, his *fidelis minister*: grant of land in Staffordshire	Burton
610	King Eadwig to Bath Abbey: grant of land in Gloucestershire	Bath
611	King Eadwig to Brihtnoth *princeps*, his *fidelis*: grant of land in Oxfordshire	Abingdon
612	King Eadwig to Byrnric, his *minister*: grant of land in Wiltshire	Wilton
613	King Eadwig to Byrnric, his *fidelis minister*: grant of land in Hampshire	Old Minster Winchester
619	King Eadwig to Eadric, his *fidelis minister*: grant of land in Hampshire	Old Minster Winchester
620	King Eadwig to Eadric, his *homo*: grant of land in Berkshire	Abingdon
661	King Eadwig to Bath Abbey: restoration of land in Somerset	Bath

	S 587	588	591	602	610	611	612	613	619	620	661
KING EADWIG	1	1	1	1	1	1	1	1	1	1	1
EDGAR	2	2	2	2	2		2	2	2	2	2
Bishops											
Archbishop ODA	1	1	1	1	1	1	1	1	1	1	1
ÆLFSIGE	2	2	2	2	2	3	2	2	2	2	2
BRIHTHELM	3	3	4?	3	3	2	3	3	5?		4?
CENWALD				4	4	4	4	4		3	
OSCETEL	4	4	3	5	5	5	5	5	3	4	3
OSULF	5	5		6	6	6	6	6	4	5	
BRIHTHELM			4?	7	7	8	7	7	5?		4?
WULFSIGE						8	7			7	
ÆLFWOLD	6	6				9	9			6	
ATHULF						8	10	8	8	8	6
DANIEL	7	7	5			10	11		9	7	5
Ealdormen											
ÆTHELSTAN	1	1	1	1	1		1	1	1	1	1
EDMUND	2	2	2			2	2	2	2	2	2
ÆTHELSTAN	3	3				3	3	3	3		
ÆLFHERE			3	2	3	1	4	4	4	5	3
ÆTHELSIGE	4	4	4	3	4	5	5	5	5	4	4
ÆTHELMUND			5				4				5
ÆTHELWOLD	5	5	6	4	5	3	6	6	6		6
BRIHTNOTH						5	6	6			
Ministri											
ÆLFHEAH	1	1	3	1	1	1	3	3	1	1	3
ÆLFSIGE	4	4	1	2	2	2	1	1	2	2	1
ÆTHELGEARD			4		6	3	2	2	11		5
ALFRED	2	2			4	5			10		
ÆLFGAR						3			8		
BRIHTFERTH			2			4	7		12		2
ÆLFRIC					3	8	5	6	6	3	4
ÆLFSIGE					5	9			5	5	4
EADRIC	8	8				8	10	4	4	4	8
ÆLFWINE	5	5	5			7	8	8	5	3	6
ÆLFWIG						7	14	7	7	15	7
ÆTHELMÆR	3	3							14		4
WULFSTAN	6	6									
WULFGAR	7	7				12				6	6
ÆTHELRIC				6							
ÆLFNOTH						6		9			
BYRNRIC						9	11				
WULFRIC						13	8			7	
ÆLFWOLD							6			18	
ÆLFMÆR									9	9	5
ÆLFHEAH										9	
ÆLFRIC										13	
ÆLFRIC										16	
ÆLFSIGE										17	
EADWOLD										19	

Note

S 619: the first *minister* occurs as the last ealdorman.

6 The diplomas of King Eadwig issued in 956: Group Four

The relative order of the bishops is much the same as for the diplomas assigned to Group Two, except that in the present group Brihthelm of London occurs higher up, ahead of Cenwald and Oscetel, and Daniel normally occurs at the end. Occasionally two bishops called Brihthelm subscribe; three diplomas (S 591, 619 and 661) which have the subscription of only one Bishop Brihthelm may refer to the bishop of Wells, for he occurs after Oscetel, but one would then have to accept that the bishop of London was coincidentally omitted, and of course the relative order of the bishops may not have been rigidly observed. The lists of ealdormen are headed by Æthelstan and Edmund, with Æthelsige and Æthelwold towards the end; the subscriptions of Ealdorman Brihtnoth occur in three diplomas, always in the final position. The general appearance of the lists of *ministri* shows one significant change from the lists assigned to Group Two: Ælfsige, Æthelgeard and Ælfheah are still prominent (though Ælfheah more so than he had been in Group Two), but Wulfric seems not to appear at all – for the three occurrences of a Wulfric (in S 610, 611 and 619) are in a relatively low position and probably represent the second Wulfric known to have witnessed diplomas in Group Two (S 583, 590, 596 and 606). Other frequent witnesses are Ælfwine, Eadric and (to a lesser extent) Ælfwig, none of whom is common in earlier lists. One may finally observe that Ælfgar and Brihtferth, who occur often and generally together in Groups One, Two and Three, are included much less frequently in the diplomas of Group Four. S 611 is dated 29 November and was issued at the royal 'palace' at Cheddar in Somerset, giving the time of year and location for the whole group.[106]

This classification of King Eadwig's diplomas issued in 956 is based entirely on the analysis of their witness lists.[107] In establishing the successive groups I have adopted the proposition that there would have been only a few occasions during the year on which most of the bishops, ealdormen and prominent king's thegns in the kingdom

---

[106] It should be observed, however, that the atheling Edgar and Ealdorman Æthelstan were apparently omitted from the list attached to S 611, differing in this respect from the other diplomas assigned to the group.

[107] Cf. Liebermann, *National Assembly*, p. 47, for an alternative classification which seems rather crude; cf. also the classification which underlies Hart, 'Athelstan "Half-King" ', pp. 126–8.

would have been collectively available for witnessing diplomas, and in order to retain this historical perspective it is necessary to make allowance for some variation within the groups: for it would be mistaken to attach significance to all the differences and so to multiply the groups, since it is perfectly conceivable that more than one memorandum was made on a single occasion, and since much of the variation can probably be attributed to differing standards of accuracy achieved by the cartulary copyists.[108] The fact that the suggested classification of the diplomas is compatible with the available indications of relative chronology constitutes a guarantee that the groups are more than fortuitous, and it seems reasonable therefore to argue that each represents a separate gathering of the king and his council. The diplomas of Group One were probably produced in January; those of Group Two in February; and those of Group Four in November. So it emerges that there were exceptionally productive meetings, in terms of diplomas issued, at the beginning and at the end of the year, which together account for the great majority of the extant diplomas dated 956, and perhaps two other gatherings during the spring and summer months at which a more normal amount of business was conducted.[109]

Analysis of formulation provides some striking support for the suggested classification, since the diplomatic similarities that do exist generally involve diplomas which have been assigned to the same group. The diplomas assigned to Group One are remarkably homogeneous in formulation and structure. In the first place, their proems are concerned with interrelated themes, so that the same ideas and considerations are sometimes expressed in similar wording.[110] Secondly, they share a perfunctory dispositive section, in which each operative element (the royal superscription, the clauses naming the beneficiary and estate concerned, the dispositive clause itself, the list of appurtenances, the clause establishing the beneficiary's power to alienate the estate, and the clause reserving the

---

[108] I have omitted from the discussion those diplomas with anomalous lists (S 581, 593, 616, 630, 633 and 659) and also those with truncated lists (S 595, 599, 625–6, 628 and 632). The list in S 605 seems to fall between that in S 582 issued in the closing weeks of 955 and those in the diplomas of Group One.

[109] Unfortunately there is not the space to discuss here the historical significance of the large number of diplomas issued in 956, but I intend to do so in a future paper.

[110] E.g. there are verbal parallels in S 597 and 629 (and cf. S 644, dated 957), in S 629 and 627, in S 629 and 666, and in S 594 and 608 (and cf. S 630, also issued in 956).

common burdens) is expressed in the simplest possible way, contrasting with the degree of elaboration often attained in the same context in diplomas of the 930s and 940s. We may notice in addition that the beneficiary is never described as the king's *minister*: he is styled more intimately the king's *fidelis* or *familiarissimus*. And thirdly, the diplomas share the structural irregularity of having the sanction (with combined blessing) after the list of witnesses: there are only a few scattered examples of diplomas with a similar structure dated before and after 956, yet there are nine such diplomas dated 956, comprising nine of the ten diplomas assigned on other grounds to Group One.[111] All these features of the Group One diplomas recur in S 672, ostensibly a diploma issued by King Edgar, with the subscription of Archbishop Dunstan, but in fact clearly a forgery modelled on an authentic instrument of 956.[112] It is difficult to avoid the conclusion that the diplomas of Group One were produced by a single agency on the same occasion.[113] Estates in Berkshire, Hampshire, Somerset and Wiltshire were involved, and the diplomas were preserved in the archives of six religious houses.

The diplomas assigned to Group Two, so clearly defined by the analysis of witness lists, are not collectively as homogeneous in terms of their formulation, but smaller groups can be identified within the series. The most remarkable sub-group comprises S 590, 606, 624 and 635, disposing of land in Berkshire, Somerset, Sussex and Wiltshire respectively, and preserved in the archives of Abingdon and the Old Minster Winchester. These diplomas share the unusual structural feature of placing a statement of the pious

---

111 The exception is S 597, of which one version (BCS 950) has a declaration by the king after the witness list. Dumville, 'The Ætheling', pp. 8–9, identifies a development in diplomatic usage whereby the form *cliton* used for an attesting atheling during the reigns of Æthelstan, Edmund and Eadred gives way to (*indoles*) *clito* in 956, and his evidence accords very well with my classification of Eadwig's diplomas: the new terminology is characteristic of diplomas assigned to Group One, and occurs otherwise in one Group Three diploma (S 623, which has other Group One associations), in two Group Four diplomas (S 591 and 661), and in three texts classified as anomalous (S 593, 616 and 630); in Groups Two, Three and Four the atheling Edgar is normally described simply as *regis frater*.

112 Its proem is very closely related to that in S 637; the grant is to Ælfstan, the king's *familiarissimus miles*, and is dated 956, 'in the first year of our reign'.

113 Note that some of the diplomas include *dictavi* amongst the styles of subscription for the bishops: S 589 (Daniel), 594 (Osulf), 597 (Daniel), 614 (Daniel) and 637 (Oscetel). Coupled with the diplomatic evidence, this suggests that *dictavi* cannot be interpreted literally and that it is in fact only one of the available styles for the act of subscription.

consideration behind the grant after the invocation and royal superscription; verbal parallels link S 590 with S 624, and S 624 with S 606 and 635. But the most significant common denominator is the use in S 590, 624 and 635 of a rhyming couplet as a blessing-cum-anathema:

Gloria consentientibus
Tartarum nolentibus   (S 590)

Augens fruatur domino
minuens ipse zabulo   (S 624)

Coelum scandat cupiens
Ima petat rennuens   (S 635)[114]

It is possible that such verses were conscious, if not entirely success-ful, attempts at imitation of the rhythmic octosyllables popular amongst the Anglo-Saxons in the eighth century;[115] certainly they cannot be paralleled in tenth-century diplomas,[116] and they must be regarded as the work of a single draftsman. Another sub-group of Group Two comprises S 600 and 601, both of which are in favour of Æthelhild, a *nobilis femina*, though preserved in the archives of the Old Minster Winchester and Horton respectively since estates covered by the diplomas subsequently came into the possession of these houses. Apart from two omissions in S 601, the witness lists are identical, and a common draftsman is guaranteed by the use of identical formulation as well. The threat contained in the sanction ('Si quis vero minuerit hanc meam donationem sciat se reum omni hora vitæ suæ et tenebrosum Tartarum non evadere') recalls the couplet in S 590 and introduces a formula that enjoyed especial popularity in Eadwig's reign.[117] A third sub-group comprises S 615 and 621, both from the Abingdon archives but for different beneficiaries and concerning estates in Northamptonshire and Surrey respectively: the diplomas share the same proem[118] and sanction. The sanction recurs in three other diplomas assigned to Group Two,

---

[114] This couplet recurs in S 1005 (dated 1044).

[115] On which see Lapidge, 'Liber Epigrammatum', p. 818.

[116] The closest analogy seems to be the lines attributed to Aldhelm in S 230, a forgery of the tenth century.

[117] Besides S 600–1, see S 571, 575, 577, 620, 628, 642, 645, 667, 691 and 723.

[118] It appears to be a conflation of two proems popular in the 940s: cf., e.g., S 442 for the opening, and S 523 for the continuation.

S 592, 609 and 622,[119] which themselves have a comparable structure (with attenuated proem) and share smaller elements of their formulation; S 599 (which has a truncated witness list) may belong to the same group, given its diplomatic connections with S 592, though it has a different sanction (itself found in S 603 and 663, assigned to Group Two).[120] Another sub-group might comprise S 596, 598 and 604, which apart from having admittedly conventional proems on worldly transitoriness also have related sanctions; a comparable proem occurs in S 583 and a comparable sanction occurs in S 636.[121] There are further similarities of formulation amongst the diplomas assigned to Group Two which cut across these subsidiary groups. For example, many of the formulae used to describe the beneficiaries are distinctive: 'cuidam meorum optimatum' (S 609), 'cuidam meorum charorum propinquorum' (S 615), 'uni meorum carorum' (S 621), 'cuidam meorum optimatum' (S 624), 'uni meorum procerum' (S 635) and 'cuidam meorum principum' (S 636), and compare 'uni meorum karorum' in S 599. Again, we find that the majority of the diplomas employ the same range of styles of subscription for the leading witnesses.[122] A different and more distinctive combination of formulae of attestation occurs in S 583, 609, 622 and 624, recurring in S 595, which has a truncated list. Overall it emerges that the diplomas of Group Two are intimately related to one another, and given the similarities between the witness lists one can again conclude that they were produced by a single agency on the same occasion: estates in nine counties are involved, and the diplomas were preserved in six different archives.

The diplomas assigned to Group Three have less in common than those assigned to Groups One and Two; several of the formulae employed originated in the 940s, but otherwise there is nothing distinctive about them. The diplomas of Group Four, on the other hand, have interesting associations with the earlier groups and are

---

[119] And thereafter in S 634, 910 and 1863; cf. S 553 and 1015.

[120] The sanction occurs in the following diplomas: S 552, 578, 584, 599, 603, 611, 650, 663, 727, 755, 769, 778 and 828. See also Gibson, *Reliquiæ*, p. 19, from a diploma of Edgar dated 958, and cf. S 932.

[121] The sanction recurs in S 602, 625, 649, 651, 653, 852 and 879.

[122] S 590, 592, 596, 598, 600–1, 606–7, 615, 621, 635–6 and 663; see also S 599. The formula employed for the king's subscription contains the adverb *indeclinabiliter*, used several times in Eadred's diplomas and often in the diplomas assigned to Group Four (but not in those assigned to Group One).

themselves interrelated. The proem of S 591, preserved at Abingdon, had been used before in S 618 (Group Three, also from Abingdon),[123] and its witness list is almost identical with that in S 661, a text from Bath which though spurious nevertheless suggests the existence of an authentic diploma of the same group in its archives. There can be no doubt that a single memorandum of witnesses underlies S 612 (from Wilton, for land in Wiltshire) and S 613 (from the Old Minster Winchester, for land in Hampshire), both issued in favour of Beornric; the formulation of the diplomas, however, is not related. S 587 and 588 are similarly in favour of one man, Ealdorman Ælfhere; both were preserved at Abingdon, though one is for an estate in Oxfordshire and the other for an estate in Warwickshire. In the case of this pair, the formulation[124] as well as the witnesses are identical. Some of the formulae used in these two diplomas had been used previously in S 585, in favour of Ælfheah *minister* (Ælfhere's brother, subsequently appointed an ealdorman), preserved at the Old Minster Winchester and assigned to Group Three; S 610, in favour of Bath Abbey and assigned to Group Four, is related to S 585 in a different way.[125] S 611, in favour of Ealdorman Brihtnoth, was apparently modelled on a diploma like S 603 (Group Two). In addition to the similarities of formulation, the witness lists of both diplomas omit the atheling Edgar and list the ealdormen in an unusual order: so it seems that the influence of a model on its copy might affect some aspects at least of the witness list. Each of the remaining diplomas assigned to Group Four has minor diplomatic links with others issued in 956. In general terms it is thus apparent that the later diplomas of 956 display a greater diversity of formulation than the diplomas produced in the early months of the year. This may reflect no more than a developing willingness on the part of the draftsmen to revive old formulae and to experiment with new ones; certainly, the variety is not in itself incompatible with the continued centralized production of diplomas.

---

[123] An abbreviated form occurs in S 433, a mid-eleventh-century forgery from Exeter which resembles S 591 in other ways.

[124] The distinctive structure of these diplomas had originated in the early 940s (S 465, 474–5, 481, 488) and had been used previously in 956, in S 604 (Group Two); see also S 641, 674 and 679.

[125] The structure of S 585 and 610 derives ultimately from diplomas issued in 943 (S 490 and 512); cf. S 609, dated 956 (Group Two). It recurs thereafter in S 575, 645, 650, 712, 778, 877 and 973.

It is quite inconceivable that the similarities in the formulation of the Group One and Group Two diplomas in particular, and among the witness lists of each of the four groups, could have arisen if the beneficiaries were allowed to make their own arrangements for securing a written record of the conveyance of land in their favour. The evidence demonstrates conclusively that documents in favour of different beneficiaries, referring to estates in various counties and subsequently preserved in the archives of several religious houses, were drawn up by a single agency on the same occasion: in short, the centralized drafting of royal diplomas was the norm in 956, just as it had been in the 930s and 940s. While it is possible that the same person may not have been responsible for both the drafting and the writing of a diploma, to demonstrate drafting by a central agency is tantamount to establishing the existence of a central secretariat, for obviously the texts must have been set down at the same time. The secretariat of the 940s was certainly still active during Eadwig's reign. The scribe of S 636, assigned to Group Two, is the one identified as the writer of the 951 annal in the Parker Chronicle, so he was evidently connected at one time, if not necessarily in 956, with the Winchester scriptorium. The scribe of S 624, also assigned to Group Two, is another of the supposed 'Winchester' scribes, and was employed again for the writing of royal diplomas in 957, for he has been identified as the scribe of S 646, issued on 9 May at Edington in Wiltshire.[126] These three diplomas, together with S 649 (dated 957), display the characteristic features of script and layout established in the secretariat as early as 939. Had others been preserved in their original form, they may have been of the same external appearance: for the characteristic absence of the word *Ego* after the first column of witnesses (the bishops) is reflected in several cartulary copies of diplomas from all the groups of 956,[127] and many of the diplomas employ the type of dating formula suitable for division into its constituent elements and so for spreading

---

[126] Bishop, 'A Charter of King Edwy', p. 371. The diplomas are from the archives of Abingdon and Ely respectively.

[127] S 627, 629, 631 (Group One); S 592, 598, 609, 615, 1662 (Group Two); S 584 (Group Three); S 610-12, 661 (Group Four); see also S 593, 616 and 659 (anomalous). The Abingdon and Old Minster Winchester copyists generally inserted the *egos* if they were absent: see their treatment of S 587, 611, 613 (compared with the related S 612) and 636.

across the width of the membrane.[128] It is worth adding that there may have been some innovation in the nature of the device chosen for the pictorial invocation on the original membrane. The extant originals of the first half of the tenth century invariably employ a simple cross,[129] and to judge from S 594 and 637 this was the practice adopted for the Group One diplomas of 956;[130] but in all but one of the Group Two and Group Four diplomas for which there is manuscript evidence of a pictorial invocation of any kind we find that a chrismon was used.[131] The tendency towards a greater degree of diplomatic variety which is detectable in the diplomas of 956 when compared with those of the 930s and 940s may have been paralleled in other ways by more radical experimentation with new scripts and layouts. It seems reasonable to suppose that the diplomas of Group One were produced by the same central agency as was responsible for those of Group Two, and yet the only one to survive in its original form (S 594) is markedly different in appearance from the originals of the second group: indeed, it has been cited as the earliest dated example of English Caroline minuscule, though 'evidently written by an unskilled scribe'.[132] Another apparent original of 956, S 618 (assigned to Group Three), is also distinctive in its script and design. The only respect in which these two diplomas resemble contemporary originals is in the absence of *Ego* after the first column of witnesses.[133] They raise the possibility,

---

[128] S 592, 596, 601, 603–4, 615, 621–2, 635 and perhaps 598 and 600 (Group Two); S 623 and 638 (Group Three); S 587–8, 612–13 and 619–20 (Group Four); see also S 595, 599, 625, 632 (truncated) and 659 (anomalous). This type of formula was never employed in the Group One diplomas, in which the dating formula occurs before the bounds.

[129] The only diplomas from this period with chrismons which rest on respectable manuscript authority are S 411 and 559 (and perhaps S 554, if the chrismon was not provided by the copyist).

[130] Initial crosses may have been used in Group Three, if only to judge from S 584 and 623 (the one spurious and the other an apograph).

[131] S 601, 615, 624 and 636 (Group Two); S 599 (truncated, but probably Group Two); S 587 and 602 (Group Four). The exception is S 611 (Group Four), which had an initial cross. The chrismons which appear in 956 and 957 are decorated in the same sort of way on the extant originals, so it seems likely that there was one mind behind their design as well as behind the decision to use them regularly.

[132] Bishop, *English Caroline Minuscule*, p. xix. Here, and in 'Cambridge MSS, Pt. iv', p. 333, Bishop assigns the scribe of S 594 to the Abingdon scriptorium, but the reason for so doing appears to be that the diploma was subsequently preserved there; the abbey held the estate concerned at the time of the Domesday survey.

[133] Three other diplomas of 956 are extant on single sheets, but none likely to be an original: S 587, 602 and 623. S 602 is remarkably similar in its design and appearance to S 646 (dated 957), and it is conceivable that it was modelled closely on a diploma by the same

suggested also by the diplomatic evidence, that in the 950s the personnel of the central agency became more adventurous, and perhaps more numerous as well.

The secretariat that had produced diplomas in the 930s and 940s was still in operation during the reign of King Eadwig, but it may not then have survived the political developments of 957–9 in an unchanged form. Whatever organization had evolved during the reigns of Æthelstan, Edmund, Eadred and Eadwig would presumably have remained under Eadwig's control after the division of the kingdom in 957.[134] As king of the Mercians Edgar would have had to establish a separate arrangement for the production of diplomas, though not necessarily a different kind of arrangement. 'Centralized' production can be detected in two pairs of diplomas dated 958: S 674 is a grant of an estate in Huntingdonshire to Ælfheah *minister*, subsequently preserved at Peterborough, and shares essentially the same formulation[135] and witness list with S 679, a grant of land in Nottinghamshire to Bishop Oscetel, preserved at York; S 676 is a grant of an estate in Essex to Ealdorman Æthelstan, preserved in the archives of the Old Minster Winchester, and shares its formulation[136] and witness list with S 678, a grant of an estate in Oxfordshire to Eanulf *minister*, preserved at Abingdon. An apparent original from the Wells archives, S 677 (also dated 958), suggests how different in appearance Edgar's diplomas of this period may have been from those of his predecessors:[137] of course this is hardly

---

scribe. S 587 is in a well-developed Caroline minuscule hand but may have been copied from an original of the standard square minuscule type since it reflects the features of that design.

134 Indeed, further evidence for 'centralized' production can be obtained from the diplomas issued in the closing years of Eadwig's reign: amongst the many points of contact, note the sanction common to S 641, 643, 655–6 and 1291 (all issued in 957–8), and re-used in S 730 (dated 964); cf. S 577 and 655–6 (and note that S 577 is attested by 'Wulgar leofa', the beneficiary of S 655); and cf. S 652 and 660, both attested by Brihthelm during his brief period of office at Canterbury.

135 Note the use of a regnal style ('industrius Anglorum rex ceterarumque gentium in circuitu persistentium gubernator et rector'; see also Gibson, *Reliquiæ*, p. 19, from another diploma of Edgar dated 958) which implies sway over all England at a time when Edgar was king only north of the Thames and normally employed more appropriate styles (S 576, 667, 675–8 and 681); but the style was probably taken over from the draftsman's exemplar (see above, p. 66 n. 124) without thought for its implications. Eadwig was generally styled simply 'rex Anglorum' after the division.

136 For which see above, p. 48 n. 85.

137 The hand is a square minuscule, but of a different style; a cross serves as the pictorial invocation; the bounds are written in the same size script as the rest of the text; no attempt

surprising, since the scribes would probably have been trained in different scriptoria or by different people, and so would not have been heirs to the same tradition.

Nevertheless, the contrast remains even after the reunification of the kingdom following Eadwig's death in 959, and is generally held to reflect the removal of responsibility for the production of diplomas from a single scriptorium, be it a nascent 'royal chancery' or that of Winchester, to other ecclesiastical scriptoria. There are eight diplomas dated between 960 and 963 extant as apparent originals,[138] of which five were written by a single scribe. Drögereit called him 'Edgar A' and suggested that he might be Æthelwold, abbot of Abingdon (and from 963 bishop of Winchester); Dr Chaplais also regarded him as an Abingdon scribe.[139] The connection between this scribe and Abingdon appears to depend on the fact that he practised a script different from that of the earlier diplomas located by Dr Chaplais at Winchester, and on the fact that two of his diplomas were preserved in the Abingdon archives. One of them is in favour of the abbey, but by itself this does not constitute sufficient reason for locating the scribe there. He was responsible for the following diplomas:

S	Date	Details of transaction	Archive
687	960	King Edgar to Wulfric, *minister*: restitution of lands in Berkshire, Hampshire and Sussex	Abingdon
690	961	King Edgar to Abingdon Abbey: grant of land in Hampshire	Abingdon
703	962	King Edgar to Æthelflæd, a *matrona*: grant of land in Suffolk	Bury St Edmunds
706	962	King Edgar to Titstan, *cubicularius*: grant of land in Wiltshire	uncertain
717	963	King Edgar to Ingeram, *minister*: grant of land in Essex	Christ Church Canterbury

has been made to distinguish between the different elements of the text by careful layout; *egos* occur in all the columns of witnesses; an archaic style of subscription occurs after each witness; the endorsement is not of the conventional type. There are several points of contact between the formulation of S 677 and that of S 667, from the archives of Chester, dated 958 and issued at Penkridge in Staffordshire; the same draftsman may have been responsible for S 723, dated 963, which relates to land in Salop and thus appropriately has a regnal year calculated from 957 (see also S 712, 776 and 782).

[138] S 684, 687, 690, 697, 703–4, 706 and 717. There is reason to believe that the extant 'original' version of S 702 is not in fact strictly contemporary with its purported date: see Korhammer, 'Bosworth Psalter', pp. 182–7.

[139] Drögereit, 'Königskanzlei', p. 416; Chaplais, 'Origin and Authenticity', p. 42. Also, Bishop, 'Cambridge MSS, Pt. IV', p. 333.

The work of this scribe is quite distinctive. He practised a sober insular minuscule, though generally employing Caroline forms of *a* and *s*, without the elaborate decoration of the 'Winchester-style' diplomas issued in previous decades. He used rustic capitals for the king's name, the beneficiary's name (except in S 690 and 703) and the name of the place conveyed (except in S 687), as well as for the initials in '*Anno*' and '*Ego*'. A characteristic form of chrismon occurs in all his diplomas except S 717 (which has a cross as its pictorial invocation). In external design, his diplomas do not follow the usual pattern of the 'Winchester-style' documents: for example, the word *Ego* occurs in each column of witnesses and the dating formulae he chose to employ were of types that preclude arrangement in sections across the width of the membrane. He was responsible for only the first part of S 690, for having written the text up to the end of the boundary clause he stopped, and the membrane was folded horizontally and presumably submitted for use in a ceremony of conveyance; the dating clause and witness list were added subsequently by a different scribe in an accomplished Caroline minuscule hand.[140] It is clear that another diploma written by 'Edgar A' underlies S 702, itself written either at Christ Church Canterbury or at Westminster by the scribe of the Bosworth Psalter: the formulation of this text is identical with that of S 706, dated to the same year, and the scribe imitated 'Edgar A' in the use of rustic capitals.[141]

There is some justification for regarding 'Edgar A' not only as the scribe but also as the draftsman of S 687, 690, 703, 706, 717 and the exemplar of S 702, for in terms of their formulation the diplomas are closely related to one another. The earliest of the originals, S 687 (dated 960), stands apart from the rest: the proem and sanction were adapted from formulae found in diplomas of the 940s and 950s,[142] and the dispositive section was determined by the special

---

[140] See Bishop, *English Caroline Minuscule*, p. 9. Drögereit, 'Königskanzlei', p. 417, identified the second scribe as Osgar, Æthelwold's successor as abbot of Abingdon. There is no more reason to regard the second as an Abingdon scribe than there is the first: note the close relationship of the witness list in S 690 to that in S 811 (from the Old Minster Winchester).

[141] *Ibid.* p. 355 n. 4, and Korhammer, 'Bosworth Psalter', p. 182.

[142] For the proem, cf. S 493, 497, 501, 506–7, 525 and 528; the sanction originated *c.* 940 (S 392 and 465) and occurs twenty times in the next twenty years, to be revived sporadically in the reigns of Æthelred and Cnut.

nature of the diploma, which restored certain estates to the beneficiary. The other diplomas written by 'Edgar A' between 961 and
963 are interrelated in several ways. S 690, for Abingdon Abbey
and dated 961, contains a proem that describes the act of the creation
and the loss of immortality, leading naturally into a statement of
the consideration behind the making of the grant; the same proem
recurs in S 703, for Æthelflæd and dated 962, without reference to
the consideration. The theme was popular throughout the tenth
and eleventh centuries, and a substantial number of different
formulae were developed for expressing it, but it seems that this
one was used exclusively by 'Edgar A'; it is otherwise found only
in S 688, an Abingdon forgery modelled on S 690. The proem used
for S 706, issued in 962, contains a citation of Luke xxi 10 ('Surget
gens contra gentem et regnum adversus regnum'); the same formula,
which does not occur before 962, recurs in the copy of an 'Edgar A'
diploma of 962 made by the scribe of the Bosworth Psalter (S 702).
Another proem occurs in S 717, written by 'Edgar A' in 963, and its
occurrences elsewhere are confined almost entirely to cartulary
copies of diplomas issued in the same year. The dispositive sections
of 'Edgar A' 's diplomas are closely related, if allowance is made for
necessary variation in grants to an abbey (S 690) and a woman
(S 703). The same sanction occurs in S 690, 706 and 717 (and also in
S 702); a variation of it is found in S 703. It is without doubt the
most common formula in Anglo-Saxon diplomatic, so at first sight
its use might not appear to be significant. But leaving aside two
'earlier' forgeries (S 78 and 409), its earliest occurrence in an acceptable diploma is in S 683, dated 960: thus it emerges that 'Edgar A'
used it frequently at precisely the time of its introduction. It is
found with increasing frequency in 961 and 962 in cartulary texts,[143]
and then in the majority of the extant diplomas dated 963.[144] It was
curiously little used in 964 and 965,[145] but it recurs often in the
period 966–75[146] and several times during the reigns of Æthelred

---

[143] S 688, 696, 698, 700–1 and 833; it occurs also in S 1298, a lease issued by Bishop Oswald
in 962.

[144] S 708–11, 714, 716, 718–20 and 722; a version with slight variants occurs in S 1634,
purportedly issued by Archbishop Dunstan in 963.

[145] It is found, with a variant opening, only in S 729 (which is probably spurious).

[146] S 737–8, 744, 746–8, 754, 757–60, 762, 764–7, 771–3, 777, 780–2, 789, 792, 794, 800–1,
805 and 820; see also S 749, 776, 804 and 806 for variant forms from the same period.

and his successors.[147] One is tempted to suggest that it was devised and popularized by 'Edgar A' himself, if only because the period of its most consistent use (960–3) coincides exactly with the known span of his career. Finally, with the exception of S 690 all the witness lists attached to 'Edgar A' 's diplomas have simple formulae of attestation, with the use of the same range of verbs; of course, the witness list of S 690 is known not to have been written by 'Edgar A'.

The features of formulation which characterize the diplomas written by 'Edgar A' recur in several texts dated between 960 and 963 and now preserved only in cartulary copies:

S	Date	Details of transaction	Archive
683	960	King Edgar to Bishop Brihthelm, his kinsman: grant of land in Hampshire	Old Minster Winchester
696	961	King Edgar to Byrnsige, *minister*: grant of land in Wiltshire	Old Minster Winchester
698	961	King Edgar to Eadric, *minister*: grant of land at *Hamstede* (unidentified)	Abingdon
700	962	King Edgar to Abingdon Abbey: grant of land in Berkshire	Abingdon
708	963	King Edgar to Abingdon Abbey: grant of land in Sussex	Abingdon
709	963	King Edgar to Ælfric, *minister*: grant of land in Somerset	Wells
710	963	King Edgar to Ælfsige, *minister*: grant of land in Dorset	Shaftesbury
711	963	King Edgar to Ælfsige, *decurio*: grant of land in Somerset	Bath
714	963	King Edgar to Æthelwold, bishop: grant of land in Sussex	Abingdon
716	963	King Edgar to Gunner, *dux*: grant of land in Yorkshire	York
718	963	King Edgar to the Church of St Andrew, Meon: grant of land in Sussex	Old Minster Winchester
719	963	King Edgar to Winstan, *camerarius*: grant of land in Wiltshire	Wilton
720	963	King Edgar to Wulfgeat, *minister*: grant of land in Warwickshire and Worcestershire	Burton
722	963	King Edgar to Wulfnoth, *minister*: grant of land at *Hocan edisce* (unidentified)	Abingdon

Examination of the witness lists attached to the diplomas in this

[147] S 835, 841, 864, 866–8, 887, 907, 919, 948, 967, 1014, 1058 and 1228; see also S 843, 850, 861, 938 and 1016 for variant forms.

group which were issued in 963 suggests that S 708, 709, 711, 718 and 719 may have been drawn up on the same occasion, before 29 November, when Æthelwold (who attests each one as abbot) was consecrated bishop of Winchester. Many of the same witnesses recur in S 717, also dated 963, which is one of the diplomas written by 'Edgar A'. S 714, 716 and 722 were presumably produced in December 963, since Æthelwold occurs in each as a bishop. S 710 and 720 have truncated lists: the former is impossible to place, but the latter at least has the subscription of Abbot Æthelwold, showing that it was produced before 29 November. Collectively, these diplomas display much the same range of formulae as the 'Edgar A' originals. The proem citing Luke xxi 10, already seen in S 706 (and 702), recurs in S 700, 710, 711, 714 and 716, and the proem seen in S 717 recurs in S 709, 720 and 722;[148] the argument developed in the proem in S 696 recalls that previously used in S 687, and depends on the same formulae current in the 940s and 950s. The proems in the remaining diplomas cannot be paralleled in the extant 'Edgar A' originals; those in S 708 and 719 are closely related to one another, and that in S 683 is an adaptation of formulae current in the preceding decades.[149] The dispositive sections in all of the diplomas under consideration are made up of the formulae favoured by 'Edgar A', though again allowance has to be made for variation which arises from differences in the nature of the transactions and beneficiaries involved. The sanction characteristic of the originals written by 'Edgar A' occurs in every one of them, and the styles of subscription employed in the witness lists are also of the same simple type as he used.

'Edgar A' seems to have produced a large proportion of the originals extant from the period 960–3, and it is likely that the other diplomas issued in the same period which employ the distinctive combination of formulae characteristic of the originals can be attributed to him. It emerges therefore that a single person was made responsible for the drafting and writing of the majority of the king's diplomas issued in the opening years of the reign, and certainly

---

[148] The proem in S 706 etc. recurs in S 767 and 864; see also S 782, 792, 824, 827 and 841. The proem in S 717 etc. recurs only in S 746.

[149] For the formula in S 683, cf. S 519, 638 (and 763). Variant forms of the proem in S 718 were used in a series of suspicious texts from Abingdon (S 410, 682, 689, 732–4, 829, 967, 1020 and 1023); see also S 771 and 825.

of more than one would expect were his services only exploited when the king was in the vicinity of Abingdon or if the beneficiaries were required to make their own arrangements for the production of the diplomas in their favour. Under such circumstances, it seems reasonable to regard 'Edgar A' as a scribe in permanent attendance on the king and so as one in his personal service. There is some evidence which suggests that he may already have been employed by King Edgar before the death of King Eadwig. The formulation of S 681, a diploma of King Edgar issued in 959 while he was still king of the Mercians, seems to anticipate the 'Edgar A' originals in that it provides the earliest known occurrences of features which in a slightly different form became characteristic of them. Thus its proem contains the first citation of Luke xxi 10, as the premise for a brief disquisition on the transitoriness of worldly things; the theme was perennially popular, though the formula in question had no currency in later diplomas.[150] But as we have seen, the quotation from St Luke's gospel was used frequently in the diplomas written by or here attributed to 'Edgar A', albeit in a more exclusively eschatological context; moreover, the second part of the proem in S 681 could well be regarded as the prototype of the formulae in S 708 and 719.[151] S 681 also has a sanction which incorporates, for the first time in an acceptable diploma, the phrase 'æternis baratri . . . incendiis', and which may in this and other respects be regarded as the prototype of the sanction characteristic of the 'Edgar A' diplomas.[152] There are also substantial similarities between the dispositive sections of these diplomas and the corresponding section of S 681. It may go beyond the diplomatic evidence to suggest that the draftsman of S 681 was none other than 'Edgar A' at a formative stage in his career; but one may observe that the draftsman of S 681 does seem to have remained in King Edgar's service after the reunification of the kingdom, if only to judge from the fact that substantial parts of the formulation of S 681 were repeated in S 680, a diploma issued

---

[150] The citation of Luke xxi 10 occurs in a similar context in S 401, a spurious diploma dated 929.

[151] The only earlier diploma with a related formula, S 584, is not authentic (cf. S 611 and 617–18).

[152] The same sanction occurs in a series of suspicious texts from Abingdon (S 408, 410, 607, 682, 732–4, 829, 1020 and 1023) and also in S 837; cf. S 695. Other 'early' occurrences of elements of the 'Edgar A' sanction – in S 511, 567, 583, 626, 658 and 673 – are all from suspicious texts.

later on in 959 when Edgar had become king of all England. If 'Edgar A' did work for King Edgar before Eadwig's death as well as in the early 960s, the change in the external appearance of diplomas from one reign to the next could be readily understood, and there would be further cause to dissociate 'Edgar A' from Abingdon. When Edgar succeeded to the reunited kingdom in 959 he would perhaps have preferred to maintain the arrangements established while he was king of Mercia rather than abandon them in favour of a secretariat inherited from King Eadwig: thus the continued employ-ment of the same personnel from reign to reign, which lends homogeneity to the diplomas of Æthelstan and his successors, would have been interrupted, and some changes would seem to have been inevitable.[153]

At first sight the formulation of the later diplomas issued in King Edgar's name presents a degree of variety that might seem incom-patible with their production in a central office and that might indeed be held to imply that they were drawn up in different ecclesiastical scriptoria acting independently as or for the beneficiaries. To some extent, however, the variety could be artificial. Perhaps it arises in part from the inclusion of a large number of miscellaneous documents (wills, leases, memoranda, vernacular records and agreements, etc.) amongst the series of royal diplomas as edited by Birch, which has the effect of repeatedly diverting the reader's attention from the diplomatic tradition that the diplomas represent. It also arises from the presence in the corpus of many transparent forgeries foisted on King Edgar by subsequent generations of monks anxious to demon-strate that their privileges were granted or confirmed by the secular leader of the monastic reform movement. If one concentrates on the diplomas which are or appear to be authentic, one is struck more by the uniformity of the documents than by any degree of variety. For example, substantial elements of the formulation characteristic of the diplomas written by and attributed to 'Edgar A' occur in a

---

[153] However, two diplomas extant as originals retain some of the external characteristics of the originals of the 940s and 950s: S 697 and 736. These diplomas are strikingly similar in appearance. They share several minor but significant elements of their formulation, notably the use of the auxiliary *habban* with *bocian* in the endorsement (i.e. *hæfð gebocod*: see Hart, '*Codex Wintoniensis*', p. 22). The formulation of S 697 is repeated in S 721. It is quite likely that a single agency was responsible for producing these three diplomas.

considerable number of the diplomas of King Edgar issued between 966 and 975:[154]

S	Date	Details of transaction	Archive
737	966	King Edgar to his kinswoman Ælfgifu, *matrona*: grant of land in Buckinghamshire	Abingdon
738	966	King Edgar to his kinswoman Ælfgifu, *matrona*: grant of land in Oxfordshire	?Abingdon
744	966	King Edgar to Shaftesbury Abbey: confirmation of land in Dorset	Shaftesbury
747	967	King Edgar to Ælfheah, *comes*, and Ælfswith, Ælfheah's wife: grant of land in Surrey	Glastonbury
748	967	King Edgar to Ælfsige, his *minister*: grant of land at *Eastune* (unidentified)	Old Minster Winchester
754	967	King Edgar to Winflæd, *nobilis matrona*: grant of land in Hampshire	Old Minster Winchester
762	968	King Edgar to Brihtgifu, *femina*: grant of land at *Ealderescumbe* (unidentified)	Shaftesbury
764	968	King Edgar to Glastonbury Abbey: grant of land in Dorset	Glastonbury
765	968	King Edgar to Romsey Abbey: grant of land in Wiltshire	Romsey
766	968	King Edgar to Wilton Abbey: confirmation of lands in Wiltshire and the Isle of Wight	Wilton
767	968	King Edgar to Wilton Abbey: grant of land in Wiltshire	Wilton
771	969	King Edgar to Ælfhelm, *minister*: grant of land in Oxfordshire	Old Minster Winchester
772	969	King Edgar to Ælfwold, his *fidelis minister*: grant of land in Bedfordshire	Worcester
773	969	King Edgar to Ælfwold, his *fidelis minister*: grant of land in Warwickshire	Worcester
777	970	King Edgar to Bath Abbey: grant of land in Somerset	Bath
780	970	King Edgar to Ely Abbey: grant of land in Cambridgeshire	Ely
781	970	King Edgar to Ely Abbey: grant of land in Suffolk	Ely
789	972	King Edgar to Winstan, his *cubicularius*: grant of land in Wiltshire	Wilton
794	974	King Edgar to Ælfhelm, *minister*: grant of land in Cambridgeshire	Ely
800	975	King Edgar to Ælfweard, *minister*: grant of land in Hampshire	Old Minster Winchester
801	975	King Edgar to Æthelwold, bishop: grant of land in Staffordshire	Old Minster Winchester
805	*c.* 972	King Edgar to Mangoda, *minister*: grant of land in Middlesex	Westminster

[154] Cf. Drögereit, 'Königskanzlei', pp. 402 and 417–18, and Hart, *Charters of Northern England*, pp. 25 and 70, for different interpretations of much the same evidence.

The production of Anglo-Saxon royal diplomas

If allowance is made for the inevitable differences in detail arising from the range of beneficiaries and the nature of the transactions involved, one finds amongst these diplomas remarkable consistency in the phrases used to name the beneficiary and the estate concerned, to express the conditions under which the land was to be held, to introduce the bounds, to date the document, and in the selection of the forms of attestation; furthermore, these elements occur in every case in combination with the sanction characteristic of the 'Edgar A' diplomas. There is, on the other hand, a considerable degree of variety in the choice of proems: occasionally one was selected which had been used previously in the diplomas written by or attributed to 'Edgar A' himself,[155] but generally the draftsmen appear to have preferred to express the well-worn themes in their own ways. Variety in this context might be a matter of individual taste rather than a reflection of decentralization. A common denominator seems to underlie the production of particular pairs of these diplomas: thus S 737 and 738 (with the same beneficiary), 748 and 754, and 772 and 773 (with the same beneficiary)[156] are related not only in terms of their formulation but also share the same witness lists. As it happens, each of these pairs was preserved in a single archive (Abingdon, the Old Minster Winchester and Worcester respectively). The case of S 777 and 781 is more remarkable.[157] Both are dated 970, and the similarity of the witness lists suggests that they could have been drawn up on the same occasion. A common draftsman is guaranteed by the use in both of a variation of the 'Flebilia fortiter detestanda . . .' proem of the early 930s, though from the superscription onwards the formulation follows the normal 'Edgar A' pattern. S 777 is in favour of Bath Abbey and refers to land in Somerset, whereas S 781 is in favour of Ely Abbey and refers to land in Suffolk: so here at least is an unequivocal instance of two diplomas with different – ecclesiastical – beneficiaries nevertheless produced by the same agency.[158] The continued use of some of the

---

[155] For the proems in S 738, 744 and 780, cf. those in S 708 and 719; for the proem in S 767, cf. that in S 706, etc.; for the proem in S 771, cf. that in S 718.

[156] S 772 is extant as an apparent original, and its scribe has been identified as that of a manuscript of Virgil (Bishop, *English Caroline Minuscule*, p. 17); see also Hart, *Charters o Northern England*, p. 82.

[157] See John, *Orbis Britanniae*, pp. 202–3, and Hart, *Charters of Northern England*, pp. 25–6.

[158] Note that the composition of and the order of precedence within the witness lists of the diplomas mentioned above are surprisingly consistent from one pair to the next, suggest-

78

formulae characteristic of the 'Edgar A' diplomas does not, of course, necessarily indicate that 'Edgar A' was himself still active between 966 and 975; indeed, the fact that no diplomas of this type were apparently issued in 964 and 965 might in some way reflect the end of his career as a royal scribe. It may indicate rather that the draftsmen of the later series had been trained under 'Edgar A' and regarded the type of diploma introduced by him as a convenient norm to follow in their own work. Nor should one imply that all of King Edgar's later diplomas display elements of the formulation associated with 'Edgar A'; but such overall variety as does exist remains perfectly compatible with the personal preferences of individual members of a single agency for reviving old formulae or types of diploma, and for experimenting with new ones.

CONCLUSION

The diplomatic evidence set out above indicates that in the tenth century a single agency was often entrusted with the responsibility for drawing up and writing several diplomas issued on the same occasion in favour of different beneficiaries. That such an agency existed during the reigns of Æthelstan, Edmund and Eadred is not controversial, but we have seen that there are strong grounds also for supposing that centralized production remained the norm during the reigns of Eadwig and Edgar. It has been suggested in addition that the production of diplomas was undertaken on the occasion of the gathering of the king and his council, partly on the basis of the same diplomatic evidence, but also because such an arrangement would have been in the best interests of both the king and the beneficiary and because the witness lists appear to be 'official' records of attendance at a *witenagemot*. This tends to dissociate the production of diplomas from ecclesiastical scriptoria, since it requires that the agency was mobile and could operate in the royal vills, towns and boroughs where the gatherings were commonly held. The uniformity of the documents in external design and formulation over extended periods militates against the supposition that different ecclesiastics and their entourages were entrusted by the

ing that there was a further link between them all. Note also that S 762 and 766, both dated 968, share a proem which occurs nowhere else.

king with the production of diplomas on successive occasions, and it implies rather that the agency was a permanent office whose members were employed continuously for several years. As a permanent office it is likely to have been attached to the king's household. Moreover, if centralized production persisted during the heyday of the monastic reform movement, when many ecclesiastical scriptoria were active, there is obviously less justification for arguing that it arose in the first instance out of necessity when a (supposed) decline in the number of scriptoria left only Winchester available: it may at all times have reflected the desire of the king to maintain control over the creation and distribution of privileges and of privileged estates, which directly affected the royal revenue and which must sometimes have involved politically sensitive issues. It remains uncertain, however, to what extent the move towards the centralized production of diplomas should be regarded as a phenomenon of the first half – and more particularly of the second quarter – of the tenth century. A detailed study of the diplomas issued in the ninth century may suggest that at least on some occasions royal diplomas for different beneficiaries were drawn up by an agency that appears to be independent of any ecclesiastical interest in the transactions concerned,[159] and that may therefore have been part of a royal office, but it is unlikely that such a study would detract significantly from the impression that the decisive developments in the arrangements that existed for the production of royal diplomas took place after the death of King Alfred.[160] There is evidence that King Æthelstan took various measures to consolidate royal control of the governmental machinery over which he presided,[161] perhaps as an administrative counterpart to the progress made in his reign towards

---

[159] There are intriguing links between, e.g., S 300 and 301, and between some of King Alfred's diplomas, notably S 347, 348 and 356 (and S 366, in the name of Edward the Elder), as Professor Whitelock has shown in her recent article, 'Some Charters in the Name of King Alfred'. See also Stenton, *Latin Charters*, pp. 47–8, Levison, *England and the Continent*, p. 232, Bruckner, *Ch. L. A.* IV, xviii, and Hart, '*Codex Wintoniensis*', p. 21; cf. Chaplais, 'Origin and Authenticity', pp. 37–9.

[160] The hiatus in the diplomatic tradition between 909 and 924, and the difference in the overall nature of the tradition before and after this period, is probably significant in this context: see Stenton, *Latin Charters*, pp. 52–3, Hart, *Charters of Northern England*, p. 17, and Galbraith, *Studies*, p. 37.

[161] Some of the evidence will be found in Æthelstan's coinage (Blunt, 'Coinage of Athelstan', esp. p. 116), in his legislation, and perhaps indirectly in the nature of the assemblies convened by him (on which see Stenton, *Anglo-Saxon England*, pp. 351–2).

the political reunification of England, and the emergence of a royal writing office may have been one result of this process. The nature of the output of the office would have been determined by its composition. The striking uniformity of the diplomas issued in the 930s and 940s might indicate that it was then staffed by a small number of scribes who shared a similar background or training and who used the same stock of formulae; the relatively greater degree of variety in the diplomas of the 950s might simply indicate that more scribes were employed, particularly by King Eadwig to cope with the exceptionally large number of diplomas issued during his reign; the new formulation developed early in Edgar's reign and the changes in the external appearance of the originals might reflect an interruption in the continuity of personnel employed,[162] itself determined by political considerations, while the striking uniformity of his diplomas issued between 960 and 963, contrasted with the relatively greater degree of variety thereafter, suggests that Edgar's office began on a modest scale and increased in size from the mid-960s onwards.

This can be no more than informed speculation, pending a comprehensive examination of the diplomas issued by the Anglo-Saxon kings from Æthelstan to Edgar, and always bearing in mind that the circumstances governing the production of diplomas are likely to have been more complex than we shall ever be able to detect by examination of those that have been preserved. One could not maintain that a royal office was made responsible for the production of *all* diplomas: consistency of practice was apparently never recognized by the Anglo-Saxons as something desirable for its own sake, and one can easily imagine circumstances in which the adoption of alternative arrangements would have been more appropriate. The ecclesiastics concerned may have been asked to draw up certain diplomas which defined the privileges to be enjoyed by religious communities,[163] perhaps as a continuation of the custom that had

---

[162] It is worth observing in this connection that the form of endorsement standard on royal diplomas from *c.* 940 onwards (e.g. '✠ Þis is þara .vii. hida boc æt Melebroce þe Eadwig cing gebocode Wulfrice his þegne on ece yrfe') underwent a slight modification *c.* 959: hitherto the diploma had almost invariably been described as a *boc*, but henceforth it was more commonly described as a *landboc*.

[163] E.g. the New Minster foundation charter (S 745), which can be regarded as the work of Bishop Æthelwold: see Whitelock, 'King Edgar's Establishment of Monasteries', pp. 131–3, John, *Orbis Britanniae*, pp. 272–3, and Lapidge, 'Hermeneutic Style', pp. 89–90.

prevailed before the tenth century, or perhaps because the particular requirements often put the diplomas beyond the competence of royal scribes used to producing more routine texts. It is also perfectly conceivable that under some circumstances a diploma in favour of a layman might be drawn up by an ecclesiastic, whether or not one who was directly or indirectly 'interested' in the transaction: the layman might, for example, have been unable to produce the requisite payment when the details of the transaction were ratified at the *witenagemot*, or to provide an up-to-date survey of the estate concerned for incorporation into the diploma,[164] so he might have been authorized to make his own arrangements by applying to an ecclesiastical scriptorium in his neighbourhood. Again, there might have been occasions when the writing of diplomas was entrusted to one of the bishops present at a *witenagemot*, whether of necessity because a royal scribe happened not to be available for the purpose, or by choice because the bishop seemed to be particularly suitable in the context of the transaction.[165] Or perhaps if an ecclesiastical scriptorium was given the task of drawing up a diploma, it was on an occasion when the gathering of the *witan* was being held in the

---

[164] One presumes that it was up to the beneficiary to provide the scribe with a survey of the estate in which he was interested, whether in the form of an older diploma for the same estate, or on a separate slip of parchment produced locally (see, e.g., S 1547).

[165] It is probably in this context that we should set the series of alliterative diplomas from the 940s and 950s: S 472–3, 479, 484, 520, 544, 548–50, 556–7, 566, 569, 572, 633 and 1606; cf. S 392, 404, 574 and 1497. The use of the third person in place of the first in the dispositive clause is a distinguishing feature of this series and accords well with the supposition that the diplomas were not drawn up under the normal circumstances. The series is perhaps to be associated with Cenwald, bishop of Worcester, since he occurs in all of the diplomas with full witness lists (described as *monachus* in S 544, 566, 569 and 633), since he uses elements of the formulation himself in S 1290, and since half of the estates concerned are in the west Midlands (see Whitelock, *Will of Æthelgifu*, p. 42; *idem*, *EHD*, pp. 372–3; Brooks, 'Anglo-Saxon Charters', p. 218; Sawyer, *Charters of Burton*, p. xlviii; and Chaplais, 'La chancellerie royale anglaise' (forthcoming); cf. Hart, 'Danelaw Charters', and *idem*, *Charters of Northern England*, pp. 18–20); but any future study of the alliterative diplomas will have to take into account the inscription in London, Lambeth Palace MS 1370 (see above, p. 26 n. 37), which anticipates them in certain stylistic respects. One should add that there is every reason to believe that the diplomas were not drawn up in an ecclesiastical scriptorium (e.g. Worcester), but rather on the occasion of the *witenagemot*: individual examples were issued at Colchester (S 472), Chippenham (S 473), Winchcombe (S 479), Kingston (S 520), Somerton (S 549), Cirencester (S 633) and Kirtlington (S 1497); S 544 and 548–50 are closely interrelated, and a single agency was apparently responsible for S 544 and 549, and then for S 548 and 550, on two separate occasions in 949; S 556 and 557 are also likely to have been drawn up together. One should bear in mind that once the type had been introduced, other draftsmen would have been free to imitate it: some of the diplomas in the main series may be cases in point, as is S 931 (dated 1013).

vicinity, and when it was most convenient to take advantage of the scriptorium's services. But one should emphasize that the king might not have relinquished any control in such cases: in the eleventh century, the delegation of responsibility for the production of a diploma was a matter which required authorization by royal writ,[166] and at all times the initiative might have had to come from the king.

[166] Harmer, *Writs*, pp. 39–41.

Chapter 3

THE DIPLOMAS OF KING ÆTHELRED

THE DIPLOMAS ISSUED BETWEEN 978 AND 990

There are clear signs of a continuous diplomatic tradition extending from the closing years of Edgar's reign to the opening years of Æthelred's reign, though seeming not to involve the slightly anomalous group of diplomas in the name of Edward the Martyr.[1] Many of the diplomas issued between 970 and 975, including those identified above as belonging to the series of Edgar's diplomas which conform in various respects to the pattern established by 'Edgar A' in the early 960s, can be distinguished from those issued earlier in the reign by the employment of the style 'Ego Edgar rex prefatam donationem concessi' for the king's subscription, followed by the style 'Ego Dunstan Dorovernensis ecclesiae archiepiscopus consignavi' for the archbishop of Canterbury.[2] Several of the diplomas issued at the beginning of Æthelred's reign, between 979 and 983, reflect the continued employment of this formulation in the witness lists,[3] and it is significant that the diagnostic features do not occur in combination in any diploma issued thereafter. It is also noticeable that the same early diplomas of Æthelred generally contain various elements of the formulation associated directly and indirectly with 'Edgar A', notably the formula for expressing the freedom of the estate from worldly burdens[4] and a distinctive type of dating clause;[5]

---

[1] Two diplomas of Edward from Abingdon (S 828 and 829) cannot be authentic as they stand, but the attached witness lists were probably derived from genuine texts; two from Exeter (S 830 and 832) are closely related to one another (see Chaplais, 'Diplomas of Exeter', pp. 15–16), and the former if not an apograph may be authentic; S 831, from the Old Minster Winchester, was apparently modelled on a diploma of the 940s (see, e.g., S 476) and is probably authentic. Cf. Hart, *Charters of Northern England*, pp. 26–7.

[2] S 780, 789, 794, 800–1 and 804–5; cf. S 749, 775, 777–8, 781 and 795.

[3] S 835–6, 841, 843 and 849; cf. S 837, 839–40 and 938.

[4] See S 835–7, 840–1, 843 and 938; cf. S 838.

[5] S 835, 837, 841, 843 and 849, the distinctive features being the absence of an indiction and the use of *carta* instead of *cartula* etc.; cf. S 838 and 840.

some of them have further links with later diplomas of King Edgar,[6] reinforcing the overall impression of diplomatic continuity from one reign to the next. After this initial group of Æthelred's diplomas we find a larger and more clearly defined group that comprises a substantial proportion of the diplomas issued between 983 and 990 and that appears to represent the development of a different (if not entirely new) type of formulation. The diplomas are identified in the first instance by the employment of the following styles of attestation for the king and the two archbishops:

✠ Ego Æðelred rex Anglorum huius donationis libertatem regni tocius fastigium tenens libenter concessi.

✠ Ego Dunstan Dorovernensis aecclesiae archiepiscopus cum signo sanctae crucis roboravi.

✠ Ego Oswold Eboracensis aecclesiae archiepiscopus crucis taumate adnotavi.

This combination of formulae occurs for the first time in a diploma dated 983 (S 844), and is only found thereafter in eleven diplomas issued in the period up to 990;[7] elements of this combination occur in six other diplomas issued in the same period.[8] It would be difficult to convey clearly the complexity of the further diplomatic links between particular diplomas within this group, but they extend to all parts of the formulation from the invocation and proem to the sentence introducing the bounds and the dating clause. While the styles of attestation were apparently new, it is interesting to observe that several of the formulae employed for the earlier sections of the diplomas originated in the central decades of the tenth century. A diploma of King Edmund issued in 940 probably underlies S 844 (dated 983 and preserved at the Old Minster Winchester) and S 855 (dated 984 and preserved at Abingdon): the invocation, proem,

---

[6] Cf. the statement about the earlier, lost, diploma in S 835 with a similar statement in S 744; cf. elements of the disposition in S 837, 841 and 843 with corresponding elements in any of the 'Edgar A' series in favour of religious communities; for the proem in S 841, see above, p. 74 n. 148; for the proem in S 849, see S 789 (and 649) and cf. S 835; for the sanctions in S 835, 841, 843 and 938, see above, p. 73 n. 147. Note also that substantial elements of the formulation in S 834 had been used previously in S 793; for its proem, cf., e.g., S 504 and 619.

[7] S 851, 853, 855, 856–8, 860, 863–4, 866 and 874, with only a few minor variations.

[8] S 848, 859, 861, 867–8 and 872.

superscription, dispositive section and sanction common to these two diplomas are all found in S 461–3, and the proem itself does not occur in genuine texts elsewhere.[9] The sanction, on the other hand, is found more frequently. It appears to have originated in these diplomas of 940 (S 461–3), as a variation of one that occurs for the first time in 939,[10] and it was used sporadically thereafter, in the 940s, 950s and 960s.[11] But when it was revived for use in S 844 and 855 it was simplified slightly by the omission of the clause 'quod opto absit a fidelium mentibus'; the same variation of the formula occurs in S 856 (dated 985), another of the diplomas belonging to the group under discussion, but is not found again.[12] Another old sanction, found several times in diplomas dated between 940 and 960,[13] and revived once already in 982 (S 842), occurs again in 983 (S 851, from Abingdon) and in 985 (S 860, from the Old Minster Winchester).[14] The formulation of S 860 is of interest in a further respect: it shares with S 856 a long proem which cannot be traced elsewhere, but the exposition, running from the end of the proem to the superscription and also common to both diplomas, was derived ultimately from the diplomas of King Æthelstan issued in the early 930s which employ the proem beginning 'Flebilia fortiter detestanda . . .'.[15] A variation of a sanction found in diplomas dated 928 (S 399 and 400) was used in S 858 (dated 985), which shares its dispositive section with S 844 and 855 and so with the diplomas of 940. Formulae used in S 859 and 872 can also be traced back to the second quarter of the tenth century,[16] and formulae used in S 848, 863, 864, 866, 867, 868 and 872 can be traced back to the 950s and 960s.[17] Of course the revival of old formulae is by

---

[9] It is found in S 226, an Evesham forgery; a variation occurs in S 464, dated 940; another variation, with elements from both versions used in 940, occurs in S 784, 890 and 1019.

[10] S 445, 654, 705 and 795.   [11] S 523, 619, 638, 704, 740, 763 and 770.

[12] Later occurrences of the sanction are of the full version: S 886 and 951.

[13] S 392, 465, 474–5, 502, 521, 524, 531, 534, 536, 540, 554, 558, 585, 587–8, 610, 640, 674, 679 and 687.

[14] See also S 884 (omitting the reference to frying pans), 955 and 968.

[15] See above, p. 44. See also S 728 and 919.

[16] For the proem in S 859, see S 414–15, 476 and 480; also S 83, 662, 831 and 959. The sanction in S 872 was current between 944 and 948 (S 493, 495, 497–9, 501, 506–7, 525, 529–30, 532–3, 535 and 541–2) and occurs elsewhere in S 582, 668, 671, 783 and 1010.

[17] For the proem in S 848, see S 584, 681, 701, 708, 719, 738 and 744; also S 780, 826, 830, 846, 907, 993 and 1025. For the proem in S 864, see above, p. 74 n. 148. The proem of S 872 occurs in S 554, 577, 642, 655, 730 and 800. The dispositive section common to S 863–4 and 867–8 contains elements that were already in use in the 950s (e.g. S 575 and 602). For

no means unusual in the general context of Anglo-Saxon diplomatic, but it is nowhere more marked than in Æthelred's diplomas issued between 983 and 990: given the recurrence of certain formulae (after several years of apparent disuse) almost simultaneously in two or more diplomas, and then perhaps in a slightly modified form, and given the degree of relationship between the diplomas in other respects, one cannot avoid the supposition that a common denominator underlies their production.

Further support for this supposition comes from consideration of particular pairs or groups of diplomas within this series. The witness lists attached to S 844 and 851, both dated 983 and preserved in the archives of the Old Minster Winchester and Abingdon respectively, are remarkably similar. The ten bishops and four abbots given in each list are identical, and occur in the same order (see Tables 2 and 4); the lists of *ministri* are also intimately related, since the seven names common to both are recorded in the same relative order (see Table 7). However, it is certain that these diplomas were issued on different occasions in 983, since the lists of ealdormen reveal that S 844 was produced before the death of Ealdorman Ælfhere, whereas S 851 was produced after his death and after the promotion of Ælfric from *minister* to ealdorman in his stead (see Table 6, and compare Table 7). So it would appear that the same memorandum of witnesses' names was used on two separate occasions in the year, with some necessary alterations to the lists of ealdormen and *ministri*. A very similar memorandum underlies the witness list attached to S 855, preserved in the Abingdon archives and dated 984. The group of bishops is the same as that common to S 844 and 851, though without Sigar of Wells (see Table 2); the group of abbots is identical with that common to these two earlier diplomas (see Table 4); the ealdormen are the same as in S 851, with two names transposed (see Table 6); and the nine *ministri* common to S 855 and 851 are listed in the same order, apart from the transposition of Leofwine (see Table 7). Moreover, the formulation of S 855 is almost identical with that in S 844, though these diplomas are from different archives.[18]

the sanctions in S 861, 864 and 866–8, see above, p. 73 n. 147; the sanction in S 863 was probably of the same type.

[18] Note that both diplomas incorporate a brief statement of previous ownership of the estate concerned: S 844 in the endorsement, and S 855 in the dispositive section.

Amongst the diplomas issued in 985 are three that can probably be regarded as the products of a single agency acting on the same occasion: S 856 and 860 from the Old Minster Winchester and S 858 from Abingdon. The relative order of the bishops in each of the attached witness lists is identical (see Table 2), and the lists are interlocked by the occurrence of particular bishops in S 856 and 858 (Wulfgar of Ramsbury), S 856 and 860 (Athulf of Hereford) and S 858 and 860 (Æscwig of Dorchester and Sigar of Wells). When apparent copyists' alterations and errors have been corrected,[19] it emerges that the remaining groups of witnesses in each of the diplomas are also remarkably similar. The ealdormen and the abbots are identical, and the only differences amongst the *ministri* are the omission of Ælfhelm and Leofstan from S 856 and the relative position of the latter in S 858 and 860. It is conceivable, therefore, that a single memorandum underlies the witness lists in these three diplomas: given the similarities between the lists in S 844, 851 and 855 this may not be sufficient to guarantee that the diplomas were drawn up on the same occasion, but the possibility that they were derives some support from their formulation. Up to and including the superscription and after the sanction, S 860, in favour of Wulfrun and relating to land at Wolverhampton, is cast in terms identical with S 856, in favour of Æthelric and relating to land in Berkshire. Moreover, these diplomas share a special formula condemning any other document brought forward to challenge the beneficiary's title to the estate, a formula that was apparently developed in the early 980s and that in one form or another was used several times during the course of this decade.[20] S 856 and 860 differ chiefly in the choice of sanction; that in S 856 had been used in S 844 and 855, whereas that in S 860 had been used in S 851. S 858 shares different elements of its dispositive section with S 856 and 860, and corresponds to both in the latter part of its formulation (from the sentence introducing the bounds); like them too it contains a sanction revived from diplomas of the earlier tenth century.[21]

---

[19] See Appendix 1, pp. 244–5.

[20] The formula in S 856 and 860 occurs also in S 861 and 872; cf. S 842. Its opening recurs in S 896, and the full version in S 933 and 1004. A variation occurs in S 874, 920, 930, 961 and 969; cf. S 873.

[21] There may also be a common denominator underlying the other two diplomas dated 985, S 857 and 859: they share the unusual feature (in diplomas of this period) of naming the sees of the bishops of Winchester and London (see Table 2).

There are strong grounds also for supposing that S 863, 864, 866 and 867 were drawn up by the same agency in 987, and moreover that S 864 and 867 were produced on the same occasion. The lists attached to S 864 and 867 are closely related to one another. The selection of bishops is identical, and apart from the transposition of names in one pair they are recorded in the same order (see Table 2); the abbots differ only slightly (see Table 4); the ealdormen are identical (see Table 6); and, most significantly, the first ten *ministri* are identical in both selection and order, though the lists diverge thereafter (see Table 7).[22] Unfortunately, the cartulary copyists of S 863 and 866 transcribed the witness lists only in an abbreviated form, so one cannot judge whether or not these two might have been drawn up with S 864 and 867. In terms of their formulation these four diplomas constitute a well-defined group. A proem beginning 'Annuente Dei patris ineffabili humane proli clementia...' occurs in S 863 and 866, from the Burton and Glastonbury archives respectively, and the opening words of the same formula, with a different and shorter continuation, are found in S 867, from the Old Minster Winchester. The proem was apparently a newly-composed one, so that its simultaneous appearance in three diplomas issued in the same year ought to be significant.[23] S 864 has a completely different proem, derived ultimately from one of the 'Edgar A' diplomas issued in the early 960s. The dispositive sections in S 863, 864 and 867 are closely related, while that in S 866 necessarily diverges from the others because it is a diploma in favour of an abbey rather than an individual. S 866 does, however, share its exposition with S 863 and 867, its superscription with S 863, and its dispositive clause with S 864 and 867. The sanction associated with 'Edgar A' is employed in S 864, 866 and 867 (and probably in S 863 as well, though the copyist only recorded the opening words of the formula), and of course the styles of attestation used for the king and archbishops in all four diplomas are related. It is interesting

[22] For the order of the *ministri* in S 864 and 867, cf. S 861.

[23] In its longer form (i.e. S 863 and 866) the proem recurs only in S 868 and 933. In its shorter form (i.e. S 867) it recurs only in S 804 and 1016, both of which are spurious diplomas in favour of the Old Minster Winchester, evidently forged together using S 867 as a model; they incorporate (absurdly) passages derived ultimately from *Domesday Book*, and the sanction in S 804 represents the only other occurrence of a slight variation of the sanction associated with 'Edgar A' which is found in S 867; it is significant that neither S 804 nor S 1016 was included in the *Codex Wintoniensis*.

that the formulae employed in these diplomas of 987, represented in particular by S 863, recur in S 868, issued in the following year and preserved at the Old Minster Winchester; its witness list contains basically the same selection of people as had attested the diplomas of 987, and there are some similarities in the order in which the names are recorded. This relationship adds further to the evidence for continuity in the agency behind the production of these diplomas, suggested already by the diplomatic links between S 844 and 855 and by the similarities between the witness lists attached to S 844, 851 and 855, and between those attached to S 861, 864 and 867.[24] Taking the diplomas issued between 983 and 990 which are united by their styles of attestation again as a single group, we find that they were preserved in the archives of seven religious houses and relate to estates in nine counties. Nearly all of them are in favour of laymen, and of these at least two represent the appropriation of land from a religious foundation.[25] One of the diplomas, however, is in favour of an abbey (Glastonbury: S 866), and another is in favour of the king's priest Wulfric (S 859). So apparently the agency responsible for the production of these diplomas could cater for ecclesiastical beneficiaries as well as for secular ones, and apparently it could be used for recording transactions of a decidedly secular and even anti-ecclesiastical nature.

The diplomas discussed above and assigned to two groups, one representing a continuation of the diplomatic practices prevalent in the closing years of Edgar's reign and the other representing a distinctive development within the 980s, account for about 70% of the diplomas issued in the period from 978 to 990. Those that remain seem to belong to other diplomatic traditions, though by no means are they necessarily isolated from the main groups: some may simply reflect an individual draftsman's choice of a different type of formulation rather than a different agency of production. Thus most of the formulae used in S 850, dated 984 and preserved at Shaftesbury, seem to be peculiar to this diploma, in part reflecting the special circumstances of the transaction involved. It may,

---

[24] Note in this connection that the lists in S 861 and 864 have the form *abba*, in place of the usual *abbas*, for each abbot; it is not possible to tell what form was used in S 867, since the copyist changed *abba(s)* to *dux*.

[25] S 861 (cf. S 891) and 864 (cf. S 893).

however, have been drawn up on the same occasion as S 852, from Abingdon: both were produced before 1 August in 984, since Æthelwold, bishop of Winchester (who died on that day), is included in the witness lists; the same selection of twelve bishops occurs in both lists, recorded in the same order apart from the transposition of names in two pairs (see Table 2); the ealdormen are identical (see Table 6), and the diplomas share the unusual feature of having no list of abbots; all of the *ministri* in S 852 occur in S 850, including the rare Ælfwine (see Table 7).[26] In terms of their formulation S 850 and 852 have nothing of significance in common, but the draftsman of the latter at least displays the marked tendency observed in contemporary diplomas for reviving formulae current in earlier decades.[27] There can be little doubt that S 870 (from Wilton) and S 871 (from Glastonbury) were drawn up by a single agency; they may indeed have been produced on the same occasion, for both belong to the period in 988 when there was a vacancy at Canterbury created by Archbishop Dunstan's death, and their witness lists are identical, at least as far as the truncated one in S 871 extends. Substantial elements of the formulation in S 870 were apparently derived from a diploma issued in the 940s,[28] but otherwise it shares with S 871 an unusual clause between the superscription and the disposition, and very distinctive styles of attestation in the witness list. The subject of S 870 is a messuage in Wilton and the subject of S 871 is a messuage in Winchester, so it is as if a single draftsman adopted a similar type of formulation for two transactions of a similar nature.[29] The sanctions composed for each diploma reveal close links with the main group of contemporary diplomas: that in S 870 incorporates the clause 'sciat se coram Christo titubantem tremebundumque rationem redditurum', derived from a

---

[26] The other diploma issued in 984 before 1 August, S 855, is set apart from S 850 and 852 by the inclusion of Ealdorman Thored, the king's mother and a group of abbots.

[27] S 852 may have been modelled on a diploma of King Eadwig's: for the proem, see S 647 (and cf. S 526); for the dispositive section and sanction, see S 636; for the superscription and sanction, see S 604; for the sanction alone, see above, p. 65 n. 121.

[28] Cf. its dispositive section and sanction with, e.g., S 495, 497, 501, 506, 525, 530, 532 and 541.

[29] It is remarkable that the beneficiaries of S 870–2 are the king's *minister* Æthelnoth, Æthelsige, bishop of Sherborne (with Æthelmær the king's *miles*) and the king's *minister* Leofstan: for the three men named as the negotiators of the peace between England and Normandy, in a document dated 1 March 991 (see Stubbs, *Memorials*, pp. 397–8), are Æthelsige, bishop of Sherborne, Leofstan the son of Ælfwold and Æthelnoth the son of Wigstan. If this is more than a strange coincidence, it is still inexplicable.

formula current between 944 and 948 and revived in S 872, which was issued later on in 988;[30] that in S 871 is especially distinctive and is closely related to the corresponding formula in S 857, issued in 985.[31] Accordingly, one could with some justification regard S 870 and 871 as the products of the agency responsible for most contemporary diplomas.[32]

Those diplomas of the 980s that were preserved in the archives of the New Minster Winchester seem to form a separate group. S 865, dated 987, is a grant of land in Wiltshire to Æthelwold, one of the king's *obsequentes*, and to it is appended Æthelwold's will (S 1505) bequeathing the estate to his wife, with reversion after her death to the New Minster. S 869, dated 988, is a grant of land in Sussex to Æthelgar, bishop of Selsey: part of the estate concerned came into the possession of the New Minster some time before the Conquest, doubtless through the agency of Æthelgar, who had been appointed abbot of the New Minster in 964 and who had apparently retained that office after he became bishop of Selsey in 980, relinquishing it in 988 when he was translated to Canterbury. The two diplomas have several minor but unusual and therefore significant expressions in common, from the superscription, dispositive section and sanction to the sentence introducing the bounds, the dating clause and the styles of subscription. Two earlier diplomas preserved in the New Minster archives, S 842 (dated 982) and 845 (dated 983), anticipate in some respects the distinctive formulation of S 865 and 869. S 842 is in favour of the New Minster and shares certain

---

[30] See above, p. 86 n. 16. For the date of S 872, see Appendix 1, p. 249.

[31] The formula in S 857 cites Luke xiii 27 ('Discedite a me omnes operarii iniquitatis', with the continuation 'in flammas ignium') instead of Matthew xxv 41 ('Discedite a me maledicti in ignem aeternum, qui paratus est diabolo et angelis eius', altered to '. . . qui paratus est Sathanæ et satellitibus eius' and sometimes with *maligni* for *maledicti*), which is the text used in related sanctions (e.g. S 844 and 855, on which see above, p. 87). It is therefore interesting to find similar formulae based on Luke xiii 27 in S 871 and 882, both continuing with the same variant of verse 28 ('ibi erit fletus et stridor dentium', altered by inserting *oculorum* after *fletus*). These formulae in S 857, 871 and 882 probably had a common origin.

[32] It is conceivable that the fragmentary S 1863 (*c.* 987) could be assigned to the same group: the main formulae were old ones revived (the proem occurs in S 448, 707, 727, 966, 1214 and 1379 (cf. S 440 and 445) and for the sanction see above, p. 65 n. 119); for the unusual phrase 'ceu supradiximus' in the dispositive section see S 863, dated 987; note the absence of *egos* in the column of witnesses, as in the diplomas of the 940s and 950s. S 847 and 875 stand out on their own, at least from a diplomatic point of view; for the formulation of the latter, cf. the diplomas of Æthelstan listed above, p. 44 n. 78.

features of its disposition, dating clause and witness list with S 865 and 869; S 845 is in favour of Bishop Æthelgar, apparently in his capacity as abbot of the New Minster, and shares elements of its disposition, sanction and dating clause with S 865 and 869. It seems, therefore, that the New Minster is the common denominator behind at least the two later diplomas: for whereas S 842 and 845 may have been drawn up by an independent agency, coincidentally for associated beneficiaries, it is improbable that several of the characteristics would be repeated fortuitously in two later diplomas for beneficiaries associated in the same way. Accordingly, it would appear that S 865 can be regarded as a diploma drawn up by the intended eventual beneficiary and S 869 as one drawn up by the actual beneficiary.

The interest of the New Minster diplomas does not end here. Diplomatic evidence tends to support the possibility that S 842 and 845 were not themselves products of the New Minster scriptorium, for both have intriguing links with the main group of diplomas issued between 983 and 990. S 842 contains an apparent prototype of the formula, found in some of this group, whose purpose was to annul any older document produced by another party to challenge the new one,[33] and the same diploma also contains a sanction revived from the earlier tenth century which occurs again in S 851 and 860. The proem of S 845 has some points of contact with the proem of S 858, which may be sufficient to suggest a direct link between them.[34] S 842 and 845 would presumably have been available at the New Minster when S 865 and 869 were drawn up, and the draftsman of the latter two diplomas may have been influenced by aspects of their formulation. But at the same time he seems not to have been isolated from the mainstream of contemporary diplomatic. In S 869 he expressed the reservation of the three common burdens in terms that are clearly related to an extraordinary formula in S 874:

---

[33] See above, p. 88 n. 20.

[34] A few of the minor diplomatic features which distinguish S 842, 845, 865 and 869 can be shown to have been current outside the New Minster, providing further grounds for the possible dissociation of the earlier pair from the abbey: see S 886 and 1796. The slightly anomalous order of ealdormen in S 845, 865 and 869, with Ælfric of Hampshire before Æthelweard of the Western Provinces, is found elsewhere, in S 843 and 855. For the naming of the bishops' sees in S 842, 865 and 869, see S 870 and 871 (and cf. below, p. 119).

S 869	S 874
. . . tribus tantummodo causis exceptis, quæ hujus incolæ hactenus patriæ ritu observant legali, id est, cum hostium cunei commilitonum corripere compulerint arma, vel cum recuperationem expetunt pontium vada, seu cum arcis munitionem vastitas flagitat urbana.	. . . tribus tantummodo rationabiliter rebus exceptis, que usuali ritu observantur actenus, id est cum glomerata sibi alternatim expeditioni compulerit populari commilitonum confligere castra, atque cum sua petunt pontis titubantia muniri vada, ac cum concivium turma urbium indigent muniri stabiliter septa.

It might appear that the formula in S 869 is the earlier version, of which that in S 874 is a development, since the latter diploma was issued two years after the former. But if the draftsman of S 869 devised it himself, it is perhaps unlikely that it would ever have been available for slight revision by another person. The formula in S 874 may in fact have been used before 988 in a diploma that has not survived, making the version in S 869 a variation of it; moreover, there is evidence that the version in S 874 became current, since it is found in two eleventh-century diplomas from Abbotsbury.[35] Whatever the case, the relationship between S 869 and 874 implies contact of some description between the draftsman responsible for S 865 and 869 and the agency responsible for the majority of the contemporary diplomas.

The unusual formulation of S 862, which begins directly with the date and which lacks a proem, is derived from a series of diplomas issued in the third quarter of the tenth century, some of which seem to have a particular association with the abbey of Glastonbury.[36] S 862 is the last diploma to employ the formulation, and the only authentic representative of the series to survive from the 980s.[37] Its distinctive character extends to the witness list. The order of the ealdormen is regular and the absence of a group of abbots is not exceptional, but the list is in other respects anomalous. Amongst the bishops, third place seems high for Athulf of Hereford and ninth place low for Ælfstan of London. More significantly, the group of *ministri* is composed largely of men who could not be regarded as prominent thegns on the collective evidence of contem-

---

[35] Gibson, *Reliquiæ*, pp. 19–20 (dated 1014) and S 1004.
[36] See above, p. 48.
[37] S 854 (from Bath) is not authentic; cf. Hart, *Charters of Northern England*, p. 21 n. 2.

porary diplomas, and indeed, four of the *ministri* who consistently dominate the lists in the 980s appear to be missing (see Table 7). Nevertheless, the authenticity of the list is guaranteed by the presence of Osweard, whose subscriptions are confined to the diplomas issued between 986 and 988; that the series of subscriptions of Wulfheah and Wulfgeat should commence in 986 is supported by S 861, issued in the same year. S 862 was preserved in the archives of Malmesbury Abbey, for it is a grant to the king's *minister* Wenoth of five hides at Littleton on Severn (in Gloucestershire), held by the abbey in 1066 and 1086.[38] Thus the archives should have contained such a title-deed, and it is interesting that it is the only diploma not directly in favour of the abbey that the first Malmesbury cartularist admitted into his collection, suggesting that he was at least satisfied with it as evidence for the abbey's title to the estate.[39] It seems reasonable to accept S 862 as an authentic instrument of 986, and to regard its unusual features as a sign that it was not drawn up under the normal circumstances.

THE DIPLOMAS ISSUED BETWEEN 993 AND 1016

No diplomas have survived from the years 991 and 992, but the series recommences in 993 and the diplomas produced thereafter until the end of the reign display a diversity of structure and formulation that, when set beside the uniformity of the diplomas issued in the 980s, appears at first sight to suggest that they were drawn up under different circumstances. A relatively small proportion of Æthelred's later diplomas conform to the format which had become firmly established during the reign of Æthelstan and which was standard for the great majority of diplomas issued between 925 and 990. Instead the series is dominated by a type of diploma incorporating in the dispositive section an account of the circumstances leading up to the transaction that in some cases amounts to a description of the recent history of the estate, and that considerably augments the length of the text.[40] Examples of the type had appeared occasionally

38 DB i, fo. 165v.
39 See above, p. 9.
40 On the tendency of Æthelred's diplomas to enlarge on the history of the estate concerned, see Stenton, 'St. Frideswide', pp. 226–7, *idem*, *Latin Charters*, pp. 74–82, Whitelock, *EHD*, p. 379, and Campbell, *Charters of Rochester*, p. xxvi.

in the 980s,[41] but most were produced during the second and third decades of Æthelred's reign and almost without exception are in favour of the religious houses in whose archives they were preserved:

S	Date	Details of transaction	Archive
876	993	King Æthelred to Abingdon Abbey: confirmation and grant of privileges	Abingdon
882	994	King Æthelred to Æscwig, bishop: confirmation of land in Buckinghamshire	Christ Church Canterbury
884	995	King Æthelred to Muchelney Abbey: confirmation of lands in Somerset and elsewhere	Muchelney
885	995	King Æthelred to the see of Rochester: restoration of lands in Kent	Rochester
889	996	King Æthelred to the Old Minster Winchester: restoration of land in Winchester	Old Minster Winchester
891	997	King Æthelred to the Old Minster Winchester: restoration of lands in Wiltshire	Old Minster Winchester
893	998	King Æthelred to the see of Rochester: restoration of land in Kent, with appurtenant woodland in the Weald	Rochester
937	?999	King Æthelred to Abingdon Abbey: description of circumstances behind grant of lands in Berkshire, Warwickshire, Gloucestershire and ?Oxfordshire[42]	Abingdon
899	1001	King Æthelred to Shaftesbury Abbey: grant of a *cenobium* and land in Wiltshire	Shaftesbury
909	1004	King Æthelred to St Frideswide's Abbey: confirmation of lands in Buckinghamshire and Oxfordshire	St Frideswide's
911	1005	King Æthelred to Eynsham Abbey: confirmation of foundation and endowment in various counties	Eynsham
912	1005	King Æthelred to St Albans Abbey: grant of privileges and of lands in Hertfordshire	St Albans
916	1007	King Æthelred to St Albans Abbey: grant of lands in Hertfordshire	St Albans
918	1008	King Æthelred to Abingdon Abbey: restoration and grant of lands in Wiltshire	Abingdon

[41] S 835, 850 and 869.

[42] S 937 is anomalous in form and content, but there is no conclusive objection to it. It was apparently intended to supplement S 896 (dated 999) and other (no longer extant) diplomas produced at the same time, perhaps because the common circumstances of the transactions they represented could not easily be described in the context of just one of them or in every one of them. A paragraph at the end of S 937 declares that the document should always be kept in the monastery so that the *libertas* guaranteed by the individual diplomas 'might be eternal' ('. . . sit . . . eterna', adopting the reading of B.L. Cotton Claudius C ix in preference to the nonsensical *externa* in Claudius B vi as printed by Stevenson, Kemble and Thorpe).

920	1008	King Æthelred to Burton Abbey: grant of land in Staffordshire	Burton
933	1014	King Æthelred to Sherborne Abbey: grant of land in Dorset	Sherborne[43]

These diplomas are to be distinguished carefully from a further group issued during the same period for a variety of beneficiaries and characterized by the incorporation of a narrative section describing the crimes of an individual, serving to explain why his estates had been forfeited and thus to demonstrate that the king had the right to dispose of the particular estate in question:

S	Date	Details of transaction	Archive
883	995	King Æthelred to Æthelwig, his *miles*: grant of land in Oxfordshire (apparently forfeited by three brothers)	Abingdon
886	995	King Æthelred to Wulfric, *minister*: grant of land in Gloucestershire (forfeited by Æthelsige)	Abingdon
877	996	King Æthelred to Ælfthryth, his mother: grant of lands in Kent (forfeited by Wulfbald)	New Minster Winchester
896	999	King Æthelred to Abingdon Abbey: grant of land in Gloucestershire (forfeited by Ealdorman Ælfric)	Abingdon
926	1012	King Æthelred to Godwine, bishop of Rochester: grant of land in Huntingdonshire (forfeited by Æthelflæd)	Rochester
927	1012	King Æthelred to Leofric, his *minister*: grant of land in Oxfordshire (forfeited by Leofric)	Abingdon
934	1015	King Æthelred to Brihtwold, his bishop: grant of land in Berkshire (forfeited by Wulfgeat)	Abingdon[44]

The prevailing impression of diversity in structure and formulation made on the reader of Æthelred's later diplomas is to be attributed directly to the currency during the corresponding period of these discursive documents. One should, however, hesitate before interpreting the diversity as symptomatic of some relaxation of control over the production of diplomas; for it is arguable that it

---

[43] S 838, 894, 935 and 940 have discursive elements but are spurious in their received form. There are two further examples from the reign of Cnut, S 951 and 956, on which see Stenton, *Latin Charters*, pp. 82–3.

[44] For an example of this type of diploma from the reign of Edward the Elder, see S 362. A few diplomas not included in this list refer in passing to crimes that led to forfeiture of estates: S 842, 892, 901 and 923; see also S 869, 893, 911, 916, 918 and 937, assigned to the previous group.

should be understood rather as the effect that certain historical developments in the 990s had on the nature of diplomas issued at the time. After 990 there was a marked decrease in the number of diplomas issued in favour of laymen and a no less marked increase in the number of diplomas issued in favour of religious houses. Many of the latter represented not simply fresh grants of land but involved more complex matters – for example, definition of the privileges to be enjoyed by the new foundations, the restoration of estates that had previously been appropriated, or the confirmation of endowments that had recently been made by prominent laymen. Straightforward grants of land were still made, of course, but it was now often considered desirable to explain in some detail how the king had come into possession of the estate concerned.[45] Those responsible for drafting such documents would have had to abandon the conventional format of royal diplomas where necessary, in favour of a more individually distinctive text that took the particular circumstances of the transaction fully into account.

The very nature of these discursive diplomas renders it the less surprising that there are not such extensive diplomatic links between them as were noticeable between the diplomas produced in the 980s, while the fact that they were preserved in the archives of many different religious houses could itself be held to imply that there was still some degree of contact between their respective draftsmen; and the closer one examines them, the more convinced one becomes that the draftsmen of many of them may indeed have been members of the same writing office. S 876, issued by King Æthelred in 993 to confirm and extend the privileges of Abingdon Abbey, is related diplomatically to a series of earlier diplomas known as the *Orthodoxorum* group from the initial word of their common proem: one, in the name of King Eadwig, is in favour of Abingdon (S 658), and the remaining four, in the name of King Edgar, are in favour of Abingdon (S 673), Pershore (S 786), Worcester (S 788) and Romsey (S 812). Were these earlier diplomas authentic,[46] there would clearly be grounds for asserting that S 876 was drawn up at Abingdon, by a draftsman who used as his models the *Orthodoxorum*

[45] For a discussion of the historical background, see below, pp. 200–2.

[46] John, *Orbis Britanniae*, pp. 181–209, argues that of the *Orthodoxorum* series all but S 788 are authentic, though he regards part of S 673 as an interpolation; see also Chaplais, 'Anglo-Saxon Chancery', p. 49, and Brooks, 'Anglo-Saxon Charters', pp. 229–30.

diplomas for the abbey issued by Eadwig and Edgar. However, there are good reasons for supposing the earlier diplomas to be forgeries, themselves drawn up ultimately on the basis of the authentic S 876. In the first place, the proem common to the series is related textually to that found in S 690 and 703, both originals written by 'Edgar A' in 961 and 962 respectively and therefore later than the two purported *Orthodoxorum* diplomas for Abingdon: it was suggested above that 'Edgar A' was a scribe in the king's service, and – if so – it is unlikely that he would have been in a position to adapt for his own purposes a formula used previously in the two Abingdon diplomas; it seems more likely that the *Orthodoxorum* proem is a development of the formula found in S 690 and 703 and as such makes an anachronistic appearance in S 658 and 673.[47] Secondly, all but two of the *Orthodoxorum* diplomas contain a formula which seems to arise from a specific historical context entirely appropriate to S 876 but less appropriate to the others individually and rather implausible if applied to all of them collectively. In S 876 a passage beginning 'Tempore siquidem . . .' insists on the repudiation of the 'new hereditary charters' which certain men had procured for themselves at a time when the estates now restored by King Æthelred had been unjustly appropriated from the abbey. It can be shown from independent evidence that in the 990s Æthelred restored to various religious foundations estates which had been appropriated in the 980s, and that in so doing he had to annul the earlier diplomas which he himself had issued in respect of the appropriated lands:[48] so the 'Tempore siquidem . . .' formula in S 876 makes perfect historical sense. Yet the same formula occurs in S 673, 786 and 788, differing only in the use of the verb *concessi* where S 876 has the clause 'per hoc modernum privilegium restauravi'. It would assuredly be a strange coincidence if such a formula had been devised in the first place for diplomas issued in Edgar's reign, and was found still to be appropriate for use in 993. Moreover, it is not obvious what is meant in S 673, 786 and 788 by the estates which had been unjustly appropriated from the

---

[47] On this hypothesis, the draftsman of S 876 would have had access to a diploma like S 690, used not only for the proem but also for the styles of subscription (cf. S 811); S 690 itself would have been available at Abingdon and probably served as the model for the styles of subscription in S 673 (see also S 688 and 689).

[48] See further below, pp. 176–9.

abbeys in question and for which 'new hereditary charters' had been acquired. So again it seems that the formula was taken over into these diplomas from S 876, creating in this case not only a diplomatic but also an historical anachronism.[49] Thirdly, with the exception of S 876 all of the *Orthodoxorum* diplomas have miscellaneous suspicious features of their own, which if not themselves always fatal to the authenticity of the individual documents are at least consistent with their being spurious.[50] But undoubtedly the most decisive argument against the authenticity of the *Orthodoxorum* diplomas in the names of Eadwig and Edgar turns on the existence of apparently minor but in fact significant points of contact between S 876 and other diplomas produced in the 990s, suggesting that its formulation was contemporary and generally current rather than derivative and perhaps restricted to Abingdon. It shares elements of its proem, dating clause and styles of attestation with S 880, King Æthelred's grant of privileges to the see of Cornwall drawn up in 994,[51] and it contains a sanction, also used in S 880 and (in an abbreviated form) in another diploma of the 990s (S 892), which

[49] For a different interpretation of the 'Tempore siquidem . . .' formula, which depends on the reference to appropriation applying to the period before the restoration of Abingdon Abbey in Eadred's reign (and which cannot be ruled out), see John, *Orbis Britanniae*, pp. 186, 188, 191 and 194.

[50] The regnal style in the superscription of S 658 may be anachronistic (see above, p. 69 n. 135, but cf. S 651), as may the subscription of Archbishop Oda (see O'Donovan, 'Episcopal Dates, Pt. 1', pp. 33–4); cf. John, *Orbis Britanniae*, pp. 191–3. In S 673 a section restoring certain named estates contradicts S 567 (*ibid.* pp. 195–8), and the contradiction undermines confidence in both; there is also an error in the dating clause (958 for 959). There is clearly a direct connection between the long list of *ministri* in S 658 and the list in S 673, involving both the choice of names and the relative order in which they are recorded; cf. *ibid.* p. 195. If the arguments against S 658 and 673 are allowed, it could be said that S 786, 788 and 812 fall with them, since the formulation of these diplomas as a group does seem to have originated at Abingdon. S 786 is extant as an apparent original, but it may not be contemporary with its purported date; it is diplomatically anomalous in the sense that an *Orthodoxorum* diploma seems to have been transformed into a general confirmation charter listing all the estates of the abbey; its pictorial invocation is identical with that in S 876, whence it may have been derived, since an analogous device occurs on S 880 (dated 994), suggesting that it was a current form at that time. The statement in S 812 that 900 mancuses of gold (no less, in the form of a bowl) were given to the king for woodland pertaining to the estate seems rather improbable, and a section after the bounds looks out of place in a diploma. S 788 is obviously spurious, derived directly from S 786 (*ibid.* pp. 206–7).

[51] Elements of the *Orthodoxorum* proem itself are repeated in S 948 and 971. Leaving aside S 953 and 954, both Exeter forgeries modelled on S 880, the interesting reference to the fall of Lucifer and the tenth order of angels in S 880 can be paralleled only in S 853 (dated 984). One wonders whether there is any connection between proems like those in S 853 and 880 (see also S 745 and 906) and the catechetical *narratio* (on which see Day, 'The Influence of the Catechetical *Narratio*', pp. 51–5).

seems particularly well suited to the historical conditions of the decade.[52] It is one of a group of contemporary diplomas (comprising S 876, 885, 891 and 893) in which the king is made to regret the indiscretions of his youth, and it shares an idiom in this context with S 885 (from Rochester, dated 995), which increases the likelihood that these diplomas by their very nature had a common origin.[53] And it has certain features of content in common with S 891 (from the Old Minster Winchester, dated 997), such as the references to the grants of the king's predecessors, the provision of details concerning the successive stages leading to the production of the diploma, the inclusion of a regnal year in the dating clause and the identifications provided for each of the attesting abbots (the last feature being peculiar to these two diplomas). According to the text of S 876, the decision to make the confirmation of privileges was first taken at a synodal council held at Winchester on 4 June 993, and the *auctoritas* of the document was 'concessa et corroborata . . . die xvi. kalendarum Augustarum [17 July] in oratorio vici qui usitato Gillingaham nominari solet'; it was *confirmata* after mass had been celebrated, by the act of subscription. So it would appear that the document was actually written at Gillingham.[54] There is no place of this name in Berkshire, and it is impossible to decide between the Gillinghams in Dorset, Kent and Norfolk;[55] at least it is clear that the diploma was not drawn up at or even near the abbey of Abingdon. According to the corresponding section in S 891, the king restored the land to the Old Minster at Eastertide in 997, 'collecta haud minima sapientum

---

52 The sanction may not have been developed until 993 (S 876): its 'earlier' occurrences are confined to the *Orthodoxorum* diplomas and other suspicious texts (S 553, 756, 811 and 838; cf. S 567), though some of its features are anticipated in S 836; for later occurrences, see S 953–4 and 971, and cf. S 888 and 911. The formula is directed specifically at offences 'contra sanctam Dei ecclesiam' (hence its use in S 811 and 971 is strange), and it may have originated in response to the appropriations of Church property which took place in the later 980s: the phrase 'philargiriæ seductus amentia' echoes the statement in S 876 that the *infortunia* of the period arose partly on account of the 'detestanda philargiria' of the king's associates.

53 In S 876 it is said that the *infortunia* arose 'partim . . . pro meæ juventutis ignorantia, quæ diversis uti solet moribus'; in S 885 reference is made to the things done 'iuuentutis mee tempore que diuersis solebat uti moribus'.

54 Note that the scribe of S 876, which is extant as a contemporary single sheet, did not apparently supply any initial crosses in the witness list. But they were added subsequently against the names of all the bishops in the first column, and against the names of a few of the abbots: they all differ in appearance, and it is quite possible that they are autograph.

55 Perhaps the Dorset location is the most likely, since the Gillingham there was a royal manor with a church in the eleventh century (DB i, fos. 75r and 78v).

multitudine in aula villae regiae quae nuncupative a populis et Calnæ vocitatur': that is, at Calne in Wiltshire, about fifty miles north-west of Winchester. The diploma itself was drawn up a few days later, when the *witan* had moved to Wantage in Berkshire (about fifty miles north of Winchester).[56] Thus neither of these two related diplomas was drawn up in the scriptorium of the bene-ficiary.

We have seen that S 885, by which King Æthelred restored two estates to the see of Rochester in 995, has one significant diplomatic link with S 876. It is also related to S 886, a diploma issued at about the same time in 995,[57] and preserved in the archives of Abingdon. S 885 is said to have been drawn up at the request of the king's dear bishop, 'ipsa non minus actuum probitate quam naturalis uocabuli impressione Goduuini'; S 886 is in favour of one of the king's *ministri*, 'cui parentelæ nobilitas Wlfric indidit nomen', and it describes the crimes of one who had been given the name Æthelsige, 'licet foedo nomen dehonastaverit flagitio'. There do not seem to be any other Anglo-Saxon royal diplomas in which the draftsman related to their deeds the literal meaning of the names of people concerned in the transactions, so the appearance of this feature in two diplomas from different archives produced at about the same time in a particular year is likely to reflect a common denominator behind their production. In its styles of attestation S 885 has further links with S 888 (a diploma in favour of St Albans Abbey, dated 996) and S 889 (in favour of the Old Minster Winchester and also dated 996). As the effective beneficiary, Bishop Godwine attests S 885 with the style 'hoc donum uoti compos optinui', which may be compared with the style 'hanc praefatam donationem uoti compos obtinui' used for Ælfheah, bishop of Winchester, in S 889; the expression does not occur elsewhere in Æthelred's diplomas. Another of the bishops attests S 885 with the style 'consentaneus extiti', which is

---

[56] According to S 891, the *witan* gathered at Wantage 'ob diuersarum quaestiones causarum corrigendas', conceivably an allusion to the promulgation of Æthelred's 'third' code of laws (enacted at Wantage: Liebermann, *Gesetze* I, 228). For the conditional expression 'si contingat expeditionem promoueri, arcem, pontemue recuperari' in S 891's reservation clause (and analogous expressions in S 890, 899 and 904, of the same period), cf. the conditional phrases in the same context in other laws of Æthelred (*ibid.* pp. 242 and 254): the correspondence supports the implication of S 891 that the promulgation of laws and the production of diplomas might take place at the same meeting.

[57] See Appendix I, p. 253.

found also in S 888 and 889.[58] There are further points of contact between the formulation of these two diplomas: S 888 disposes of certain lands in St Albans with nine *habitacula*, 'que patria lingua hagan appellari solent', in the town, while S 889 disposes of part of a *hospicium*, 'quae patria lingua haga solet appellari', in Winchester; the dispositive clause in S 889 is 'restituendo concedo et concedendo restituo', which may be compared with the clause 'renouando restituo, et restituendo . . . praecipio' in S 888; both contain a formula laying down in the name of Christ (S 888) or by the king's and the Lord's authority (S 889) that successors shall not presume to alter the grant;[59] finally, both contain the same range of verbs by which the bishops in the witness list express the act of attestation, and they are given in much the same order.[60] S 889 has a sentence after the witness list that represents a collective declaration by the witnesses: 'Nos uniuersi regis optimates huic regiae donationi unanimen consensum alacriter praebuimus.' Such a feature is not at all common,[61] so it is interesting to find an analogous statement ('Nos omnes optimates consensimus') after the witness list attached to S 893, a diploma by which King Æthelred restored an estate to the see of Rochester in 998. This diploma itself has some points of contact with S 885, Æthelred's earlier diploma for Rochester, which suggests that the beneficiary, Bishop Godwine, may have played some part in the drafting of S 893 (if not of S 885), but its relationship with contemporary diplomas strongly implies that it was not drawn up in isolation from them. For in addition to its connection with S 889, S 893 is also one of the group of diplomas in which the king is made to regret the indiscretions of his youth, sharing a discursive type of dating formula with S 876 and 891 (which belong to the same group); moreover, the verbs of attestation used for the bishops' subscriptions in S 893 are closely related to those in S 888 and 889.

---

[58] The style recurs in S 916, probably derived from S 888; cf. 'consentaneus fui' in S 895. 'Consentaneus extiti' occurs elsewhere in S 803; cf. S 565.

[59] Cf. formulae to a similar effect in S 876–7, 885, 891, 893, 899, 904, 916, 937 and 940.

[60] Phrases from the proem in S 888 were derived from earlier tenth-century diplomas (e.g. S 497 and 696), and phrases from the proem in S 889 similarly echo earlier diplomas (e.g. S 532–3). Note that S 889 shares elements of its dispositive section with two Winchester forgeries, S 521 and 540; the latter is extant as an eleventh-century apograph and was probably worked up from S 889 and an authentic diploma of 948 in the Old Minster's archives (e.g. S 532).

[61] Occasionally a sanction represented as the collective declaration of the witnesses is positioned at the end of the list, as in S 898. Otherwise, cf. S 62, 108, 155, 224, 319, 1041 and 1380.

Three other diplomas produced in the 990s (including S 877, in favour of King Æthelred's mother, Queen Ælfthryth), and one transparent forgery whose perpetrator seems to have had access to an authentic document of the period, are related in various ways to the diplomas already discussed and reveal further indirect links between them.[62] The overall impression thus created is of a group of diplomas dated between 993 and 998, in favour of four religious houses (Abingdon, St Albans, Wilton and the Old Minster Winchester), two episcopal sees (Cornwall and Rochester), two laymen (Wulfric and Ealdorman Leofwine) and the king's mother, which, if they display considerable diversity on a general level, are nevertheless intimately related in significant points of detail. It seems not unreasonable to infer that a single agency was responsible for their production, though it was clearly one that co-operated closely with the different beneficiaries. Two of the diplomas are said to have been drawn up at places some distance away from the abbeys in whose favour they were issued, so one can also infer that the agency was not an ecclesiastical scriptorium and that indeed it was one able to act on the occasion of the *witenagemot* when the facilities of such a scriptorium would not have been readily available. In short, it would appear that the arrangements which had been established for the production of royal diplomas in the second quarter of the tenth century still obtained in the 990s, though the nature of the documents produced had been affected in some ways by recent historical developments.

Further and decisive evidence to the same effect is forthcoming from the diplomas produced in the early years of the eleventh century. There is clearly some relationship between S 899, King Æthelred's diploma for Shaftesbury Abbey dated 1001 (after 7 October), and S 904, his diploma for Wherwell Abbey dated 1002

---

[62] S 877 shares with S 891 the odd form 'Æðelfric' for Ælfric, archbishop of Canterbury; it shares with S 888 the archaic form *dignoscuntur* (for *dinoscuntur*) in the formula listing the appurtenances of the estate. S 881 shares with S 877 the phrase 'populis et tribubus praeordinatus in regem' in the superscription; the latter, but not the former, takes this phrase and its structure from the diplomas listed above, p. 66 n. 125. S 892 shares its superscription with S 876, its sanction and some of its styles of attestation with S 876 and 880; the unusual phrase 'ab hominibus aliis notis ignotisque causis' in its immunity clause echoes 'tam in notis causis quam ignotis' in S 877 (and cf. S 898). S 1380 is spurious, but clearly an authentic document of the 990s underlies it: for Ealdorman Ælfhelm's style, cf. S 891; for Bishop Godwine's style, cf. S 885; and for the declaration following the witness list, cf. S 893 and 889.

(before 23 April). Their lengthy proems cover much the same ground, though differently worded, and each one ends with a pair of scriptural quotations. The exposition and the opening of the dispositive section in each diploma can be compared:

S 899	S 904
Talibus mandatorum Christi sentenciis a meis frequentius praemonitus consiliariis . . . , ego Æðelredus rex Anglorum . . . quoddam Christo et sancto suo germano scilicet meo Edwardo . . . cum adiacente undique uilla humili deuotione offero cenobium quod uulgariter æt Bradeforda cognominatur . . .	Huiusmodi sententiis multociens a meis praemonitus sapientibus,[63] ego Æðelred gentis gubernator Angligenae . . . quoddam nobile cenobium cum uilla circumquaque sibi connexa, Christo sanctisque omnibus humillima offero deuotione, quod uulgares suapte a uicinitate fontis æt Werewelle appellare consueuerunt . . .

The diplomas naturally diverge with the details appropriate to each grant, but there are further points of contact in the reservation clause:

tribus tantummodo exceptis communium laborum utilitatibus, si contingat expeditionem promoueri, arcem pontemque construi	sequestratis solummodo trium causis necessitatum communium, si contingat expeditionem educi, arcem seu pontem redintegrari[64]

and in the combination of a blessing with the sanction:

Quisquis autem hanc nostram munificentiam amplificare studuerit, augeatur ei . . . Qui uero euertere aut in aliud quid transferre satagerit . . .	Si quis autem hoc nostrum donum augere studuerit, augeatur ei . . .[65] Qui uero euertere seu in aliud transferre satagerit . . .

The similarities extend also to the dating clause and the formula used for the king's attestation:

---

[63] Cf. 'his et aliis praemonitus sententiis' in S 891 (after a proem which concludes with two scriptural quotations linked by 'Rursumque . . .', as in S 904); see also S 853.

[64] Cf. above, p. 102 n. 56.

[65] For this type of blessing, cf. S 712, 853, 861, 901 and 911.

Scripta est siquidem haec cartula   Scripta siquidem est haec cartula
anno dominicae incarnationis   anno dominicae incarnationis
millesimo primo. Indictione .xiiii[a].   millesimo secundo,
horum testimonio sapientum   hiis unanimi conspirantibus testimonio
quorum onomata inferius   quorum inferius subsequuntur onomata.
descripta esse cernuntur.
Ego Æðelredus rex hanc largitatem   ✠ Ego Æðelred Rex Anglorum hoc
Christo sanctoque martyri Edwardo   munus Christo
humili optuli deuotione   deuote offerens
et ne nostra oblatio obliuionem   ne forsan postero tempore obliuioni
forsan inposterum sortiretur   traderetur
omnia prout gesta sunt
hac in scedula exprimi mandaui ✠.   hac scedula titulari mandaui.

The remaining styles of attestation are not related, except in so far as S 899 uses verbs alliterating in *con-* and S 904 uses verbs alliterating in *a-*. The Wherwell diploma (S 904) is itself closely related to S 906, King Æthelred's diploma confirming the foundation of Burton Abbey, drawn up in 1004. The proem in the latter is apparently a direct expansion of the already lengthy proem in the former, and there are extensive verbal parallels which guarantee that the relationship between the two extends beyond the identity of theme. The dispositive verb in S 906 is *offero*, as in S 899 and 904, and not found elsewhere in Æthelred's diplomas; and the distinctive phrases used to describe the appurtenances of the estates can also be paralleled in S 904:

S 904	S 906
cum uniuersis appendiciis sibi	cum omnibus que sibi
iure subiacentibus, campis, siluis,	subiacent. villulis. prediis. campis.
pascuis, pratis, aquarum decursibus,	siluis. pratis. pascuis. aquarum
gronnis, piscationum hostiis . . .	decursibus piscationum hostiis . . .

The dating clause in S 906 is of the same type as that already seen in the Shaftesbury diploma (S 899):

Scripta siquidem est huius libertas
priuilegii anno ab incarnatione christi.
millesimo .iiii[to]. indictione .ii[a].
horum testimonio sapientum quorum
nomina inferius annotata esse cernuntur.

And curiously enough, the styles of attestation begin with a series of verbs alliterating in *con-* and then continue with a series alliterating in *a-*.[66]

Elements of particular formulae employed in these three diplomas recur in two others issued (like S 904) before 23 April in 1002. S 900, a diploma from the archives of St Albans and in favour of the king's *minister* Ælfhelm, shares with S 904 the unusual phrase 'his unanimi conspirantibus (consensu)' in the dating clause, and it shares with S 899 a range of verbs of attestation alliterating in *con-*.[67] S 901, from the archives of Abingdon and in favour of Archbishop Ælfric, has a proem similar in structure to those in S 899, 904, 906 (and 891), and the type of combined blessing and sanction seen in S 899 and 904; its dating formula contains the phrase 'horum consensu sapientum', which may be compared with the similar phrase in S 899 and 906, and its styles of attestation are made up of essentially the same range of verbs alliterating in *a-* as found in S 904. Moreover, S 900 and 901 share with the three remaining diplomas issued in 1002 (leaving aside S 904, in which it would not have been appropriate) the feature of stipulating the price paid by the beneficiary for the land:

S 900:   ... pro suo placabili pecunia, id est centum quinquaginta duo mancusas puri auri ...

S 901:   ... quam ipse a me cum l^a talentis exigebat, ponderosa trutinationis publicæ probatis libratione.

S 902:[68] ... pro ejus amabili obsequio et placabili mercede, id est xxx. mancusas puri auri ...

[66] A diploma of King Æthelred's for Amesbury Abbey (founded like Wherwell by Queen Ælfthryth), partially reconstructed by Finberg, *Charters of Wessex*, pp. 103–4, should clearly be associated with these texts: the abbey's name is explained, as in S 904 (and cf. S 468, 523 and 799), and the provisions for the election of a new abbess are similar to those given in the same diploma; the clause establishing the liberty of the abbey could be compared with corresponding sections in S 904 and 906.

[67] For the proem in S 900, cf. S 633, 755 and 832. Its sanction contains a phrase ('stridula clangente archangeli buccina') derived ultimately from diplomas of King Æthelstan current between 930 and 934 (cited above, p. 43 n. 74 and p. 44 nn. 77–8); it is not likely to be a mere coincidence that the phrase 'clangente tuba archangeli' occurs in S 895.

[68] The sanction in S 902 is hybrid, combining elements from a formula current in the 940s (S 470, 474–5, 487, 491, 526 and 528; also S 665 and 955) with elements from one current between 938 and 943 (S 351, 441–2, 446, 466, 480, 485 and 491; also S 665, 699, 728 and 1013). In this respect S 902 is related to S 896, which combines elements of a formula developed in the 980s (see above, p. 88 n. 20) with both of the formulae used in S 902. The earlier parts of the formulation in S 896 recur in a group of suspicious texts from Abingdon (see above, p. 11 n. 16) and also in S 1014; for the proem, cf. the diplomas cited above, p. 71 n. 142, and for some of the styles of attestation, cf. S 876.

S 903:[69] . . . hanc prefatam terram a me cum centum auri obrizi mancusis comparavit . . .

S 905:[70] . . . pro eius humili famulatu et competenti pretio hoc sunt vii. librae . . .

Of course there is nothing remarkable about such statements in the overall context of Anglo-Saxon diplomatic, and many examples could be cited from all periods. They suffice to show that the practice of paying the king for the land or privileges was common, and that the decision to incorporate a record of the payment was largely a matter of preference.[71] But the significance of the examples in the diplomas dated 1002 becomes apparent when one realizes that these are the first references to payments by the beneficiary in the diplomas of King Æthelred.[72] Five out of five diplomas which might have contained such references do contain them, and the diplomas were issued throughout the year and were preserved in the archives of four religious houses (St Albans, Abingdon, Westminster and Christ Church Canterbury). It is improbable that independent draftsmen would independently have taken the decision to insert the reference to the price paid, so one can reasonably attribute its appearance in these diplomas to the existence of a common denominator behind their production.[73]

[69] The proem in S 903 occurs in S 776; cf. S 117, 505, 847 and the formula in S 859 etc. (above, p. 86 n. 16). Its sanction recurs in S 920 and 930. The clause stating a condition on which the grant is made may be compared with a similar clause in S 905; cf. S 926.

[70] S 905 was written 'in ciuitate dorobernensis' and is extant as an apparent original; its scribe has been identified in manuscripts assigned to the Christ Church Canterbury scriptorium (Bishop, 'Cambridge MSS, Pt. vii', pp. 414, 420 and 423). But there are grounds for believing that it is not in fact the original instrument: it is misdated 1003, for 1002, not in itself fatal to its originality but equally the type of error that might arise were it a contemporary copy made in Christ Church owing to the community's reversionary interest in the estate; its formulation accords well with the other diplomas produced in 1002; for its proem, cf. S 907; a Christ Church scribe or draftsman of an original may not have felt it necessary to explain that Canterbury is the *metropolis* of the men of Kent; the names of three witnesses are crammed into the margin, as if the parchment chosen for the copy was not quite the same size as the original.

[71] See above, p. 33.

[72] The only exceptions are exceptional: S 836 (Bishop Æthelwold's purchase of a fishery with a golden bracelet) and S 842, 866, 884 and 894 (references to earlier transactions). The practice of recording payment continued after 1002: S 910, 912, 915, 919, 923, 930 and 943; see also S 916 and 960.

[73] King Æthelred and his councillors arranged at the beginning of 1002 to make a payment of 24,000 pounds to the Danes: the payment was apparently made at roughly the same time as the banishment of Ealdorman Leofsige, and since all of the diplomas in question were issued after his banishment it may be that the king was trying to recoup some of his

No less distinctive in terms of their formulation than the group of diplomas in favour of Shaftesbury, Wherwell and Burton (and the related group issued in 1002) are three diplomas from the archives of Evesham (S 1664, dated 1003),[74] St Albans (S 912, dated 1005)[75] and Burton (S 917, dated 1007).[76] These diplomas may be associated in the first instance by the occurrence in each of a remarkable type of dating formula:

S 1664

Scripta est autem hec cartula decursis annis ab incarnatione domini nostri nongentis bisque binis, in cursu millenario equidem tertio, indictione .iᵃ. his testibus assensum prebentibus quorum hic caraxantur onomata.

S 912

Scripta est autem huius libertatis cartula decursis annis ab incarnatione Christi .dcccc.xc. nouenis terque binis in cursu millenario equidem sexto, his testibus fauentibus quorum hic dignitates cum onomate contemplari ualebis.

S 917

Scripta est hec cartula decursis annis ab incarnatione Christi .dcccc.xc. bisque quinis necne septenis indictione .v. hiis fauentibus quorum hic subtus onomata et dignitatum vides officia.

In S 912, a base value of 990 plus nine and thrice two gives 1005, in the sixth year of the millennium, also for 1005. In S 917, the same base value of 990 plus twice five and seven gives 1007, correctly corresponding to the fifth indiction. The formula in S 1664 requires some emendation if it is to make any sense. On the analogy of S 912 and 917 one has to supply a base value – in this case 99 – added to which 900 and twice two gives 1003, corresponding to the first indiction; but the indiction contradicts the 'in cursu millenario' formula, which (if used in the same way as in S 912) should imply

recent expenses by selling an unusually large amount of land and privileges; cf. below, p. 202 n. 182.

[74] S 1664 is now no more than a fragment, since the first part of the text was erased by a later user of the register in which it was entered, to make room for S 1174: it is not therefore known in whose favour the diploma was issued, though to judge from the dispositive section it was an individual rather than Evesham Abbey.

[75] S 912 is in favour of St Albans and implements provisions made for the abbey in the will of Archbishop Ælfric (S 1488), who was a former abbot and brother of the then abbot, Leofric. The diploma may have been interpolated, for the formula describing the privileges to be enjoyed occurs otherwise in a suspicious series of diplomas (S 774, 1000, 1031 and 1450) and includes exemption from the common burdens.

[76] S 917 is, like S 1664, incomplete: see further below, p. 115 n. 110.

1002. The confusion may indicate that the formula in S 1664 is a blundered attempt to imitate an expression found in an authentic diploma in the Evesham archives. Further parallels between S 1664, 912 and 917 lend considerable support to the obvious inference that the diplomas were the work of a single draftsman. The proems in S 912 and 917 begin in a similar way:

S 912	S 917
Cum nos in extrema pene huius uitae margine cernamus sistere, et ultima quaeque senescentis mundi pericula indesinenter luere . . .[77]	Cum enim nos liquide in extrema decrepitacione huius senescentis mundi viteque momentanee tamquam ultime prosapie abortiuos filios procreatos nouerimus . . .

The superscription in S 917 ('Hec ego Æþelredus regali infula Anglorum populis Christo allubescente subth[r]onizatus') may be compared with that in S 912 ('Quapropter ego Æðelredus . . . rex subthronizatus');[78] both use *condono* as the dispositive verb. At this point in the formulation the text of S 917 is no longer available for comparison, but the text of S 1664 begins. There are several similarities between S 912 and 1664 in their dispositive sections and blessings,[79] but of most significance is the use in the sanctions of *Herebus* as a euphemism for Hell.[80] After the circumlocutory type of dating formula common to all three diplomas, we find related formulae used for the king's subscription:

S 1664

Ego Æðelred regali prosapia comptus hanc meae dapsilitatis donationem signo agie crucis confirmo.

[77] Note the use in S 912's proem of the phrase 'per bonorum operum exhibitionem', echoing the phrase 'cum exhibitione operum bonorum' in S 859, itself adapted from the formula in the diplomas cited above, p. 86 n. 16; and cf. the phrase 'cum continua bonorum operum exhibitione' in S 911, issued (like S 912) in 1005.

[78] *Subthronizatus* is not used elsewhere in Æthelred's diplomas; cf. S 951, 955 and 962; for the phrase 'regali infula', cf. S 430 and the king's subscription in S 912.

[79] See also S 962.

[80] It does not occur elsewhere in the sanctions used during Æthelred's reign; cf. the invocation in S 886, and the sanctions in S 346, 471, 486–7, 489, 492, 496, 547 and 571. The sanction in S 912 occurs in S 138 (a spurious diploma from St Albans, perhaps based in part on S 912) and that in S 1664 occurs in S 112 (a spurious diploma from Evesham, perhaps based in part on S 1664). Note the clause 'quorum vermis mordax et ignis fumicus nunquam per saecula cessat' in S 1664, and cf. 'ubi vermis est non moriens et ignis indeficiens' in S 906 (issued in the following year), both paraphrasing Mark ix 43 (and for proper quotation see S 1028 and 1231).

S 912

Ego Æðelredus regia infula comptus propriae munificentiae donum stabiliter confirmo.

S 917

Ego Æþelred regia munificientia fretus[81] hoc datum quod dedi agye crucis signamine perpetualiter confirmo.

Finally, it is interesting to find that *comes* is used to describe the ealdormen in the witness lists attached to these three diplomas, since they are invariably designated *dux* in the other diplomas of King Æthelred.

King Æthelred's diploma for the see of Cornwall (S 880) and the diploma for the abbey of St Albans (S 912), both discussed above in different contexts, together reflect an important development in Anglo-Saxon diplomatic which can be traced in other texts of the same period. A diploma is generally presented as a statement in the first person of a completed royal action, and since the intended function of the document as a title-deed meant that it was directed implicitly at posterity as well as at contemporaries, it does not contain any limiting address to specific parties. In this respect, the diploma is to be distinguished from the vernacular writ, which as a practical instrument of royal government is invariably addressed to the principal ecclesiastical and secular officers in the locality concerned and cast in the form of a notification (often 'ic cyþe eow þæt . . .') of royal action or will. However, it seems that in the late tenth and early eleventh centuries there was a tendency to incorporate a general notification clause into the dispositive section of the royal diploma:[82]

S 880 (994):	Qua de re nunc patefacio omnibus catholicis, quod . . .
S 883 (995):	cunctis meis volo notum adesse fidelibus, quod . . .
S 937 (?999):	palam cunctis innotesco, quod . . .
S 912 (1005):	Notum etiam uobis cupio fore quantum . . .

[81] Cf. 'regali fretus a Domino dignitate' in the superscription of S 887 (and see also S 242, 250, 269, 272–3, 276, 284, 309, 684, 713, 934, 998 and 1044).

[82] Instances of a specific address to readers of the document (e.g. S 549, 603, 611, 769, 886, 891 and 909) are here excluded.

S 915 (1007):   notum affore cupio omnibus Anglicæ fines regionis circumquaque incolentibus, quod . . .

S 943 (1006 × 11):   meis notum uolo adesse fidelibus, quod . . .[83]

The diplomas containing these formulae were preserved in the archives of Exeter, Abingdon, St Albans and Thorney, and when one admits occurrences in texts which though spurious in their received form nevertheless reflect pre-Conquest diplomatic practices,[84] it becomes apparent that the notification formulae were even more widely dispersed: the clause 'cunctis gentis nostræ fidelibus innotesco' is found in three texts from the New Minster Winchester, one of which is extant as an early eleventh-century apograph;[85] a text from the Burton cartulary contains the clause 'Unde ego Eadredus . . . rex omnibus meis notum uolo 7esse fidelibus quod . . .';[86] and one from the Wilton cartulary contains the clause 'nunc omnibus vobis notum facio quod . . .'.[87] Further instances of notification formulae could be cited from diplomas in the name of King Æthelred that are probably spurious, preserved in the archives of Abingdon, Christ Church Canterbury, St Paul's and Westminster.[88]

In some respects the significance of the appearance of notification formulae in the 990s is difficult to assess. The formulae are not exactly analogous to the specific notifications one finds in the vernacular writs, weakening the otherwise attractive supposition that they reflect the influence of the writ form on the royal diploma.[89] They might on the other hand represent an adaptation of the notification formulae employed in some law codes and private vernacular documents,[90] or even reflect the influence of continental

---

[83] See also S 882 (994): 'sed et hoc fidelibus quibuslibet, ut necessarium aestimamus, intimare curamus qua . . .'.

[84] The usages in, e.g., S 3, 456, 537, 728 and 798 probably derive from post-Conquest or continental diplomatic practices.

[85] S 360, 370 and 648, probably forged together.

[86] S 545. The '7', if for *et*, is nonsensical; perhaps the Burton copyist, in a moment of distraction, read *adesse* (cf. S 883, 918 and 943) as *andesse* and wrote that in turn as *7esse*.

[87] S 586. The only objection to this diploma (that it is dated 956, contradicting the regnal year, indiction and witness list, all for 959) is not conclusive; an argument that its notification formula is a diplomatic anachronism might be adduced, but it would be unavoidably circular.

[88] See S 894, 897, 908, 914 and 918.

[89] But note in this connection the opening lines of S 911, which seem to approximate to the initial greeting formula of the writ.

[90] Cf., e.g., the opening clauses of II Edmund, and S 1807–8 and 1810.

diplomatic practices.[91] But whatever their origin, they are distinctive enough in Anglo-Saxon diplomatic to warrant attributing their introduction, apparently in the 990s, to a particular agency. Obviously one could not argue that all instances derive from the same source, as the idea, once introduced, could have been adopted by other draftsmen.[92] But a few of the diplomas that contain notification formulae are related to one another in other respects as well, suggesting that they at least may belong to a more restricted tradition. S 883, dated 995 and preserved at Abingdon,[93] shares several features of its formulation with S 943, issued between 1006 and 1011 and preserved at Thorney: namely, a short proem on the advantages of recording things in writing,[94] the use of the form *mansos* (as opposed to the grammatically correct form *mansas*), and particular types of reservation clause[95] and sanction.[96] The same types of proem, notification formula and reservation clause occur in S 545, a spurious text from Burton, which in addition shares with S 943 a distinctive formula introducing the king's subscription:[97] perhaps a text drawn up at about the same time (and by the same agency?) as S 883 and 943 was used by the person who concocted

---

91 See, e.g., Tessier, *Diplomatique royale française*, pp. 89 and 217.

92 There are, nevertheless, very few (if any) examples of notification formulae in authentic diplomas of Cnut, Harthacnut and Edward the Confessor: see S 1006–7, and otherwise a host of spurious documents (S 995, 1000, 1002, 1041, 1043, 1045–7 and 1060).

93 Note that S 883 has an interesting link with S 887, also preserved at Abingdon: both give the style 'Australium ecclesiæ præsul' for Ordbriht of Selsey, omitting 'Saxonum'. The formulation of S 887 has many points of contact with the diplomas of King Edgar associated with 'Edgar A': if the similarities extended to the presentation of the witness list, it may well have had simple styles of attestation; so it is conceivable that the styles in S 887 were added by the Abingdon copyist from S 883, which he had transcribed earlier in the manuscript, in order to rectify what was felt to be a deficiency.

94 The sentiment in S 943 ('ne forte iniuste iniquorum perdatur consilio, quod iuste cum bonorum uirorum adquiritur testimonio') might be compared with remarks balanced in the same way in S 893 ('ut qui iniuste rapuit aliena . iuste amitteret propria') and S 918 ('quæ injuste adquisierunt omnia juste perdiderunt'); see also S 545.

95 'exceptis tribus, populari expedicione, pontis restauracione, regie arcis constructione' (S 943); 'tribus tamen rebus exceptis, populari scilicet expeditione, arcis constructione, pontis restauratione' (S 883).

96 The clause 'sit anathema maranatha' (I Corinthians xvi 22) had occurred in sanctions in the eighth and ninth centuries (S 35–6, 130, 164, 337 and 363), but never with the gloss 'hoc est alienato a consortio Christianorum'; cf. S 761, 964 and 967.

97 'Et ut hoc scriptum inuiolabilem semper obtineat firmitatem, ego primus Rex propria manu confirmo . . .' (S 943); 'Et ut hec cartula inuiolabile robur firmitatis optineat. ✠ Ego Eadredus rex primus regali manu confirmo' (S 545). Note that the verbs of subscription are in the present tense in S 545 and 943.

S 545.[98] Some elements of the formulation recur in S 915, dated 1007 and preserved at Abingdon: it has a notification formula, uses *mansos* instead of *mansas*, and like S 943 employs 'hoc testificor' as a style of attestation.[99]

A significant degree of relationship between diplomas preserved in different archives persists until the very end of Æthelred's reign. One could compare the form of the atheling Æthelstan's subscription in S 907 (dated 1004, from Ely)[100] with that in S 909 (dated 1004, from St Frideswide's),[101] the styles of attestation for all the athelings as well as for the queen in S 910 (dated 1005, from Horton)[102] with the same feature in S 911 (dated 1005, from Eynsham),[103] and all the styles of attestation in the list (datable *c.* 1007) attached to the spurious S 854 (dated 984, from Bath)[104] with those in S 922 (dated 1009, from Burton).[105] One might observe that the appearance of a remarkable form of chrismon with conjoined A in S 923 (dated 1011, from Burton) almost exactly coincides with the occurrence of an

[98] Cf. Hart, *Charters of Northern England*, pp. 92–3.

[99] Elements of the formulation in S 545, 883, 915 and 943 occur in several diplomas preserved at Abingdon: S 355 (note the amusing error 'cum Iuda apostata', for '. . . Juliano . . .' or '. . . proditore', in the sanction), 761, 897, 918 (probably modelled largely on S 915), 964 (proem and sanction as in S 897), 967, 993, 999 (perhaps authentic, with sanction as in S 545) and 1025; for some of these diplomas, see above, p. 11 n. 16.

[100] S 907 is probably not authentic as it stands, since the bounds include land that was not acquired until 1008 (Blake, *Liber Eliensis*, p. 417). The formulation was derived at least in part from S 780, an earlier diploma for Ely, though interpolating a sentence ('sicut . . . marcescit') in the proem, perhaps on analogy with S 919, another diploma for Ely; on the other hand, there can be no doubt that a genuine text of 1004 provided the witness list, and some minor divergences of the proem in S 907 from that in S 780 find support elsewhere (e.g. S 848), while the inserted sentence may have been a contemporary theme (cf. S 905).

[101] S 907: 'regis filius una cum fratribus meis.' S 909: 'regalium primogenitus filiorum, cum fratribus meis.' Cf. S 916. It was not normal practice to list only Æthelstan (see Table 1).

[102] Elements of S 910 are derived ultimately from mid-tenth-century diplomas: see S 625 for the conditions of the grant, S 691 for the immunity and reservation clauses, and above, p. 65 n. 119, for the sanction. Some of its styles of attestation recur in S 977.

[103] S 911 has an interesting formulation, sharing elements with the so-called 'First Decimation Charters' (S 294, 314 and 322: but these are spurious, and the formula in question, bemoaning heavy Viking attacks, looks more like an early eleventh- than a mid-ninth-century theme), with some diplomas of the second quarter of the tenth century (S 429, 438 and 470: for the theme 'Duo quippe sunt . . .'; cf. Boethius, *De Consolatione Philosophiae* IV, 2), and with the dubious Thorney diploma, S 792 (echoing the *Regularis Concordia*: see Symons, *Concordia*, p. 6); see also above, p. 110 n. 77 and p. 112 n. 89. Further similarities in its blessing and sanction with S 899 and 904, in its sanction with S 876 etc., and its relationship with S 910, strongly support its authenticity.

[104] For the formulation of this diploma, see above, p. 48 n. 89.

[105] The proem of S 922 cites II Corinthians iv 18, a text used frequently in ninth- and tenth-century diplomas; see, e.g., S 334.

analogous form of chrismon in S 926 (dated 1012, from Rochester);[106] and one could also compare the opening of the proem in S 923 with that in S 932 (dated 1014, from Pershore).[107] Finally, one could record an intriguing correspondence between the dispositive sections in S 933 (dated 1013, from Sherborne) and S 934 (dated 1015, from Abingdon), supported by a further link in the styles of attestation used for the abbots.[108]

A survey of the diplomas of King Æthelred thus shows that facilities for the centralized production of royal diplomas still existed during his reign, and it suggests in particular that the facilities were exploited for drawing up some of the most important of the privileges for religious houses issued in the late tenth and early eleventh centuries. The diplomatic evidence would only be compatible with the notion that the production of diplomas was by this time decentralized and distributed amongst various ecclesiastical scriptoria if one were to imagine that the separate draftsmen had access to and were required to use formularies. But while it is true that some draftsmen seem to have had access to copies of continental formularies (such as the papal *Liber Diurnus* or the Merovingian formulary of Marculf[109]), or at least to documents themselves based on these collections, it remains the case that no Anglo-Saxon formulary has survived, and there is no evidence that one ever existed.[110] The negative argument is not strong, of course, since a

---

106 On the significance of these chrismons, see Keynes, 'An Interpretation of the *Pacx, Pax* and *Paxs* Pennies', pp. 169–70. The formulation of S 926 is connected in a few minor ways with contemporary diplomas: see S 927 (immunity and reservation clauses) and 929 (clause following the superscription).

107 For the reservation clause in S 932, cf. S 934 (and also S 851 and 860).

108 Abbots are not normally listed with verbs of subscription, but we find *libenter annotaui, consensi* and *subarraui* in S 933, and *libenter consensi, adnotaui* and *subarraui* in S 934; cf. S 935. S 933 shares several features of its structure and formulation with S 969 (originally from Horton, but at Sherborne from the first half of the twelfth century): it is possible that S 933 is a forgery concocted at Sherborne using S 969 as a model, or that S 969 was written at Sherborne on behalf of its lay beneficiary, using S 933 as a model; on the other hand, both diplomas accord well with respectively contemporary texts, so the relationship between them may only be indirect.

109 Chaplais, 'Diplomas on Single Sheets', p. 87, has suggested that there was a copy of the *Liber Diurnus* at Winchcombe, and he has pointed out, *ibid.* p. 79, that a formula from Marculf's formulary occurs in S 617.

110 Two documents that seem at first sight to represent blanks for royal diplomas might be cited in this connection: S 913 (from Worcester) and 917 (from Burton). The former is dated and refers to a specific estate and beneficiary: thus it is abbreviated rather than not completed; the formula 'Ego .N. episcopus .N.' which follows in the manuscript appears

practical handbook of use in the tenth and eleventh centuries but not thereafter would have had limited chances of preservation. Even so,

to be a separate text, perhaps the superscription of a blank for an episcopal charter. Moreover, it may be no more than a Worcester forgery: its formulation bears little resemblance to contemporary diplomas, and for its sanction, cf. S 1185. The transcription of the dispositive section in S 917 is restricted to the sentence 'Hec ego Æþelredus regali infula Anglorum populis Cristo allubescente subthonizatus condono cuidam meo ministro talem terram. et cetera', and it then continues with the dating clause and witness list, concluding with the sentence 'Ego Winsye monachus qui hoc testamentum dictitaui atque perscripsi'. Since there is no apparent reason why the Burton copyist should himself have abbreviated this one text in this particular way, we must assume that he found it already in this form. What significance, then, are we to attach to the presence in a monastic archive of a document that looks like a blank for a royal diploma and that is said to have been drafted and written by a named monk? Its diplomatic connections with S 912 and 1664 (above, pp. 109–11) demonstrate that it emanated from a central source, so there appear to be two main possibilities. In the first place, Winsye was a member of a monastic community serving (temporarily?) in the central writing office; he drafted all three diplomas, attaching his own subscription to one from which, for some reason, the operative details were omitted; the blank was either sent to Burton to serve as a model (anticipating a need?), or found its way there amongst the personal effects of Winsye when he returned or retired to the monastery. One can certainly envisage circumstances in which it may have been necessary to send a blank (perhaps by entrusting it to the intended beneficiary) to a monastic scriptorium for completion; e.g., a boundary clause may not have been available when the transaction itself was ratified at the *witenagemot* (and cf. above, pp. 81–3). Moreover, the implication that personnel from leading churches or monasteries were seconded to serve in the central writing office accords well enough with the identification of the scribe of S 636 as a one-time member of the Winchester scriptorium (above, pp. 20–1) and with a tradition recorded in the *Liber Eliensis* (discussed below, pp. 151–2). On the other hand, if S 917 *is* a blank sent from a central source, it is not clear why it was preserved after use, why it alone was signed by its draftsman and scribe, and why (above all) it did not contain the other important elements of the diploma (e.g. immunity clause, reservation clause and sanction); it is conceivable that the Burton copyist abbreviated his exemplar (he almost invariably abbreviated boundary clauses and witness lists, and he abbreviated other elements of the text in, e.g., S 484, 739, 863, 878–9, 922–3 and 1606), but one would not expect him to have left no trace of these elements (cf. his treatment of the diplomas just listed). The second possibility is that Winsye was a member of the Burton community who for reasons best known to himself took an authentic diploma from the archives and, using it as his model, produced a modified version in which he left out the elements between the superscription and the dating clause, and to which he added his own subscription. There is no evidence that he produced his version to serve as a model for a forgery or forgeries in Burton's interests; his motive may simply have been to try his hand at producing a royal diploma, whether as a writing exercise or for the sake of elaborating (according to his own taste) on the theme expressed in the proem of his exemplar, and he may not have copied out the dispositive section either because he had no interest in doing so or because he realized that it would be improper (and even unwise) to duplicate an existing title-deed. We would then have to assume that his exemplar was subsequently lost or destroyed, that the estate was alienated from Burton and the diploma handed over to the new owner, or that a layman who had deposited the diploma in the monastery's archives resumed possession of it when he wanted to dispose of the estate.

There seem to be no conclusive reasons for accepting or rejecting either of these two suggestions; nor (it must be added) do they exhaust the possibilities presented by S 917. I am particularly grateful to Dr Brooks for discussing this document with me.

several copies would have been produced and circulated, and such dispersal would naturally increase the chances that one might survive, if only to be recorded in a medieval library catalogue or to be mentioned in some other context. It is difficult anyway to reconcile some general aspects of Anglo-Saxon diplomatic with the supposition that formularies underlie the production of diplomas. If series of formulae for the successive components of a royal diploma were recorded in a manual which was continually available in the ecclesiastical scriptoria throughout the country, one would expect occurrences of all the formulae to be distributed fairly evenly over the same extended period, as different draftsmen selected them independently for use in their own diplomas; in other words, one would not expect to find that particular formulae enjoyed special popularity for short periods and then fell into disuse, to be revived sporadically thereafter, unless one were to suppose that the manual was periodically revised by the deletion of old formulae and the addition of new ones. Yet it is often possible to show that a given formula was introduced at a certain time and was used quite frequently in the following decade or so, then suddenly to pass out of fashion. This applies to all constituent parts of the diplomas issued in the tenth and eleventh centuries, but it is particularly true of the proems and sanctions.[111] It is arguable that the concentration of occurrences of a formula in a fairly limited period is more readily compatible with its development and use by a single draftsman than with its incorporation into a formulary for the use of all over a longer period; its revival subsequently would have been determined no less by personal preference. Of course, the same formula might be used simultaneously by more than one draftsman, but this need only reflect the draftsman's use of an existing diploma as a model.

It is especially difficult to believe that the draftsmen of King Æthelred's later diplomas had recourse to formularies. They appear to have favoured originality of expression as if for its own sake, modifying existing formulae or developing new ones suited to their own purposes, and it would be entirely inappropriate to suppose that they were required to make their texts conform to a predetermined structure or to employ formulae supplied from any kind of

---

111 Each formula needs to be thoroughly investigated, with a view to establishing its origins, its period of greatest use, and the instances of its revival; for examples of the application of this approach in the text and footnotes above, see General Index, under *diplomas*.

manual. Moreover, many of the diplomatic features which suggest the existence of a common denominator behind the production of the diplomas are of a nature that could hardly involve a formulary. In the first place, the group of diplomas in which the king is made to regret the indiscretions of his youth must have emanated from a single source close to the king himself, for it is unlikely that the personal and apologetic tone adopted by the draftsmen on the king's behalf could have arisen without direct royal approbation and could have been employed without direct royal authority. Similarly, some of the accounts of the crimes of individuals which led to the forfeiture of their estates are expressed in such personal terms and with such indignation that it is difficult to imagine the draftsmen producing them except under royal supervision. In the second place, the similarities between diplomas from different archives very often extend to details of the presentation of the witness list which, one imagines, would not be covered in a formulary. For example, it is noticeable that the position of the abbots relative to the other groups of witnesses changed during the course of the reign. In the great majority of the extant diplomas issued in the 980s they are placed after the ealdormen; during the 990s the abbots occur as often before the ealdormen as after them; and in the early eleventh century (until the end of the reign) we find that the majority of the extant diplomas then issued place the abbots before the ealdormen. Since the abbots had almost invariably been positioned between the bishops and the ealdormen in Edgar's diplomas, it is possible that the reversal of this tendency in the 980s reflected a change in the relative respect accorded to abbots and ealdormen during Æthelred's youth; one can easily appreciate how this might have been implemented as a policy in a central office, but it would indeed be a curious phenomenon had the diplomas been drawn up in various ecclesiastical scriptoria. The gradual return in the 990s and thereafter to the situation in Edgar's reign might well indicate that abbots were recovering their prestige, or it might have been dictated simply by a desire, which soon developed into a convention, to keep the ecclesiastical and secular witnesses distinct from one another.[112] Again, one might observe that the witness lists tend to be longer in diplomas issued in the second half of the reign than they

[112] See further below, pp. 156–7.

were in the first: this is as likely to reflect a change in the general habits of the draftsmen (in the size or proportions of the parchment they selected for the diploma) as to reflect a change in attendance at meetings of the king's council. The practice of specifying the sees of the majority of the subscribing bishops is largely characteristic of the diplomas produced in the 990s,[113] and it is interesting to note that amongst the diplomas with this feature the style of the bishop of Ramsbury is first consistently 'Coruinensis ecclesiae episcopus'[114] and then consistently 'Wiltunensis ecclesiae episcopus',[115] apparently reflecting a decision made in 993/4 to change the title of his see.[116] It is unlikely that the identifications were added by later copyists, given the chronological and archival distribution of the diplomas in question, and besides, it is highly doubtful that anyone but a contemporary (or a modern scholar with all the resources at his disposal) would have been able to make the identifications in the first place.[117]

---

[113] See Tables 2 and 3, where an asterisk against a subscription indicates that the bishop's see is identified. There are very few authentic diplomas of King Edgar with this feature: see, e.g., S 726.

[114] See S 865, 869–70, 871 and 876; for later occurrences, see S 959 and 979. The appellation is from *corvus*, 'raven', for 'Hræfn's *burh*' or Ramsbury: see Gover *et al.*, *Place-Names of Wiltshire*, pp. 287–8.

[115] See S 880–2, 1379 and 883; there are no further forms for the 990s, since Ælfric retained the see of Ramsbury while he was archbishop of Canterbury; for later occurrences, see S 934 and the great majority of the diplomas of Cnut, Harthacnut and Edward the Confessor in which the bishops' sees are identified. The form in S 880 ('episcopus uuiltane ciuitatis') is curious, since it appears to refer specifically to Wilton, the eponymous city of Wiltshire. There are various references to bishops of *Wiltunscire* in the *Anglo-Saxon Chronicle*, and 'Wiltuniensis ecclesiae' is the form in the late tenth-century episcopal list in the Parker manuscript of the *Chronicle*. Only one diploma breaks the pattern of *Coruinensis* up to 993 and *Wiltunensis* thereafter: the spurious S 1380 gives Ælfric as 'Corfensis ecclesiæ episcopus', but it seems that a list of *c.* 995 in which he would have appeared as archbishop was used to produce a list in which he was bishop of Ramsbury, so that the forger had to add the style himself (see below, Appendix 1, p. 252).

[116] The Ramsbury styles should be compared with those for the sees of Selsey and Wells. Æthelgar of Selsey is consistently 'bishop of the South Saxons' (S 842, 865 and 869–71), but his successor Ordbriht occurs either as 'bishop of the South Saxons' (S 876, 878, 883, 887, 891, 899, 909 and 916) or as 'bishop of Selsey' (S 1379–80, 882 and 885); the draftsman of S 905 apparently did not know what to call him, and left a blank space. Sigar of Wells is styled bishop 'Fontanae ecclesiae' in S 870, 884 and 1380, but is otherwise bishop 'Uuillensis ecclesiae' (S 876, 1379, 878, 882 and 885); his successor Ælfwine is bishop 'Fontanae ecclesiae' in S 891, and the same style was used for Lyfing (S 899 and 909).

[117] S 876 (dated 993) and 891 (dated 997) also identify the subscribing abbots by their respective abbeys; S 891 is further distinguished by the unique feature of naming the provinces controlled by each of the ealdormen, and there is no reason why these should not be regarded as contemporary attributions (cf. Campbell, *Chronicle of Æthelweard*, p. xv n. 8, and *idem*, *Charters of Rochester*, p. 45 n. 2).

It also seems improbable that such a feature should be attributed to the circulation of instructions to different scriptoria, but one might argue that it could arise naturally in a central office.

While the tenor of the evidence suggests the existence of a diplomatic tradition that envelops diplomas for many different beneficiaries, that develops on a chronological basis irrespective of archival or geographical factors, and that is therefore most readily interpreted in terms of a central agency for the production of diplomas, it remains to consider whether any instances of production under apparently different circumstances can be adduced from amongst King Æthelred's later diplomas. S 884 (dated 995), a confirmation of land in favour of the abbey of Muchelney in Somerset, was written by a scribe whose hand reappears in manuscripts assigned to the scriptorium of Christ Church Canterbury.[118] This fact not only tends to guarantee the authenticity of the original diploma; it also reveals that a diploma in favour of a religious house was in this case not drawn up retrospectively in the scriptorium of the beneficiary, but was for some reason produced by a scribe apparently attached to a different scriptorium. S 884 is the first diploma attested by Ælfric as archbishop of Canterbury,[119] and it is conceivable that it was written at Christ Church when the *witan* had gathered there to attend his consecration. It is interesting that it has no significant diplomatic links with contemporary diplomas,[120] and an unusually short witness list.[121] There are extant on single sheets two other royal diplomas (S 890 and 905) whose scribes have been identified as members of ecclesiastical scriptoria: if the single sheets are indeed original both could be regarded as diplomas drawn up by 'interested ecclesiastics',[122] but there are grounds for believing

[118] Bishop, *English Caroline Minuscule*, pp. xxvi and 7.

[119] His style is 'Dorobernensis æcclesie episcopus', perhaps indicating that he had not yet received his pallium (cf. Lyfing's subscriptions in 1013–16). According to *ASC* MS 'F', Ælfric went to Rome to collect the pallium in 997, though he subscribes the diplomas of 996 as 'archbishop': perhaps the Christ Church scribe was more punctilious than the others.

[120] For the proem, see S 197 and 364, and cf., e.g., S 467, 532 and 1005. S 884 does, however, have some points of contact (in its superscription, sanction and immunity clause) with S 851 (dated 983, from Abingdon).

[121] It seems that the names were selected in accordance with the nature of the transaction, for the inclusion (in preference to many others) of Sigar, bishop of Wells, and Wulfsige, bishop of Sherborne, would otherwise be unusual.

[122] See above, pp. 19–20.

that they are in fact near-contemporary copies and as such they would not directly reflect the agency of their production in the first instance.[123]

There is, in addition, diplomatic evidence which suggests that certain diplomas were drawn up in close co-operation with the beneficiaries, if not necessarily by the beneficiaries themselves. It is apparent from the incorporation of information on the traditional history of the houses concerned that the beneficiaries played some part in the drafting of S 876 (for Abingdon),[124] S 888 (for St Albans) and S 891 (for the Old Minster Winchester), though the overall formulation of these diplomas associates them with the mainstream of contemporary diplomatic practice. The influence of the beneficiary on the draftsman may sometimes have extended to more general aspects of the formulation of the diploma. Thus S 885 and 893 (two diplomas for the see of Rochester, dated 995 and 998 respectively) contain similar passages in which the king is made to insist that the terms of the diploma shall not be challenged and that

---

[123] For S 905, see above, p. 108 n. 70. S 890, dated 25 July 997, is in favour of Ælfwold, bishop of Crediton, and was written by the scribe who wrote Bishop Ælfwold's will (S 1492), and who might therefore be located in the Crediton scriptorium: Chaplais, 'Origin and Authenticity', p. 42, and *idem*, 'Diplomas of Exeter', p. 21. The grounds for regarding S 890 as an apograph are as follows: (1) Bishop Ælfwold's will contains remarks which suggest that it was written during his last illness, so between 1011 (when he attests for the last time) and 1015 (when his successor makes his first certain appearance: see Table 3); the reference to the 'atheling' amongst the beneficiaries implies a well-known adult and is consistent with the period 1011 × 15 (cf. S 1422). The will begins with the bequest of land at Sandford, part to Crediton and part to Godric; it is thus closely connected with the diploma, by which the king gave the land at Sandford to the bishop. It would be a coincidence if a scribe of a diploma issued in 997 was employed perhaps fifteen years later to write the will which was concerned with the same estate; it would be more natural to suppose that the extant version of S 890 was written at the same time as the will, perhaps in connection with the division of the estate. (2) The omission of the immunity clause, leaving the reservation clause pendent, and the textual corruption of the blessing and sanction (*ibid.* p. 21), while not necessarily indicating that the diploma is not an original, are at least consistent with its being a copy (Finberg, *Studies*, p. 39). One might add that S 890, whether an apograph or not, is unlikely to have been drawn up *at Crediton* in the summer of 997, a time when the Danes were ravaging extensively in the south-west: for Ealdorman Æthelweard (of the Western Provinces) is conspicuously absent from the witness list (see Table 6), suggesting that he was away looking after his own interests and in turn implying that the council had gathered elsewhere. Note incidentally that S 405, another Sandford diploma but not for the same part of the parish as S 890 (*ibid.* pp. 29–44), was probably fabricated in the early eleventh century (Chaplais, 'Diplomas of Exeter', p. 11).

[124] Hence Abbot Wulfgar's style of attestation: 'hoc sintagma triumphans dictavi'. According to the dating clause, the diploma was written 'humillimo rogatu . . . abbatis Uulfgari', which could be taken to imply that it was actually written on his behalf, not by him.

the land shall always belong to the bishops of Rochester: perhaps Bishop Godwine was careful to ensure that such a passage was inserted in both diplomas. The relationship between S 888 (a diploma for St Albans, dated 996) and S 916 (another diploma for the abbey, dated 1007) could be interpreted in a similar way. The superscription and exposition in the later diploma seem to echo the corresponding elements in the earlier one, if not closely enough to suggest direct borrowing:

S 888	S 916
Quapropter ego Æðelredus,	Qua propter ego ÆÐELRED
totius Albionis	totius albionis
caeterarumque gentium	
in circuitu persistentium,	
munificente superno largitore	superna largiente gratia
basileus,	basileus .
incertum futurorum temporum	
considerans euentum . . .	
ut ipse in tremendo magni	ut in tremendo magni
iudicii die, sanctorum	iudicii die sanctorum
patrociniis suffragantibus	patrociniis interuenientibus
haereditatis supernae	superni regni
cohaeres effici merear . . .[125]	coheres existere merear . . .

The diplomas also contain similar passages expressing the king's insistence that no one should presume to appropriate the land from the abbey, and the conditions for repentance in the sanctions are given in much the same terms:

. . . nisi digna et congrua	. . . nisi digne
satisfactione citius	citius
emendauerit quod contra	emendauerit, quod contra
deum et sanctum martyrem	deum et sanctum martyrem
eius delinquere non timuit.	eius ALBANUM deliquit.

Finally, the styles of attestation for the archbishops and bishops are almost identical. S 916 is extant as an apparent original,[126] and it seems that its authenticity cannot be impugned. S 888 presents some problems, for the indiction is wrong and there is no explicit reference to the reservation of the three common burdens: consequently it

---

[125] Does this clause reflect apprehension before the millennium? The theme is not restricted to the years around 1000 (see S 617, if authentic), but it may have been especially 'popular' then: see S 895 (dated 998) and 904 (dated 1002), and also the spurious S 894 (dated 998, but apparently modelled in part on S 895).

[126] Bishop, *English Caroline Minuscule*, p. 15, and *idem*, 'Copenhagen Gospel Book', p. 39 n.

might be thought to be a forgery modelled in part on S 916 and concocted to provide a direct title-deed for estates certainly connected with the abbey. However, the relationship described above between S 888 and 889, issued in the same year, weighs strongly in support of the authenticity of S 888.[127] Thus it would appear that S 916 was drawn up either at St Albans by a draftsman who had one eye on S 888, or elsewhere in co-operation with someone acquainted with the terms of an earlier privilege for the abbey.

In some cases, a prospective beneficiary seems to have supplied the draftsman with a diploma already in his possession when procuring another diploma from the king. There is no reason to question the authenticity of S 920, King Æthelred's diploma in favour of Abbot Wulfgeat and Burton Abbey, issued in 1008. Yet its styles of attestation are closely related to those used in S 906, the Burton foundation charter (dated 1004), and the obvious inference is that a copy of S 906 was used in the drafting of S 920. It might then follow that S 920 was drawn up in the Burton scriptorium, but it is no less likely that Abbot Wulfgeat himself supplied a copy of S 906 when S 920 was drawn up, in order to demonstrate the abbey's right to the two estates he was exchanging with the king.[128] And there is no reason to question the authenticity of S 924 (dated 1011), a diploma granting an estate at *Ufre* to the king's *minister* Morcar. Yet in its witness list the last nine bishops are listed in exactly the same order as the fifth to the thirteenth bishops in S 922, another diploma in favour of Morcar but issued two years previously, in 1009; moreover, the first abbot in S 924 is the same as in S 922, and a statement at the end of the text of S 924 suggests that the numbers of the other witnesses were also very similar. This degree of relationship could not have arisen fortuitously, and it may indicate that Morcar submitted his earlier diploma to the draftsman of his new one.[129]

---

[127] See above, pp. 102–3. Note that (like S 888) S 889 contains no reference to the reservation of the *trimoda necessitas*: both diplomas are for urban estates which may have been assessed for their military services in a different way (but cf. S 870 and 871).

[128] Other elements in the formulation of S 920 derive from earlier diplomas of Æthelred: for the formula condemning other charters, see above, p. 88 n. 20, and for the sanction, see S 903. S 930 is a Burton forgery modelled on S 920; its additional formula referring to the beneficiary's service and payment is of a standard type (cf. S 471).

[129] The entire formulation of S 924 was apparently derived from a diploma of King Edgar, with some variation in the first part of the proem: see S 784, and also S 890.

An account of a lawsuit settled apparently in the early years of Cnut's reign describes how King Æthelred had once entrusted the production of a *boc* to Archbishop Wulfstan,[130] and there may have been other occasions when a member of the episcopacy was employed in a similar role. S 880 is said to have been written (*scripta*) by Archbishop Sigeric, and since the diploma directly concerns the privileges to be enjoyed by one of the southern dioceses, it is easy to believe that he played some part in the drawing up of the text; but the overall formulation accords well with that of contemporary diplomas,[131] and Sigeric's contribution may have been restricted to deciding the terms of its operative elements. It is also possible that S 882, a diploma in favour of Æscwig, bishop of Dorchester, and preserved in the archives of Christ Church Canterbury, was drawn up by Æscwig himself or by one of his entourage. Its witness list is identical with that in S 1379, representing a grant of land by Bishop Æscwig to his man Ælfstan, suggesting that a single memorandum underlies both documents; and since officers of the king would be unlikely to undertake the production of an episcopal charter, the immediate inference seems to be that both were drawn up under Bishop Æscwig's supervision. But alternatively one might suppose that, having received S 882 from the king, Bishop Æscwig also received the king's permission to use it on the same occasion for drawing up a diploma of his own: S 1379 was issued 'cum consensu ac licentia Æðylredi regis atque senatorum', and the king subscribes 'Æscwio episcopo desiderante', a phrase not found in S 882.[132] S 931, from the archives of Thorney and dated 1013, more certainly represents an example of a diploma drawn up by a bishop who was indirectly 'interested' in the transaction. It concerns an estate in Northamptonshire, and the diocesan bishop, Eadnoth of Dorchester, attests with the style 'hanc scedulam dictitans . Rege

---

130 S 1460. See Harmer, *Writs*, pp. 38–41.
131 See above, pp. 100 and 111.
132 S 882 and 1379 share an error in the dating clause, giving 995 for 994: this may imply that a completed document, rather than simply a memorandum of witnesses, was the common denominator, and since S 882 gives the correct indiction it may well have been the document in question; the distinctive sanction in S 882 (see above, p. 92 n. 31) suggests that it belongs to the diplomatic mainstream. S 1378 is a spurious Christ Church charter concocted to represent the return of the estate at Risborough (with S 882 itself) to the community: the estate was in fact returned to Archbishop Ælfric, who bequeathed it to Christ Church in his will (S 1488).

suisque præcipientibus perscribere iussi'. The formulation of the diploma is derived from the alliterative diplomas of the mid tenth century,[133] and like them it casts the grant in the third person, creating an impression of indirectness that is consistent with the production of the diploma by an agency independent of the king. The diploma stands well outside the norm of contemporary diplomatic practice, perhaps indicating that the circumstances under which it was drawn up were exceptional.[134]

A few other diplomas are made up largely of formulae that cannot be traced elsewhere amongst the extant diplomas issued during Æthelred's reign, and thus that cannot be associated in any way with the diplomatic mainstream; some of them are couched in terms that seem indeed to be unique.[135] Such diplomas may be the work of particularly adventurous draftsmen, and in certain cases their distinctive features may reflect their production by independent agencies. But a perusal of all the diplomas surviving from the reign of King Æthelred serves to put them in their proper perspective: while the initial impression may be one of diplomatic diversity, especially in the diplomas issued from 993 onwards, it soon emerges that there are significant factors linking a large proportion of the diplomas and suggesting strongly that they were the products of a central office. In the light of the diplomatic evidence from the period between 925 and 975 assembled above,

---

[133] See Hart, *Charters of Eastern England*, pp. 196–8, and above, p. 27 n. 39 and p. 82 n. 165.

[134] S 931 belongs to a group of late tenth- and eleventh-century diplomas in which the bishop of Dorchester of the day attests with one or other of the styles that seem to imply some hand in the drafting of the text (see above, pp. 26–8); in each case the land concerned is (or is probably) in the diocese of Dorchester: see S 834, 883, 887 (though the style in this diploma may have been copied from S 883: above, p. 113 n. 93), 931, 977 and 983 (and see also S 1105 in this connection). One wonders whether the phenomenon should be attributed at least in part to the tendency of certain styles of attestation to attach themselves to particular bishops and sees (cf., e.g., Bishop Cynesige's subscriptions in S 565, 712 and 1213), or regarded as evidence that the production of diplomas was the responsibility of the diocesan bishop; if the latter, why does the evidence concern Dorchester in particular and not any of the other sees to the same extent, and why are the styles in question as often as not attached to a bishop other than the diocesan?

[135] S 878, 898 (for its pictorial invocation, cf. S 139, 646 and 853), 925 (a dubious text which grants exemption from the *trimoda necessitas*, but as it is in favour of the queen we might expect some exceptional features), 929 (its proem reappears in S 975 and 979) and 940 (cf. S 353, and for the king's subscription, cf. S 914). Three diplomas are linked by the presence of formulae derived ultimately from the diplomas of Æthelstan: S 919 (exposition and superscription), 921 (king's subscription; elements of the dispositive section in this diploma recur in S 343, a spurious diploma from the same archive) and 928 (whole text).

there is nothing particularly remarkable about this: if most of Æthelred's diplomas were drawn up in a central office of some description, it was only in continuation of long-established arrangements.[136]

ROYAL DIPLOMAS AND THE WITENAGEMOT

It is unfortunate that the draftsmen of King Æthelred's diplomas only rarely indicate where the documents were drawn up, for the formulae most commonly used for expressing the date did not extend to a note of the location. So it is often the case that those draftsmen who were more informative were those who had chosen to depart from the norm in other respects as well and who were incorporating more circumstantial detail than usual. S 915 might be called an 'Abingdon charter' because it was preserved in one of the cartularies of that house and because it concerns land in Berkshire, but it is quite clear that it was not produced there. Its connection with the abbey may indeed be fortuitous, since it belongs to a group of texts which relate to lands with no known association with Abingdon, raising the possibility that it was deposited in the archives by a layman for safe-keeping.[137] The diploma begins with a proem to the effect that the Creator 'tantæ ... caritatem dulcedinis dominorum ac prælatorum cordibus inmiscuit, ut servulos ac subditos utpote proprios diligerent filiolos'. The dispositive section

---

[136] The further development of the diplomatic tradition demands more detailed discussion than would be strictly relevant here. The overall impression is one of diversity, but this may be attributable largely to the fact that relatively few diplomas were produced after Æthelred's death (see further below, pp. 140–5). There remain various intriguing points of contact between diplomas from different parts of the country (e.g. the appearance, in a considerable proportion of them, of particularly detailed dating formulae and of witness lists which specify with unusual precision the status of the witnesses and which often include priests; the occurrence of elements of a sanction current between 930 and 934 in S 994, 1006, 1010 and 1044; and links between the formulation in S 970, 1000 and 1001, in S 1015 and 1032, in S 1026 and 1048, and in S 1033, 1036 and 1038), but there are several no less intriguing instances of linked pairs or groups of diplomas where the common denominator appears to be regional (cf. the formulation in S 947 and 948, and in S 975 and 979; cf. the witness lists in S 980 and 984; cf. the styles of attestation in S 953, 962–3, 971, 998 and 1019), as well as instances of diplomas which were or appear to have been drawn up in ecclesiastical scriptoria (S 950; S 1019, if modelled on S 890) and instances of diplomas written by the same scribe (S 963 and 971, perhaps from Crediton; S 994 and 1008, perhaps from the Old Minster Winchester). In short, the evidence seems to point simultaneously and equally in different directions.

[137] See above, pp. 12–13.

describes how the king's reeve Ælfgar approached King Æthelred and offered him gold and silver valued at 300 golden mancuses for eight hides of land *æt Wealtham*.[138] Seeing the devotion of his mind and recalling his good service – and doubtless unable to resist the offer – the king granted him the land. Thus the transaction took place entirely in a secular context, for it was arranged on a personal basis between the king and one of his reeves, and the diploma by which it was duly recorded was *acta* in 1007, 'in novo videlicet oppido, quod regis vocatur vocabulo Beorchore':[139] the question whether or not it was produced in an ecclesiastical scriptorium acting for the beneficiary does not arise. It is more surprising that two diplomas which seem at first sight to be ideal candidates for production in the scriptoria of the respective beneficiaries were in fact drawn up at a distance from the abbeys concerned: for as we have seen, S 876, in favour of Abingdon, was *confirmata* at Gillingham (perhaps in Dorset), after an earlier meeting at Winchester, and S 891, in favour of the Old Minster Winchester, was written at Wantage in Berkshire, after an earlier meeting on the royal estate of Calne in Wiltshire.[140] Moreover, it seems that even when the *witan* had gathered in the vicinity of an abbey destined to become the beneficiary of a diploma, the diploma might nevertheless be drawn up at a place other than the beneficiary's scriptorium: S 909, King Æthelred's confirmation of lands to St Frideswide's in Oxford, was 'scripta . . . iussu prefati Regis in villa regia que Hedyndon appellatur die octauarum B. Andree Apostoli', and Headington, which was one of the estates involved, is only a few miles north-east of Oxford.[141] To these diplomas said to have been drawn up at

---

138 For Ælfgar the reeve, see below, p. 183 n. 110. The estate was at Waltham St Lawrence (Gelling, *Place-Names of Berkshire* III, 635–9); it was assessed at eight hides in the Domesday survey, and was held by the king; it had been held by Queen Edith (DB i, fo. 56v).

139 This place cannot be identified. Presumably it represents OE *beorc-ōra*, meaning 'slope covered with birch trees'; cf. Birchover (Derbyshire) and Bircher (Herefordshire), with *i*-mutated forms of the first element and with *ofer* as opposed to *ōra* (Cameron, *Place-Names of Derbyshire* I, 45, and Smith, *Elements* I, 28–9, 36, and II, 53–5); note also the minor place-name Barker's Hill (*beorcora* in S 582) in Semley in Wiltshire (Gover *et al.*, *Place-Names of Wiltshire*, p. 209).

140 See above, pp. 101–2.

141 At the time of the Domesday survey, Headington was a royal manor of ten hides (DB i, fo. 154v). According to a local tradition, Æthelred was born at Headington and christened there by Archbishop Dunstan: the remains of an ancient building there are known to the Ordnance Survey as 'Ethelred's Palace', but otherwise the tradition appears to be without foundation.

Beorchore, Gillingham, Wantage and Headington one can add
S 1796, a fragment of a diploma dated 986 which was 'acta . . . in
urbe nobilium heroum, scilicet Londonia', and S 905, written in
1002 'in ciuitate dorobernensis quae est metropolis cantuariorum'.[142]
The references to the meeting places of the *witan* in royal diplomas
hardly enable one to reconstruct an itinerary of King Æthelred,
but they do suggest that he and his *witan* gathered more often on
royal estates than in the major ecclesiastical and urban centres of the
kingdom.[143] This impression is confirmed by other references to
gatherings of the *witan* held during Æthelred's reign. Thus the
king's coronation in May 979 took place 'mid mycclum gefean
Angelcynnes witon', at Kingston upon Thames in Surrey;[144]
shortly before the rededication of the Old Minster at Winchester in
October 980, there had been a council 'uico regis in Andeferan'
(Andover in Hampshire) attended by 'proceresque ducesque, gentis
et Anglorum maxima pars comitum';[145] in 985 a 'synodal council'
attended by bishops, ealdormen and all the *optimates* of the kingdom
was held on the royal estate of Cirencester;[146] at Easter in 995
Ælfric, bishop of Ramsbury, was elected archbishop of Canterbury
'fram Ægelrede cinge. 7 fram eallan his witan', at Amesbury in
Wiltshire;[147] the king convened his *witan* at Cookham in Berkshire
c. 997;[148] codes of laws were promulgated at Woodstock in Oxford-

---

[142] We may disregard the statement in Kemble's text of S 888 (KCD 696) that the diploma
was 'conscriptus . . . in loco qui dicitur Celchyð in synodo publico', since the statement
properly forms part of S 150. The spurious S 894 was 'scripta . . . quando ad classem
proficiscens illud monasterium [*sc.* Westminster] visitarem', and the spurious S 1382 was
'Data Lundoniae, indictione .xi. [in this case for 998] praesente rege coram omni concilio'.

[143] According to VIII Æthelred 37 (Liebermann, *Gesetze* I, 267) meetings since the death of
King Edgar had been held advisedly 'on namcuðan stowan'; see also above, p. 35, and
Fig. 1; see further Appendix 2.

[144] *ASC* MSS 'D' and 'E'; also MS 'C'. Kingston was, of course, a royal estate: DB i, fo. 30v.

[145] Wulfstan Cantor, 'Narratio de Sancto Swithuno', lines 75–80 (Campbell, *Breuiloquium*,
p. 67); for the rededication itself, celebrated by Archbishop Dunstan and eight bishops
'in presentia regis Aðelredi et in conuentu omnium pene ducum, abbatum, comitum,
primorumque optimatum uniuerse gentis Anglorum', see also Wulfstan's *Vita Æðelwoldi*,
c. 40 (Winterbottom, *Three Lives*, pp. 58–9), and Sheerin, 'Dedication of the Old Minster'.
For Andover as a royal residence in the Anglo-Saxon period, see Biddle, *Winchester*,
p. 466; it was a royal estate in the eleventh century: DB i, fo. 39r.

[146] S 896 and 937: the meeting decided on the banishment of Ealdorman Ælfric, which took
place in 985. Cirencester was still a royal estate in the eleventh century: DB i, fo. 162v.

[147] *ASC* MS 'F'. Amesbury was a royal manor during the reign of Edward the Confessor:
DB i, fo. 64v.

[148] S 939; see Gelling, *Place-Names of Berkshire* I, 79–80. Cookham was a royal manor during
the reign of Edward the Confessor: DB i, fo. 56v.

shire[149] and at Wantage in Berkshire[150] – both probably before the last decade of the reign and the latter perhaps in 997[151] – and reference is made in them to an earlier meeting held at *Bromdune* (the location of which is uncertain);[152] further codes of laws were promulgated at Enham, in Hampshire, *c.* 1008,[153] at Bath in 1009,[154] and again at Woodstock.[155] Finally, in 1015 the scene of the betrayal of Sigeferth and Morcar by Ealdorman Eadric was a 'mycele gemot' convened at Oxford.[156]

These meetings of the *witan* were recorded in connection with a variety of specific activities, but there is of course no reason to assume that only the specified business was conducted on each occasion: any one *witenagemot* might see a combination of such activities, whether the discussion and settlement of disputes, the promulgation of legislation, the election of higher ecclesiastics, political, administrative and military decisions, internal intrigue, or the authorization of grants of land and privileges. Certain of these activities presuppose the availability of means for the production of written instruments at the meeting. An agreed text of any new laws enacted would have to be recorded prior to general circulation,[157] and it would be necessary to set down some account of the settlement of legal proceedings: indeed, S 939 (the document by which the king granted that Æthelric of Bocking's will might stand) must have

¿Not in ecclesiastical court??

---

149 I Æthelred: Liebermann, *Gesetze* I, 216. Woodstock was assessed as royal forestland at the time of the Domesday survey: DB i, fo. 154v.

150 III Æthelred: Liebermann, *Gesetze* I, 228. Wantage was a royal manor during the reign of Edward the Confessor: DB i, fo. 57r.

151 See Whitelock, *EHD*, p. 439, and above, p. 102 n. 56.

152 Liebermann, *Gesetze* I, 216 and 228.

153 VI Æthelred: see *ibid.* p. 247, and the reference in X Æthelred to an earlier meeting at Enham, *ibid.* p. 269. VI Æthelred is closely related to V Æthelred, dated 1008 in one manuscript; see Whitelock, *EHD*, p. 442, and Wormald, 'Æthelred the Lawmaker', pp. 49–58. Land at (Knight's) Enham was held by certain people from Edward the Confessor (DB i, fo. 50r); part of the estate is known as King's Enham.

154 VII Æthelred: Liebermann, *Gesetze* I, 262, and Whitelock, *EHD*, p. 447.

155 IX Æthelred: Liebermann, *Gesetze* I, 269.

156 *ASC* MSS 'C', 'D' and 'E'. It is unfortunate that the several references to the deliberations of the king and his councillors in the *Chronicle* (*s.a.* 992, 994, 999, 1002, 1006 and 1010–11) are not given a location. There was a 'great meeting' at London in the 980s and a 'great synod' there in 988 × 90 (S 877), but it is not clear whether the king was himself present on either occasion (though it seems likely that he was).

157 Note in this connection the penultimate clause of IV Edgar, which lays down that 'write man manega gewrita be þisum 7 sende ægþer ge to Ælfhere ealdormen ge to Æþelwine ealdormen, 7 hy gehwider' (Liebermann, *Gesetze* I, 214).

been written during the meeting at Cookham where the deliberations took place, for it contains a statement that 'þeos swutelung
wæs þærrihte gewriten 7 beforan þam cincge and þam witon
gerædd'. One suspects that records of the circumstances under
which certain estates were forfeited to the king were also made on
the occasion of the meeting where the forfeiture was decided, for
incorporation sooner or later into the diplomas by which the king
granted the estates to others.[158] Accordingly it is not at all unlikely
that diplomas might also have been written on the occasion of a
witenagemot: in one instance it is explicitly stated that the diploma
was itself written on the king's instructions and then handed over
by the king to the beneficiary at the assembly and in the presence
of the king's *optimates* (S 893). But if arrangements could be made
for the production of written instruments there and then, what
form did they take? It is evident that the peregrinations of the king
often took him and his council outside the orbit of any religious
house, so that he could not have been dependent on the facilities
offered by an ecclesiastical scriptorium; he might have taken
advantage of the skills of a particular bishop (or abbot) and his
entourage (though the continuity of diplomatic practice from
meeting to meeting and from year to year militates against this),
or there might have been a writing office attached to his own
household.

Examination of the witness lists attached to Æthelred's diplomas
provides support from another direction for the possibility that the
diplomas arose directly from the proceedings of a *witenagemot*. We
may discard at once the notion that the lists were the product of
informed speculation or wishful thinking on the part of scribes
working independently or retrospectively in ecclesiastical scriptoria,
for they fit together in a way that can only reflect the existence of
recognized conventions in their compilation,[159] as applied by scribes
who were themselves present and so in a position to observe the

---

[158] The narrative sections in diplomas describing forfeitures are generally in Latin (S 883,
896, 926, 927 and 934), but occasionally in English (S 877 and 886); some of those in Latin
could have been adapted from English originals. Such narratives may originally have had
a separate existence: the detailed account of Wulfbald's crimes in S 877 was presumably
drawn up *c*. 990 on the occasion of the synod at London where the forfeiture of his son's
property was decided, and then kept by the king until he disposed of some of Wulfbald's
property in 996.

[159] For the conventions that determined general features of the lists, see above, pp. 118–20.

actual attendance at the meetings. In some respects, perhaps, the regularity of the witness lists attached to diplomas with different provenances may not be especially significant, for the names of contemporary bishops and prominent abbots or *ministri* would be known to many, and the strict order of precedency detectable in the lists of ealdormen and athelings was based on the criterion of seniority and could possibly be established without too much difficulty: but while such features *could* be compatible with the notion that the lists were idealized, it is improbable that the great majority of scribes would independently take the necessary care over the protocol, and so it would still be more natural to attribute the features to the conventions practised in some kind of central office. When one considers the subscriptions of particular individuals one is left with no doubt that the lists are, as they purport to be, statements of those who were present at a *witenagemot* and who had witnessed the transaction concerned. It is often the case that successive stages in the career of an individual can be followed with remarkable ease, as he was promoted from the ranks of the *ministri* to the ranks of the ealdormen,[160] as he climbed in the hierarchy of ealdormen (see Table 6), or as he was promoted from the ranks of the abbots to the episcopal bench and then perhaps translated to one of the archbishoprics;[161] the details that emerge elegantly reflect events recorded in narrative sources, and those concerning one person might establish a relative order within a series of diplomas issued in the same year which is then found to accord perfectly with the details concerning someone else.[162] It would be astonishing if scribes working independently and without direct knowledge were nevertheless collectively so well-informed that they were able to produce lists that now fit so well together: they might have heard about appointments, promotions and deaths amongst the

---

[160] See, e.g., the subscriptions of Ælfric, Ealdorman Ælfhere's successor, in Tables 7 (up to S 844) and 6 (from S 851).

[161] See the subscriptions of Æthelgar (abbot of New Minster Winchester, bishop of Selsey, archbishop of Canterbury), Sigeric (abbot of St Augustine's Canterbury, bishop of Ramsbury, archbishop of Canterbury), Ælfheah (abbot of Bath, bishop of Winchester, archbishop of Canterbury), Ælfric (abbot of St Albans, bishop of Ramsbury, archbishop of Canterbury), Ealdulf (abbot of Peterborough, bishop of Worcester, archbishop of York) and Lyfing (abbot of Chertsey, bishop of Wells, archbishop of Canterbury) in Tables 2–5.

[162] See Appendix 1, *passim*.

131

higher ecclesiastics, but it is less likely that they would have been keenly and immediately aware of events such as the appointment, promotion, banishment or death of an ealdorman, or of the temporary absence (for one reason or another) of particular people from the meetings of the *witan*.[163] Again, it is striking and encouraging to find a group of subscriptions in the name of a particular *minister* concentrated in a brief period, especially when the position of the subscriptions does not suggest that he could be numbered amongst the prominent laymen.[164] And it is improbable that the tendency of brothers or kinsmen to occur together in the lists[165] could have arisen in any way other than by their own preference for associating with one another at a *witenagemot*, thus ensuring that the lists are based on direct knowledge: for scribes could not be expected to be aware of family relationships or to be concerned to group brothers and kinsmen together.

A group of four diplomas taken from different archives serves to illustrate how the witness lists can reflect historical detail in such a way as to guarantee their status as reliable records of attendance at meetings of the *witan*. Siweard and Sired, two *ministri* who can be identified as brothers from Kent,[166] occur together in several diplomas issued in the late tenth and early eleventh centuries, ranging from S 885 (dated 995 and in favour of Rochester) to S 910 and 911 (both dated 1005, and in favour of Eadsige the reeve and Eynsham Abbey respectively). Their presence in S 885, and also in S 893 (another diploma for Rochester, dated 998), might be attributable to the selection of witnesses considered especially suitable and useful in the context of the transaction concerned (for there is

---

[163] For the absence of Ælfstan, bishop of Rochester, see below, pp. 178–9, and for that of Queen Ælfthryth, see below, pp. 176 and 181–2.

[164] See, e.g., the subscriptions of Osweard in Table 7, and those of Æthelnoth in Table 8.

[165] For this tendency in the diplomas of kings Eadwig and Edgar, note the subscriptions of Ælfgar and Brihtferth (said to be brothers in S 651), and of Osweard and Osulf (said to be brothers in S 652). It is exemplified in Æthelred's diplomas by the subscriptions of Æthelmær, Brihtwold and Ordulf; of Wulfric, Wulfheah and Ælfhelm; of Æthelmær and Æthelwold; of Siweard and Sired; and of Eadric Streona and his family: see further below, pp. 188–9, 209 and 212–13.

[166] 'Siweard . 7 Sired his broðor' occur in S 1455 and 1456; 'Sigeward on Cent' occurs in the list of those present at the synod of London *c*. 990 (S 877), where the forfeiture of Kentish estates was discussed; S 875 is a diploma granting land in Kent to the king's *minister* Sigered in 990; see also Hart, *Charters of Northern England*, pp. 358–9.

evidence that such a practice was adopted on some occasions[167]), or it might simply reflect that the diplomas were drawn up in Kent, and that the Kentish brothers had attended a meeting in their own locality; alternatively, it might be a coincidence, if the diplomas were drawn up elsewhere at meetings which the brothers happened to have attended.[168] The remaining diplomas attested by Siweard and Sired are S 878 (dated 996, for Wulfric Spot), 899 (dated 1001, for Shaftesbury), 904 (dated 1002, for Wherwell) and 905 (also dated 1002, for Æthelred, the king's man), and the final names amongst the *ministri* in the attached witness lists are as follows:

S 878: Leofwine, Leofwine R, Siweard, SIRED, GODWINE

S 899: Æthelric, Siweard, Sired, Wulfgar, Leofwine

S 904: Leofwine, Siweard, Sired, Lyfing, Leofwine, Æthelric

S 905: Leofwine, Æthelric, Lyfing, Leofstan, Siweard, Wulfstan, Sired[169]

It is interesting to find that in addition to Siweard and Sired, seven of the eight other names grouped together at the end of these witness lists occur in contemporary documents with Kentish provenances and interests, and so could belong to contemporary Kentish thegns. S 1456, a document recording the settlement of a dispute between a certain Leofwine and the church of Rochester, drawn up during the archiepiscopate of Ælfric (995–1005), includes amongst its witnesses 'Lyfing of Malling and Siweard and Sired his brother and Leofstan of Mersham and Godwine, Wulfheah's son, and Wulfstan of Saltwood . . . and Leofwine of Ditton';[170] the witnesses to S 1455, a document of the same general period as S 1456 and involving the community of St Augustine's Canterbury, includes amongst its witnesses a thegn called Lyfing, Siweard and

---

[167] See above, p. 120 n. 121, and Hart, *Charters of Northern England*, p. 336 (for Frythegyst).

[168] It is perhaps worth mentioning that they do not occur in S 891, drawn up in Berkshire, nor in S 909, drawn up in Oxfordshire.

[169] Sired is the last *minister* in S 905, but the names of three men (Wulfstan, Wærelm, Guthwold) without titles are crammed into the right-hand margin; it is not clear whether they are *ministri*, but they are certainly Kentish (see S 1456 and Ward, 'Witan at Canterbury', pp. 45–7). I have omitted S 914 (a Christ Church forgery) from the group, though it would fit well: in the OE version the last names are Siward, Sired 'Siwardes broðor', Wulfstan *ealda*, Wulfstan *geonga*, Lyfing and Leofstan.

[170] The remaining witnesses include Æthelred the reeve of Canterbury, perhaps the beneficiary of S 905 (which is a grant of land in Canterbury).

his brother Sired, and Wulfstan of Saltwood; S 1220, a document drawn up between 1013 and 1018, records a grant of land in Kent by Godwine to Leofwine the Red and is witnessed by Sired and Æthelric, amongst others; finally, S 1461, a Kentish marriage agreement of the period 1016–20, includes amongst its witnesses Sired the Old and Godwine, Wulfheah's son, and mentions Leofwine the Red as one of those who acted as security for the agreement. The identification of the *ministri* who attested S 878, 899, 904 and 905 as the Kentish thegns of these documents depends on their occurrence together, in association with Siweard and Sired, rather than simply on shared personal names. Of the four diplomas concerned, S 905 is said to have been drawn up in Canterbury, so it is no surprise to find a group of Kentish thegns at the end of the witness list. On the analogy of this diploma, it seems reasonable to suggest that the grouping of apparently Kentish names at the ends of the lists in S 878, 899 and 904 indicates that these diplomas too were drawn up in Kent: the capitalization of Sired and Godwine in S 878 and the informed distinction of one of the Leofwines as 'Leofwine R' (for Leofwine the Red?) might reflect the scribe's special treatment of the local thegns. It is obvious that scribes working independently in different scriptoria would be neither concerned nor able to reconstruct a group of relatively minor thegns whose local associations have nothing to do with the beneficiaries of the diplomas: so S 878, 899 and 904, preserved in the archives of Burton, Shaftesbury and Wherwell respectively, suggest strongly that witness lists were based directly on information recorded on the occasion of the *witenagemot* and presumably incorporated into the diploma at the same time.

THE CENTRAL WRITING OFFICE

The evidence of the diplomas themselves takes us only thus far: it demonstrates that the centralized production of diplomas, by an agency able to operate on the royal estates where the meetings of the *witan* were commonly held, remained the norm (if not the rule) during Æthelred's reign, but it does not indicate the nature of the agency entrusted with the responsibility for issuing diplomas on each occasion, beyond creating the presumption that it was an office attached to the king's household. So it is important finally to enquire whether there is any other evidence for the existence of such an office which might lend substance to the presumption from a different direction.[171]

Isolated and incidental references to writers in the service of the king are at first sight of limited value, as they suggest nothing about the way in which the written business of the court was conducted, and give no indication of the responsibilities of the writer.[172] It is well known that King Æthelred numbered amongst his *ministri* a *scriptor* called Ælfwine, to whom he granted an estate in Oxfordshire in 984. The dispositive section of the diploma (S 853) refers to the beneficiary in customarily warm terms:

cuidam mihi oppido dilecto fidelique ministro videlicet meo scriptori qui a notis noto Elfwine nuncupatur vocabulo pro eius amabili humilique obsequio quo iugiter instanter deseruit

One should emphasize the implications of the description of Ælfwine as a faithful *minister* of the king. In the first place, one suspects that the term *minister* conceals distinctions between the several officials in a king's household who are known from other incidental references to have existed in the tenth century,[173] so that if only we knew in what capacity other men described simply as *ministri* served the king it might emerge that Ælfwine the writer was not alone. Secondly, it would appear that Ælfwine, as a *minister*, was probably a layman,[174] and we have to infer that ecclesiastics may not have had the monopoly of literacy. It is true that one should not overestimate the extent of secular learning and culture in Anglo-Saxon England, even after the example had been set by

---

171 No two of the extant (apparently) original diplomas issued in Æthelred's name are written by the same scribe, so one cannot complement the diplomatic and historical approaches with conclusive palaeographical evidence; since there are not more than eight originals (S 864, 876, 878, 880, 892, 898, 916 and 922) conceivably from the central office, spread over 20 years of a 38-year reign, it is perhaps not surprising that this should be so. However, further study of the scripts in these diplomas may cast some light on the training and affiliations of the individual scribes, and so on the composition of the central office.

172 We may disregard the statement in S 1380, the Wolverhampton foundation charter, that it was written 'per calamum & atramentum & manum notarii & scriniarii Ethelredi Regis Anglorum', since the charter is clearly a forgery: the forger tried to produce an archiepiscopal privilege by adapting a papal one, and in the process created a 'notarius et scriniarius' of King Æthelred from the equivalent official at the Lateran palace.

173 See further below, pp. 158–61.

174 Cf. Harmer, *Writs*, p. 58 n. 2.

King Alfred,[175] but there were important exceptions: Æthelweard, one of King Æthelred's ealdormen, produced an extraordinary Latin 'translation' of a version of the *Anglo-Saxon Chronicle* which affords a clear indication that the hermeneutic style characteristic of tenth-century Anglo-Latin literature, including many royal diplomas, was not exclusively the property of learned and pedantic ecclesiastics.[176] This renders rather less improbable, at least in principle, the incidental reference in a post-Conquest St Albans source to Ælfric, one-time abbot of St Albans and archbishop of Canterbury, who purchased land from the king 'cum adhuc sæcularis, et Regis Etheldredi cancellarius, extitisset'.[177]

However, we can but guess at the nature of the work entrusted to men like these. Æthelwulf, king of Wessex, had a person in his service called Felix, 'qui epistolarum vestrarum officio fungebatur',[178] and Æthelred's *scriptor* may similarly have been responsible for the king's correspondence. But one of the major tasks of a royal writer in the later Anglo-Saxon period must have been the production of administrative communications. In his vernacular version of St Augustine's *Soliloquies*, King Alfred refers in passing to a lord's 'ærendgewrit and hys insegel'[179] as if it were a commonplace in the late ninth century for the king, and perhaps any other lord, to make known his will by means of a written document associated, whether physically or not, with the impression of a seal.[180] And the same can be said of the reign of King Æthelred. In his homily *De populo Israhel*, Ælfric remarks that there are many men who refuse to listen to the Lord's instruction, lest they should be punished more severely for being aware of it and yet not living by it. The homilist offers an objection to this attitude, drawn from the secular world:

[175] Wormald, 'Literacy in Anglo-Saxon England', pp. 104–14.

[176] On Æthelweard and his style, see Lapidge, 'Hermeneutic Style', pp. 97–8 (and also pp. 99–101 for the style of diplomas), Winterbottom, 'Style of Aethelweard', and Campbell, *Chronicle of Æthelweard*, pp. xlv–lv.

[177] Riley, *Gesta Abbatum* I, 32 and III, 399; but it is possible that *sæcularis* in this context means that Ælfric was a member of the secular clergy (as Dr Brooks points out to me). Ealdulf, who became archbishop of York, is said to have been King Edgar's chancellor before he became a monk: Mellows, *Hugh Candidus*, pp. 29–31 (and see Hart, *Charters of Northern England*, pp. 326–7, and Barlow, *English Church*, p. 125).

[178] Haddan and Stubbs, *Councils* III, 648.

[179] Carnicelli, *Soliloquies*, p. 62; Harmer, *Writs*, p. 10.

[180] Chaplais, 'Anglo-Saxon Chancery', pp. 51–4, makes a plausible case for questioning the assumption that the *insegel* was necessarily attached to the *ærendgewrit*; see also Barraclough, 'Anglo-Saxon Writ', pp. 203–4.

Nu cweðe we þærtogeanes, þæt gif se cyning asent gewrit
to sumon his þegena, and he hit forsyhð swa swyðe
þæt he hit nele gehyran, ne his aseon,
þæt se cyning ne byð na swyðe bliðe him,
þonne he geaxað hu he hine forseah.[181]

The clause 'ne his aseon' makes no sense as it stands, because the verb requires an object. It is tempting to suppose that a word for 'seal' has been omitted accidentally, giving the sense 'nor look at its seal'; but it is difficult to see how a word of such import could have dropped out. Other alternatives are that *his* is an error for *hit*, or that a word such as *aht* has been omitted: 'ne his aht aseon' would give 'nor look at any of it',[182] perhaps with the implication 'that he will not hear it, let alone look at it', and it has the advantage that *aht* is not such a substantial word. At least the passage demonstrates conclusively that it was common in Ælfric's time, and therefore in Æthelred's reign, for the king to send a written instruction (*gewrit*) to one of his thegns, which would be read out for him to hear (*gehyran*)[183] and which was substantial, so that he would have been able, had he been so inclined, to look at (*aseon*) it. Indeed, a dependence on oral messages would be surprising when one reflects on the complexity of the information which a messenger might have to convey, and on the greater safety to be obtained by the simple and obvious expedient of having it written down.[184] Accordingly, it is no surprise to find a statement that King Æthelred sent a 'gewrit and his insegel' to Archbishop Ælfric, ordering that a certain dispute should be settled;[185] on another occasion he seems to have

---

181 Pope, *Homilies of Ælfric* II, 659 (and see Harmer, *Writs*, p. 14). 'Now we say against this, that if the king sends his writ to any one of his thegns, and he despises it so greatly that he will not hear it, nor look at [any] of it, the king will not be very gracious to him when he learns how he scorned him' (Whitelock, *EHD*, p. 380 n. 3).

182 Pope, *Homilies of Ælfric* II, 666.

183 Apparently the thegn was not expected to read the *gewrit* himself, so perhaps he depended on a member of his household: cf. the situation in Alfred's reign described by Asser (Stevenson, *Asser*, pp. 92–5; Whitelock, *EHD*, p. 303), and cf. also Harmer, *Writs*, p. 545 no. 21 (which implies that 'seal' could be shorthand for 'sealed writ').

184 The Anglo-Saxons were well aware of the advantages of written letters, and often extolled them in the proems of royal diplomas: see, e.g., S 883.

185 S 1456, discussed by Chaplais, 'Anglo-Saxon Chancery', p. 56. The inclusion of a possessive pronoun in the expression 'gewrit and his insegel', as in King Alfred's reference to the 'ærendgewrit and hys insegel', could be taken to imply that the document and the seal were separate; cf. the references to the 'gewrite and insegle' in the *Chronicle* and the 'brevis et sigillum' of *Domesday Book*, applying to sealed writs of Edward the Confessor (Harmer, *Writs*, pp. 542–5).

relied on an oral message delivered by a person whose position may have guaranteed its authority and authenticity and who was entrusted with the king's *insegel* as a token of credence.[186] Clearly a variety of procedures might be adopted for the communication of the king's will to his subjects: it is always hazardous to assume consistency of practice in an Anglo-Saxon context.

The use of written instruments can be observed at other levels of the hierarchy in King Æthelred's reign, reinforcing the impression that it was a standard method of communication. Archbishop Dunstan sent a *gewrit* to King Æthelred concerning the estates of the bishop of Cornwall, and a contemporary copy of the document was preserved in the Crediton archives.[187] Queen Ælfthryth made a declaration to Archbishop Ælfric and Ealdorman Æthelweard concerning the manor of Taunton, and it was probably written down at the time since a copy was subsequently entered in the *Codex Wintoniensis*.[188] Again, Bishop Æthelric made a declaration to Ealdorman Æthelmær complaining of losses sustained by the bishopric of Sherborne: the text was recorded by a contemporary hand in the Sherborne Pontifical, perhaps as the equivalent of a file copy, and we may reasonably assume that the original was sent to the ealdorman.[189] The second and third documents are epistolary in form, but it has been suggested nevertheless that they originated as oral declarations, written down retrospectively by the 'beneficiary' in one case and by the sender in the other.[190] In each case the formula of address is indistinguishable from that employed in Edward the Confessor's written and sealed writs, and though the formula might well be used for oral declarations and in written versions of the same, the more natural explanation does seem to be that the messages were conveyed in the first instance in a written form, as in the case of Dunstan's *gewrit*.

It is significant also that the use of seals seems to have been common during the reign of Æthelred. We know that the king had one himself,[191] and it is certain that he was not unique in this respect.

---

[186] S 1454, discussed by Chaplais, 'Anglo-Saxon Chancery', pp. 56–7; but cf. n. 183 above.

[187] Napier and Stevenson, *Crawford Charters*, pp. 18–19, 102–10; Chaplais, 'Anglo-Saxon Chancery', p. 57.

[188] S 1242 (Harmer, *Writs*, no. 108).   [189] S 1383 (Harmer, *Writs*, no. 63).

[190] Chaplais, 'Anglo-Saxon Chancery', pp. 57–9.

[191] S 1454 and 1456.

Three seal matrices that can probably be assigned to the late tenth and early eleventh centuries have survived: the first, of ivory, was found at Wallingford in Berkshire and has on one side the inscription '✠ SIGILLUM B GODWINI MINISTRI';[192] the second, of bronze, was found at Weeke in Hampshire and reads '✠ SIGILLUM ÆLFRICI ⋙ ';[193] and the third, of ivory, came to light recently at Sittingbourne in Kent and has the inscription '✠ SIGILLUM WULFRICI'.[194] All three bear portraits of men brandishing swords, and there is no reason to doubt that they belonged to laymen.[195] But for what purposes were these seal matrices used? To imagine that they were of the kind for so mundane a function as sealing jars or other receptacles[196] would be to demean them, while to assume that they were used for sealing and authenticating written documents would involve some wishful thinking.[197] They may have been used loose in the same way the king's seal was sometimes used, as tokens of credence to support oral messages and written documents (letters, depositions to courts, etc.) conveyed by others. The letter of Pope John XV describing the reconciliation between King Æthelred and Duke Richard of Normandy concludes with the statement that 'de hominibus regis vel inimicis suis, nullum Ricardus recipiat, nec rex de suis sine sigillo eorum',[198] suggesting that one of the king's (or the duke's) men might approach the duke (or the king) bearing his lord's seal as an assurance that he came on official

---

[192] Tonnochy, *Seal-Dies*, no. 2, Okasha, *Handlist*, no. 117, Beckwith, *Ivory Carvings*, p. 53 and no. 41, and Cramp, 'Anglo-Saxon Sculpture', p. 197. The meaning of 'B' in the inscription is unclear; Okasha suggests that it could be 'decoration or an error, especially in view of the lack of space at the end of the text'. The inscription '✠ SIGILLUM GODGYÐE MONACHE DEO DATE' occurs on the other side, and probably reflects secondary use of the matrix; that the Godwine inscription is primary is suggested by the fact that the design on the headpiece is on the same side (as in the Wulfric seal mentioned below).

[193] Tonnochy, *Seal-Dies*, no. 3, Okasha, *Handlist*, no. 119, and Wilson, *Ornamental Metalwork*, no. 104.

[194] The seal is described and illustrated in the catalogue of a sale of Fine Antiquities at Christie's, 16 March 1977, Lot 179 and Plate 18. Its provenance may not be significant, for the yellow patination on the matrix suggests that it has been out of the ground for some time.

[195] See Tables 7 and 8 for subscriptions of *ministri* called Godwine, Ælfric and Wulfric in Æthelred's diplomas.

[196] See references in Toller, *Dictionary*, s.v. *insegel*.

[197] Cf. Harmer, *Writs*, pp. 19–20, and Galbraith, 'Monastic Foundation Charters', p. 213.

[198] Stubbs, *Memorials*, p. 398. On the use of loose seals in Anglo-Saxon England, see Chaplais, 'Anglo-Saxon Chancery', pp. 52–3.

business and to guarantee that he would be treated with appropriate respect: the duties and responsibilities of prominent laymen, and of *ministri* in particular, may have been such that it was necessary for them too to have their own seals for use in much the same way. One might speculate in this connection that the matrices were commissioned and supplied on an official basis: details of their epigraphy and iconography can be paralleled quite closely on coins of the same period,[199] and it is conceivable that those responsible for engraving the dies of coins undertook the production of seal matrices like these in the years between recoinages;[200] the similarity of the general appearance of the matrices themselves supports the possibility that they emanated from a common source.

The evidence for the use of written mandates and seals by the king, supplemented by evidence for the use of letters and seals at other levels of Anglo-Saxon society, shows that one should not underestimate the degree of sophistication in the management of private and official business during Æthelred's reign.[201] It is next worth considering the possibility that the sealed writ–charter was a current diplomatic form in this period. It is often assumed that the emergence of the writ should be understood in terms of a decline in the value attached to royal diplomas during the first half of the eleventh century. It is indeed a striking fact that there is a progressive fall in the average number of royal diplomas preserved from year to year in the eleventh century, when compared with the tenth century, presumably reflecting a reduction in the number of diplomas then issued (see Fig. 2): several of the cartularies that provided extensive series of tenth-century diplomas contain only isolated documents assigned to the reigns of Cnut, Harthacnut and Edward the Confessor,[202] and it is only the major collections from Abingdon and

---

[199] The parallels between the Ælfric and Wulfric matrices and the *First Hand* pennies of King Æthelred are especially striking.

[200] See Dolley, 'The Coins', pp. 362–3.

[201] I beg, therefore, to differ from some of the general observations made by Clanchy, *Memory to Written Record*, pp. 1–3 and 12–17, esp. 17 ('It seems unlikely that England was governed by a bureaucracy using documents in its routine procedures before 1066'). One might recall in this context Galbraith's remark that 'the Anglo-Saxon financial system, which collected the Danegeld, was not run from a box under the bed' (*Studies*, p. 45).

[202] The only eleventh-century diploma in the Wilton cartulary is one of Edward the Confessor dated 1045 (S 1010); apart from a diploma of Edward dated 1048 (S 1017), there

the Old Minster Winchester that include several eleventh-century royal diplomas apiece (though in relative terms the drop is still significant). Given the chronological coincidence between this phenomenon and the appearance of royal writs in large numbers, in the second quarter of the eleventh century, one might reasonably suppose either that the development of the more efficient writ rendered the diploma redundant as an instrument for the conveyance of land and privileges,[203] or that the natural decline of the diploma precipitated the emergence of the writ as a better alternative.[204]

Such a view would imply that, from the reign of Cnut onwards, the writ was used increasingly to the exclusion of the diploma, and so in turn that the two types of document served the same purpose. However, while several writs convey information that would be quite incompatible with the intended function of the royal diploma, those that do concern the transfer of land or the granting of privileges seem to complement the diploma, rather than make it redundant.[205] The diploma was a solemn document by which an immunity was created and possession of which was tantamount to possession of the land: its value was permanent, and a diploma first drawn up in the reign of Æthelred or before could serve as the title-deed for several generations thereafter. Once an estate had been 'booked' – once the immunity had been created – subsequent changes of possession would be effected simply by the handing over of the diploma to the new owner. Thus when the monasteries of Abbotsbury and Horton were founded, during the reigns of Cnut and Edward the Confessor respectively, some diplomas issued in the tenth century were transferred to each new house to serve as title-deeds for their estates.[206] It follows that the so-called 'decline' of the diploma is an illusion: the drop in the numbers produced may reflect rather the adequacy of earlier diplomas for transactions involving the conveyance of property, and it is also possible that

is nothing later than 1012 in the Burton collection in National Library of Wales, Peniarth 390; apart from a spurious diploma of Cnut (S 966) interpolated at the beginning, there was nothing later than the reign of Æthelred entered in the Glastonbury *Liber Terrarum*; the latest diploma entered in the *Textus Roffensis* is dated 1012 (S 926).

[203] Chaplais, 'Origin and Authenticity', p. 35, and *idem*, 'Anglo-Saxon Chancery', p. 50; also Galbraith, 'Monastic Foundation Charters', pp. 210–11.

[204] Chaplais, 'Anglo-Saxon Chancery', p. 60.

[205] See Harmer, *Writs*, pp. 34–8, and Chaplais, 'Anglo-Saxon Chancery', p. 50.

[206] See above, pp. 33–4.

by then less land was available for booking afresh.[207] At the same time, it would have been necessary to notify the shire court that a transaction had taken place, and for this purpose it seems that the writ–charter was used. Several extant writs serve to notify those concerned that a certain estate has been given by the king (or someone else) to an individual or to an ecclesiastical foundation. In this respect the writ is purely evidentiary: it announces that the conveyance of a privileged estate has been authorized, but its publication does not appear to represent the act of conveyance itself. A dispositive counterpart is required, and is supplied by the diploma: dispositive in the sense that it was used to symbolize the transfer of the estate. The diploma needed the writ to make explicit the fact of the recent change of ownership, and perhaps to provide supplementary evidence of direct interest in the estate; the writ needed the diploma as the title-deed for the estate, as the document that both established the terms on which it was to be held and defined its boundaries.[208]

If it were true that the writ eclipsed the diploma during the course of the eleventh century, one would expect to find some reflection of the change in the contents of cartularies, as their compilers switched from a dependence on diplomas to a dependence on writs. But it transpires that the manuscript sources for the one type of instrument are largely different from the sources for the other, and any account of the origin of the writ and of its relationship to the diploma must accommodate this fact. Many of the archives that provide extensive series of royal diplomas do not supply the text of a single writ: none has been preserved from Burton, Exeter, Glastonbury,

---

207 One would like to know how great a proportion of each county is covered by the extant royal diplomas: the Index map in Gelling, *Place-Names of Berkshire*, suggests that at least one-third of that county had been booked by the close of the Anglo-Saxon period (and of course many diplomas for other estates have doubtless been lost).

208 Thus the endowment of Abbotsbury was effected by the transfer of earlier diplomas to the community (as one can tell from Spelman's citations of diplomas from the lost Abbotsbury cartulary: Gibson, *Reliquiæ*, pp. 19–20), duly announced by King Edward in a writ (S 1064: Harmer, *Writs*, no. 2). The diploma and the writ may still have been used together after the Conquest. The series of claims in Lincolnshire recorded in *Domesday Book* includes one concerning land at Well: 'Homines de Treding dicunt quod T.R.E. habuit Turolf cum saca et soca. et post habuit Tonna. et ista terra fuit deliberata episcopo Odoni per cartam. sed non viderunt inde brevem regis.' (DB i, fo. 375r.) This may imply that Odo had received the title-deed for the estate, but that the men of the Riding had not seen the king's writ, which provided the only evidence for his direct interest in it.

Malmesbury, Rochester, St Albans, Shaftesbury, Thorney or Wilton; the *Codex Wintoniensis* contains the texts of four writs, three of which are later insertions,[209] while the Abingdon cartularies contain only three.[210] Indeed, a cursory survey of the contexts in which writs were preserved reveals how exceptional they might be: they are found, for example, in cartularies that contain no other pre-Conquest documents, in charter rolls or later confirmations, or entered in blank spaces in service books. Writs were, however, preserved in remarkable quantity at Bury St Edmunds and Westminster: of the ninety-nine examples purportedly issued by Edward the Confessor, no less than eighteen come from the archives of the former house and thirty-four from the archives of the latter.[211] Since both houses accumulated the greater part of their respective endowments during the eleventh century, and since very few royal diplomas have been preserved from either,[212] it might at first seem to follow that, by the time these houses began to prosper, the writ had replaced the diploma as the principal means of effecting or announcing the conveyance of land. But the situation can probably be attributed to circumstances peculiar to the process of the endowment of each foundation, which determined the nature of the documents deposited in their archives. To judge from *Domesday Book*, the Bury estates consisted of a large number of comparatively small holdings, for which separate title-deeds may not have existed, whether simply because the estates had become too fragmented or perhaps because conditions of land tenure in the eastern counties differed in some respects from the conditions that prevailed in the

---

[209] S 1242 (Harmer, *Writs*, no. 108) is entered by the main hand, and is authentic; S 946, 1154 and 1428 (*ibid.* nos. 107 and 112–13) are insertions, and are all dubious. Three other writs from the Old Minster (S 1151–3: *ibid.* nos. 109–11) are the only pre-Conquest documents entered in a mid-thirteenth-century cartulary.

[210] S 1065–6 and 1404 (*ibid.* nos. 3–5); the two royal writs are both spurious. See also *ibid.* p. 543, no. 10.

[211] The rest are derived from nineteen different archives. The texts from Bury are generally reliable, but the Westminster series is replete with forgeries: following Dr Harmer's judgements, it would appear that between fifteen and twenty are acceptable – in other words about the same number as from Bury.

[212] From Bury: S 483 and 703 (in favour of individuals), and S 507, 980 and 995 (in favour of Bury, and all dubious). A considerable number of documents on single sheets dated before the Conquest have survived from the Westminster archives, but they do not include any royal diplomas that could be accepted without hesitation as original instruments: see S 670, 702, 753, 1031 and 1450–1; S 903, entered in a cartulary, is probably authentic.

West Saxon and Mercian parts of the kingdom. There is no obvious reason why so few diplomas should have entered the archives of Westminster, but one should not forget that many of the abbey's estates were acquired through the direct patronage of Edward the Confessor,[213] who was in a position to endow his abbey with estates scattered all over the country: it seems that he transferred blocks of estates by the simplest expedient of announcing the fact in a writ and apparently without the simultaneous transfer of earlier deeds.[214] In order to compensate for the scarcity of diplomas, the monks of Bury and Westminster may have been particularly careful to recover the writs issued in their favour once they had been 'published' in the shire court; certainly it would appear that they were more careful in this respect than most other religious communities. For unless one is to suppose that only selected communities were the recipients of writs in the eleventh century, it cannot be a mere coincidence that so many archives from which diplomas have been preserved (whether in cartulary copies or in their original form) do not – and apparently did not – contain any writs,[215] while the houses which did preserve examples of writs in their cartularies are the houses from which the extant originals have survived and which at the same time provide very few diplomas. Perhaps the communities without writs were able to enjoy – and were satisfied with – the security of tenure guaranteed by the possession of royal diplomas.

The concentration of writs in the period for which there are relatively few diplomas does not therefore reflect a dissatisfaction with the diploma and its replacement by the writ.[216] Rather it

---

[213] See Whitelock, *Bishops of London*, pp. 22–3, Knowles, *Monastic Order*, pp. 72 and 102, and Harvey, *Westminster Abbey*, pp. 24 and 27.

[214] S 1143 (Harmer, *Writs*, no. 99).

[215] The Burton scribe who put together the collection of royal diplomas in National Library of Wales, Peniarth 390, and who was therefore well acquainted with Anglo-Saxon documents, remarks in the Annals he also compiled that seals were never used in England (before the Conquest), implying that no writs had been preserved in the archives (Luard, *Annales* I, 183). Thomas of Elmham remarks on the absence of pre-Conquest sealed documents in the archives of St Augustine's Canterbury, with the exception of a document in the name of King Cnut (Hardwick, *Thomas of Elmham*, p. 118). Note also the reference in a St Albans source to the discovery of King Edward's seal at Westminster as contradicting statements that the Anglo-Saxons did not use seals (Riley, *Gesta Abbatum* I, 151).

[216] Archbishop Lyfing might complain to King Cnut that 'he freolsas genoge hæfde gyf hi aht forstodan', but even so the *mund* of Christ Church was confirmed by the king's

arises in part from a drop in the number of diplomas issued (perhaps, as we have seen, because the older ones were still in use and because less land was available for booking afresh) and in part from the combination of local and archival factors that led to the preservation of writs at certain places – and not at others – in the eleventh century. This re-establishes the possibility that the writ may have been a current form for some time before the date of the earliest examples known today: if in the middle of the eleventh century greater importance was attached in some quarters than in others to the explicit and outwardly authenticated evidence of title to land and privileges afforded by a writ, it may be that during the reign of Æthelred, for example, the relative value attached to diplomas and putative writs was generally different, and that there was less incentive to retrieve the writs once their contents had been announced before the local officers and suitors of the shire courts. We have seen that in Æthelred's reign written documents and seals were used for private and official purposes, that the king is known to have issued writ–mandates, that he is known to have had a writer in his service, and that he is known to have had a seal, for which he would have required a keeper. There may be little to be said in favour of the authenticity of the two extant writs attributed to King Æthelred,[217] but at least we do not seem in his reign to be far from the world of sealed writ–charters, with all the attendant implications for the existence of some kind of office capable of producing them.

We may introduce in this connection the evidence of a Latin–Old English glossary entered in the margins of a manuscript of *Excerptiones de Prisciano*, almost certainly at Abingdon in the first half of the eleventh century.[218] Some of the material in this confused and

---

placing the charters on the altar, and the proceedings were announced in a writ (S 985: Harmer, *Writs*, no. 26, on which see Chaplais, 'Anglo-Saxon Chancery', p. 59). Those writs that give an ecclesiastic permission to draw up a diploma themselves testify to the continued value attached to the diploma as a permanent record: S 985, 1067, 1105 and 1115 (Harmer, *Writs*, nos. 26, 7, 55 and 68).

[217] S 945 and 946 (*ibid.* nos. 52 and 107); see Chaplais, 'Anglo-Saxon Chancery', pp. 55–6.
[218] For the curious history of the glossary in manuscript and print, see Ladd, 'The "Rubens" Manuscript', and Buckalew, 'Leland's Transcript', p. 157 n. 1 and p. 164; I have not yet been able to see L. Kindschi, 'The Latin–Old English Glossaries in Plantin–Moretus MS 32 and British Museum MS Additional 32,246' (unpublished Ph.D. dissertation, Stanford University, 1955). The text, described variously as 'Abbot Ælfric's Vocabulary' and 'Archbishop Ælfric's Vocabulary', in Wright and Wülcker, *Vocabularies* I, cols. 104–67

confusing work seems to have been derived from the glossary by Ælfric the homilist, but the greater part of it appears to be an original compilation. Since it is a class glossary, whose compiler seems himself to have been responsible for selecting the Latin lemmata, we may derive some indication of his thought process from the associations that he makes and from his choice of both lemmata and glosses. For it is important to appreciate that (as far as we know) the lemmata were not suggested by any particular work, and so the glossarist was not required to find equivalents for difficult Latin words that might have had no application in an Anglo-Saxon context.[219] The relevant group of glosses is as follows:

> Cancellarius *id est* Scriniarius. burþen
> Scrinium *vel* Cancellaria. idem *sunt.*
> hordfæt. Primiscrinius. yldest burþen
> Et sacriscriniarius. cyrcweard[220]

The words associated in this equation form a potentially most interesting group. *Burþen* itself has no scribal connotations, and perhaps we should infer that the glossarist knew of no word in Old English suitable for application to the exalted official known as a chancellor, whose business it was to produce written documents. On the other hand, the choice of a gloss that is not a literal equivalent of the lemma might mean that the glossarist was offering conceptual equivalents and so suggest that he did have some knowledge of the offices he was considering. The fact that he selected *cancellarius* as a lemma in the first place is arguably of some significance, and since he provided a gloss which implies that a chancellor was a person

(no. IV), is there distinguished from a 'Supplement to Alfric's Vocabulary', *ibid.* cols. 168–91 (no. V). In fact, neither represents the work of Ælfric, whether abbot or archbishop, and both are part of a single collection (Ker, *Catalogue*, no. 2 art. d). Moreover, Wright incorporated a distinct alphabetical glossary (*ibid.* no. 2 art. c) into the work. In fairness to him, the manuscript was known only from an inaccurate and muddled transcript by Junius before the main part of it came to light in 1884: see Thomson, 'Ælfric's Vocabulary' and Kluge, 'Glossen'.

219 The selection of lemmata may in fact have been derived from a general acquaintance with the terminology used in the papal chancery for its offices and officials (on which see Poole, *Papal Chancery*, pp. 12ff and 51ff).

220 B.L. Add. 32246, fo. 21v. Junius apparently omitted the second and third lines by homoeoteleuton, so the text given in Wright and Wülcker, *Vocabularies* I, col. 190, is incorrect. Previous discussions of the glosses (e.g. Larson, *King's Household*, pp. 133 n. 60 and 143, and Barlow, *English Church*, pp. 122 and 124) have been based on this edition.

who served in the chamber, it may be that he thought that it was this characteristic that set him apart from an ordinary scribe. Moreover, the gloss as applied to *cancellarius* is indirect. The glossarist explicitly qualifies the *cancellarius* as a *scriniarius*, implying that the two offices were united under one man, and only then provides the appropriate gloss, *burþen*. The word *scriniarius* is ambiguous, denoting either 'archivist' or 'custodian of books' from the primary meaning of *scrinium* ('chest, for storage of books'), or 'keeper or custodian of relics' from its secondary meaning ('reliquary' or 'shrine'). It was apparently the second meaning of *scriniarius* that was intended by the Abingdon glossarist, with an extension to cover the guardianship of precious things in general. For as he had equated the *cancellarius* with the *scriniarius*, and both with the chamber-thegn, so did he equate the *cancellaria* with the *scrinium*, and both with the *hordfæt*, or 'treasure-chest'. The concept of the *scriniarius* and the *scrinium* is then developed in the gloss *sacriscriniarius: cyrcweard*. Clearly it would be mistaken to regard *scriniarius* simply as an alternative term for 'notary', and so the phrase *cancellarius id est scriniarius* as a variation of the tautological formula *notarius et scriniarius* familiar from papal contexts. Thus we emerge with the impression that the exalted official with responsibilities for producing written documents (*cancellarius*) was identical with the custodian of the relics and other treasures (*scriniarius*), and that the *scrinium* could accordingly be identified with the *cancellaria*. Moreover, he was a thegn characterized by service in the chamber (*burþen*) and so the *Primiscrinius* could be described as the *yldest burþen*. One should recall that Ælfwine the king's *scriptor* was himself one of the king's faithful thegns and perhaps a member of his household.

The potential significance of the Abingdon glossary as historical evidence turns on the validity of the assumption that the glossarist was arranging and interpreting the lemmata in terms of contemporary Anglo-Saxon practices, and it is obvious that as evidence the glossary cannot stand on its own. But some corroboration for the impression that it creates can be derived from other sources. In the earliest *Vita Dunstani* it is said that King Eadred

commisit illi [*sc.* to Dunstan] . . . optima quæque suorum suppellectilium, quamplures scilicet rurales cartulas, etiam veteres præcedentium regum thesauros, necnon et diversas propriæ adeptionis suæ gazas, sub munimine monasterii sui fideliter custodiendum.[221]

We learn also that King Eadred, suffering from an illness and fearing for his life,

misit circumquaque ad congregandas facultates suas, quas dum posset spontaneo liberoque dictatu ipse suis vivendo disponeret; per hoc enim vir Dei Dunstanus, velut alii regalium gazarum custodes ibat; ut quas causa custodiendi secum habuerat regi reportaret.[222]

These two passages show that for a period during the reign of Eadred, the king's *suppellectiles*, comprising charters and treasures, were entrusted for safe-keeping to various people (and so were presumably kept at various places), of whom Dunstan (at Glastonbury) was one, though he received the 'best'. It was a temporary rather than a permanent arrangement, for the king eventually instructed the 'keepers of the royal treasures' to return the goods to him on his deathbed for distribution.[223] The interesting feature of the tradition in the present context is the association of the royal archives and the royal treasures: and while it is not entirely clear what objects are referred to as the ancient *thesauri* of preceding kings and the *gazae* acquired by Eadred himself,[224] it is not unlikely that they included some of the surplus holy relics in the royal collection. More explicit references to the keeping of documents with the king's relics appear from the late tenth century onwards. S 939, by which King Æthelred granted that the will of Æthelric of Bocking might stand, ends with the declaration:

þissa gewrita syndon þreo. an is æt x̄pes cyrcean. oðer æt þæs cinges haligdome. þridde hæfð seo wuduwe.

Haligdom had the meaning 'relics' or 'holy things', but it could also denote a sanctuary or holy place. Thus the second copy of S 939 was to be kept 'at the king's sanctuary'. Such an expression does not necessarily imply that the *haligdom* where the archives were kept was

---

[221] Stubbs, *Memorials*, p. 29; Whitelock, *EHD*, p. 900.
[222] Stubbs, *Memorials*, p. 31; Whitelock, *EHD*, p. 900.
[223] For possible diplomatic repercussions of this arrangement, see above, pp. 46–8
[224] Mr Eric John, in a personal communication, suggests to me that the distinction here between the *thesauri* of preceding kings and the *gazae* acquired by Eadred himself may anticipate the post-Conquest legal distinction between inherited property and property acquired *ex conquestu*.

a fixed place: other analogous statements are generally to be translated 'with the king's relics' or 'amongst the king's treasures',[225] and in this sense it seems that the archives, like the relics and treasures, would be peripatetic with the king.[226] Documents may have been kept with the relics because they gained additional strength from the association,[227] for ease of access should reference need to be made to them, or because their intrinsic value meant that they were regarded as properly a part of the royal treasures. It would appear to follow that custody of the king's relics would have involved an additional responsibility for the royal archives, and herein lies the interest of the Abingdon glossarist's equation of the *scrinium* with the *cancellaria* and of the *scriniarius* with the *cancellarius*: the association seems entirely appropriate, for it is clear that one prerequisite for the production of official documents, including royal diplomas, was access to a store of other documents for use as models.

One should not discount the possibility that the office of *cancellarius* was known in Anglo-Saxon England, though its holder might not always have been dignified with so specific a title. King Æthelred's *scriptor* Ælfwine was described as a *minister*, and the *cancellarius* of the Abingdon glossary was described as a *burþen*: if the person who discharged the function of a chancellor was regarded first and foremost as a member of the king's household, it would be impossible to distinguish him from the other *ministri* who attested royal diplomas; indeed, whether he was a *minister* or one of the king's priests we should not necessarily expect him to have been included amongst the witnesses at all.[228] But in the reign of Edward the

---

225 See S 981, 1478 and 1521; also Blake, *Liber Eliensis*, p. 158, and Macray, *Chronicon*, p. 172.

226 Hart, 'Codex Wintoniensis', pp. 18–19, locates the *haligdom* and the royal archives at Winchester; but valid objections to the argument were raised by Brooks, 'Anglo-Saxon Charters', p. 228. Of the diplomas in the *Codex Wintoniensis* marked by Hart as possibly derived from the royal archives, several are clearly earlier title-deeds for estates acquired by the Old Minster, while some of those that relate to estates with no known connection with the Old Minster were probably deposited in the archives by laymen for safe-keeping.

227 As implied by Wormald, 'Sherborne "Cartulary" ', p. 107.

228 Titstan and Winstan, respectively *cubicularius* and *camerarius/cubicularius* (and thus *burðegnas*) of King Edgar (see below, p. 159 n. 24), do not appear to have attested any of his diplomas. Priests occur quite regularly in the lists attached to the diplomas of Edward the Elder, but thereafter they are rarely included amongst the witnesses until the reigns of Cnut, Harthacnut and Edward the Confessor: see Larson, *King's Household*, pp. 138–42, and Barlow, *English Church*, pp. 130–4.

Confessor the draftsmen of diplomas were sometimes prepared to specify the positions held by particular witnesses in the king's household, and to include the king's priests in the witness lists. Many of the diplomas in question are demonstrably spurious, but their witness lists seem to be based on genuine pre-Conquest material; moreover, the diplomas have different provenances and therefore tend to corroborate one another, while some of the identified officials also occur in other contexts. In a group of diplomas probably forged by Osbert de Clare in the twelfth century one finds a reference to 'Wulfwius regie dignitatis cancellarius'[229] and three references to 'Reinbaldus (regis) cancellarius';[230] in two instances Reinbald (Regenbald) is associated with a *notarius* called Swithgar who seems to have been responsible for the actual writing of the text,[231] and in the third with a *notarius* called Ælfgeat.[232] Two diplomas that appear to be independent of this group and of each other suggest that Osbert was not inventing these officials. S 1033 (in favour of St Mary's Rouen) has the subscription of 'Regenboldus regis sigillarius', and S 1036 (in favour of Waltham Abbey) has the subscription of 'Regenbaldus regis cancellarius', as well as the statement 'Hec ego conscripsi Swidgar sub nomine Cristi ✠' at the bottom of the witness list.[233] Several of the other royal officials mentioned in S 1036 recur with the same status in S 1042, from Wells,[234] and some of the identifications in both diplomas find support from incidental references to pre-Conquest officials given in *Domesday Book*:[235] if we can accept on this evidence

---

[229] S 1011; for 'Wulfwius', see Harmer, *Writs*, pp. 60–1.

[230] S 1030, 1041 and 1043.

[231] S 1030 and 1043.   [232] S 1041.

[233] Note that Kemble's text of S 1036 (KCD 813) is printed from a manuscript (S, MS 1) in which several of the witnesses' names are given in a corrupt form; the orthography in S, MSS 2 and 3, is clearly pre-Conquest.

[234] Cf. 'Esgarus regie procurator aulae', 'Radulphus regis aulicus' and 'Bundinus regis palatinus' in S 1036 with 'Esgar procur'', 'Raulf procur'' and 'Bundi procur'' in S 1042; 'Wigodus regis pincerna' and 'Herdingus regine pincerna' in S 1036 with 'Wigod pinc'' and 'Heardyng pinc'' in S 1042.

[235] Asgar and Raulf occur frequently in *Domesday Book* described as stallers; each occurs as 'regis dapifer' in S 1029. Bondig occurs as *constabularius* in DB i, fo. 151r, and as *stalr* in DB i, fo. 218v; he occurs as a *stabulator* in S 1235. All three are described as stallers in S 1426. S 1042 has the subscription of 'Winsi cubicul'', doubtless the 'Wenesi camerarius R.E.' of DB i, fo. 151r. The (queen's) butler Herding of S 1036 and 1042 is perhaps the Herding who held land from Queen Edith (DB i, fo. 63v). It is against this background that we should judge the description of Regenbald as *canceler* in an Edwardian context in DB i, fo. 180v.

that the draftsman of the witness list attached to S 1036 had in front of him a genuine pre-Conquest text that specified the offices held by certain witnesses, it would seem entirely reasonable to allow that his description of Regenbald as *cancellarius* and his reference to Swithgar came from the same source, and in turn therefore to accept that Edward the Confessor had an official at court known to some as his *cancellarius*,[236] assisted by a person who described himself as a *notarius*. The description elsewhere of this official as the king's *sigillarius* suggests that the office of chancellor involved custody of the king's seal and is not at all far-fetched given the fact that sealed writs were certainly produced during this period. Perhaps it would be hazardous to argue from this evidence that because King Æthelred too is known to have had a seal he may also have had an official who discharged the responsibilities associated with a chancellor; yet the argument would not stand without support from other directions, and if such an official is not actually mentioned by name before Edward's reign it may only be because the draftsmen of royal diplomas were not then accustomed to be so specific.

The evidence from pre-Conquest sources discussed above puts in perspective a well-known passage from the *Liber Eliensis*, probably written in the mid twelfth century, in a chapter whose theme is the good relations enjoyed by Ely Abbey with King Æthelred as benefactor:

Statuit vero atque concessit, quatenus ecclesia de Ely ex tunc et semper in regis curia cancellarii ageret dignitatem, quod etiam aliis, Sancti videlicet Augustini et Glestonie, ecclesiis constituit, ut abbates istorum cenobiorum vicissim adsignatis succedendo temporibus annum tripharie dividerent, cum sanctuariis et ceteris ornatibus altaris ministrando. Abbas quoque Elyensis cenobii semper in die purificationis sancte Marie ad administratorium opus procedebat in ipso Februarii mensis initio et sic ipse abbas, vel quem de fratribus destinaret, quantum temporis ei suppetebat per iiii menses, tertiam videlicet anni partem, cum summa diligentia illic officium reverenter supplevit, deinde alii, quos diximus, residuum anni per adsignata sibi tempora explicabant.[237]

---

[236] Harmer, *Writs*, pp. 59–60, Bishop and Chaplais, *Facsimiles of Writs*, p. xiii, Barraclough, 'Anglo-Saxon Writ', p. 213, Hall, *Studies*, pp. 164–5, Barlow, *English Church*, pp. 120–1 and 129, Stenton, *Latin Charters*, pp. 86–7, Chrimes, *Administrative History*, p. 16 n. 2, and others, are more sceptical about the evidence for the existence of the office of *cancellarius* before the Conquest. Cf. Round, *Feudal England*, pp. 421–30, Larson, *King's Household*, pp. 143–5, and Davis, *Regesta*, pp. xiii–xv.

[237] Blake, *Liber Eliensis*, pp. 146–7; see also Galbraith, *Studies*, pp. 39–40, Chaplais, 'Anglo-Saxon Chancery', p. 49, and Gransden, *Historical Writing*, p. 276.

This arrangement, whereby the abbots of Ely, St Augustine's Canterbury and Glastonbury were to discharge in rotation the office of chancellor in the king's court, is said to have been established by King Æthelred and to have lasted until the Norman Conquest. In his account of King Cnut's visit to Ely to celebrate the Purification of St Mary, the author of the *Liber Eliensis* refers again to the arrangement, remarking that the visit took place at the time when the abbots of Ely were accustomed to begin their 'ministerium in regis curia'.[238] It is difficult to disregard this Ely tradition entirely, as an anachronistic figment of a fertile post-Conquest imagination, but equally it is difficult to accept the tradition as it stands, for it finds no corroboration in the recorded traditions of the two other houses involved,[239] and no apparent reflection in the diplomas of the late tenth and eleventh centuries.[240] At least we can say that a monk of Ely in the mid twelfth century had no reason not to believe that there was an office of *cancellarius* in the later Anglo-Saxon period, that indeed he thought there was such an office, and that he associated it with the custody of the sanctuaries and of other ornaments of the altar.

To summarize the foregoing: there is evidence for the existence, during the reign of King Æthelred, of a royal secretariat responsible for the production of administrative communications and other documents associated with the exercise of government, and there is also evidence that Æthelred had a seal and that his archives were kept with the royal collection of relics; a glossarist at Abingdon in the first half of the eleventh century equated the office of *scriniarius*, implying custody of the relics (and so significantly of the royal archives as well), with the office of *cancellarius*, and certain diplomas

---

238 Blake, *Liber Eliensis*, p. 153.

239 *Ibid.* p. 146 n. 1.

240 This may not be significant, for one could not justify the required assumptions that the draftsman of a diploma was accorded special prominence in the witness list or that the work of the different abbots would be individually distinctive; moreover, one would not expect the abbots of two of the houses concerned to be absent from meetings of the king's council during that part of the year in which they were not discharging the office of chancellor, and therefore the operation of the rotation would not necessarily be reflected in the witness lists (cf. Barlow, *English Church*, p. 125); again, one could not assume that all the abbots present at a meeting would be included in a witness list. For what they are worth, the subscriptions of the abbots of Ely, St Augustine's Canterbury and Glastonbury in Æthelred's diplomas may be studied in Tables 4 and 5; see also below, pp. 190 (Sigeric of St Augustine's Canterbury) and 191 (Ælfweard of Glastonbury).

of King Edward the Confessor appear to confirm that the office of *cancellarius* was a familiar one in his reign. It therefore seems reasonable to interpret in terms of a central and royal writing office the extensive diplomatic evidence for the production of royal diplomas by an agency that catered for all types of beneficiary and that was able to operate on the occasion of the *witenagemot*: it may have been less well developed in the tenth century than in the eleventh century, and it may never have had a complete monopoly of the production of royal diplomas, but by the close of the Anglo-Saxon period it had become an organization which contemporaries could dignify with the officials and status of a *cancellaria*. Thus when the author of the *Constitutio Domus Regis*, describing the composition of the king's household in the reign of Henry I, indicated that the chancellor and the *magister scriptorii* were closely associated with the 'chaplain in charge of the chapel and of the relics',[241] he was depicting an office that had been developing throughout the tenth and eleventh centuries.[242]

[241] Johnson, *Dialogus*, p. 129; see also Galbraith, *Studies*, pp. 40–1.
[242] I should emphasize that the concept of a royal secretariat or central writing office is introduced above for the sake of convenience (cf. the usage of Tessier, *Diplomatique royale française*, p. 2), and not because there is any conclusive evidence that the presumed royal scribes were organized into a department. It is likely that the king's household clerks played an important part in the royal secretariat: for an excellent account of Anglo-Saxon court ecclesiastics (though differing in some respects from the views above), see Barlow, *English Church*, pp. 119–34; on the Continent (and doubtless to some extent also in England) the function of a royal writing office was discharged by members of the royal chapel, and not by scribes organized into an independent department (see Fleckenstein, *Die Hofkapelle*, pp. 74–95, for the ninth century; also Klewitz, 'Cancellaria', pp. 13–40, and Tessier, *Diplomatique royale française*, pp. 55–7 and 130–2, covering wider ground).

Chapter 4

A FRAMEWORK FOR THE REIGN OF KING ÆTHELRED

THE COMPOSITION OF THE WITNESS LISTS

King Æthelred II became best known to posterity as a king without a well-planned and well-executed stratagem to his credit, or as one continually misled and periodically betrayed by his ill-chosen councillors, a reputation itself epitomized by his epithet *unræd*, latterly 'the Unready'.[1] The annals of the *Anglo-Saxon Chronicle* portray the king acting with his *witan* on several occasions, but while the chronicler was often ready to bemoan the dire political and military consequences of the decisions they took, he affords little idea of the circumstances or people behind them. The witness lists attached to the royal diplomas issued in King Æthelred's name provide invaluable and largely untapped evidence for establishing who was in attendance on the king at any one time, and therefore who may have influenced him and participated in the decisions; in fact, they enable the historian to perceive developments at the level of the king's council which serve to modify in certain respects the traditional and prevailing picture of the reign.

The witness lists are not, however, without their limitations as sources of information about the identity of those in closest personal contact with the king. This is not because they are the products of wishful thinking, for as we have seen there are good grounds for believing that they reflect actual attendance at meetings of the *witan*.[2] It is rather because we are so often dependent on cartulary texts and have to admit the possibility that a list has become corrupt or has been abbreviated during the course of transmission,[3] and also because the arrangement and scope of the list on the original diploma were directly affected by certain external factors and

[1] See further Keynes, 'Declining Reputation'.
[2] See above, pp. 130–4.
[3] The instances of such corruption and abbreviation are discussed in Appendix 1.

conventions. The overall length of a list was determined in the first instance by the dimensions of the membrane selected for use,[4] and so by the amount of space left after the text itself had been inscribed. The number of names included in each category of witnesses was then determined by the convention that the successive columns should balance one another and should be discrete in their composition:[5] for example, the bishops might be given in the first column, the abbots and the ealdormen in the second, and the *ministri* in the third and fourth. Consequently, while we may assume that those named in a witness list were present together at a *witenage-mot*, we cannot assume that the list is proportionally representative of *all* those present.[6] The holders of high ecclesiastical and secular office are represented best, probably at the expense of several abbots and a large number of thegns who had gathered for the occasion but who were not sufficiently prominent to be included in the list. These considerations in turn affect the more specific problem of identifying in the witness lists those men most likely to have exercised an important influence over the king. The only criteria available for judging whether one man was arguably more influential than another are the frequency of his subscriptions combined with the relative position accorded to him in the lists, and both criteria are admittedly fallible. The inclusion of some witnesses was doubtless little more than a formality and could not be taken to indicate that they necessarily played any part in the deliberations of king and council; equally, we may imagine that the king numbered amongst his advisers and associates men (and women) who may have had no place in the witness lists of royal diplomas. But many of the holders of high office in the kingdom (whether archbishop, bishop, abbot

---

[4] Stenton, *Anglo-Saxon England*, p. 551. Oleson, *Witenagemot*, pp. 39–40, asserts that 'the scribe would first inscribe the charter and only then cut the parchment. Thus the length of the charter with its witness list would determine the size of the parchment'. But examination of the originals generally reveals that the scribe pricked and ruled the parchment before inscribing it, and that the extent of preparation (i.e. number of lines ruled) was determined by the size of the parchment; sometimes it appears that a certain area was prepared, and then the parchment was cut. Oleson's view implies that the scribe would rule the lines as he inscribed the text, which seems rather unlikely.

[5] Bishop Ælfgar attests S 916 'cum reliquis coepiscopis', and since his name occurs at the bottom of a column one suspects that the scribe did not want to continue with the bishops into the next column. Thus absence from a list need not automatically imply absence from the *witenagemot*.

[6] Note in this connection the formula introducing the witness lists in S 661 and 694.

or ealdorman) would presumably have owed their appointment in the first place to royal patronage, and would have been in regular attendance at meetings of the *witan* by virtue of the offices they held and so in a position to influence the king in matters of policy; they would have been consulted if not by right then at least by good custom and because their opinions were valued by the king who had appointed them.[7] Their position in this respect may not always have been maintained during the reign of a succeeding king with different inclinations and sympathies, though they would have continued to attest his diplomas. In seeking to identify those who were numbered amongst a king's influential advisers one should therefore be careful to bear in mind a distinction between office-holders appointed by the king himself and office-holders inherited from his predecessors. One should also bear in mind the possibility that the position of a witness within his respective group was affected by the relative distinction of the office he held or by his seniority of appointment.

In the case of the episcopacy, it is noticeable that the more recently appointed bishops often appear in the lower reach of a list, and that the bishops of some geographically peripheral sees also tend to occur towards the end (see Tables 2 and 3), but there are enough exceptions and anomalies to suggest that positioning was not determined in every instance by the application of such impersonal factors;[8] indeed, it is doubtful that the sees other than Canterbury and York could be arranged in an order of their relative importance. Accordingly, the factor underlying the order of precedence that can sometimes be detected in the higher reaches of the lists was probably the personal influence of the bishops in question, and did not affect the greater part of the episcopacy in any obvious way. The composition of the groups of abbots differs from that of the groups of bishops in that a much smaller proportion of the full complement occurs

---

[7] It is worth recalling that Dunstan was ordained bishop 'eotenus maxime quo regali præsentiæ propter provida prudentiarum suarum consilia jugiter adfuisset' (Stubbs, *Memorials*, p. 36).

[8] Note in particular the subscriptions of Ælfhun, bishop of London, and of Æthelwold II, bishop of Winchester, compared with those of their respective predecessors. It was some time before the long-serving Athulf of Hereford ascended to the upper reaches of the lists, but Wulfstan of London is consistently prominent from the occasion of his first appearance. See also Barlow, *English Church*, p. 238.

consistently: there appear to have been between twenty-five and thirty religious houses (not all of which can be identified) whose abbots attested diplomas during Æthelred's reign, but only three or four of the abbots are ever prominent for an extended period, and the majority occur only sporadically. One should remember, of course, that the king would have had less control over appointments to abbacies than to the other high offices, and this may have meant that abbots in general were not given an opportunity to exert a degree of influence comparable with that of the bishops and ealdormen,[9] unless they first gained the confidence of the king in their own right. Since there is no indication that certain abbeys, and therefore their abbots, were accorded precedence over others, a case could be made for regarding the abbots who do occur consistently and prominently as those who had gained a special position in the king's council, at least in relation to their colleagues.

The lists of ealdormen constitute the most regular of the various groups of witnesses, and it is clear that an order of precedency based essentially on seniority of appointment was generally observed. One could divide the period from 978 until 1009 × 12[10] into four shorter terms, defined by the precedency of Ælfhere of Mercia (978–83), Æthelwine of East Anglia (983–92), Æthelweard of the Western Provinces (992–8) and Ælfric of Hampshire (999–1009× 12): when, during this period, an ealdorman died or went into exile, the one immediately after him in the lists took over his place, leaving the relative order of the rest undisturbed; new appointees were invariably introduced at the bottom of the lists (see Table 6). Since ealdormen who died (or went into exile) were not always replaced at once, if at all, the total number attesting from one period to another tends to vary, but between such events it is generally constant, suggesting that it was normal practice for all the current ealdormen to attend meetings of the *witan* and to be included in the witness lists; the only ealdormen who do not appear consistently

---

[9] It appears from the omission of abbots in some diplomas (S 838, 842, 850, 852, 862, 885 and 889, leaving aside truncated or unreliable lists) that their position in councils was not assured; see above, p. 118. The reference to the council at Cirencester in 985 (above, p. 128) seems to imply that no abbots were present; see also below, p. 181 n. 103. For provisions for the appointment of abbots, see Barlow, *English Church*, pp. 316, 318, 320–1, Bates, *Muchelney*, p. 41 n., and John, *Orbis Britanniae*, pp. 185, 187–8, 208 n.

[10] The later limit is unclear because there are no diplomas dated 1010 and because the only ones for 1011 do not name the ealdormen individually.

during their periods of office are some of northern origin.[11] Against the background of such regularity determined by seniority, it is very difficult to penetrate the lists of ealdormen in an attempt to discern their relative influence with the king. However, the regularity was dramatically broken in the period 1009 × 12–1016, with considerable historical implications to be discussed presently.

Especial interest attaches to the groups of *ministri* who subscribe Æthelred's diplomas, because they are the most likely to include men who owed their presence to a personal link with the king, perhaps consolidated by tenure of office within the king's household. Writing in the 990s, Ælfric reminded Ealdorman Æthelweard that

> An woruld-cynincg hæfð fela þegna
> and mislice wicneras . he ne mæg beon wurðful cynincg
> buton he hæbbe þa geþincðe þe him gebyriað.
> and swylce þening-men . þe þeawfæstnysse him gebeodon.[12]

The few available references which bear on the organization of the king's household suggest that there was some degree of specialization amongst the thegns and officials of Ælfric's text. Asser refers to the noble thegns (*ministri nobiles*) of King Alfred who resided in turn at the royal court, 'in pluribus ministrantes ministeriis', and he describes how the king allotted one-sixth of his annual income to his fighting men and to his household thegns, 'unicuique tamen secundum propriam dignitatem et etiam secundum proprium ministerium';[13] likewise in his will, Alfred bequeathes 200 pounds to 'þam mannum þe me folgiað . . . ælcum swa him to gebyrian wille æfter þære wisan þe ic him nu dælde'.[14] So apparently the thegns discharged various offices and were rewarded accordingly in different proportions, though very little can be glimpsed of the nature of this specialization.[15] In the will of King Eadred, however,

---

[11] Ælfhelm and Uhtred occur quite frequently (during the periods 993–1005 and 1009–15 respectively), but Thored is 'absent' in 980–2 and again in 986–8, while Northman and Waltheof make only a single appearance each, in 994.

[12] Skeat, *Lives of Saints* I, 6.

[13] Stevenson, *Asser*, pp. 86–7; Whitelock, *EHD*, p. 301.

[14] S 1507 (Harmer, *Select Documents*, no. XI, p. 18).

[15] The witness list of S 348 (purportedly issued in 892) includes the subscriptions of Deormod *cell[erarius]*, Ælfric *thes[aurariu]s* and Sigewulf *pinc[erna]*, between two priests and several *milites*. There may be a genuine basis to these identifications: Deormod occurs quite frequently as a prominent *minister* in the late ninth and early tenth centuries; Ælfric the 'treasurer' is conceivably the Ælfric *hrælðen* who was apparently an official of King Alfred's (S 1445); a Sigulf *minister* occurs in S 1508, dated between 871 and 888.

bequests are made more specifically to 'ælcan gesettan discðegne and gesettan hræglðene and gesettan biriele', as well as to 'ælcan minra mæssepreosta . . . ælcan þæra oþerra preosta . . . ælcan gesettan stigweard . . . and ælcan þæra þe is on minnum hirede, si swilcre note nyt swilc he sy'.[16] The *discðegnas*, *hræglðegnas* and *byrelas* were presumably the most important among these officials of the king's household, but little more is heard of them in other vernacular sources. They are, however, more familiar under their respective Latin titles: Ælfric used the word *discðen*, 'seneschal' as a gloss for *discifer*, and the word *byrle*, 'butler', for *pincerna*;[17] if a *hræglðegn*, who was by definition responsible for the king's wardrobe, was more generally regarded as the keeper of the king's chamber, he may be better known as a *burðegn*, that is, as a *camerarius* or *cubicularius*.[18] Occurrences of men designated by these Latin titles are not uncommon in the royal diplomas of the tenth century:[19] *disciferi* occur amongst the witnesses to diplomas of Æthelstan,[20] Eadwig[21] and Edgar;[22] *pincernae* occur in the diplomas of Eadwig;[23] and the beneficiaries of Edgar's diplomas include *cubicularii* and *camerarii*.[24]

[16] S 1515 (Harmer, *Select Documents*, no. XXI, p. 35).

[17] Zupitza, *Grammatik*, pp. 315 and 303. The eleventh-century glossary in B.L. Add. 32246 (above, p. 145 n. 218) provides *discþen* for *discifer uel discoforus*, and *byrle* for *pincerna* (Wright and Wülcker, *Vocabularies* I, cols. 126 and 189). In another glossary, B.L. Harley 3376, the words *discoforus, discifer* are glossed *stiweard* (*ibid.* col. 223): so the *stigweardas* of Eadred's will may have performed the same function as the *discðegnas*, though they were clearly of inferior status. (In S 835 there is a reference to Æthelbriht, an *oeconomus* who had given land to King Edgar: *economus* is the lemma for *stiward* in B.L. Add. 32246 (*ibid.* col. 129).)

[18] See Larson, *King's Household*, pp. 128–9, and Harmer, *Select Documents*, p. 122. *Hræglðegn* does not seem to occur in the glossaries; in B.L. Cotton Cleopatra A iii, *vestiarius* is glossed *hræglweard* (Wright and Wülcker, *Vocabularies* I, col. 279). *Burþen* is the gloss for *cubicularius* in B.L. Add. 32246 and for *camerarius* in B.L. Harley 3376 (*ibid.* cols. 124 and 198); *bedþen* is the gloss for *camerarius* in B.L. Add. 32246 and for *cubicularius, custos cubili* in B.L. Harley 3376 (*ibid.* cols. 124 and 216).

[19] For earlier occurrences of *pincernae*, see S 24, 57 and 164; the subscription of 'Eatta dux et regis discifer' occurs in S 124.

[20] S 396–7 and 450; see also Barker, 'Two Lost Documents', pp. 138–41.

[21] S 597, 651 and 658.

[22] S 768, 782 (in which the *disc*' of the copyist's exemplar was expanded incorrectly to *discipulus*) and 792.

[23] S 651 and 658. In the latter, three witnesses are described as *custos*, perhaps for *custos cubilis*, i.e. *cubicularius* (above, n. 18).

[24] S 706 (Titstan *cubicularius*); S 713 (Æthelsige *camerarius*); S 719 (Winstan *camerarius*); S 789 (Winstan *cubicularius*); the endorsements on S 706 and 789 describe the beneficiary as the king's *burðen*. The Æthelsige *camerarius* of S 713 may be the Æthelsige *pedisecus* of S 768, and *pedisequi* also occur as the beneficiaries of S 520 and 569, in the name of King Eadred: the word *pedisequus* was used in the ninth century apparently as a synonym for *minister* (see Larson, *King's Household*, pp. 123–4, and S 168–70, 188, 328, 1434, 1436 and

Where such officials are found in the witness lists they are generally positioned immediately after the ealdormen and so at the head of the groups of *ministri*.[25] Indeed, it seems that they were normally described simply as *ministri*,[26] since they bear the names of contemporary and prominent thegns who would otherwise be conspicuously absent from the lists in which the distinctive titles occur; the use of these titles would thus have depended on particular draftsmen deciding at random to be more specific. It follows that the consistency in the composition of the upper reaches of the lists of *ministri*, so noticeable in the diplomas of the tenth and early eleventh centuries, can be regarded as a reflection of the membership of the king's household;[27] this 'official' element in the lists might be supplemented by other laymen who owed their prominence to, for example, a family relationship with the king and who may not also have held office in his household.[28]

Consistency of composition is nowhere more striking than in the lists of *ministri* attached to the diplomas of King Æthelred (see Tables 7 and 8). In S 853, dated 984 and (perhaps significantly?) issued in favour of the king's *scriptor* Ælfwine, a distinction unique in them is made between four *disciferi*, four *pincernae* and eleven *ministri*, and if we may assume that the men given these titles, unfortunately not named by the copyist, were the same ones who consistently occur at the head of the lists of *ministri* in the 980s,

---

1861), but in S 768 a distinction seems to be implied between the *pedisecus* and the other *ministri*.

[25] As in S 396–7, 450, 597 (in the manuscript, though arrangement in BCS is muddling), 768, 782 and 792. In S 651 they occur after the king's kinsmen Ælfgar and Brihtferth, and in S 658 three *ministri*, including Ælfgar and Brihtferth, occur between the *custodes* (who follow the second ealdorman) and the *discifer*.

[26] The word *minister* could clearly conceal more subtle distinctions of status: S 853 is in favour of the king's *minister*, 'videlicet meo scriptori'; S 910 and 969 are both in favour of *ministri*, but we discover from their endorsements that the beneficiaries were respectively a reeve and a housecarl.

[27] It is difficult to detect in tenth-century diplomas any sign of rotation amongst the household thegns (as practised in Alfred's court: Stevenson, *Asser*, pp. 86–7). During the reign of Cnut, and particularly during the reign of Edward the Confessor, there seems to have been a greater degree of fluctuation in the composition of the attesting groups of *ministri*: this may reflect rotation, or it may suggest that the element in permanent or frequent attendance on the king had been considerably reduced, and that a greater proportion of the thegns was derived from the area where the *witenagemot* was held; cf. Oleson, *Witenagemot*, pp. 55–9.

[28] This statement probably applies to the king's kinsman Ælfgar and his brother Brihtferth (S 651; in S 692 both are called *consul*), who were prominent during the reigns of Eadwig and Edgar: see Hart, *Charters of Northern England*, pp. 254–5 and 301.

then we may infer that the lists were dominated by members of the king's household.[29] The same interpretation should hold good for the later diplomas of King Æthelred: the vernacular version of S 914 – spurious as it stands, but with a witness list that must derive from a genuine source and that was written down in the first half of the eleventh century – describes the consistently prominent Æthelmær as 'mines hlafordes discðen' and Leofric as *hrægelðen*, though the Latin version describes each simply as *minister*. The witness lists thus serve as an invaluable guide to the composition of a group of laymen who would have been in frequent and intimate attendance on the king, and who as his personal officials may have exerted considerable influence on his decisions.

The eleven *ministri* who followed the *disciferi* and *pincernae* in S 853 perhaps represent an 'unofficial' element in attendance at a *witenagemot*, whose composition varied considerably as the king moved from one place to another. We have seen that in some cases the lower reach of a witness list contains a group of thegns who can be identified as 'local', that is, as thegns whose interests lay in a particular area and whose presence might identify the locality where the *witenagemot* was held.[30] It is this element, together with the many thegns who must have gathered from other parts of the country for important meetings, that is least well represented in the witness lists of tenth- and eleventh-century diplomas: for on average the lists of *ministri* are of such a length that (on the analogy of S 853) they would largely comprise members of the king's household. The document confirming the will of Æthelric of Bocking in the late tenth century (S 939) suggests the problem: those actually mentioned as present at the *witenagemot* (held at Cookham in Berkshire) are those whose subscriptions are commonly recorded in contemporary diplomas, but a remark which follows this list reveals that many other thegns from all over the country were present, though too numerous to be named individually: 'and ealle ða ðegnas ðe þær widan gegæderode wæron ægðer. ge of Westsexan. ge of Myrcean. ge of Denon. ge. of Englon.' The reference to

---

[29] According to the spurious S 897, King Æthelred had a *pincerna* called Wulfgar, who received a grant of land in 983 (S 851, in which he is called the king's *homo*); there are, however, no subscriptions of a Wulfgar in the reign before 997.

[30] See above, pp. 132–4.

'Danes', presumably a generic term for the inhabitants of the Danelaw, is of much interest. There are only two diplomas of King Æthelred which include several *ministri* with Scandinavian names amongst the witnesses, and these are the two with the longest witness lists of all.[31] Because the diplomas are in this respect exceptional, we cannot tell whether the presence of 'Danes' (as at the Cookham meeting) was itself exceptional: they may represent unusually large meetings, attended by *ministri* from all over the country, for which correspondingly large pieces of parchment were chosen, or they may represent ordinary meetings, but again attended by *ministri* from all over the country, for which unusually large pieces of parchment were chosen.

Under normal circumstances, one would expect the selection of *ministri* who frequently attest Æthelred's diplomas to change almost imperceptibly, as at different times individuals died or left the royal service and were replaced by others: the respective periods during which particular *ministri* were prominent should begin and end at various points throughout the reign as if at random. But the circumstances do not appear to have been normal, for the witness lists suggest rather that distinctive *groups* of *ministri* were prominent in successive periods. When these developments are synchronized with developments in the other categories of witnesses, and when all are set against the background provided by such narrative sources as are available, it emerges that there were certain events in Æthelred's reign which apparently led to significant changes of policy or attitude on the part of the king, reflected by the prominence at different times of particular factions, each of which was presumably in a position to have exercised a dominant influence over him in its own interests. In this way we may establish for the reign of King Æthelred a working framework which serves to restore a sense of perspective to the interpretation of a period known otherwise only from sources written at its close.[32]

---

[31] S 911 and 922. See Stenton, 'Danes in England', p. 153 n. 1, and *idem, Anglo-Saxon England*, p. 551 n. 1.

[32] On the date of the account of the reign in the *Anglo-Saxon Chronicle*, see Keynes, 'Declining Reputation', pp. 229–31.

THE PERIOD OF TUTELAGE, 978-984

DCCCCLXXVIII Her wearð Eadweard cyning ofslegen. On þis ylcan geare feng Æðelred æðeling his broðor to rice.[33]

The laconic annal in the Parker Chronicle gives little away itself, but later generations of historians were to find the key to the understanding of Æthelred's unhappy reign in the circumstances of his accession, following the murder of his half-brother Edward on 18 March 978.[34] Already in the eleventh century, and then throughout the Middle Ages, the series of unrelenting Danish invasions which eventually brought about the fall of Æthelred's kingdom was regarded as divine punishment for the crime. More rational historians have attributed the success of the Danes in part to the incapacity of King Æthelred for organizing any effective opposition to them, and in part to the disloyalty shown by the English towards their king and his cause: Æthelred's own behaviour is regarded as that of a king aware of his subjects' distrust, which in turn is said to have arisen from their dismay about Edward's murder.[35] It is therefore a matter of some importance to establish if possible what factors lay behind the murder of Edward, and to ascertain whether or not contemporaries attached any blame for the crime to Æthelred himself.

The problem of choosing a successor to King Edgar in 975 could not be resolved by the application of any clearly-defined principles. The eldest son of a king did not automatically succeed to the kingdom on his father's death, but rather the succession belonged to that member of the royal family who was considered the most 'throne-worthy' by those left in effective control. Edgar was survived by two sons, born of different mothers. According to Osbern of Canterbury, writing in the 1080s, Edward was his son by a nameless veiled virgin of Wilton Abbey whom he had seduced,[36] but according to Eadmer of Canterbury, writing a generation later than Osbern, Edward was the legitimate son of Edgar's wife Æthelflæd

---

[33] Plummer, *Chronicles* I, 122.
[34] For the date of Edward's murder, see Appendix 1, p. 233 n. 7.
[35] See, e.g., Stenton, *Anglo-Saxon England*, pp. 373-4.
[36] Stubbs, *Memorials*, pp. xcix–c and 111–12.

'the White';[37] Edgar had married again by 964,[38] so Edward was probably born before then, making him at least eleven years old on his father's death. Æthelred was Edgar's son by his wife Ælfthryth, the one whom the king had married by 964; there was a first son of this marriage called Edmund, who died in 971,[39] so Æthelred himself may not have been born before 966, making him a child not more than nine years old when his father died.[40] Between two such young children there may not have been much to choose, and it is clear that the question of which one should succeed Edgar in 975 was hotly disputed by the leading men of the kingdom. The controversy appears to have turned (at least outwardly) on one or more of three issues, each conceived as an objection to Edward rather than as a positive point in favour of Æthelred. In the first place, there seem to have been some doubts about the legitimacy of Edward. As we have seen, Osbern of Canterbury asserted that Edward was the offspring of an illicit union between Edgar and a nun of Wilton, and there is further evidence that Edward's status was considered dubious even during Edgar's lifetime. His mother does not attest any of Edgar's diplomas, whereas Ælfthryth occurs as queen in 964 and several times thereafter; in the New Minster foundation charter (S 745, dated 966) Ælfthryth is described in the witness list as 'legitima prefati regis conjuncx', seeming to imply a distinction between herself and a wife who was not legitimate. In the same list Edmund, Edgar's eldest son by Ælfthryth, is described as 'clito legitimus prefati regis filius', and is positioned in front of his elder half-brother Edward, who is described simply as 'eodem rege clito procreatus', so the distinction between the wives may have extended to the sons.[41] Again, in the will of Ealdorman Ælfheah (S 1485) bequests are made to the Lord (represented by three abbeys), to King Edgar and to Queen Ælfthryth, followed by bequests to

[37] *Ibid.* p. 210; see also Stafford, 'A Study in Limitations', p. 40 n. 26.

[38] See Whitelock, *Wills*, p. 121.

[39] The manuscripts of the *Chronicle* place Edmund's death variously in 970, 971 or 972, but all agree in placing it two years before the coronation of Edgar, dated variously 972, 973 or 974 (for 973).

[40] According to William of Malmesbury, Æthelred was seven years old in 975 (Stubbs, *De Gestis Regum Anglorum* I, 181), but the authority for this statement is uncertain. It may be significant that Æthelred was not included in the witness list of S 745, issued in 966.

[41] John, *Orbis Britanniae*, pp. 274–5; see also Finberg, *Tavistock*, p. 279 n. 10, and Dumville, 'The Ætheling', pp. 30–1, and cf. Fisher, 'Anti-monastic Reaction', p. 269.

'þam yldran æþælingæ þæs cyngæs suna. and hiræ', i.e. Edmund, and to 'þam gincgran' (atheling), i.e. Æthelred, perhaps pointedly omitting any mention of their elder half-brother Edward. In short, it may have been Edmund who was regarded as heir apparent until his premature death in 971, and since his position appears to have been determined by his legitimacy it would then arguably have been inherited by his younger brother Æthelred. A second objection to Edward arose even if it was conceded that he was the son of a legitimate union between Edgar and Æthelflæd the White: for according to Eadmer, some of the leading men opposed the choice of Edward 'quia matrem ejus, licet legaliter nuptam, in regnum tamen non magis quam patrem ejus, dum eum genuit, sacratam fuisse sciebant';[42] put another way, Edward, though legitimate, was born at a time when neither his mother nor his father had been consecrated, and in the eyes of some this made him the less suitable as a candidate for the throne.[43] Presumably the same objection did not apply to Æthelred, though it is not otherwise known that both Edgar and Ælfthryth had been consecrated before his birth.[44] The third objection to Edward arose from the reputed severity of his character. According to the *Vita Oswaldi*, a work which can be attributed with some confidence to Byrhtferth of Ramsey and which can be dated on internal evidence to the decade 995–1005,[45]

Quidam enim ex primatibus hujusce regionis eligere volebant seniorem regis filium ad regem, nomine Eadweardum; nonnulli ex principibus desiderabant juniorem, (i.e. Æthelredum,) quia mitior apparuit omnibus in sermone et opere. Senior vero non solum timorem sed etiam terrorem incussit cunctis, qui non verbis tantum, verum etiam diris verberibus, et maxime suos secum mansitantes.[46]

In deciding who was the more 'throne-worthy' candidate, the

---

[42] Stubbs, *Memorials*, p. 214; Eadmer derived his information from Prior Nicholas of Worcester, *ibid.* p. 423.

[43] See Chaney, *Cult of Kingship*, p. 25; cf. Brooke, *Saxon and Norman Kings*, pp. 128–9.

[44] See Nelson, 'Inauguration Rituals', p. 67.

[45] Lapidge, 'Hermeneutic Style', pp. 91–5. Fisher, 'Anti-monastic Reaction', pp. 258–9, has suggested that the passage in question should be regarded as an interpolation made 'by a later writer probably resident in one of the Mercian monasteries', but Dr Lapidge assures me that the stylistic uniformity of the *Vita* outweighs the errors of detail that occur in this section and that one would not expect to find in a Ramsey author writing *c.* 1000; he points out that some of the errors might be attributable to the demonstrably inaccurate scribe of the unique manuscript (B.L. Cotton Nero E i). See also John, *Orbis Britanniae*, pp. 290–1.

[46] Raine, *Historians of York* I, 449; Whitelock, *EHD*, p. 914. Eadmer's statement to the same effect (Stubbs, *Memorials*, p. 214) may have been derived from the *Vita Oswaldi*.

leading men may thus have had a difficult choice between Æthelred, a boy about nine years old and probably something of an unknown quantity, and his slightly older half-brother Edward, who if not illegitimate had nevertheless been born before his parents were consecrated and who had already alienated many by his overbearing behaviour; but one suspects that the allegiance of many of them would have been determined not so much by any of these considerations as by rivalries which had their roots elsewhere. The case for Æthelred was presumably advocated by his mother Ælfthryth, and she may have had the support of Æthelwold, bishop of Winchester, since it was probably he who drafted the diploma which implied the illegitimacy of Edward.[47] But it was the case for Edward that prevailed, perhaps because he was after all the elder of the two, but also because he had the considerable advantage of Archbishop Dunstan's support.[48] There may in the event have been a compromise, since a diploma of 999 (S 937) reveals that Æthelred received for his personal use the lands set aside for 'royal sons',[49] but of course his more ardent supporters may have continued to harbour resentment towards King Edward while he reigned.

It seems likely that the murder of Edward was the ultimate expression of such feelings, and that is certainly the impression left by the earliest circumstantial account of the crime, given by Byrhtferth in the *Vita Oswaldi*. The author asserts that on an occasion when Edward had gone to visit his half-brother, who was staying at an unnamed place with his mother, the 'zelantes . . . ministri' of Æthelred rose up against the king and killed him. Edward's corpse was given a secret burial in the house of a certain unimportant person, where it apparently remained for almost a year until Ealdorman Ælfhere translated it to a more honourable place.[50] Byrhtferth offers no explanation for the action of the zealous thegns, but by juxtaposing his account of the disputed succession and his account

---

47 See Whitelock, 'King Edgar's Establishment of Monasteries', p. 131, and Lapidge, 'Hermeneutic Style', p. 89.

48 The author of the *Passio Sancti Eadwardi* (Fell, *Edward*, p. 2), Osbern (Stubbs, *Memorials*, p. 114) and Eadmer (*ibid*. p. 214) describe Dunstan's decisive role in securing Edward's coronation; see also Stafford, 'A Study in Limitations', p. 40 n. 30.

49 The draftsman of S 937 chose to gloss over the disputed election of 975, asserting that 'omnes utriusque ordinis optimates ad regni gubernacula moderna fratrem meum Eaduuardum unanimiter elegerunt'.

50 Raine, *Historians of York* I, 449–51; Whitelock, *EHD*, pp. 914–15.

of the murder he seems content to allow his readers to believe that the thegns murdered the king because they preferred to have the gentler Æthelred as their lord. Nor does he implicate either Ælfthryth or Æthelred in the crime, and indeed he takes pains to stress the love between the two half-brothers. Were one to assume that the *Vita Oswaldi* was intended for wide circulation and that the author's indiscretions would be punished, one could argue that he was merely anxious not to give offence to parties still alive, but it would have been simpler to avoid the issue altogether than to misrepresent what was known to have been the truth. The other early references to the murder of Edward are more immediately incompatible with the notion that it was associated with those who inevitably benefited most directly from it. A brief lament on the holy king, probably written in the late tenth century and now incorporated in the northern recension of the *Chronicle*, implies that the crime was perpetrated by a group of men who refused to acknowledge Edward's position, but it distinguishes his *eorðlican banan* from his *eorðlican magas* who would not avenge him, and so seems to dissociate the members of the royal family from the deed.[51] Most important is the reference to the crime in Archbishop Wulfstan's *Sermo ad Anglos*, first preached in 1014:

and ful micel hlafordswice eac bið on worolde þæt man his hlaford of life forræde, oððon of lande lifiendne drife; and ægþer is geworden on þysan earde: Eadweard man forrædde and syððan acwealde and æfter þam forbærnde, and Æþelred man dræfde ut of his earde.[52]

The murder of Edward is here introduced as an example of a man's betrayal of his lord, and the juxtaposition of a reference to the expulsion of Æthelred would hardly seem appropriate if Æthelred had himself been involved in some way in the earlier crime. The statement that the body was burned finds no support in later sources,[53] but the authority of Wulfstan is considerable, and the discrepancy only emphasizes the existence of more than one tradition about Edward's death.

---

[51] Plummer, *Chronicles* I, 123. Byrhtferth also implies that those who had killed the king were allowed to live on, to suffer punishment on earth.

[52] Whitelock, *Sermo Lupi*, pp. 56–7, and see n. 78; cf. Bethurum, *Homilies*, pp. 361–2.

[53] Fell, *Edward*, p. xxviii n. 44, points out that a cult needs relics. There was indeed no shortage of Edward's relics in the Middle Ages: we find references to them at Shaftesbury, Abingdon, Exeter, Leominster, Reading and St Albans. And some (from Shaftesbury) may still survive: see Stowell, 'Bones of Edward'.

The very vagueness of the earliest accounts of the murder suggests how much room there was for speculation and the development of rumours, and a multiplicity of legends subsequently grew up around the crime. It was once thought that they represented differently-developed versions of traditions circulating orally about the murder, but it has been shown more recently that most are derived ultimately from the *Passio Sancti Eadwardi Regis et Martyris*, an account of Edward's life, murder and miracles written probably in the 1070s by the Anglo-Norman hagiographer Goscelin and itself based partly on an earlier account of St Edward which may have been written at Shaftesbury in the early years of the eleventh century.[54] According to the *Passio*, it was Queen Ælfthryth, envious of Edward's success as a ruler, who plotted his murder in order to substitute her own son Æthelred on the throne; the later accounts that are dependent on the *Passio* embroider the story in various respects and are no more restrained in presenting the queen as the prime culprit, whether as instigator or as perpetrator of the crime. Accusations against Ælfthryth are not, however, confined to the *Passio* and its derivatives. Adam of Bremen and Osbern of Canterbury, writing at about the same time as Goscelin, both implicate her;[55] and in the next generation, Florence of Worcester declares that Edward was killed on her orders[56] and Henry of Huntingdon reports the story that she stabbed the king herself while offering him a drink.[57] It is not difficult to understand why belief in Ælfthryth's complicity had become widespread by the late eleventh century. Æthelred and Ælfthryth were respectively the direct and indirect beneficiaries of the murder, so we have motive; the crime occurred on an estate belonging to Ælfthryth, so we have opportunity; and Ælfthryth was after all the victim's step-mother, so it might be said that we even have expectation.[58] These factors alone would suffice to

---

[54] Fell, *Edward*, pp. iii, xiv–xx.

[55] *Ibid.* p. xvi.

[56] Thorpe, *Chronicon* I, 145.

[57] Arnold, *Historia Anglorum*, p. 167.

[58] Writing of the hardships of Sverri's youth, the author of Sverri's Saga likened his condition to that of the proverbial royal children under the curse of step-mothers: 'var þvi licazt sem i fornum sogum er sagt at verit hæfði. þa er konunga born urðo fyrir stiup-mæðra skopum' (Indrebø, *Sverris Saga*, p. 7). Ælfthryth was credited in addition with other murders and acts of witchcraft: see Wilson, *Lost Literature*, pp. 45–7 and 101–3. See also Fell, 'Anglo-Saxon Hagiographic Tradition', pp. 10–11.

explain why she attracted suspicion, but the decisive stage in the reasoning that led to belief in her guilt probably involved some extrapolation from the known outcome of Æthelred's reign. King Æthelred had evidently incurred God's displeasure to deserve the dire punishment inflicted on him and his kingdom by the Vikings, and the mysterious circumstances surrounding his accession were duly exploited to provide the explanation. Edward was not just murdered by person or persons unknown; he was murdered on Ælfthryth's orders so that Æthelred might become king, and ever thereafter king and country paid the penalty. Thus the same late-eleventh- and early-twelfth-century historians who accuse Ælfthryth of the crime also report a story that on the occasion of Æthelred's coronation Archbishop Dunstan predicted the coming disasters of his reign, because Æthelred had aspired to the kingdom through the death of his half-brother; and William of Malmesbury informs us that it was believed and commonly reported in his day that the country suffered for a long time on account of Ælfthryth's crime.[59] Indeed, Æthelred and Ælfthryth were not given the benefit of any doubt: every act that they may have done from pious and honourable motives has since been interpreted as an act of atonement for their alleged part in the murder of Edward. In recent years a case implying Ælfthryth's involvement in the crime has been developed on more rational grounds, with the suggestion that in pressing the claims of Æthelred when the succession was disputed in 975 she had enjoyed the support of Ealdorman Ælfhere of Mercia, and that after the 'unsuccessful' outcome of the dispute they had together orchestrated an attack on the monasteries in an attempt to hurt their political opponents (namely Dunstan and his fellow-bishops) who had supported Edward, though ultimately achieving their objective with the murder of the king.[60]

It is difficult to reconcile the traditions that arose concerning the murder of Edward with the early development of his cult as a saint. To some extent, of course, it was a wave of popular emotion that swept Edward into the ranks of sainthood.[61] The antithetical

[59] See Keynes, 'Declining Reputation', pp. 236–9.
[60] Fisher, 'Anti-monastic Reaction', pp. 255, 269–70; Hart, *Charters of Northern England*, p. 274.
[61] Stenton *Anglo-Saxon England*, p. 374.

passage on the murder incorporated in the northern recension of the *Chronicle* was written during the lifetime of the murderers and thus testifies to the rapid development of the cult:

Ne wearð Angel cynne nan wærsa dæd gedon, þonne þeos wæs, syððon hi ærest Bryton land gesohton. Men hine ofmyrðrodon; ac God hine mærsode. He wæs on life eorðlic cing; he is nu æfter deaðe heofonlice sanct.[62]

In his *Vita Dunstani*, written between 996 and 1011, Adelard of Ghent makes passing reference to 'sanctum Eadwardum martyrem',[63] while Byrhtferth of Ramsey, in his roughly contemporary *Vita Oswaldi*, invests his account of Edward's murder with the conventions of hagiography, describing how the body was found to be incorrupt when raised in 979 and recounting the miracles performed through the martyr's ministrations.[64] But the cult of Edward was also promoted with the direct encouragement and approbation of those in authority. Ælfhere of Mercia, the senior ealdorman and perhaps the most powerful laymen in the kingdom, was instrumental in the translation of the king's remains from Wareham to Shaftesbury in February 979, apparently acting on behalf of Æthelred:

Audiens itaque quidam comes magnificus, Ælfere nomine, sanctum corpus tam praeclaro indicio inuentum, immenso perfusus gaudio, dominoque suo tanquam adhuc uiuo fidele obsequium praebere desiderans, in digniorem locum illud transferre decreuit. Erat enim uir illustris magnam de crudeli eius interitu compassionem habens, et nimis indigne ferens tam pretiosam margaritam in tam uili loco obfuscari.[65]

About five years later, in 984, King Æthelred himself made a grant of land to Shaftesbury Abbey (S 850), which may or may not be significant, and according to the *Passio* the translation of Edward's remains from their resting-place in the churchyard to a more secure place within the abbey, on 20 June 1001, was conducted on the instructions of the king.[66] A few months after that event

[62] Plummer, *Chronicles* I, 123.
[63] Stubbs, *Memorials*, p. 61.
[64] Raine, *Historians of York* I, 450–2.
[65] Fell, *Edward*, p. 8. See also below, p. 214 n. 216.
[66] *Ibid.* pp. 12–13. The author of the *Passio* states that King Æthelred was not himself able to be present at the translation because he was hemmed in on all sides by the Danes (and see also the exposition in S 899), a detail that accords well with the extensive fighting recorded in *ASC* MS 'A', *s.a.* 1001 (and for the day, 23 May, of the battle of Æthelingadene, see Dickins, 'Battle of Æthelingadene'). Æthelred entrusted the task to Wulfsige, bishop of Sherborne, and to 'a certain *praesul* of great sanctity' called Ælfsige, amongst others: but there was no bishop called Ælfsige at the time. According to Goscelin, in his

Æthelred issued a further diploma in favour of Shaftesbury, and the grant was specified as one to Christ and to 'sancto suo germano scilicet meo Edwardo, quem proprio cruore perfusum per multiplicia uirtutum signa ipse dominus nostris mirificare dignatus est temporibus' (S 899); the diploma gave the nuns of Shaftesbury jurisdiction over the abbey of Bradford-on-Avon in Wiltshire, for use as a place of refuge for the community and its relics in times of Viking attack. The cult of Edward was given further royal approval when it was established, apparently in a code of laws promulgated in 1008, that his festival was to be celebrated throughout England on 18 March.[67] At no point is there any suggestion that King Æthelred was atoning for the crime. If there were any feelings amongst his contemporaries and subjects that Edward had been murdered as the result of a plot against him hatched within the royal family, the glorification of the victim as a martyr could serve only to diminish the security of Æthelred's own position, by drawing attention to the circumstances of Edward's martyrdom. If there were no such feelings, the king would naturally profit materially from the cult of a royal saint so closely related to him.[68]

It is especially difficult to believe that Ælfthryth could have engineered the crime with the support of a party that pursued an anti-monastic policy to secure its ends. The suggestion raises more problems than it seems to resolve, not least because resentment towards the monks and the litigation over their estates lingered well on into Æthelred's reign and was rooted more deeply elsewhere than in the political issue, but above all because the apparent distribution of support between Edward and Æthelred respectively is not readily compatible with the composition of the different parties on

Life of St Ive, it was Archbishop Sigeric (990–4) who encouraged the king to commemorate Edward at Shaftesbury (Migne, *PL* CLV, cols. 87–8).

[67] V Æthelred 16 (Liebermann, *Gesetze* I, 240–1; cf. *ibid.* p. 252); but there is a possibility that the operative clause is an interpolation (Wormald, 'Æthelred the Lawmaker', pp. 53–4). For the festival of Edward in pre-Conquest calendars, see Fell, *Edward*, p. xxii, and Korhammer, 'Bosworth Psalter', p. 175.

[68] Æthelred may have been motivated by genuine compassion for his half-brother, but he may also have been indignant that the royal office which he himself held had been so assailed, and by affirming the inviolability of the royal office (on which see the late eighth-century report of the papal legates to Pope Hadrian, in Haddan and Stubbs, *Councils* III, 453–4; Whitelock, *EHD*, pp. 837–8) in this way he may have sought to strengthen his own position. One should note that Æthelred's son Æthelstan, who had been brought up by Ælfthryth, made a bequest in his will (S 1503) to the Holy Cross and St Edward at Shaftesbury.

the monastic issue. Queen Ælfthryth in particular fits badly in anti-monastic clothes, for she was intimately associated with the activity of her husband King Edgar in the reform movement.[69] According to the *Liber Eliensis*, she and Edgar commissioned Bishop Æthelwold to prepare a translation of the Rule of St Benedict,[70] and it is recorded in the Preface to the *Regularis Concordia* that Ælfthryth was made the 'protectress and fearless guardian of the communities of nuns'.[71] There is no evidence that she reversed her position following Edgar's death. In his account of the reform movement, probably written during or after the period of the anti-monastic disturbances, Bishop Æthelwold still mentions the role of Ælfthryth as the guardian of the nunneries;[72] moreover, it is recorded that Bishop Æthelwold, Ælfthryth and the young Æthelred visited Ely Abbey during the reign of Edward.[73] Perhaps it is unlikely that Æthelwold would have written kindly of Ælfthryth or visited Ely in her company if at the time she had been connected with a party openly hostile to the monks. Against this background, it is no surprise to find that Ælfthryth founded two nunneries during the reign of Æthelred, at Amesbury in Wiltshire and at Wherwell in Hampshire, though medieval chroniclers naturally preferred to see this as an attempt at expiation for her part in the murder. The author of the *Passio* fully appreciated the incongruity in this respect of associating Ælfthryth with the crime: he borrowed the passage from the *Regularis Concordia* mentioning Edgar's wife as the protectress of the nunneries, but by implication he substituted Æthelflæd, Edward's mother, for Ælfthryth.[74] Ealdorman Ælfhere, for his part, was no friend of the monks and by that token alone an improbable accomplice for Queen Ælfthryth. His only demonstrable connection with the fate of King Edward was his involvement in the translation of Edward's remains to Shaftesbury in 979, and it would be difficult to explain how the description of the ealdorman's

---

[69] Hart, 'Two Queens', pp. 14–15, and *idem*, *Charters of Northern England*, pp. 272–4; also Meyer, 'Women and the Monastic Reform', pp. 51–61.
[70] Blake, *Liber Eliensis*, p. 111.
[71] Symons, *Concordia*, p. 2.
[72] Whitelock, *EHD*, p. 922; for its date, see *ibid.* p. 920, and *idem*, 'King Edgar's Establishment of Monasteries', p. 136.
[73] Blake, *Liber Eliensis*, p. 146.
[74] Fell, *Edward*, pp. 1–2; see also p. xviii.

motives given in the *Passio* (and cited above) could have arisen had he in fact been party to the murder.[75]

The murder of Edward might well have been regarded by contemporaries as the worst deed that had been committed since the English first came to Britain, but it would be mistaken nevertheless to assume that they attached any blame to the young Æthelred, and that as a result Æthelred was thereafter unsure of himself and his subjects disinclined to rally round him when the security of the country was threatened; it also seems improbable (though one could not press the case on this ground alone) that Ælfthryth, so prominent amongst the leaders of the monastic reform movement, would have countenanced murder on her behalf. It seems more advisable to dismiss the later traditions for what they are and to suppose that the zealous thegns of Æthelred who resorted to regicide probably did so in their own interests, perhaps through a personal dislike of Edward and in the hope that their own lord would prove more amenable; this would accord with the three earliest sources which describe or allude to the circumstances of the murder (the *Vita Oswaldi*, the northern recension of the *Chronicle*, and the *Sermo ad Anglos*), each of which can indeed be construed as exonerating Edward's kinsmen. The most puzzling aspect of the affair remains the statement, explicit in the *Chronicle* and also implicit in the *Vita Oswaldi*, that no revenge was taken on the culprits: technically, the responsibility was Æthelred's, but as a young boy at the time he may not have been in a position to single out and punish those of his thegns who had done the deed; he may not even have known who they were. At least one should consider these possibilities before leaping to the conclusion that no revenge was taken because the crime had been carried out on the orders of Ælfthryth and Æthelred. Similarly, though we are told that Edward was buried 'butan ælcum cynelicum wurðscipe',[76] the inference should not be that his successor omitted to pay him due respect, pointing to his own complicity, for the reference is to the secret burial in 978, and since the body was not discovered until February 979 Æthelred was

---

[75] Note, however, that William of Malmesbury, apparently drawing his own conclusions from Ælfhere's involvement in the translation, states that it was he who murdered Edward (and in so doing contradicts himself): Stubbs, *De Gestis Regum Anglorum* I, 189.

[76] Plummer, *Chronicles* I, 123, from *ASC* MSS 'D' and 'E'.

hardly in a position to oblige; as soon as the body was discovered, it was taken at first to Wareham, and translated five days later to Shaftesbury, 'mid mycclum wurðscipe'.[77] The very fact that Æthelred's coronation was delayed for over a year after his accession[78] may reflect the general confusion and dismay occasioned by the crime, for had it been planned at a high level, in order that Æthelred should become king, one might expect a hasty coronation to seal the matter: as Ælfric remarked, once a king had been consecrated he had sole authority over the people and they could not shake his yoke off their necks.[79] It would otherwise have been only respectful to Edward to wait for some time before the consecration of his successor, and it is not impossible that it was the rediscovery of the body in February 979, nearly a year after the murder, and his re-burial 'with great honour' at Shaftesbury, that finally settled the matter and set in motion the train of events that led to Æthelred's coronation, at Kingston and in the presence of two archbishops and ten diocesan bishops, on 4 May following. According to the *Vita Oswaldi*, there was great rejoicing at Æthelred's coronation, 'ipse enim juvenis extitit annorum circulis, moribus elegans, pulcher vultu, decorus aspectu',[80] and according to the northern recension of the *Chronicle* he was consecrated 'mid mycclum gefean Angel cynnes witon'.[81]

Æthelred would have been a boy not more than twelve years old when he became king. He was probably too young and inexperienced to take an executive part in the government of the kingdom, and too young in relation to those in effective control to have had any personal influence on the choice of his councillors. It is generally and not unreasonably assumed that Ælfthryth played an important role in protecting and advancing the interests of her son during his youth,[82] and there is a suggestion that the influence of Æthelwold,

77 Fell, *Edward*, pp. 7–10, and Plummer, *Chronicles* I, 125, from *ASC* MSS 'D' and 'E'.
78 For the date of Æthelred's coronation, see Appendix I, p. 233 n. 7.
79 Thorpe, *Homilies* I, 212; Whitelock, *EHD*, pp. 925–6.
80 Raine, *Historians of York* I, 455; Whitelock, *EHD*, p. 916.
81 Plummer, *Chronicles* I, 123. Had Æthelred's succession been secured by a royal and dastardly plot, one would not perhaps expect such a popular response.
82 E.g. Fisher, 'Anti-monastic Reaction', p. 270; Fell, *Edward*, p. xxvii n. 33; Meyer, 'Women and the Monastic Reform', pp. 52–3; and Stafford, 'Sons and Mothers', pp. 91–2. Attempts have been made (e.g. by Campbell, *Encomium Emmae*, pp. 62–5) to establish Ælfthryth's status as reflected in the relative position accorded to her in the witness lists: during Edgar's reign she generally occurs after the bishops, but in Æthelred's reign (especially up

bishop of Winchester, may also have been particularly important at this time.[83] Otherwise, a study of the witnesses to Æthelred's early diplomas conveys the general impression that he was surrounded, as one would expect, by people who had achieved prominence during the reigns of Edgar and Edward; certainly there are no signs of an upheaval in the composition of the king's council. The archbishops and bishops naturally remained in office. The groups of ealdormen represent a continuation of the position established in Edgar's reign, as modified by new appointments made during the reign of Edward,[84] and several of the prominent *ministri* who attest these diplomas can probably be identified amongst those in the lists attached to the diplomas of Æthelred's two predecessors.[85] There were, on the other hand, some developments in the ranks of the abbots, though it is not clear what we should make of them. Æscwig of Bath, Osgar of Abingdon and Æthelgar of the New Minster Winchester had been prominent since the early years of Edgar's reign, and remained so during the reign of Edward: the first was promoted to the see of Dorchester *c.* 979, the second remained prominent until 980 (though he did not die until 984) and the third was promoted to the see of Selsey in 980. Their 'places' were taken by Ordbriht of Chertsey, Sigeric of St Augustine's Canterbury and Æthelweard of Malmesbury (see Table 4). Ordbriht had been appointed abbot of Chertsey in 964, and whereas he is to be found as a witness to several diplomas issued in the 960s, he is largely 'absent' throughout the 970s:[86] hence his reappearance in 980, and

to 984) she often occurs immediately after the king or the archbishops. This may indicate some improvement in her position, but it cannot be said that the material is conclusive.

[83] See further below, pp. 176 and 181. Æthelwold was the beneficiary of Æthelred's first grant to the Church after his coronation (S 835); he was also the beneficiary of S 849, dated 983, and the Old Minster was the beneficiary of S 836 and 837, dated 980.

[84] King Edgar's last diplomas were attested by Ælfhere of Mercia, Æthelwine of East Anglia, Brihtnoth of Essex and Oslac of Northumbria (who was banished in 975). Southern and western England were not apparently represented, unless one accepts the rather poor evidence that Æthelweard of the Western Provinces was appointed before Edgar's death (S 751, 798 and 800, against the silence of the other diplomas); see also Barker, 'Æthelweard', pp. 85–6. The situation was rectified by the appointment during Edward's reign of (?)Æthelweard, Æthelmær of Hampshire and Eadwine of Sussex; the Leofwine of S 830 and 832 cannot be identified. Cf. Table 6.

[85] With the exceptions of Ælfgar and Wulfsige, all the prominent *ministri* of the early 980s in Table 7 *could* be amongst the consistent witnesses to the diplomas of Edgar and Edward, but of course definite identifications are impossible. Ælfgar occurs from the reign of Edward onwards, and Wulfsige's subscriptions commence in Æthelred's reign.

[86] See Knowles *et al.*, *Heads of Houses*, p. 38, and Hart, *Charters of Northern England*, pp. 350–1.

his position at the head of all but one of the extant lists dated between 983 and 988, seems to indicate that he suddenly recovered his position as one of the king's advisers; he became bishop of Selsey when Æthelgar was translated to Canterbury (see Table 2). Both Sigeric and Æthelweard make their first appearances in Æthelred's reign, and thus come directly into prominence; the former became bishop of Ramsbury in 985 × 6 and was translated thence to Canterbury in 990.[87]

THE PERIOD OF YOUTHFUL INDISCRETIONS, 984–c. 993

During the opening years of Æthelred's reign, his mother Queen Ælfthryth occurs ten times as a witness to the royal diplomas issued in the name of her son.[88] It is a remarkable fact, therefore, that she does not attest any of the extant diplomas dated from 985 to 990 inclusive, and since she 'returns' in 993 and witnesses several diplomas issued thereafter until 999, it seems that she was for some reason temporarily absent from the meetings of the king and his council. It is no less remarkable that her disappearance from the witness lists seems to coincide generally with the death of Æthelwold, bishop of Winchester, on 1 August 984, for her only subscription in that year occurs on a diploma (S 855) issued before the prelate's death. In S 876, the diploma of 993 which marks the 'return' of Ælfthryth, the king draws attention to Æthelwold's death as if it had been a turning-point in his reign:

Ego . . . Athelredus . . . non inmemor angustiarum mihi meæque nationi septimo regni mei anno et deinceps frequenter ac multipliciter accidentium, post decessum videlicet beatæ memoriæ mihique interno amore dilectissimi Atheluuoldi episcopi . . .

The death of Æthelwold deprived the country of one 'whose industry and pastoral care administered not only to my interest but also to that of all inhabitants of this country, the common people (*subditi*) as well as the leading men (*praelati*)'. The king describes how he began to turn over many things in his mind, and to consider what might be the cause of the afflictions occasioned by Æthelwold's

---

[87] It is not clear which of the subscriptions of an Abbot Leofric in the 980s belong to the abbot of Exeter and which to the abbot of Muchelney, so one cannot tell whether one or the other (if not both) was prominent at the time: see Table 4.

[88] S 835, 837–8, 840–3, 845, 849 and 855.

death, and how he has reached the conclusion that they occurred 'partly on account of the ignorance of my youth . . . and partly on account of the abhorrent greed of certain of those men who ought to administer to my interest'. In short, it appears that the death of Æthelwold ushered in a period of wrongdoing, when some men took advantage of the king's youth in their own interests, a period which by 993 the king had come to regret.[89]

The wrongdoings involved the maltreatment of certain churches, the reduction of their privileges and the appropriation of their property. In S 876 King Æthelred specifies the role of the late Bishop Wulfgar (bishop of Ramsbury, 981 – 985 × 6) and of Ealdorman Ælfric ('qui adhuc superest': so presumably the ealdorman of Hampshire,[90] 982–1016) in persuading him to reduce the *libertas* of Abingdon Abbey *in servitutem*, and he then renounces the price that Ealdorman Ælfric paid him in order to secure the abbacy for his brother Eadwine (abbot of Abingdon, 985–90).[91] It transpires also that S 876 served to restore certain estates to the abbey, for the king repudiates the 'new hereditary charters' which perfidious men had obtained when the estates now restored had been unjustly appropriated;[92] and in S 918 we hear of an Abingdon estate that

---

[89] S 876 refers to 'afflictions', 'perils' and 'misfortunes', and at first sight it seems as if the draftsman meant Viking attacks: but it is apparent from Æthelred's explanation that other types of misfortune were intended; and besides, it was normally held to have been Dunstan's death that presaged the attacks.

[90] Thus Napier and Stevenson, *Crawford Charters*, p. 121, though see next note. Ælfric's interests and authority probably extended beyond Hampshire: he is styled 'Wentaniensium Prouinciarum dux' in S 891, but in 1003 he was entrusted with the leadership of an army gathered from Wiltshire as well as from Hampshire; see also below, p. 182 n. 104.

[91] An addition to the Abingdon manuscript of Florence of Worcester states that 'major domus regiæ Ælfricus quidam præpotens' secured the abbacy for his brother Eadwine by making payment to the king (Thorpe, *Chronicon* I, 147 n. 5). The Abingdon chronicler, enlarging on this statement, identifies Ælfric (wrongly called Eadric) with the Ealdorman Ælfric of Mercia who was thought to be the son of Ealdorman Ælfhere, who was exiled in 985, and who allegedly returned to England soon afterwards with a group of Danes and ravaged the country for some time thereafter (Stevenson, *Chronicon* I, 357). It is tempting to connect the reference in S 876 to Ealdorman Ælfric, 'qui adhuc superest', with this tradition that the exiled Ælfric returned, and so to identify the Ælfric of S 876 with the exile, thus avoiding the apparent difficulty that Ælfric of Hampshire remained in office after a deal in which he had been involved was publicly denounced. However, it seems from *ASC* MS 'C', *s.a.* 985, that Ælfric of Mercia may already have been in exile when Eadwine became abbot of Abingdon (though cf. Stevenson, *Chronicon* I, 357), and the Abingdon tradition does not actually imply that the exile was still active in 993, when S 876 was drawn up; moreover, in the context of Æthelred's reign it is not essentially unlikely that Ælfric of Hampshire would have survived impeachment on the issue in question.

[92] See above, pp. 99–100.

had been 'unjustly' acquired by one of the king's reeves during the abbacy of Eadwine, with King Æthelred's acquiescence.[93] It is clear that Abingdon was not the only religious foundation to suffer during the latter half of the 980s. According to the *Anglo-Saxon Chronicle*, King Æthelred laid waste (*fordyde*) the diocese of Rochester in 986,[94] though the circumstances that led up to the event are obscure. Osbern, in his *Vita Dunstani* (written 1080 × 93), states that the king besieged the city of Rochester 'propter quasdam dissensiones', and, unable to capture it, proceeded to ravage the estates of the diocese, desisting only when Archbishop Dunstan offered him a bribe;[95] William of Malmesbury, following Osbern, declares that a *simultas* which had arisen between the king and Ælfstan, bishop of Rochester, precipitated the king's attack, though its cause was unknown ('incertum qua de causa').[96] Sulcard of Westminster, writing between 1076 and *c.* 1085, so probably before Osbern (and William), provides important information not found elsewhere:

Hic ergo Adelredus, pontificante prefato Dunstano presule, commotus insolencius succendit igne Rofacen. vrbem et ecclesiam sancti Andree, omnesque terras ad eiusdem vrbis episcopum attinentes et depredacione vastauit et igne, vtque breuiter supra attinguimus. Idem rex mansionem vnam eiusdem presulis petenti cuidam suo militi dederat, cuius donacionis nescius pontifex eum inde cum suis turpiter eiecerat; et ex hoc illa commocio regis erat. Episcopum eciam si posset comprehendere, multo, vt aiebat, dampnasset dedecore.[97]

According to Sulcard, Archbishop Dunstan told the king that he had given the lands of St Andrew to his *miles* unjustly, and that he had not acted *regaliter* in the burning of his kingdom. But Æthelred became only more incensed, whereupon Dunstan prophesied that 'quoad vixeris non deerit tibi combustio ignis et effusio sanguinis'.[98] The animosity between King Æthelred and Bishop Ælfstan is reflected neatly in the witness lists attached to diplomas issued between 984 and 987: for though the bishop attests consistently in

[93] See further below, pp. 183–4.
[94] Plummer, *Chronicles* I, 125, from MSS 'C', 'D' and 'E'.
[95] Stubbs, *Memorials*, p. 117.
[96] *Ibid.* p. 310.
[97] Scholz, 'Sulcard', p. 89; cf. pp. 74–6. The remark 'vtque breuiter supra attinguimus' has no antecedent in Sulcard's tract, and so it may suggest that he had taken the story from some other written source which included an earlier allusion to it.
[98] *Ibid.* pp. 89–90; cf. p. 76 n. 68.

the early years of the reign, he disappears from the lists in 984 (but not, apparently, until after the death of Bishop Æthelwold) and does not occur at all in 985, 986 and 987, reappearing in 988 (see Table 2).[99] We may infer that Ælfstan did not attend or was excluded from meetings of the king's council for at least three years, according well with Sulcard's statement that the king used to say that he would punish the bishop severely if he could apprehend him. A group of royal diplomas from the archives of Rochester throws further light on King Æthelred's antagonism to Bishop Ælfstan and his diocese. In S 885, dated 995, the king adopts the contrite tone already seen in S 876, regretting the indiscretions of his youth and resolving to mend his ways:

Ea que neglegenter iuuentutis mee tempore que diuersis solebat uti moribus excessi dum me diuina praeueniente gratia in uirilis robur aetatis euasi . totis uiribus ad melioris arbitrii cultum mutare studui . ut et reatum prioris ignorantie salubriter euaderem . et ne tante benignitati ingratus sed tota mentis intentione gratus existerem.

In so doing, Æthelred restores an estate to the see of Rochester, and we may infer that during his youth he had been party to its appropriation. Another Rochester diploma (S 893, dated 998) is more specific. The king restores land which 'in tempore iuuentutis mee a Hrofensis ecclesie diocesi quibusdam instigantibus abstraxi', explaining that he had authorized the appropriation 'not so much cruelly as ignorantly', and especially at the instigation of a certain Æthelsige, who is said to have taken advantage of the king's 'boyish ignorance'. Greater maturity of age brought with it greater maturity of judgement:

[99] The position is complicated by the fact that there was a contemporary Bishop Ælfstan, of London, whose subscriptions cannot be immediately distinguished from those of his namesake. However, the consistency with which Ælfstan of London subscribes during the 960s, 970s and early 980s, and the relative position in which he does so (nearly always either before or after Æthelwold of Winchester; and invariably before Ælfstan of Rochester when the two are explicitly distinguished, as in S 671, 737-8, 745, 820, 838 and 842), argue strongly for the identification of the Ælfstan who subscribes between 985 and 987 (generally in third place, after the archbishop of York) as the bishop of London: he is identified as such in S 857, 859, 1450 and 861. Certainly it would be strange if any diplomas of 985-7 witnessed by Ælfstan of Rochester were not witnessed by Ælfstan of London. The only anomaly is the ninth place in S 862, but for this diploma, see above, p. 94. Ælfstan of Rochester is identified in the list of 984 × 8 incorporated in the spurious S 1293 (of purported date 959): he occurs between Oswald of York and Ælfheah of Winchester, and there is no second Ælfstan, so it seems likely that the identification of Ælfstan's see was the forger's own and mistaken contribution.

Nunc autem quia superna michi parcente clementia ad intelligibilem etatem perueni . et que pueriliter gessi in melius emendare decreui . . .

In this case the diploma by which the appropriation was effected has survived, and it is dated 987.[100]

The Old Minster at Winchester was also deprived of some of its estates during the king's youth. S 891, dated 997, reveals that Æthelred had appropriated a hundred hides at Downton and Ebbesborne from the church:

Quam uidelicet telluris portionem ipse ob enormem pueritiae meae iuuentutem mihimet aliquandiu usurpaui; sed tandem crebris meorum sapientum instinctus ammonitionibus, dumque stabilitatem mentis aetas caperet iam adulta, cognoui me hanc iniuste possidere, et supernum metuens examen, furoremque apostolicum incurrere, huius nunc scedulae renouatione constituo, ut . . .

Thus the king yet again attributes his action to his youthful condition, and declares that he realized his error when he came of age. He also repudiates the older documents relating to the estates, including those 'quas ipse pro iuuenili aetate dictaui': one such diploma must be S 861, by which King Æthelred had given five hides at Ebbesborne to a faithful *minister* called Ælfgar, in 986.[101]

Finally, it seems that the abbey of Glastonbury was another of the religious foundations to suffer at this time. William of Malmesbury, whose researches into the history of Glastonbury had made him familiar with its archives and traditions and who therefore has some authority, describes how a certain rich man called Ælfwold joined the community at Glastonbury when he was afflicted with disease, at the same time handing over certain of his possessions to the abbey. After a while Ælfwold recovered his health (and duly lost his zeal), abandoned the monastic life and pestered the community for the return of his property.

Cum nihil promoueret, regis Egelredi animum oblatione nummorum tentauit.

---

[100] S 864. Dolley, 'Æthelræd's Rochester Ravaging', observes that the Rochester moneyer Sidewine resorted to the irregular expedient of altering a *First Hand* obverse die into one of *Second Hand*, *c.* 985, and he connects this with difficulties over the supply of new dies at a time when the king and the bishop of Rochester were at loggerheads.

[101] S 876, 885, 891 and 893 comprise the distinct group of diplomas in which the king is made to regret the indiscretions of his youth, and it is arguable that they have a common origin: see above, p. 101. A passage in S 838, in which the king confesses that he was powerless in his infancy to prevent attacks on Tavistock Abbey, might have been derived from or suggested by another diploma in this group; S 838 itself is dated 981 – much too early in the reign, one might suppose, for this air of retrospection.

Ille, sub cujus regimine magnus erat labor justitiæ, sub quo nullus tutus nisi pecuniosus, missis apparitoribus Alwoldo quicquid interrogabat in solidum restituit. Ita rusticus invadens omnia, etiam multa præter hæc monasterio inflixit incommoda, ut est agrestium cum incipiunt sævire protervia.

The monks appealed to Archbishop Dunstan, who replied: 'a Domini matre ultionem exigite; illum comedant vulpes.' Ælfwold fell mortally ill, and – that he might humbly rest when dead at the place he had arrogantly forsaken while alive – he left instruction that he should be buried at Glastonbury; his wish was respected, but as his body was being transported to the abbey it was (needless to say) attacked and devoured by a pack of foxes.[102] The story may not deserve much trust in detail, but at least it is consonant with a period, which included the years before Dunstan's death in 988, when the king was prepared to be party to the maltreatment of certain churches and when others were fully disposed to take advantage of the situation.[103] The pronounced emphasis on laymen as the beneficiaries of royal diplomas between 984 and 990 may reflect the king's sympathies at this time.

That the death of Bishop Æthelwold should have ushered in a period when churches were abused in these ways suggests indirectly how important his influence may have been in Æthelred's early years. Similarly, that Queen Ælfthryth should cease to attend meetings of the king and his council for a period after Æthelwold's death suggests that her control over her son's actions was by no means completely effective: since she was so closely associated with the reform movement in general – and perhaps with Æthelwold in particular – her absence elicits no surprise, though it is not apparent whether she had fallen temporarily from favour or whether, powerless to influence her son, she had on her own initiative dissociated herself from his activity. It is entirely appropriate that she should have returned by 993 – when the king had decided to

---

[102] Stubbs, *Memorials*, pp. 313–14, being the only part of William's *Vita Dunstani* that is really new: see Farmer, 'Two Biographies', p. 164. William does not indicate precisely when the events took place, but he positions them between an account of Bishop Æthelwold's death in 984 and a general description of Dunstan's virtues which leads into the account of the archbishop's death in 988.

[103] Note the account in S 884 (dated 995) of how the community of Muchelney had *inepte* loaned an estate for three lives, and how the lessees wrongfully obtained a hereditary charter (presumably from the king) in respect of the land: the fraud was subsequently discovered, and the charter was annulled by the bishops, ealdormen and *optimates*.

mend his ways and to repair the damage that he had done. Apart from the case of Ælfstan, bishop of Rochester, there is, however, no sign of a general (or even partial) desertion of the bishops and abbots from the king's councils during the later 980s, and it is particularly striking to find Ælfheah, bishop of Winchester, amongst the witnesses to S 861, by which an estate was appropriated from his own church. Some ecclesiastics – for example, Wulfgar, bishop of Ramsbury, and Eadwine, abbot of Abingdon – were themselves party to the various abuses, and there may have been others; but since one can hardly impugn the integrity of the bishops and abbots collectively, one has to infer that their attendance at meetings of the *witan*, and their subscriptions to royal diplomas, were at certain times little more than a formality.

It seems likely that laymen would have been primarily responsible for leading the king astray, since they appear to have been the principal beneficiaries of his indiscretions, and in the light of Æthelred's assertion in S 876 that a contributory factor was the 'abhorrent greed of certain of those men who ought to administer to my interest' – with the implication that they were in a position of authority and influence – we may focus our attention on the lists of *ministri* in an attempt to discover who these laymen may have been. There are five *ministri* who can be regarded as consistent and prominent witnesses during the 980s (see Table 7),[104] and on the analogy of S 853 it is possible that they held office in the king's household.[105] ÆLFWEARD could be regarded as the dominant *minister* of the opening years of Æthelred's reign, occurring consistently and generally in first place until 986. He had been prominent during the reigns of Edgar and Edward the Martyr, and is described as a *discifer* in S 782 (dated 971);[106] if the list in S 796 (dated 974) has

---

[104] I leave aside Ælfric: prominent as a *minister* up to 983, when he succeeded Ælfhere as ealdorman of Mercia, and banished from the country in 985 for his manifold crimes (on which see S 896 and 937). One could not discount the possibility that it was this Ælfric who, as ealdorman, was rebuked by the Pope for appropriating land from Glastonbury Abbey (Stubbs, *Memorials*, p. 396): the only question is whether there is sufficient time between Ælfric's appointment in 983 and his banishment in 985 for him to act, for the news to reach Rome, and for the Pope to react. The alternative candidate for the identification is Ealdorman Ælfric of Hampshire, no less suitably disreputable; were it he, the appropriations could not be dated more closely than between 983 and 1009 (see Whitelock, *EHD*, p. 895).

[105] See above, pp. 160–1.

[106] See also the closely related list in S 792.

an authentic basis, he appears to have been the brother of Æthelweard, another prominent *minister* of Edgar and Edward and also
described as a *discifer* in S 782.[107] ÆLFSIGE attests consistently from
the beginning of Æthelred's reign until 995, and from 985 he is often
first in the lists. Like Ælfweard he had been prominent during the
reigns of Edgar and Edward, and is described as a *discifer* in S 782.
ÆLFGAR was a consistent and prominent witness between 982 and
990. He does not seem to occur amongst the witnesses to Edgar's
diplomas, but is probably the Ælfgar who attests S 830 and 832,
diplomas of Edward purportedly issued in 976 and 977 respectively.
Three of King Æthelred's early diplomas are in favour of an Ælfgar
minister: S 839, dated 982 and concerning land at Charlton in
Berkshire; S 861, dated 986 and concerning land at Ebbesborne
in Wiltshire probably appropriated from the Old Minster Winchester; and S 868, dated 988 and concerning land at Wylye in
Wiltshire.[108] It is possible that the beneficiary of S 861 was the
prominent witness, if we may attach any significance to the statement that the grant was made 'ob eius fidele obsequium quod erga
me sedulus exhibuit';[109] the other Wiltshire grant was made to
Ælfgar 'pro sua humillima deuotione', though no analogous remark
occurs in S 839 (issued at the time when the main series of subscriptions in Ælfgar's name begins). It is also possible that the prominent
Ælfgar of the witness lists can be identified as the king's 'præpositus
atque prætiosus' who persuaded the king to grant him a Wiltshire
estate belonging to Abingdon Abbey, during the abbacy of Eadwine
(985–90); Ælfgar gave the land to his wife Ælfgifu, who subsequently married Wulfgeat, and the land was forfeited to the king
on account of Wulfgeat's crimes.[110] The subscriptions of the

---

[107] It is presumably this Æthelweard who attests some of Æthelred's early diplomas, high
up amongst the *ministri* and twice beside Ælfweard: see Table 7.

[108] Twelve hides at Wylye had been granted to the Old Minster Winchester by Ealdorman
Æthelwold, *c.* 947 (S 1504, and see Hart, 'Athelstan "Half King"', p. 119 n. 5). But it
does not follow that S 868 is an appropriation of Winchester property: the estate covered
by S 868 was part of that granted by King Edward to Ælfric in 977 (S 831); a statement
in the bounds of S 868 reveals that the land had been held by 'Æðelwold and Ælfhelm
his broðor'.

[109] The same clause occurs in S 695.

[110] The diploma recording these events and restoring the estate to Abingdon, S 918 (dated
1008), is certainly spurious: it is linked textually with S 915, dated 1007 and in favour of
Ælfgar the reeve, which seems to be authentic. One might infer that the Ælfgar of S 915
was the Ælfgar of S 918: but that would leave only a year or so for the sequence of
events, and it is likely anyway that the Wulfgeat of S 918 is the person who had suffered

prominent Ælfgar cease in 990, and there are no diplomas of 991 or 992; we read in the *Anglo-Saxon Chronicle* that the king had Ælfgar, the son of Ealdorman Ælfric, blinded in 993.[111] It is at least conceivable that the *prætiosus* reeve who encouraged the king to appropriate land in Wiltshire from Abingdon between 985 and 990 was the *sedulus minister* who secured from the king in 986 an estate in Wiltshire belonging to the Old Minster Winchester, that he was, moreover, the prominent *minister* of the 980s, and that it was he who was blinded in 993: if the *minister* was therefore the son of the ealdorman, it would then be significant that his prominence in the lists dates from the time of Ealdorman Ælfric's appointment, and it would also follow that the simoniacal Eadwine, abbot of Abingdon, was his uncle (and all three thus party in their different ways to the exploitation of that abbey). Against such a background, the blinding of Ælfgar in 993 would represent not simply a barbarous and arbitrary act of revenge for Ealdorman Ælfric's behaviour in 992,[112] but rather would seem to have been one stage in the king's escape from the influence of those who had misled him in his youth, reflected simultaneously in the production of the great diploma for Abingdon Abbey (S 876). The fourth prominent *minister* of the 980s was WULFSIGE, who occurs amongst the leading *ministri* in most of the diplomas issued between 980 and 988. He may have attested one or two of Edgar's diplomas, in a relatively low position, but his prominence clearly dates from Æthelred's reign. Unfortunately he cannot be identified in other contexts. The fifth and last prominent *minister* was ÆTHELSIGE, who occurs in the majority of the diplomas issued between 984 and 994, generally positioned amongst the first five *ministri* in the lists. He is presumably the Æthelsige who had occurred less consistently in the early years of Æthelred's reign, and perhaps the Æthelsige who had occurred sporadically and without prominence in the

forfeiture of his estates in 1006. The discursive section in S 918 seems plausible enough, and it is possible that a genuine tradition was incorporated in a diploma modelled on S 915 because of the reeve Ælfgar common to them. See S 1454 (990 × 93) for an Ælfgar, king's reeve, in a Berkshire context. 'Ælfgyfu coniunx Ælfgari presidis' and 'Wulfgyð mater Ælfgari procuratoris' were commemorated in the *Liber Vitae* of the New Minster Winchester: Birch, *Liber Vitae*, p. 58.

111 Plummer, *Chronicles* I, 127, from MSS 'C', 'D' and 'E'.

112 Cf. William of Malmesbury, in Stubbs, *De Gestis Regum Anglorum* I, 187, and later historians: e.g. Plummer, *Chronicles* II, 177, and Freeman, *Norman Conquest* I, 278.

diplomas of Edgar and Edward. A *minister* called Æthelsige was the beneficiary of S 863 (dated 987), referring to an estate which has not been identified, and also of S 864 (again dated 987), representing the appropriation of land at Bromley in Kent from the see of Rochester. It seems quite likely that the beneficiary of S 864, at least, was the prominent Æthelsige of the witness lists, for remarks made about him in S 893, by which Bromley was restored to Rochester, suggest that he had been in a position to exercise a considerable influence over the king. He was a 'miserable enemy of Almighty God and of all the people' who perpetrated various (unspecified) crimes of theft and plunder, who tricked the king into appropriating the land from Rochester, and who killed a loyal reeve who was defending the king's possessions against his attack; the last crime was regarded as especially heinous, and Æthelsige was deservedly deprived of all *dignitas* (perhaps indicating that he had held some official position). The crimes of an Æthelsige are also mentioned in S 886: he was outlawed for stealing swine from Æthelwine, the son of Ealdorman Æthelmær, and all his property, including an estate in Gloucestershire, was forfeited to the king. It is not impossible that a single thegn could have held land in Gloucestershire and Kent, but the only reason for identifying the two Æthelsiges as the same man arises from the fact that both were thieves;[113] against the identification stands the difference between a man said to have lost his *dignitas* for murder and a man said to have been outlawed for the comparatively petty crime of pig-rustling. Moreover, the forfeited estate in Gloucestershire had first been given by the king to his man Hawas, before the Wulfric who was the beneficiary of S 886 secured it for himself, so some time must have elapsed between the conviction of Æthelsige and the date (995) of the diploma. Æthelsige *minister* does not attest in a prominent position after 994; two subscriptions in a lower position occur in 995 and 997 and may suggest that by then he was gradually losing his influence, or they may belong to a different person. Whatever the case, the subscriptions seem to continue too late for them to belong to the Æthelsige of S 886; S 893, on the other hand, accords well with them, since it was issued in 998.

[113] The identification is made by Campbell, *Charters of Rochester*, p. xxvii, and by Barker, 'Bromley Charters', pp. 182–3; cf. Sawyer, *Charters of Burton*, p. 42.

The period from the death of Bishop Æthelwold in 984 until *c.* 993 was thus one in which the adolescent King Æthelred was apparently manipulated by a group of men in their own interests and at the expense of various churches.[114] It is important to emphasize that the diplomas in which the king complains about the councillors who had misled him refer specifically to this period and specifically to the abuse of ecclesiastical privileges and estates, since they are often cited as if they referred to the reign as a whole and to more varied activities of the king.

THE YEARS OF MATURITY, *c.* 993–1006

The grant of privileges to Abingdon Abbey in 993 (S 876) provides the first sure indication that the king had come to regret the indiscretions of his youth, though it is conceivable that he had been taking stock of the situation for some time, if any significance can be attached to the apparent drop between 989 and 992 in the number of diplomas issued by him. One could not claim that the composition of the king's council as reflected in the witness lists shows a clean break with the past, as if one group of prominent advisers had suddenly been ousted by another; for although it probably was Ælfgar who was blinded in 993 and although the influence of Æthelsige was clearly on the wane after 994, to some extent it must have been natural causes that reduced the numbers and so perhaps the influence of the faction in ascendancy since 984, enabling others to come to the fore. It is more significant that the rise to prominence of the group of *ministri* who were to dominate the witness lists until 1006 can be located securely in the early 990s. In 993 Æthelred would have been in his twenties, and so, one might suppose, of sufficient maturity and independence of judgement to free himself from the influence of those who had taken advantage of him in his teens, and better able to choose his own associates and to make his own way in the deliberations of the council. The deaths of Ealdorman Brihtnoth at Maldon in 991 and of Ealdorman Æthelwine and

114 Cf. Stafford, 'A Study in Limitations', p. 27. Æthelred was not alone in being misled: 'inimici homines' instructed Brihtwulf, king of Mercia, to take land away from Worcester (S 192), and an inhabitant of Winchester, 'adolescens, animosus et instabilis', tricked King Cnut into believing that land rightfully belonging to the New Minster was in fact his to give away (S 956).

Archbishop Oswald in 992 may have had some additional effect on Æthelred's position, for the loss of the country's two senior and most experienced ealdormen, and of the last of the great triumvirate of monastic reformers, perhaps left him isolated and more directly responsible for the management of the kingdom's affairs.

Æthelred seems to have turned to his family for support. His mother Ælfthryth apparently renewed her attendance at the king's councils *c.* 990,[115] and when attesting diplomas between 993 and 999 she generally occurs in company with the athelings,[116] perhaps having been entrusted with their upbringing;[117] but curiously enough, Æthelred's first wife Ælfgifu does not occur at all.[118] Following the deaths of Æthelwine and Brihtnoth, the senior

---

[115] S 1454: the context is datable 990 × 93. In her will (S 1497), Æthelgifu appeals to 'her royal lord' and to 'her lady', apparently with reference to King Æthelred and Queen Ælfthryth (see Whitelock, *Will of Æthelgifu*, pp. 23–4); unfortunately the will cannot be dated more closely than *c.* 990 × 1001.

[116] S 876, 878, 891 and 896; she occurs without the athelings in S 888, and she was the beneficiary of S 877. For the athelings, see Table 1, which shows clearly how well observed was the order of precedence within the group. It was presumably based on their relative ages: Æthelstan attests S 909 as 'regalium primogenitus filiorum', and as Barlow, *Edward the Confessor*, p. 28, has pointed out, the names follow the sequence of Æthelred's predecessors on the throne (beginning with Æthelstan, and excepting Ecgbert, who is out of series; when Æthelred reached his immediate predecessor he reverted to 'Alfred' as the name for his eighth son); cf. Sawyer, *From Roman Britain*, p. 128. On the relative ages of Alfred and Edward, see Scholz, 'Sulcard', pp. 76–9. Æthelred must have started his family quite young, to have had four sons (and perhaps some daughters) by 993 (S 876); of course there may have been twins. The document recording the truce between Æthelred and Richard of Normandy in 991 refers already to the king's 'sons and daughters, present and future' (Stubbs, *Memorials*, p. 398), and S 1454 reveals that the athelings had a seneschal by 990 × 93.

[117] In his will (S 1503), the atheling Æthelstan refers to his grandmother, Queen Ælfthryth, 'who brought me up'. S 904 reveals that Ælfthryth had used *Æðelingedene* (Dean in Sussex: see Mawer and Stenton, *Place-Names of Sussex* I, xlv) 'in usus proprios', and one is tempted to suggest that this is where she raised Æthelstan, and presumably his brothers as well. There was a battle at *Æpelingadene* in 1001 (on which see Dickins, 'Day of Æthelingadene').

[118] Florence of Worcester states that the mother of Edmund, Eadwig and Æthelstan was Ælfgifu, daughter of a *comes* called Æthelberht (Thorpe, *Chronicon* I, 275): but little reliance can be placed on this statement, since no ealdorman of that name is known from the second half of the tenth century. Ailred of Rievaulx (Migne, *PL* cxcv, col. 741) describes Æthelred's first wife (without naming her) as the daughter of Ealdorman Thored (of Northumbria), and this is altogether more plausible (see Whitelock, *EHD*, p. 48). Unless one is to imagine that Æthelred married more than once before 1002, when he married Emma of Normandy, it seems necessary to suppose that Ælfgifu survived into the late 990s: for to judge from the date of their first appearances in the witness lists, Eadwig and Edgar were born about then. Ælfgifu's absence from the lists is curious because Emma appears several times; the atheling Æthelstan's failure to mention her in his will may be significant, since he does refer to his grandmother and to his foster-mother (see Barlow, *Edward the Confessor*, p. 29 n. 1).

ealdorman was Æthelweard, descended from Æthelred I, king of Wessex (865–71),[119] and thus a kinsman of Æthelred II. More significantly, the groups of *ministri* are dominated from 990 × 93 until 1005 by Æthelred's kinsman Æthelmær (son of Ealdorman Æthelweard) and by his uncle Ordulf (brother of Queen Ælfthryth), and until 999 these two are often joined by Brihtwold, who may also be regarded as one of the king's kinsmen.[120] This royal trio had begun to coalesce during the 980s (see Table 7). Æthelmær's subscriptions begin in 983 and he occurs consistently thereafter, though before 990 often near the bottom of the lists; Ordulf also occurs from the beginning of the reign, sporadically though sometimes prominently up to 986, and consistently between 986 and 990; Brihtwold first occurs in 980 and sporadically thereafter, but not with marked prominence before 990.[121] Æthelmær and Brihtwold occur adjacent to one another in 983 (S 843) and are separated by one man (Leofric) in 984 (S 850); Æthelmær and Ordulf occur together in 987 (S 864, 865); Ordulf and Brihtwold are separated by one man (Ælfwine) in 984 (S 852); all three occur together in 986 (S 861) and 988 (S 868); one man (Leofstan) separates Brihtwold from Ordulf and Æthelmær in S 867, dated 987. Their collective prominence is unmistakable from 990 (S 942, 944), though it was not apparently assured until the disappearance of Ælfgar, Æthelsige and Ælfsige.

Æthelmær, Ordulf and Brihtwold were generally joined by a second trio, comprising Wulfric, Wulfgeat and Wulfheah. The attestations of a Wulfric commence in 980[122] and occur regularly thereafter until 1002. The name is common, and of course not all of these attestations necessarily belong to a single man: two of the name subscribe in 982, 986 and 988, and a Wulfric also occurs in 1009. Nevertheless, it is most likely that the majority of the attestations between 980 and 1002 belong to Wulfric Spot, the founder of

---

[119] Campbell, *Chronicle of Æthelweard*, pp. xii and 2.

[120] This suggestion depends in the first instance on the commemoration of 'Eadgyfu coniunx Byrhtwoldi propinqui regis' in the *Liber Vitae* of the New Minster Winchester (Birch, *Liber Vitae*, p. 58); in context, the king would have been Æthelred. The identification derives support from Brihtwold's association with Æthelmær and Ordulf in the witness lists, on which see further below.

[121] Each of the trio may occur in the last five years of Edgar's reign: for Æthelmær, see S 671, 786, 795 and 801; for Ordulf, see S 802; for Brihtwold, see S 799.

[122] There are several attestations in the same name in the last few years of Edgar's reign.

Burton Abbey in Staffordshire and the brother of the Ælfhelm who by 993 had been appointed ealdorman of Northumbria.[123] In the 980s Wulfric *minister* occurs three times in company with Ælfhelm *minister*, and several times in company with either Æthelmær or Ordulf (see Table 7), perhaps suggesting the development of a personal association between them; he can be regarded as a consistent and prominent witness during the 990s and until his disappearance in 1002. The attestations of Wulfheah commence in 986[124] and continue until 1005; he occurs six times in the 980s, and on four occasions he is positioned immediately after Ælfhelm, suggesting strongly his identification as the Wulfheah named by Florence of Worcester as Ealdorman Ælfhelm's son.[125] Thus we find a second family group – the brothers Wulfric and Ælfhelm, and Wulfheah, son of Ælfhelm – appearing occasionally during the course of the 980s; they were accorded collective prominence by the end of the decade, for the document recording the decisions of the synod of London held in 988 × 90 (S 877) shows Ælfhelm, Wulfheah and Wulfric, Wulfrun's son, at the head of the list of thegns present, and shortly afterwards Ælfhelm was promoted to the office of ealdorman, making his first appearance in S 876 (dated 993). The subscriptions of Wulfgeat commence in 986,[126] though he occurs without particular associations and without prominence until 993; from 993 onwards he is associated consistently with Wulfric and Wulfheah, and though his origins appear to have been different it seems therefore that he developed a particular relationship with these two.

Taking the evidence of the witness lists as a whole, one cannot avoid the impression that during the 990s and early 1000s the king was surrounded by men of considerable calibre, many of whom turn out to have been closely associated with the advancement of the monastic cause. Amongst the ecclesiastics we may single out

---

[123] The prominent Wulfric of S 877 and 939, at meetings of the *witan*, is described as the son of Wulfrun; S 886 is a grant of land at Dumbleton to Wulfric son of Wulfrun, and since the land was disposed of by Wulfric Spot in his will (S 1536), the identification of the son of Wulfrun as the founder of Burton is established. See also Sawyer, *Charters of Burton*, pp. xxxviii–xliii.

[124] Attestations in the same name are rare in the last decade of Edgar's reign: see S 782 and 787.

[125] Thorpe, *Chronicon* I, 158, and Whitelock, *Wills*, p. 153.

[126] There are, however, several attestations in the name of a Wulfgeat during the reigns of Edgar and Edward the Martyr.

Sigeric, archbishop of Canterbury from 990 until his death in October 994, best known, perhaps, as the dedicatee of Ælfric's first and second series of Catholic Homilies.[127] He is said to have been instrumental in persuading Æthelred to found the abbey of Cholsey, for the soul of King Edward,[128] and also to commemorate Edward at Shaftesbury.[129] On the political front, he is known twice to have been engaged in negotiations with Viking armies, once after the Maldon campaign in 991, when he initiated the policy of paying *gafol* to the enemy, and again in the autumn of 994, when he was forced to buy them off in order to save the city of Canterbury.[130] He gained much posthumous notoriety for such actions, and appears with the nickname (Sigeric) 'Danegeld' in a late fourteenth-century history of the archbishops of Canterbury.[131] Wulfstan the homilist makes an unheralded appearance as bishop of London in 996, and at once he is regularly accorded a place in the lists after the archbishops and the bishop of Winchester, before his translation to the see of York in 1002:[132] his promotion was thus rapid, doubtless in recognition of his prodigious abilities. Wulfstan's importance as one of the king's legislators has in recent years been firmly established.[133] He was no less important (at least in an Anglo-Saxon context) as a political theorist, and one only has to read his tract on the *Institutes of Polity* to gain some idea of the counsel he may have proffered to Æthelred on the nature of a king's responsibilities and on the proper paths to follow for the government of the kingdom;[134]

---

[127] See Sisam, *Studies*, pp. 156–60. Ælfric invited the archbishop to correct any heresies or fallacious statements that he might find in the homilies (Thorpe, *Homilies* I, 3).

[128] Vaughan, *John of Wallingford*, p. 59. King Æthelred had been given land at Cholsey by Queen Ælfthryth, some time before 996 (S 877); Germanus attests as abbot of Ramsey in 993 (S 876), but as abbot of Cholsey by 997 (S 891).

[129] Goscelin, in his *Life* of St Ive (Migne, *PL* CLV, cols. 87–8).

[130] *ASC* MSS 'C', 'D', 'E' *s.a.* 991, and S 882. Reference is made in II Æthelred (Liebermann, *Gesetze* I, 220) to the local truce that Sigeric made with the Vikings, probably an allusion to the agreement of 994: see Gordon, 'Date of Æthelred's Treaty', pp. 26–31, and cf. John, 'War and Society', p. 175 n. 13.

[131] Wharton, *Anglia Sacra* I, 4. See also the remarks of William of Malmesbury, in Stubbs, *De Gestis Regum Anglorum* I, 187, and of Freeman, *Norman Conquest* I, 276.

[132] For Wulfstan at London, see Whitelock, *Bishops of London*, pp. 25–31. The only diploma in which Wulfstan does not occur immediately after Ælfheah of Winchester is S 893, dated 998; in S 892, Ælfheah of Lichfield occurs before Ælfheah of Winchester and Wulfstan.

[133] See, e.g., Whitelock, 'Archbishop Wulfstan, Homilist and Statesman', and Bethurum, 'Wulfstan'.

[134] See Bethurum Loomis, '*Regnum* and *Sacerdotium*', and Loyn, 'Church and State'.

one suspects, however, that his advice was more notable for its ideology than valuable for its practicability. Ælfweard, abbot of Glastonbury, appears amongst the witnesses to royal diplomas for the first time in 987, though he had been made abbot about ten years earlier when his predecessor Sigar became bishop of Wells; he attests consistently thereafter until his death in 1009 and almost invariably in first or second place. It is not clear why Ælfweard should have gained this pre-eminence over his fellow abbots so suddenly and yet so long after his appointment, but one might speculate that Sigeric had a hand in his advancement. For Sigeric himself had been a monk at Glastonbury before his appointment *c.* 980 as abbot of St Augustine's Canterbury[135] – so perhaps in the early years of Ælfweard's abbacy – and as bishop of Ramsbury from 985 × 6 to 990 he may have been in a position to bring his former abbot into prominence; two letters written by Ælfweard offering congratulations and advice to Sigeric on the occasion of the latter's promotion to the see of Canterbury demonstrate that there was a close relationship between the two men, and reveal Ælfweard as an enthusiastic exponent of the hermeneutic style so popular in the tenth century.[136] Wulfgar, abbot of Abingdon (990–1016), was a prominent witness from 993 until the end of the reign, and according to the traditions of his abbey he played an important part in persuading the king to abandon his hostile attitude towards Abingdon and instead to make good the losses it had recently suffered;[137] he is mentioned in S 937 as the king's abbot, 'friendly to me with complete devotion',[138] who was wont loyally and gratefully to show humble and friendly obedience to him. Ælfweard and Wulfgar were joined at the top of the lists of abbots by Ælfsige, abbot of the New Minster Winchester from 988 until his death in 1007: little is known of him, but he can presumably be identified as the Abbot Ælfsige specially named in the text of S 876 as a witness to the proceedings at Gillingham. Amongst the laymen prominent in the late tenth and early eleventh centuries we may single out the king's

135 Hearne, *Domerham* I, 92.
136 See Stubbs, *Memorials*, pp. 399–403, and Lapidge, 'Hermeneutic Style', p. 97; note also Dumville, 'Anglian Collection', pp. 43–4.
137 Stevenson, *Chronicon* I, 357–8; see also S 876, 918 and 937.
138 The expression 'tota mihi devotione benignus' in S 937 may be compared with the description of Wulfgar as 'mihi humillima devotione subjectus' in S 876.

kinsman Æthelweard, ealdorman of the Western Provinces, the patron of Ælfric the homilist and the author of a Latin translation of the *Anglo-Saxon Chronicle*: he was thus evidently a cultured and literate man, and as the senior ealdorman from 993 until his death *c.* 998[139] he may have been in a position to provide useful secular backing for the more favourable attitude adopted by the king towards the Church. Æthelmær, son of Ealdorman Æthelweard, was the founder of Cerne Abbey in Dorset and of Eynsham Abbey in Oxfordshire, and like his father was the patron of Ælfric, who declares them both to be enthusiastic readers of his translations;[140] it seems that Æthelmær was a *discðegn* in King Æthelred's household.[141] Ordulf, the king's uncle, was the founder of Tavistock Abbey in Devon, and if we may identify him as the Ordulf named in the will of Ælfwold, bishop of Crediton, he too was a literate man, assuming he was expected to read the 'Hrabanus and a martyrology' bequeathed to him.[142] There is no reason to doubt that Æthelmær and Ordulf were, as their subscriptions to royal diplomas suggest, amongst the king's principal advisers and associates in the 990s and in the early years of the eleventh century: in the Abingdon diploma of 993 (S 876), they are named specifically in the text, together with Abbot Ælfsige, as witnesses to the proceedings at Gillingham, and in another Abingdon diploma (S 937) the king identifies them as being amongst the loyal men who had encouraged him to compensate the abbey for the loss of some of its estates. The only other layman mentioned in the same connection was Wulfgeat, doubtless the prominent thegn of the witness lists: he is described as the king's *dilectus minister*, according well with Florence of Worcester's reference to the thegn as one whom the

---

[139] The consistency of his subscriptions as an ealdorman make it likely that he would have died soon after his last attestation (see Table 6); cf. Barker, 'Æthelweard', pp. 87–9. It is sometimes said that Æthelweard was alive during the episcopate of Buruhwold, bishop of Cornwall, since the two names occur together in a St Petroc's manumission (Haddan and Stubbs, *Councils* I, 678–9). But in the light of a revised episcopal succession for Cornwall (see Appendix 1, p. 264), the manumission should be dated post 1011 × 12: the Ealdorman Æthelweard of the 990s was certainly dead by 1005 (see S 911), so the one of the manumission must have been someone else, perhaps the earlier Æthelweard's son's son-in-law (cf. Campbell, *Chronicle of Æthelweard*, pp. xv–xvi).

[140] Skeat, *Lives of Saints* I, 4.

[141] S 914. In S 884, dated 995, mention is made of Æthelmær the king's *satrapa* (a word used in glossaries as a lemma for *þegn*) as having given land to Muchelney Abbey.

[142] S 1492; Wormald, 'Literacy in Anglo-Saxon England', p. 110.

king loved almost more than anyone.[143] And finally, we should recall in this connection that the prominent Wulfric of the lists was Wulfric Spot, who founded Burton Abbey in Staffordshire and endowed it with a large proportion of his very substantial landed wealth.[144] Many of these men had been present at, but not prominent in, the king's councils during the later 980s, and one cannot avoid the impression that they gradually acquired greater influence over Æthelred and that by c. 993 they had effectively become his principal advisers,[145] encouraging a change in his attitudes at a time when he was anyway of greater maturity of mind: thus the witness lists neatly reflect the explicit statements in S 876, 885, 891 and 893 to the effect that the king had come to regret the indiscretions of his youth and had resolved to mend his ways. And if Æthelred complained about the councillors who had misled him in the later 980s, he readily praised the wisdom, loyalty and goodness of those who advised him in the 990s.

Against this background, a case could be made for regarding the 990s in particular as a period when the internal affairs of Æthelred's kingdom prospered, under the guidance of the king acting with the assistance and advice of a group of distinguished ecclesiastics and laymen. The mechanics of the reformed system of coinage had been perfected in the opening years of Æthelred's reign, presumably by those responsible for devising the details of the reform in the last years of Edgar's reign: the system depended in part on the periodic changing of the type in circulation, and it appears that the first two such recoinages were achieved c. 979 and c. 985.[146] That the system continued to operate successfully in the 990s is thus not in itself of particular significance, but it is important to appreciate just how

---

[143] Thorpe, *Chronicon* I, 158. As Whitelock, 'Two Notes', p. 124, has pointed out, there are no grounds for identifying Ælfric's correspondent 'Wulfget æt Ylmandune' as the prominent thegn; cf., e.g., Hurt, *Ælfric*, p. 38 (and the other identifications made *ibid.* pp. 38–9, of Ælfric's correspondents 'Sigwerd æt Eastheolon' and 'Sigefyrð' as *ministri* who attested S 911, are equally insecure).

[144] It is worth noting that the names of Æthelmær, Ordulf and Wulfric are recorded amongst the friends and benefactors of the New Minster Winchester (Birch, *Liber Vitae*, p. 54). In addition, we find there the names of Brihtwold, Wulfheah and Fræna, all of whom were amongst the consistent witnesses in the 990s.

[145] Note that the list of attesting *ministri* in S 876 seems to reflect a transitional phase between the lists of the 980s and those of the 990s.

[146] The *locus classicus* for Edgar's reform of the coinage remains Dolley and Metcalf, 'Reform of the English Coinage'.

well it fared at this time under apparently adverse political circumstances.[147] The introduction of the *Crux* type *c.* 991 marked a return to a heavier initial weight standard,[148] and at most mints the mean weight of coins struck during the currency of the type was relatively high, despite the demand for it occasioned by the payments of geld in 991 and 994.[149] The *Intermediate Small Cross* and *Transitional Crux* types appear to represent experimental issues produced late in the currency of *Crux* proper, but it seems that when the recoinage was undertaken *c.* 997, it was managed with complete efficiency, and there are no mules between *Crux* and the succeeding *Long Cross* pennies to suggest any failure in the supply of the new dies. Moreover, the early *Long Cross* pennies were struck at a weight standard that made them the heaviest since King Edgar's reform, and again the mean weight for the type was relatively high, despite the pressure of Viking raids and the demands on the kingdom's resources entailed in resisting them (including a large payment of geld in 1002).[150] Further evidence for effective control of the coinage during the 990s can be derived from the analysis of the

---

[147] For what follows, see Butler, 'Metrology', pp. 201–4; Petersson, *Anglo-Saxon Currency*, pp. 107–13; Lyon, 'Some Problems', pp. 197–201; and Dolley, 'Coinage of Æthelræd II', pp. 118–29.

[148] One should note, however, that the increase in weight standard that the *Crux* type represents could only be regarded as significant if it were certain that the type replaced the *Second Hand* type in particular, and not the *Hand* types in general: see Lyon, 'Some Problems', Fig. 2 and note on p. 199.

[149] *Crux* pennies are the first to occur in substantial quantities in Scandinavian hoards, according well with the historical evidence that the payments in the 990s were the first ones made to the Vikings. Metcalf, 'Ranking of Boroughs', pp. 179–80, has made the very interesting suggestion that the large volume of silver bullion used for minting *Crux* pennies in the 990s might reflect economic prosperity at this time; as evidence for trade, this would correspond with IV Æthelred 2 – 2,12 (on which see Wormald, 'Æthelred the Lawmaker, p. 62), dated by Liebermann to the period *c.* 991–*c.* 1002 (*Gesetze* III, 162).

[150] Lyon, 'Some Problems', p. 200, seeks to explain the heavy standard of the type in terms of a tribute paid early in its currency, but it remains that the only *recorded* payment within the currency of *Long Cross* was the one of 24,000 pounds in 1002. There does seem to have been a progressive reduction of weight standard during the currency of the *Crux* and *Long Cross* types, but it is less marked than in earlier and later types, and to some extent it is to be understood (on Petersson's thesis) as a reduction planned by the authorities for its beneficial economic effects. Five hoards deposited in different parts of England at about the turn of the tenth century and made up exclusively of *Long Cross* pennies (see Dolley, *Hiberno-Norse Coins*, p. 39) may reflect at one level the turmoil of the period, but at another level they show how the regulation that only one type should be in circulation at any time was successfully observed; see further Metcalf, 'Ranking of Boroughs', pp. 168–70.

patterns of die-production in Æthelred's reign. It is apparent from the identification of stylistic variations in certain types that the production of dies was organized on a regional basis in the opening years and closing decades of the reign, during the currency of the *First Small Cross* and *First Hand* types (i.e. from 978 up to *c.* 985) and during the currency of the *Long Cross, Helmet* and *Last Small Cross* types (together covering the period from *c.* 997 to 1016).[151] It is certainly tempting to connect the initial period of decentralization with relaxation of royal authority during Æthelred's minority,[152] and to regard the subsequent period of decentralization as indicating that it was then felt desirable to spread responsibility for the production of dies in order to avoid the danger that the system might be paralysed by a Viking attack on a centralized organization (for example, at London).[153] The years between *c.* 985 and *c.* 997, when the *Second Hand* and *Crux* types seem successively to have been in circulation, would thus be left as a period when it was feasible both to contemplate and to exercise firm royal control,[154] and this in turn would accord well with the evidence of the royal diplomas. However, it may be logically inconsistent to regard decentralization of die-production as symptomatic of administrative weakness between 978 and *c.* 985 and as indicative of administrative flexibility between *c.* 997 and 1016. Since the decentralization of die-production makes such good sense, as a practical expedient to match the profusion of mints, it would arguably be more natural to regard it at all times as suggesting that the coinage was under effective control, though just as the pattern of minting changes during the reign (often in response to political circumstances) so one would expect the regional organization of die-production to be modified accordingly. It is quite clear that the *Second Hand* and *Crux* types convey a striking impression of uniformity which gives them a special place in Æthelred's series, but until the outcome of current numismatic research is known it would be hazardous to attach particular

---

151 See Dolley, 'The Coins', pp. 358–9; and *idem*, 'Coinage of Æthelræd II', pp. 118–20 and 125–9.

152 Dolley, 'The Coins', p. 358.

153 See Dolley, 'Reflections on Hildebrand Type A', pp. 34 and 40, apropos the decentralization of die-production which he discovered in the *Last Small Cross* type.

154 Dolley, 'Coinage of Æthelræd II', pp. 121–3; see also Wormald, 'Æthelred the Lawmaker', pp. 62–3.

historical significance to this circumstance. Some numismatists would still claim that the *Second Hand* type was but a regional variety (not struck at York or Lincoln) of a general *Hand* type current during the 980s,[155] and it is emerging that dies were cut at more than one centre at least in the closing phase of the currency of the *Crux* type.[156] Even if it does turn out that *Second Hand*, like *Crux*, was a substantive type, it would remain to consider under what circumstances such uniformity of style might be achieved: did a system used in the opening years of the reign fall into temporary abeyance while one die-cutting centre or even one man took sole responsibility for the manufacture of all the dies for a type, and was there subsequently a reversion to the earlier system, or was it simply that regional die-cutters employed for the *Second Hand* and *Crux* types followed their patterns (which presumably were issued by a central authority) particularly carefully? Whatever the solution may prove to be, there can be no mistaking the quality of the coinage in the 990s, and indeed the reformed system of coinage as a whole demonstrates the remarkable sophistication attained in one area of royal government in the late tenth century, and thus suggests to the historian what he can reasonably expect in others.[157]

His expectations are not disappointed on investigation of the other aspects of royal government as practised in the 990s. In the first place, the period may have seen some of the finest legislation ever produced by the Anglo-Saxon kings. According to S 891, the *witan* gathered at Wantage in Berkshire in the spring of 997 'ob diuersarum quaestiones causarum corrigendas', and it may well have been on this occasion that Æthelred's so-called 'third' code of laws was drawn up, since it opens with the statement that it was promulgated at Wantage.[158] The code sets out in particular to define some of the customs relating to legal procedure in the Danelaw, and the degree of Norse influence on the terminology and practice of the law shows clearly how it was legislation sympathetic to the distinc-

[155] See Lyon,   ms', p. 197 and 200.
[156] See Dolle   f Æthelræd II', p. 123, citing unpublished work by Mr Mark Blackburn.
[157] While I must remain responsible for the above presentation of the numismatic evidence, I should like to record my indebtedness to Mr Mark Blackburn, Professor Michael Dolley and Dr Michael Metcalf for their guidance on these matters.
[158] See above, p. 102 n. 56.

tive Anglo-Danish community that had grown up in eastern
England during the course of the tenth century.[159] Its provisions
in many ways complement those for legal procedure given in
Æthelred's so-called 'first' code of laws, enacted at Woodstock in
Oxfordshire and specifically said to have followed English custom.[160]
It seems therefore not unreasonable to regard these two codes as
contemporary pieces of legislation and both as part of an overall
attempt to define procedural aspects of the distinction in legal terms
between the English and 'Danish' areas of the kingdom. Secondly,
there are signs that the king reorganized the structure of secular
authority in the 990s, perhaps in response to the deaths of Ealdorman
Brihtnoth in 991 and of Ealdorman Æthelwine in 992, which had
left only Æthelweard, 'Occidentalium Prouinciarum dux' (S 891),
and Ælfric, 'Wentaniensium Prouinciarum dux', as ealdormen south
of the Humber; Thored of Northumbria is not heard of again after
his part in the military fiasco of 992.[161] A series of new appointments
followed swiftly. Ælfhelm was made ealdorman of Northumbria
('Norðanhumbrensium Prouinciarum dux' in S 891), and it is
interesting to find the king promoting a member of a Mercian
family – and so perhaps someone without excessive vested interests
in the area of his authority – who seems to have been a long-standing
associate of the royal family.[162] Ælfhelm first appears as ealdorman
in 993, and in the following year we find the first subscriptions of
Leofsige, 'Orientalium-Saxonum dux' (S 891), a prompt successor to
Brihtnoth on the vulnerable eastern coast by the Thames estuary, and
also of Leofwine, 'Wicciarum Prouinciarum dux', covering an area
(around Gloucestershire) that had not previously been represented
in Æthelred's reign.[163] Even these appointments left substantial

---

[159] I incline more towards the traditional interpretation of III Æthelred as the codification
of existing provincial custom (Stenton, *Anglo-Saxon England*, pp. 508–12) than I do
towards its interpretation as 'a flagrant encroachment on the legal autonomy of the
Danelaw' by the extension to it of English practices (Lund, 'King Edgar and the Danelaw',
pp. 192–4; see also Richardson and Sayles, *Law and Legislation*, p. 25).

[160] Liebermann, *Gesetze* I, 216.

[161] Thored's responsibilities may in fact have been restricted to southern Northumbria: see
Hart, *Charters of Northern England*, p. 258, and John, 'War and Society', pp. 194–5. See
also Whitelock, 'Dealings of the Kings of England', pp. 79–80.

[162] *Ibid.* pp. 80–1, and *idem*, *EHD*, pp. 48–9.

[163] Note that it appears to have been Æthelred's practice not automatically to appoint a
successor when one of his ealdormen died (or went into exile): there were no successors
to Eadwine of Sussex (died 982), Æthelwine of East Anglia (died 992) or Leofsige of

parts of the kingdom without high-ranking secular officials, and it may have been to compensate for this deficiency and to improve the articulation of central with local government that the king gave further impetus to the development of the shire as a unit of administration[164] by encouraging the emergence of the shire-reeve as his representative at that level,[165] apparently in the late tenth and early eleventh centuries (though it has to be admitted that the evidence on this point is far from conclusive). And thirdly, a substantial number of important diplomas for the Church were produced during the 990s and early 1000s, reflecting the king's changed attitudes and the influence of his prominent advisers. The beneficiaries include Abingdon Abbey in 993 and 999 (S 876, 896 and 937), the see of Cornwall and Wilton Abbey in 994 (S 880 and 881), Muchelney Abbey in 995 (S 884), the see of Rochester in 995 and 998 (S 885 and 893), the Old Minster Winchester in 996 and 997 (S 889 and 891), St Albans Abbey in 996 and 1005 (S 888 and 912), Sherborne Abbey in 998 (S 895), Shaftesbury Abbey in 1001 (S 899), the abbeys of Westminster and Wherwell in 1002 (S 903 and 904), the abbeys of Burton and St Frideswide's in 1004 (S 906 and 909) and Eynsham Abbey in 1005 (S 911).[166] Together, the diplomas

Essex (banished 1002), and several years elapsed before the appointment of successors to Ælfric of Mercia (banished 985; succeeded by Eadric in 1007) and Æthelweard of the Western Provinces (died *c.* 998; succeeded by Æthelmær *c.* 1012). If the practice can be dignified as a policy, it seems that the king may have been trying to break the hold of local families on the ealdormanries, and by so doing affirm that the office of ealdorman was a personal one held at his pleasure.

[164] The shiring of western Mercia was effected at an indeterminable point in the tenth century, though probably earlier rather than later: see Stenton, *Anglo-Saxon England*, pp. 336–7, Kirby, *Making of Early England*, p. 176, and Hart, *Hidation of Northamptonshire*, pp. 13–14; Taylor, 'Mercian Shires', p. 24, assigns the shiring of Mercia to Ealdorman Eadric in 1007–8, and his views were endorsed by Finberg, *Charters of West Midlands*, p. 230. A document known as the County Hidage (on which see Maitland, *DB and Beyond*, pp. 455–7) is sometimes regarded as a product of Æthelred's reign (e.g. Kirby, *Making of Early England*, pp. 176–7), though not on any specific grounds.

[165] The official known as the *sciresman* appears in the last decades of the tenth century (S 1456, 1458) and is probably the equivalent of the shire-reeve known from Cnut's reign onwards (see Whitelock, *Wills*, p. 191); there is a plethora of references to reeves (king's reeves, reeves of boroughs, high-reeves) in sources relating to the late tenth and early eleventh centuries (e.g. S 883, 893–4, 908, 910, 915, 918, 925–6, 1454 and 1456; *ASC* MS 'A', *s.a.* 1001; *ASC* MSS 'C', 'D', 'E', *s.a.* 1002, 1003 and 1011) that may reflect their increasing importance as royal officials; and for friction between ealdormen and reeves in Æthelred's reign, see S 883 and *ASC* MSS 'C', 'D', 'E', *s.a.* 1002 (and S 926). See further Stenton, *Anglo-Saxon England*, pp. 548–50, and Morris, *Medieval English Sheriff*, pp. 22–3.

[166] See also Hart, *Charters of Eastern England*, p. 253, for a record that Æthelred confirmed the foundation of Cranborne Abbey in 1000; Finberg, *Charters of Wessex*, pp. 103–4,

issued in favour of the Church during this period account for the majority of such diplomas issued throughout Æthelred's reign, and the earlier emphasis on grants to laymen was thus reversed. One might even consider the possibility that the period was one of the most prosperous for the advancement of the ecclesiastical cause before the Norman Conquest. The emphasis on the reign of King Edgar as the zenith of the reform movement may to some extent be artificial, for if the large number of spurious diplomas engendered in the wake of the movement could be isolated and set aside, the impression would probably emerge that many were fathered on Edgar (in particular) as the king principally associated in the historical sources with its propagation,[167] leaving the diplomas of the middle years of Æthelred's reign to represent a significant further contribution to its progress; one should, however, maintain a distinction between the reign of Edgar as the period *par excellence* of the reform itself, and this part of the reign of Æthelred as a period when – after setbacks during the reign of Edward the Martyr and during the later 980s – the spirit that had activated the reform was kindled afresh in the hearts of those with the power to advance its material interests.[168] Not only were privileges confirmed, lands restored and houses founded and endowed; the period also saw extensive English missionary activity in Scandinavia[169] and, now appropriately rather than paradoxically, was marked by notable achievements in the realms of material culture and scholarship. The opinion of palaeographers and art-historians gravitates towards the turn of the tenth century as the period during which many of the finest decorated manuscripts to survive from Anglo-Saxon England were produced, and the same is true of other (undecorated) manuscripts of Latin and vernacular works, including some (if not all) of

---

for a reference to a diploma for Amesbury Abbey that may have been issued *c.* 1002; and Mellows, *Hugh Candidus*, p. 39, for a statement that Æthelred confirmed various estates to Peterborough Abbey during the abbacy of Cenulf, i.e. between 992 × 3 and 1006.

[167] This may be especially true at Abingdon: see the diplomas cited above, p. 11 nn. 15–17.

[168] For a judicious assessment of the reform movement in the late tenth and early eleventh centuries, see Knowles, *Monastic Order*, pp. 58–69; see also Gem, 'A Recession in English Architecture', pp. 28–9; cf. John, 'War and Society', p. 191.

[169] See Knowles, *Monastic Order*, pp. 67–8, and Birkeli, 'Earliest Missionary Activities'; see also Gjerløw, *Adoratio Crucis*, pp. 35–7, for Anglo-Saxon service books of the late tenth to early eleventh century in Norway and Sweden.

the four great poetical codices.[170] There was marked flowering of original composition in Anglo-Latin, including the *Vita Dunstani* by 'B', Byrhtferth's *Vita Oswaldi* and the *Lives* of St Æthelwold by Wulfstan of Winchester and by Ælfric.[171] The royal diplomas of the 990s and 1000s themselves display much originality and even a certain quality in their drafting, and arguably testify to the level of culture available at the king's court.[172] But above all, of course, the period witnessed the publication of some of Ælfric's most important and ambitious works.[173]

It is ironical that the diplomas which provide a tangible historical context for these achievements are also those used to suggest that Æthelred's reign was a period in which lawlessness and weakness of government prevailed. For the tendency of the draftsmen of diplomas to provide some account of the circumstances leading up to the transaction, and in so doing sometimes to describe criminal acts that led to the forfeiture of property, is characteristic of these years.[174] The tendency could be explained in different ways. Perhaps the general stability of land tenure in the last quarter of the tenth century was affected by the increase in litigation over titles to estates, which itself arose from the rapid changes of ownership during the reign of King Eadwig followed by the large-scale acquisition of land by the reformed religious houses. Under such circumstances, it would have been in the interests of the beneficiary to ensure that his title was fully protected, not only by the religious penalties threatened by the sanction of his diploma, but also by the incorporation of a statement of the king's right to possess and to grant the land to him in the first place.[175] For the narrative sections were undoubtedly intended to forestall potentially awkward

---

170 An element of special pleading may be involved here, but this is my impression from perusing the works of T.A.M. Bishop, Francis Wormald and Elżbieta Temple (for references, see Temple, *Anglo-Saxon Manuscripts*, pp. 32–3 and her catalogue, pp. 54–84); on the poetical codices (Ker, *Catalogue*, nos. 116, 216, 334 and 394) see Sisam, *Studies*, pp. 99–100.

171 See, e.g., Lapidge, 'Hermeneutic Style', pp. 81–3, 87 and 91–4, and Winterbottom, *Three Lives*.

172 One can but look forward to a detailed study of the language and content of (in particular) the proems and sanctions in tenth- and eleventh-century diplomas, and to the revelations about the background, affiliations and interests of their draftsmen that such a study would doubtless provide.

173 See especially Clemoes, 'Chronology', and *idem*, 'Ælfric'; also Pope, *Homilies* I and II.

174 See above, pp. 95–8.

175 See Stenton, *Latin Charters*, p. 82.

situations in which disappointed heirs came forward to claim (perhaps with older title-deeds) estates that had been forfeited to the king and that they had expected to inherit, or in which the recent history of the estate had been complicated enough to offer scope for counter-claims.[176] However, the concentration of the narrative diplomas in the late tenth and early eleventh centuries tends to dissociate their appearance from the litigation that followed the activities of Eadwig and Edgar, for they are rare in the 980s, even after the disturbances of Edward's reign. So the explanation for their proliferation may lie rather in the developments within Æthelred's reign: in reversing certain decisions and grants made in his youth, the king may himself have created the conditions that necessitated this degree of explanation in his diplomas. Whatever the case, one should hesitate before interpreting the accounts of crimes contained in Æthelred's diplomas as a sign that lawlessness prevailed in his reign and that the king was powerless to prevent such behaviour. It seems likely that lands which had been forfeited to the king through the processes of the law had always constituted an important source of land for redistribution to the king's subjects and to religious houses,[177] but it was only under special circumstances that the draftsmen of diplomas would choose to specify the crimes that led to the forfeiture. Of course one should not belittle the significance of the particular crimes described in Æthelred's diplomas,[178] but it is

---

[176] Note the occurrence in S 883, 896 and 927 of formulae whose purpose was to annul older charters for the estates in question: one suspects that the owners of lands forfeited to or confiscated by the king (or their kinsmen) might often secrete their title-deeds with the intention of using them subsequently to recover their lands, making the inclusion of these formulae in the new diplomas an advisable precaution; cf. in this connection the circumstances anticipated in S 443. The inclusion of a formula annulling older charters should not normally have been necessary or even appropriate, and it is possible that the occurrence of one can therefore be taken as a sign that some contention surrounded the recent history of the estate; but one should note that such formulae often occur, no less appropriately, in diplomas drawn up to replace older title-deeds that had been mislaid.

[177] II Cnut 13 and 77 (Liebermann, *Gesetze* I, 316, 364) describe circumstances in which bookland was forfeited to the king; see also Adams *et al.*, *Essays*, pp. 64–7, and Napier and Stevenson, *Crawford Charters*, p. 113 (citing S 138, 155, 254, 362, 375, 443, 753, 792, 814, 883, 886, 892–3, 901, 911, 916, 918, 926–7, 934, 937, 939, 991, 1026, 1211–12, 1377 and 1457, to which one might add S 842, 869, 877, 896, 923, 1229 and 1447) for instances of forfeiture from before, during and after the reign of Æthelred.

[178] The account of Wulfbald's crimes in S 877 appears to be particularly damning (see Whitelock, *EHD*, p. 575): three times he ignored the king's instructions, and when he did so on a fourth occasion all his property was assigned to the king; even so, Wulfbald managed to retain it until his death. It is important to appreciate that the events described took place in the 980s, for Wulfbald died some time before the synod of London in

important to emphasize that a development in the habits of draftsmen of diplomas has created a misleading impression that wicked
deeds were especially or even uniquely characteristic of his reign.

Nevertheless, the sorry tale of military disaster recounted in the
Anglo-Saxon Chronicle can hardly be discounted as a complete
misrepresentation of the truth, and it precludes one from regarding
the late tenth and early eleventh centuries as a period of prosperity
in all respects. The period saw the inception of the policy of paying
tribute to the Viking forces and the extraordinary decision in 1002
to kill 'all the Danish men who were in England'; neither of these
measures seems to reflect creditably on the quality of the decisions
being taken at a high level, and both have been duly censured by
historians.[179] The payments are regarded as an admission of weakness and as a demonstration of incapacity to resist, calculated only to
encourage further attacks for more tribute; the massacre is regarded
as a vicious and even paranoid outburst of incredible magnitude,
and as one of no less incredible folly since it was bound to incite acts
of reprisal. Some attempt, however, should be made to consider what
factors led the king and his councillors to take these decisions and
to ascertain how they were regarded by those in a position to
understand the military and political background to them. The
payments represented the application in King Æthelred's reign of a
policy that had been applied already in the ninth century,[180] and
that had been envisaged earlier on in the tenth century.[181] It is clear
from the support that the king received from his subjects in raising
the money, and from similar measures taken by other secular and
ecclesiastical leaders for the preservation of their own localities,[182]

988 × 90, and should therefore be used as evidence only for conditions during Æthelred's
youth. But one might also question whether Wulfbald's behaviour is indicative of a
weakness peculiar to this period: III Æthelstan 6 (Liebermann, *Gesetze* I, 170) reveals that
King Æthelstan was confronted with rich men or men of powerful family who could
repeatedly commit crimes (see also IV Æthelstan 3 and V Æthelstan Prol., 1; the king's
remedy was to remove such offenders to other parts of the kingdom), and I Edgar (i.e.
the Hundred Ordinance) 3 (*ibid.* p. 192) envisages circumstances in which someone might
ignore the authority of the Hundred three times, before suffering forfeiture and outlawry
on the fourth occasion; see also II Cnut 83–83.2.

[179] See further Keynes, 'Declining Reputation', p. 239.

[180] *ASC s.a.* 865; S 1278.

[181] In his will (S 1515) King Eadred allotted 16,000 pounds to be used for the good of his
people, should they need to purchase relief from hunger and from the heathen army.

[182] See Keynes, 'Declining Reputation', p. 250 n. 66. For evidence that the king had the
co-operation of his subjects in raising the money, see S 912 (Leofric, abbot of St Albans,

that the policy was not merely the defeatist reaction of an individual (King Æthelred) shirking his responsibilities, but rather was the reaction of the whole nation to the military predicament of the day: direct military action on its own could never contain the unprovoked and unpredictable attacks of the Vikings, and anyway risked the inevitable and irreversible consequences of a decisive defeat in the field; in such desperate straits it may have seemed more advisable for a wealthy nation to divest itself of some of its riches in order to gain immediate relief from the threat of devastation and to gain valuable time for making better preparations.[183] The policy certainly achieved its intended effect, for the absence of recorded raids in 995–6, 1002, 1005 and 1007–8 follows the making of payments; and one should not forget that some resistance was offered,[184] however futile it may have seemed in retrospect to the chronicler. Of course the policy was to no avail in the long run, because no payment to one Viking force could prevent any other Viking force under different leadership from attacking the country subsequently in the hope of getting rewards for itself; but in this respect it was little different from more determined military action, for while the defeat of one force might discourage further attacks, it could not prevent them all. In short, the problem that confronted King Æthelred was that he had more than one enemy.[185] Like the payments of geld, the massacre of St Brice's Day also needs to be understood against the background of the contemporary situation. The chronicler reports simply that in 1002 'the king ordered to be slain all the Danish men who were in England . . . because the king had been informed that they would treacherously deprive him, and

purchased an estate from the king 'quando illud graue uectigal Danis exsoluebamus'), S 943 (a Dane called Toti gave the king 'in adiutorium unius libre argenti appensionem de auro purissimo ad reddendum tributum', for which he received an estate in return) and above, p. 108 n. 73. For similar measures taken by others, see S 882 (Archbishop Sigeric), II Æthelred 1 (Archbishop Sigeric, Ealdorman Æthelweard and Ealdorman Ælfric), ASC MSS 'C', 'D', 'E', s.a. 1004 (Ulfcetel), 1009 (people of East Kent) and 1016 (Londoners). There is some evidence that religious houses might have been obliged to sell land in order to raise money for payment to the Danes: see Hamilton, *De Gestis Pontificum*, p. 411 (Brihtwold, abbot of Malmesbury), Mellows, *Hugh Candidus*, pp. 64–5 (Ælfsige, abbot of Peterborough) and S 933 (Æthelric, bishop of Sherborne).

[183] See Brooke, *Saxon and Norman Kings*, pp. 131–2.
[184] See Keynes, 'Declining Reputation', p. 246 n. 30.
[185] Thus the rune stone at Yttergärde in Uppland, Sweden: 'And Ulv has in England taken three gelds. That was the first which Tosti paid. Then Thorkel paid. Then Cnut paid.' (Jansson, *Swedish Vikings in England*, p. 12.)

then all his councillors, of life, and possess this kingdom afterwards', and that the order was carried out on St Brice's Day (13 November). But if the chronicler was prepared to justify the massacre as intended to forestall a specific plot, later commentators were to elaborate considerably on the basic fact and, apparently on the assumption that its victims included the inhabitants of the Danelaw, to present it more as an act of genocide in which men, women and children were variously jugulated, disembowelled, mutilated by bears or simply battered against door-posts.[186] The diploma for St Frideswide's (S 909) reveals that the victims included Danes settled in Oxford, so the measure was certainly implemented outside the Danelaw; and the draftsman states that it was directed against 'all the Danes who had sprung up in this island, sprouting like cockle amongst the wheat',[187] a remark perhaps hardly applicable to the fifth- or sixth-generation descendants of the Danes who had settled in eastern England in the late ninth century. Moreover, the original settlers and their progeny had probably intermarried gradually with the indigenous population, so that by the turn of the tenth century racial distinctions would have become blurred in a veritable Anglo-Danish community which, though retaining an historical identity as Danish, was nevertheless an integral part of the English kingdom and for that reason unlikely to have been in this case the object of the king's anger. One might also bear in mind that the Viking forces ravaged the Danelaw as much as the other parts of the kingdom, and observe both that there is no discernible mortality in 1002 amongst putative Danelaw thegns who attest royal diplomas and that the moneyers who minted *Long Cross* pennies at the Danelaw mints seem to have survived the massacre to mint pennies of the succeeding *Helmet* type. On the whole it is more readily conceivable that the order was directed against Danes who had recently settled in various parts of England, whether as traders, as mercenaries, or even simply as paid-off and provisioned members of the armies that had been ravaging the kingdom.[188] It may have been precipitated

---

[186] See Freeman, *Norman Conquest* I, 634–8.

[187] Whitelock, *EHD*, p. 591.

[188] Dolley, 'Shaftesbury Hoard', pp. 273–4, raises the possibility that the hoard of *Long Cross* pennies (many from the mints of York and Lincoln) found on the outskirts of Shaftesbury may have been deposited there by a merchant from the Danelaw who on entering the borough fell victim to the massacre. Æthelred's treaty with the Vikings (II Æthelred)

in part by the treacherous behaviour of Pallig, the brother-in-law of Swein Forkbeard, who appears to have promised his services to King Æthelred at some time before 1001: in the annal for that year in the Parker Chronicle it is recorded that Pallig opposed the English army in Devon 'with the ships which he could collect, because he had deserted King Æthelred in spite of all the pledges which he had given him', and William of Malmesbury avers that Pallig, his wife Gunhild and their son were amongst the victims of the massacre.[189] The massacre might well offend modern sensibilities and appear as the despicably cruel reaction of a paranoid king to a reported threat against him, but no act of violence on such a scale could have been carried out unless it had general support. In S 909 it is described as a 'most just extermination' ordered by the king with the advice of his leading men and thegns ('cum consilio optimatum satrapumque meorum') and it is evident that the men of Oxford rounded up the Danes with considerable enthusiasm. Feelings would certainly have been running high against them in 1002, particularly after the heavy fighting and extensive ravaging in 1001,[190] and there can be little doubt that the order would have been welcomed by King Æthelred's beleaguered subjects everywhere as justifiable and timely revenge for the Danes' unprovoked aggression and treacherous behaviour.

In the opinion of the chronicler, one of the factors underlying the successive defeats suffered by the English armies during the 990s and the early 1000s was the cowardice and duplicity of those entrusted with their leadership. He describes how Ealdorman Ælfric twice betrayed the men under his command, once in 992 when the ealdorman's behaviour enabled a Viking force to escape from a trap, and again in 1003 when the ealdorman abandoned an army he should have led, leaving a Viking force under Swein to ravage and burn the borough of Wilton; he describes how Fræna, Godwine and Frythegyst, entrusted with the leadership of a 'very large English army' in 993, were the first to start the flight; and he generalizes on the failure of the English to withstand the enemy in

appears to envisage circumstances in which members of the Viking army would remain in England.

[189] Stubbs, *De Gestis Regum Anglorum* I, 207 (and see Keynes, 'Declining Reputation', p. 248 n. 54).

[190] See above, p. 170 n. 66.

connection with the warfare in 998, 999 and 1001. It would appear
to be difficult to salvage anything from this tale of defeat, but one
does wonder how reliable and representative in these matters were
the opinions of the chronicler, writing from his vantage-point after
the end of the reign and presenting his account of the period as if it
were a continuous slide towards the ultimate Danish conquest.[191]
For if in particular Ealdorman Ælfric, Fræna, Godwine and Frythegyst were known to have been responsible in the ways described for
the failure of the expeditions in which they were involved, it is
indeed remarkable that no action was apparently taken against
them: Ealdorman Ælfric remained in office, and eventually died
defending the kingdom at the battle of *Assandun* in 1016; to judge
from witness lists to royal diplomas, Fræna, Godwine and Frythegyst
continued to attend meetings of the *witan* and so were apparently not
disgraced.[192] If the evidence available is interpreted on the basis of
the assumption that the king was an incompetent, one is certainly
at liberty to draw the conclusion that the king was powerless to
discharge from his service men known to have betrayed his interests,
though it hardly seems credible that he should have been so powerless or that he would not have discharged them had their culpability
been established. An alternative explanation is that the chronicler
was himself mistaken in attributing the defeats simply to the
cowardice of the leaders, and that those in possession of the facts
at the time knew differently. It is worth remarking in this connection
on a fragmentary text known as *Wyrdwriteras*, attributed to Ælfric
the homilist and assigned to the early years of the eleventh century.[193]
It describes the policy whereby kings had in the past delegated the
leadership of military expeditions to the 'ealdormen' they had set
under them, with successful results:

Wyrdwriteras us secgað, ða ðe awritan be cyningum,
þæt þa ealdan cyningas on ðam ærran timan
hogodon hu hi mihton heora byrðena alihtan,
for þan ðe an man ne mæg æghwar beon, and ætsomne

---

[191] Keynes, 'Declining Reputation', pp. 233–5.   [192] *Ibid.* p. 247 n. 32.
[193] Edited by Pope, *Homilies* II, 728–32. The limits 998–1002, given (implicitly) by Clemoes,
'Chronology', p. 244 n. 6, are perhaps to be preferred to the alternative limits 1002–5
given by him in the text of the same paper, p. 244; for it does seem likely that Ealdorman
Æthelweard's death can be placed *c.* 998 (above, p. 192 n. 139) and not in 1002. Pope
Homilies II, 726, is inclined, tentatively and 'on general grounds', to assign *Wyrdwriteras*
to the period of Ælfric's abbacy.

ealle þing aberan, þeah ðe he anweald hæbbe.
Ða gesetton þa cyningas, him sylfum to fultume,
ealdormen under him, and hi oft asendon
to manegum gewinnum, swa swa hit awriten is
ge on hæþenum bocum ge on Bibliothecan;
and þa ealdormen gewyldon þa onwinnendan fynd,
swa swa we wyllað secgan sume bysne be þam
of þam Leden-bocum, þæt man us ne lihnige.[194]

Ælfric proceeds to provide several instances of victories gained by generals (*heretogan*) who had been entrusted by their kings with the leadership of armies, and the text concludes with a general statement that 'our guidance and our defence shall be from God, and we should seek our advice from God himself with unwavering spirit'. If we may infer from this last admonition that the fragment does have a contemporary application, it would seem that Ælfric was either advocating the adoption of the policy of delegation, or defending its continued implementation.[195] The former possibility is perhaps the less likely, since by the time the piece was written the English forces had often been led by men other than the king. If, therefore, Ælfric was defending the policy, one might then consider whether there is anything in his arguments that suggests why criticism of it had arisen in the first place. Given the chronicler's account of the warfare in the 990s, it might be that the ealdormen selected for leadership had failed in their responsibilities: but in that case, merely to catalogue instances of the successful implementation of the policy would not have been the most subtle or judicious way to defend it. Besides, Ælfric appears to justify the policy not so much on the grounds that it had worked in the past as on the grounds that it released the king for his other responsibilities, and in one of the examples he describes how King David's followers swore that the king should never accompany them into battle lest he be killed to the cost of his people.[196] It seems possible therefore that the criticism had arisen from the disappointment of the armies that the king all

---

194 *Ibid.* p. 728: 'Historians who write about kings tell us that ancient kings in former times considered how they might alleviate their burdens, because a single man cannot be everywhere, and sustain all things at once, though he might have sole authority. Then the kings appointed ealdormen under them, as support for themselves, and they often sent them to many battles, as it is written in heathen books and in the Bible; and the ealdormen conquered the attacking enemies, as we shall recount (with) some examples about it from Latin books so that no one may contradict us.'

195 *Ibid.* pp. 727 and 733, and Braekman, 'Wyrdwriteras', pp. 963–4.

196 Pope, *Homilies* II, 728 lines 4–5, 729–30 lines 46–50 and 731 lines 85–6.

too rarely led them into battle, and it is clear from the annal for 1016 in the *Chronicle* that the English army did attach great importance to his presence.[197] Since *Wyrdwriteras* is no more than a fragment whose exact meaning may have been clearer – and different – had the rest of the text survived, it would obviously be hazardous to attach much weight to an argument which depends on identifying the circumstances under which it was written. It is only the absence in the text as preserved of any indication that recent English experience had departed radically from the tenor of the examples cited, and the fact that Ælfric felt able to defend the policy of delegation at all in the early eleventh century against criticism which had arisen on such grounds, that suggest its interpretation as a sign that not all may have shared the views of the chronicler on the management of the warfare in the period.

The last decade of the tenth century and the opening years of the eleventh will always remain in some respects paradoxical: the interests and sympathies of those who surrounded the king at this time may suffice to explain how and why the internal and cultural affairs of the kingdom were able to prosper, but though there might be good cause if not to applaud then at least to condone rather than to deplore the making of payments to the Vikings and the massacre of St Brice's Day, it is nevertheless undeniable on the evidence available that the external and military affairs of the kingdom were not conducted during these years with comparable success.[198] Some reassurance can, however, be drawn from the (albeit reckless) courage and loyalty displayed by Ealdorman Brihtnoth at the battle of Maldon in 991, from the fact that the army ravaging between 997 and 999 appears to have left the kingdom in 1000 without receiving any payment of tribute, from the possibility that the ravaging of Cumberland in 1000 was undertaken by Æthelred to counter a Norse threat from the north-west, and from the fierce resistance offered to the Danes by Ulfcetel of East Anglia in 1004.[199]

[197] See further Hollister, *Anglo-Saxon Military Institutions*, pp. 89–91.

[198] Support for the disaffection of some of Æthelred's subjects at this time comes from S 939, with reference to the alleged complicity of Æthelric in the *unræd* to receive Swein in Essex 'when first he came there with a fleet' (perhaps in 991: see Whitelock, *EHD*, p. 579): it appears that during his life Æthelric neither cleared himself of the charge nor admitted to it by making amends, and it was left to his widow to persuade the king to drop it.

[199] Ulfcetel resisted the Danes with less effect in 1010, and was killed at *Assandun* in 1016. According to Florence, he was ealdorman of the East Angles (Thorpe, *Chronicon* I,

THE CLOSING DECADE, 1006–1016

A striking change comes over the composition of the witness lists in 1005–6. Some of the laymen who had been prominent in the 990s had already disappeared by this time: Ealdorman Æthelweard attested for the last time in 998, and it is likely that he died in the same year;[200] Brihtwold attested for the last time in the following year, and Wulfric Spot died perhaps in 1002. The king's uncle Ordulf, however, vanishes in 1005, and it is possible that he had retired to his monastery at Tavistock, for if (as is likely) he is the Ordulf mentioned as a beneficiary in the will of Ælfwold, bishop of Crediton, he seems to have lived on for some years afterwards.[201] The king's kinsman Æthelmær may have entered his community at Eynsham at about the same time, for in the diploma of 1005 confirming the foundation (S 911) he is made to declare: 'and ic me sylf wille mid þære geferrædene gemænelice libban. and þære are mid him notian þa hwile þe min lif bið.' The evidence of the witness lists is not incompatible with Æthelmær's retirement in 1005, despite the appearance of a prominent Æthelmær amongst the *ministri* in the following years. For at least one other Æthelmær had occurred since 994. In S 896 (dated 999) an Æthelmær is specified as the son of Æthelwold, and he is followed immediately by an Æthelwold who was presumably his father; this association recurs in S 901 (dated 1002) and 911 (dated 1005). Æthelmær and Æthelwold were followed by one Ælfgar Mæw in S 896, and the trio recurs in S 902 (dated 1002) and 906 (dated 1004); Æthelmær and Ælfgar occur together without Æthelwold in S 890 (dated 997) and 893 (dated 998). It seems reasonable to identify the prominent Æthelmær of 1005–9 as this son of Æthelwold and associate of Ælfgar, since he occurs together with men of these names in the diplomas of 1007 and 1009 (see Table 8).[202] Nevertheless, it appears that Æthelmær son of

---

157–8), but his appearance in the witness lists (between 1002 and 1016, with especial prominence in the final years of the reign) as a *minister* and the silence of the chronicler, *s.a.* 1004, 1010 and 1016, suggests that while he may have had the power he did not have the title of ealdorman. See also Hart, *Charters of Northern England*, p. 363.

[200] Above, p. 192 n. 139.

[201] On the date of Bishop Ælfwold's will (S 1492), see above, p. 121 n. 123. See also Hart, *Charters of Northern England*, p. 353.

[202] The prominent subscriptions of an Æthelmær in S 922 (1009), S 926 (1012) and S 927 (c. 1012) could belong to the son of Æthelwold or to the Æthelmær who was a brother

Æthelweard subsequently came out of retirement, for he occurs as an ealdorman in the south-west in the last years of Æthelred's reign.[203]

The suggested simultaneous retirement of Ordulf and Æthelmær in 1005 would have left only Wulfgeat and Wulfheah out of the prominent *ministri* who had apparently enjoyed a close relationship with King Æthelred in the 990s and early 1000s, and it is remarkable to find that the series of subscriptions in their names come to an end at about the same time, in 1005. The subscriptions of Ealdorman Ælfhelm, Wulfheah's father and the second ealdorman in the hierarchy, also cease in this year. The annal for 1006 in the *Anglo-Saxon Chronicle* contains the following statement:

> and on þam ilcan geare wæs Wulfgeate ealle his ar ongenumen, and Wulfheah and Ufegeat wæron ablende, and Ælfelm ealdorman ofslagen.[204]

Florence of Worcester remarks in this connection that the king had loved Wulfgeat, whom he calls Leofeca's son, almost more than anyone, reminding one of the reference to Wulfgeat, the king's *dilectus minister*, in S 937, and he adds that Wulfgeat suffered forfeiture and the loss of all honour 'propter injusta judicia, et superba quæ gesserat opera'.[205] Two diplomas may refer to Wulfgeat's forfeiture.[206] S 918 (dated 1008) is spurious as it stands, but the narrative section seems to represent a genuine tradition.[207] It

---

of Eadric Streona; cf. Robertson, *Charters*, p. 386. For Ælfgar Mæw, see further below, p. 227 n. 265.

203 S 933, 1422; *ASC* MSS 'C', 'D', 'E', *s.a.* 1013. In the will of Ælfflæd (S 1486) 'Ealdorman' Æthelmær occurs as a contemporary of Queen Ælfthryth. Ælfthryth does not occur in datable contexts after 999, and it seems that she died on 17 November (Birch, *Liber Vitae*, p. 272) in that year or in 1000 or 1001, since S 904 (issued before 23 April in 1002: below, p. 258) refers to her as dead; an entry in the Wherwell cartulary (B.L. Egerton 2104 A, fo. 43r) places her death on 17 November 1002, the day presumably derived from a calendar obit and the year estimated by conflation with S 904, entered in the cartulary. Æthelmær occurs as a *minister* in S 904, and as a '*dux*' in S 902, issued later on in 1002; he occurs as a *minister* in diplomas dated 1004 and 1005, and reappears as a *dux* in 1013. It seems unlikely, therefore, that Æthelmær was ever an ealdorman during Ælfthryth's lifetime; his style in S 902 is most probably the result of scribal error. His description as '*æealdorman*' in the extant original version of S 1486 may in fact be a later insertion, made after his appointment: the word is squashed into the right-hand margin, and the duct of the writing changes. Cf. Whitelock, *Wills*, pp. 144–5, Robertson, *Charters*, pp. 386–7, and Harmer, *Writs*, p. 553.

204 Ashdown, *English and Norse Documents*, p. 50, from MS 'C'.

205 Thorpe, *Chronicon* I, 158.

206 See Whitelock, *Wills*, p. 164, and Robertson, *Charters*, p. 376.

207 See above, p. 183 n. 110.

describes how Wulfgeat married Ælfgifu, the widow of Ælfgar (the reeve who in the later 980s had persuaded the king to give him some land in Wiltshire belonging to Abingdon Abbey):

Qui ambo crimine pessimo juste ab omni incusati sunt populo, causa suæ machinationis propriæ, de qua modo non est dicendum per singula. Propter quam vero machinationem, quæ injuste adquisierunt omnia juste perdiderunt.

The second diploma referring to the crimes of someone called Wulfgeat (S 934) is dated 1015 and describes the forfeiture of a Berkshire estate:

Nam quidam minister, Wulfget vulgari relatu nomine, præfatam terram aliquando possederat, sed quia inimicis regis se in insidiis socium applicavit, et in facinore inficiendi etiam legis satisfactio ei defecit, ideo hereditatis substantiam penitus amisit.

Such general references to Wulfgeat's crimes, if indeed they do refer to the same person, afford no precise indication of the circumstances of his forfeiture in 1006. Florence's allusion to 'unjust judgements' suggests that he had exercised and abused some kind of legal authority, and the 'arrogant deeds' might be compatible with the treachery mentioned in S 934. Florence supplies some additional information about the other dramatic events of 1006. He describes how the 'dolosus et perfidius' Eadric Streona devised a trap for Ealdorman Ælfhelm by inviting him to a feast at Shrewsbury, and then arranged for him to be murdered while they were all out hunting in the forest.[208] He states further that it was shortly after this that Ælfhelm's sons Wulfheah and Ufegeat were blinded, on the king's orders and at Cookham, where the king was then staying.[209]

The coincidence in time between the apparent retirement of Ordulf and Æthelmær in 1005 and the alarming sequence of events in 1006 which left Wulfgeat disgraced, Ealdorman Ælfhelm murdered and Wulfheah and Ufegeat blinded, is certainly remarkable – and one might be forgiven for suspecting that it is not entirely fortuitous. Indeed, it seems to reflect something approaching a palace revolution amongst the principal lay associates of King

---

[208] Thorpe, *Chronicon* I, 158; see Wilson, *Lost Literature*, p. 52.
[209] The statement that Wulfheah and Ufegeat were Ælfhelm's sons depends on Florence, but it is entirely plausible: see Whitelock, *Wills*, p. 153. Cookham is known from S 939 to have been a royal manor in Æthelred's reign. Thus it is not unlikely that a genuine tradition underlies Florence's remarks.

Æthelred, and, if we may trust Florence of Worcester, one that had perhaps been engineered by Eadric Streona. This intriguing possibility derives some support from an investigation of the witness lists attached to the diplomas of King Æthelred issued in the early years of the eleventh century, for they suggest that if anyone or any group was associated with these events and profited by them, it was Eadric Streona and his family. Florence states that Eadric was the son of Æthelric, and names his brothers as Brihtric, Ælfric, Goda, Æthelwine, Æthelweard and Æthelmær.[210] A series of subscriptions in the name of Æthelric commences in 986 and extends thereafter to the final years of the reign; the subscriptions of an Eadric occur between 997 and 1007, while those of a Brihtric occur between 997 and 1009; no *minister* called Ælfric occurs at all in the diplomas of Æthelred issued after 990; a few subscriptions of a man called Goda occur in the early eleventh century; a series of subscriptions in the name of Æthelwine seems to commence in 996, with a concentration between 1004 and 1013; subscriptions in the name of Æthelweard are distributed throughout the reign, but there are concentrations between 995 and 998 and between 1004 and 1015; finally, an Æthelmær who was neither the son of Æthelweard nor the son of Æthelwold can possibly be identified in the 990s and may have been prominent in the period 1009–12.[211] The names of Eadric's father and brothers are not especially uncommon, and each of the series of subscriptions mentioned above may naturally represent more than one man. Nevertheless, it is significant that all but one of the names given by Florence do occur in the lists, and that they are collectively most consistent as witnesses in the closing years of the reign. Moreover, examination of the subscriptions in question as set out in Table 8 reveals that the names occur quite often in groups of twos and threes, and since it is a well-established principle that brothers and kinsmen tend to subscribe beside one another in the lists[212] it seems reasonable to conclude that members

---

[210] Thorpe, *Chronicon* I, 160. In both of the manuscripts of Florence that I have examined (Oxford, Corpus Christi College MS 157 and London, Lambeth Palace MS 42), the words 'vel Leofwini' are written above the name of Æthelric by the scribe of the text; both also have a blank space between Ælfric and Goda, as if for the name of another brother.

[211] See above, p. 209 n. 202.

[212] See above, p. 132.

of Eadric's family were indeed in fairly frequent attendance at meetings of the *witan* in the second half of Æthelred's reign. It is especially interesting that the family seems to have been present in strength at the meetings in 1005: one can but guess, however, whether they were taking advantage of the imminent retirement of Ordulf and Æthelmær to advance their own interests, or whether Ordulf and Æthelmær retired because they could not countenance the growing influence of Eadric and his family.

The events of 1006 undoubtedly look like the exposed tip of an iceberg of intrigue; it is unfortunate, though perhaps significant, that there are no diplomas for that year. After 1006, Eadric himself rose rapidly to prominence, and it is only appropriate that the removal of the influential Mercian family of Ealdorman Ælfhelm should have paved his way to power. At some point he married King Æthelred's daughter Edith, reflecting or explaining his influence and that of his family.[213] He occurs first amongst the *ministri* in S 916, an apparent original in favour of St Albans Abbey and dated 1007, and it is recorded in the *Anglo-Saxon Chronicle* that he was appointed ealdorman of Mercia in the same year.[214] At first Eadric seems to have taken his proper place in the hierarchy of ealdormen, positioned between Ælfric and Leofwine in 1007 and between Leofwine and Uhtred in 1009. But an extraordinary development took place within the period 1009 × 12, while Thorkell's army was devastating the country and doubtless causing much disruption. Hitherto the order of precedency amongst the ealdormen had been entirely regular, based essentially on seniority of appointment.[215] Ælfric had become the senior ealdorman following the (?)death of Æthelweard *c.* 998, and he occurs first on every diploma issued between 999 and 1009. Ælfhelm of Northumbria had been second before his murder in 1006, and Leofwine, 'Wicciarum Prouinciarum dux', had accordingly moved from third to second place after that date. However, by 1012, and thence

---

[213] Florence of Worcester, in Thorpe, *Chronicon* I, 161; Freeman, *Norman Conquest* I, 640–4, has much useful information on the rise of Eadric.

[214] S 917, dated 1007, had the subscription of a *patricius* (unnamed) between the ealdormen and the *ministri*, but since there are said to have been *three* ealdormen (unnamed, but presumably Ælfric and Leofwine, perhaps with Eadric), it seems unlikely that this *patricius* was Eadric before his promotion.

[215] See above, p. 157.

until the end of the reign, the relative order of the ealdormen was completely upset: the only common denominator in the lists is the presence of Eadric at the top of them all, displacing both Ælfric and Leofwine (see Table 6). Against the background of the earlier regularity one cannot avoid the inference that Eadric had effected a considerable coup at the expense of his colleagues. His prominence at this time is reflected clearly in the *Anglo-Saxon Chronicle*: the annal for 1012 records that 'Eadric ealdorman and ealle þa yldestan witan gehadode and læwede Angelcynnes' came to London and remained there until a tribute had been paid.[216] According to the Worcester monk Hemming, writing in the period 1062–95, Eadric 'presided over the whole kingdom of the English and had dominion as if a sub-king, to such an extent that he amalgamated estates and joined provinces to provinces at his will', besides appropriating estates from Worcester.[217] Hemming also records that Eadric was known as 'Streona', an epithet he glossed correctly as '*adquisitor*'.[218] Whether this connotes an ambitious and self-seeking grasper or merely greed for other people's property is not clear; but amongst the other things that Eadric acquired was a notoriety unmatched in Anglo-Saxon history, for his complicity in an assortment of murders, base stratagems and acts of treachery.[219] His treacherous streak is given full play already in the *Anglo-Saxon Chronicle*, in the annals for 1009, 1015 and 1016, and he is directly associated in the same source with the murders of Sigeferth and Morcar in 1015 and of Earl Uhtred of Northumbria in 1016; by the early twelfth century he had come to be associated in different sources with the murders of Gunhild (wife of Pallig and sister of King Swein), Ealdorman Ælfhelm and even Edmund Ironside.

[216] Ashdown, *English and Norse Documents*, p. 58, from MS 'C'. It may have been for the leading ealdorman of the day to assume the king's responsibilities during the absence or incapacity of the king himself: Æthelred may not have been able to be present at the meeting at London in 1012, leaving Eadric to take charge, and Eadric may have collected the army in 1015 because the king was then lying unwell at Cosham; similarly, perhaps, Ealdorman Æthelwine presided at a 'great meeting' at London held during the king's youth in the 980s (S 877); one wonders, therefore, whether Ealdorman Ælfhere, in translating the body of Edward to Shaftesbury in 979, was acting in his capacity as the senior ealdorman of the day.

[217] Hearne, *Hemingi Chartularium*, pp. 280–1; see Finberg, *Charters of West Midlands*, p. 234.

[218] See also Tengvik, *Bynames*, pp. 355–6, and Toller, *Dictionary*, p. 713; cf. Stenton, *Anglo-Saxon England*, p. 381 n. 3.

[219] See Wilson, *Lost Literature*, pp. 52–4; cf. Stafford, 'A Study in Limitations', pp. 36–7.

Without meaning to imply that there was always a direct connection, there can be no doubt that Eadric presided over a period of almost unmitigated military disaster.[220] Something of the frame of mind of the English at this time can be gleaned from the proem of S 911, the diploma by which the king confirmed the foundation of Eynsham Abbey in 1005. It contains what must be an early instance of characteristically English understatement:

Et quia in nostris temporibus bellorum incendia direptionesque opum nostrarum patimur, necnon & uastantium crudelissima depredatione hostium barbarorum, paganorumque gentium multiplici tribulatione, affligentiumque nos usque ad internitionem, tempora cernimus incumbere periculosa.

The situation cannot have been helped by the great famine throughout England, also in 1005, 'such that no man ever remembered one so cruel': the possible effects of a natural disaster on this scale are suggested by the Alfredian chronicler's statement that the degree to which the Danes had afflicted the English between 893 and 895 was nothing beside the degree to which the English had been afflicted 'by the mortality of cattle and men, and most of all in that many of the best king's thegns who were in the land died in those three years', and Archbishop Wulfstan, in his *Sermo ad Anglos*, refers to famine, murrain, disease and crop-failure in the same breath as devastation, burning, bloodshed and spoliation. After midsummer in 1006, the year following the great famine, a Viking force known to the chronicler as 'the great fleet' or 'the Danish fleet' arrived at Sandwich and ravaged extensively during the autumn: the English resistance is said to have been ineffective, and by Christmas the Vikings had inspired such terror 'that no one could think or conceive how to drive them from this country, or to defend this country from them, for they had cruelly left their mark on every shire of Wessex with their burning and their harrying'; so in order to save the country before it was completely destroyed, the king and his councillors reluctantly resolved to buy them off. The payment of 36,000 pounds in 1007 brought two years' respite from Viking attack, and time for feverish military preparations in 1008: every district of 300 or 310 hides throughout the country was made

---

[220] See Gem, 'A Recession in English Architecture', pp. 40–9, for the very interesting suggestion that the apparent decline in ecclesiastical building in the early eleventh century can be related to the conditions then prevailing; see also Pope, *Homilies* II, 512–14.

responsible for providing one war-ship, and in addition every unit of eight hides had to furnish a helmet and a corselet, presumably as equipment for the crews.[221] By 1009 the ships were ready, and in the words of the chronicler, 'there were more of them than ever before, from what books tell us, had been in England in any king's time; and they were all brought together at Sandwich and were to stay there and protect this country from every invading army'. The decision to concentrate the ships at Sandwich was evidently dictated by its suitability as a point of disembarkation for the Vikings,[222] for the great fleet of 1006 had arrived there: thus it appears that the English intended to engage the enemy directly and at sea, before they had an opportunity to land, take horses and so gain freedom of movement through the countryside. But all the hard work of the preparations was effectively undone by Brihtric, one of the brothers of Eadric Streona. According to the chronicler, Brihtric levelled an accusation against Wulfnoth the South Saxon in front of the king, prompting Wulfnoth to entice twenty ships from the naval force and with them to set about ravaging the south coast. Brihtric then took eighty ships and 'intending to make a big reputation for himself' endeavoured to capture the renegade Wulfnoth, but his fleet was wrecked in a severe storm and thereupon burnt by his quarry. The loss of a hundred ships in this way must have been a very serious blow to the king, and the naval force dispersed in confusion shortly afterwards: the king, ealdormen and chief councillors went home, and the remaining ships were taken back to London. Brihtric himself, if he survived the storm and the destruction of his fleet, may have been disgraced, for whereas he had attested several diplomas between 997 and 1009,[223] he does not occur thereafter.

The chronicler's account of the ship-levy in 1009, gathered to protect the country from every invading army and abandoned when everything seemed to be *rædleas*, stands in ironic juxtaposition to the account of the arrival at Sandwich (once the levy had returned to London) of Thorkell's 'immense raiding army', immediately after Lammas (1 August). The arrival of this army can probably be

---

[221] See further Hollister, *Anglo-Saxon Military Institutions*, pp. 108–15.

[222] On the importance of Sandwich, see *ibid.* p. 125.

[223] He attested S 921 in 1009, but not S 922 issued later in the same year.

regarded as one of the most catastrophic events of the reign, and it appears to have precipitated a remarkable programme of public prayer. King Æthelred's so-called 'seventh' code of laws was promulgated at Bath on an occasion when, according to the rubric of the Old English version, 'the great army came to the land', and it transpires from the first clause that this took place in a year in which Michaelmas fell on a Thursday; these conditions are best met in 1009.[224] The code begins with the proposition that 'all of us have need eagerly to labour that we may obtain God's mercy and his compassion and that we may through his help withstand our enemies'. There follows a series of provisions to be implemented on the three days before Michaelmas (that is, on 26, 27 and 28 September) and directed towards the said ends:[225] the whole nation was to observe a penitential fast on bread, herbs and water, and everyone was to process barefoot to church for confession on each of the three days; one penny was to be paid from each hide of land, brought to church and distributed for God's sake, and the food saved in the fast was also to be distributed afterwards to the sick and needy; each member of a household was to pay one penny as alms, and the householders themselves were to pay tithes; slaves were to be freed from work during the three days so that they too could join the processions and participate more readily in the fast; the communities of every minster were to sing their psalters during the three days, and every priest was to say mass for the king and his people; a mass which referred in particular to the need of the times was to be said daily in every minster until things should improve,[226]

---

[224] If the expression 'on Monday and on Tuesday and on Wednesday before Michaelmas' in the Old English version of the code is held to imply only that Michaelmas fell between Thursday and Sunday, the possible years of issue (irrespective of the historical condition) would be 992–5, 998–1000, 1004–6, 1009–11 and 1015–16 (as Liebermann and others have observed); but in the Latin version of the code the three days are said to have been *proximi* before Michaelmas, and it seems natural to infer that the feast fell on a Thursday. This cuts down the available options to 992, 998, 1009 and 1015; the armies ravaging in 992 and 998 had actually arrived in previous years, leaving 1009 and 1015; of these, 1009 is to be preferred if only because the arrival of the 'immense raiding army' in that year corresponds so well with the code's reference to the arrival of the 'great army'; 1006, in which Michaelmas fell on a Sunday, should be admitted as a third alternative, given that a 'great fleet' arrived in that year.

[225] There are various differences of organization and content between the Old English and Latin versions of the code (see Liebermann, *Gesetze* I, 260–2, and Whitelock, *EHD*, pp. 447–8), but for present purposes it is sufficient to convey its general import.

[226] In the Latin version of the code, the mass is specified as the one entitled 'Contra Paganos'. It is found amongst the votive masses in, e.g., Warren, *Leofric Missal*, pp. 185–6; Wilson,

and at each service the community was to sing the psalm 'O Lord how they are multiplied', with prayers and collect. After general injunctions that all should turn to God and deserve his mercy, and that God's dues should be paid annually in order that he may have mercy on the people and grant victory over the enemy, the code ends with the appeal 'God help us. Amen.' According to the Latin version of the code, the people were to be accompanied by their priest on the daily processions to church, and from the Old English version we learn that they were to take relics with them and 'to call on Christ eagerly from their inmost hearts'. These provisions seem to imply that litanies were to be recited on each occasion,[227] and we may turn to service books used in the early eleventh century for some indication of what this involved. After the opening *Kyrie eleison*, invocations of Christ and of the appropriate saints, the members of the procession would have made several obsecrations for deliverance from various evils, followed by supplications for (amongst other things) the prosperity of the Church and the fertility of the land, for health and propitious weather, and perhaps some for victory over enemies and peace: the obsecration 'a persecutione paganorum et omnium inimicorum nostrorum insidiis . libera nos domine' and the supplication 'ut regi nostro et principibus nostris pacem et uictoriam nobis dones . te rogamus' occur in a litany in a manuscript from the New Minster Winchester,[228] and are admittedly conventional, but the more particular supplication 'ut æþelredum regem & exercitum anglorum conseruare digneris te rogamus' is found in a litany in the Winchester Troper.[229] After the supplications, those processing would have joined in a three-fold invocation of the *Agnus Dei*, as (for example) in the Winchester Troper: 'Agnus Dei qui tollis peccata mundi parce nobis domine. Agnus Dei dona nobis pacem. Agnus Dei miserere nobis.' And the service would have concluded with another *Kyrie eleison*, the Lord's Prayer, and perhaps

---

Missal of Robert of Jumièges, p. 268; Cambridge, Corpus Christi College MS 41, p. 483, under the rubric 'For þone cyng 7 for þone bysceop 7 for eall cris[. . .]'; and Cambridge, Corpus Christi College MS 422, p. 237.

[227] Cf. the processions of the medieval Church, which took place annually on the Rogation days and on special occasions – as required – to avert disasters of any kind, during the course of which litanies would be recited (see Owst, *Preaching*, pp. 200–8).

[228] Birch, *Liber Vitae*, pp. 265–6, from B.L. Cotton Titus D xxvi.

[229] Oxford, Bodleian Library, Bodley 775, fo. 18v; see further Keynes, 'Declining Reputation', p. 253 n. 89.

a series of suffrages and collects. The invocation of the *Agnus Dei* is of especial interest: for it is undoubtedly in this context that we should place the remarkable *Agnus Dei* coinage, known on numismatic grounds to have been issued (like Æthelred's 'seventh' code) in 1009, and so most likely to have been an integral part of the intensive programme of national penitence:[230] the design on the obverse represents the Lamb of God, while that on the reverse represents the Dove, symbol of the Holy Spirit and thus of Peace. The drafting of the code itself has been attributed on stylistic grounds to Archbishop Wulfstan,[231] and certainly it accords perfectly with the emphasis recurrent in his works on the importance of moral regeneration as the means to save the nation from its troubles.[232] Of course the programme of penitence laid down for the three days before Michaelmas in 1009 would have been no substitute for direct military action, but then it was not intended to be so: it is analogous to the periodic campaigns for peace through prayer mounted in recent years in Northern Ireland, and from the historian's point of view it provides eloquent and moving testimony to the seriousness of the situation which confronted the English at that time.

The choice of Psalm 3 ('O Lord how they are multiplied that trouble me') as part of the programme is itself an indication that Thorkell's army was a force of unprecedented magnitude, and it is apparent also from the *Anglo-Saxon Chronicle* that the invading army, in its size and organization, was quite unlike any that had previously ravaged in the country. Its main contingent was probably gathered from Denmark. According to the *Encomium Emmae*, Thorkell was King Swein's military commander and had with the king's permission taken a large part of the Danish army to England in order to avenge the death of his own brother.[233] This alleged reason for the invasion enables one to identify him as Thorkell the Tall, a prominent figure in the legend of the Jómsvíkings and in the sagas of St Olaf, and if only on that evidence therefore a warrior

[230] See Dolley, 'Nummular Brooch', pp. 337–45, from which this suggestion is developed; for two recent additions to the extant corpus of *Agnus Dei* pennies, see Dolley and Talvio, 'Agnus Dei Pennies', and a forthcoming note by the same authors in *British Numismatic Journal*.

[231] See Jost, *Wulfstanstudien*, pp. 211–16; Bethurum, *Homilies*, p. 38; Whitelock, *Sermo Lupi*, p. 21.

[232] See Bethurum, *Homilies*, pp. 62–3, and also, e.g., Whitelock, *Sermo Lupi*, pp. 34–5.

[233] Campbell, *Encomium Emmae*, p. 10, and comment on p. lii.

of considerable experience.[234] Florence of Worcester states that Thorkell's army was in fact a combined force of two fleets, one led by Thorkell himself and the other by two earls called Hemming and Eglaf;[235] the former can probably be identified as Thorkell's younger brother, named in *Jómsvíkingasaga*,[236] and the latter is perhaps identical with the 'Eglaf dux' who attested several diplomas issued in the opening years of Cnut's reign.[237] The invasion force also included Olaf Haraldsson, subsequently and better known as St Olaf, king of Norway, for in the *Víkingavísur* of Sigvatr Þórðarson – a series of scaldic verses describing the adventures of Olaf in his youth – there are several allusions to his participation in battles in England which can be identified as part of the campaign of 1009–12.[238] Finally, a rune stone at Yttergärde in Uppland, Sweden, reveals that a man called Ulv had taken Thorkell's geld in England, suggesting that some Swedish mercenaries may have joined the invasion force.[239] It is then no surprise to read in the *Chronicle* that Thorkell's 'immense raiding army' dispersed in 1012, 'as widely as it had been collected'.

The main criticism of the quality of the measures adopted by the king and his councillors in response to the Viking threat (as distinct from criticism of the behaviour of those who were entrusted with the execution of the measures) covers the period between 1009 and 1012 when Thorkell's army was at large in the country. The king ordered the whole nation to be called out in 1009, but nevertheless the Vikings 'journeyed just as they pleased'; according to the chronicler, Ealdorman Eadric was instrumental in frustrating the efforts of the English, and we may recall that it was during these years that he appears to have established his precedency over the other ealdormen, in defiance of seniority. In the annal for 1010, the chronicler specifies the failure of the councillors to agree on a lasting stratagem and the failure of the shires to co-operate with one another. In the annal for 1011 he declares that 'all the disasters befell

---

[234] Campbell, *Encomium Emmae*, p. 73.

[235] Thorpe, *Chronicon* I, 160–1.

[236] Blake, *Jomsvikings*, pp. 27–8; Campbell, *Encomium Emmae*, pp. 73 and 87.

[237] S 951, 953–6, 958–61, 977, 980–1, 984 and 1424; see also Campbell, *Encomium Emmae*, pp. 86–7.

[238] See Campbell, *Skaldic Verse*, pp. 8–11.

[239] See Jansson, *Swedish Vikings in England*, pp. 12–14.

us through bad policies (*unrædas*), in that they were never offered tribute in time nor fought against; but when they had done most to our injury, peace and truce were made with them; and for all this truce and tribute they journeyed none the less in bands everywhere, and harried our wretched people, and plundered and killed them'. The extensive list of counties overrun by Thorkell's army, provided in this connection, corresponds precisely to the area of the recorded activity of the army since its arrival in 1009, and the reference to the *unrædas* can therefore be taken to apply to the period of the campaign generally. The Vikings occupied Canterbury in September 1011 and captured Archbishop Ælfheah; in April 1012 the archbishop was put to death, the army collected an enormous tribute of 48,000 pounds, and then dispersed 'as widely as it had been collected'. A contemporary German chronicler, Thietmar, bishop of Merseburg, writing soon after 1012, describes on the authority of a certain Sewald how Thorkell had tried to prevent the murder of Archbishop Ælfheah,[240] and it may have been his horror at the cruelty of his men that led Thorkell to take forty-five ships from his force and pledge his services to King Æthelred for the defence of the country, in return for sustenance.[241] It was presumably on this occasion that Æthelred instituted the tax known as the *heregeld*, later referred to as the Danegeld and said to have been levied annually at the rate of 12 pence from each hide of land.[242] Thorkell received the first payment of *heregeld* in 1013, and a further payment (of 21,000 pounds) in 1014.

There can be little doubt that the period when Thorkell's army was ravaging the country was the turning-point in the history of King Æthelred's struggles against the Vikings. The account of the warfare up to 1009 given by the chronicler may create the impression that things ever went from bad to worse, but one should not be

---

[240] Whitelock, *EHD*, pp. 349–50.

[241] Though the chronicler does not make it explicit that the 45 ships were led by Thorkell, it is apparent from the annal for 1013 that Thorkell himself changed sides and was paid for his services; the encomiast states clearly that Thorkell became an ally of the English, with 40 ships (Campbell, *Encomium Emmae*, p. 10).

[242] According to *ASC* MS 'D', *s.a.* 1052 (*recte* 1051), the *heregeld* was abolished in that year 'in the thirty-ninth year after it had been instituted', implying that it had first been imposed in 1012. The rate at which it was levied is mentioned in Downer, *Leges Henrici Primi*, p. 120, and in Liebermann, *Gesetze* I, 634 (from the *Leges Edwardi Confessoris*); cf. Johnson, *Dialogus*, pp. 55–6, where the rate is specified as 2 shillings per hide (and see also Hollister, *Anglo-Saxon Military Institutions*, p. 20).

deceived by his defeatism.[243] Successive bands of raiders were resisted, sometimes stoutly, and beaten or bought off, and there were periods of respite when time was found to overhaul the defences of the country: so it was not without justification that the English people had hoped for or expected victory in 1009, before all was frustrated by the behaviour of Wulfnoth and Brihtric. All was then changed by the events of 1009–12, for though disastrous enough in themselves they had even more calamitous consequences: it seems that they seriously damaged the will of the English to resist and indeed their capacity for resistance at all. In 1013, so soon after the dispersal of Thorkell's army, the English kingdom was invaded by one of Æthelred's oldest adversaries, Swein Forkbeard, king of Denmark. Swein is first mentioned by name in the *Anglo-Saxon Chronicle* in the annal for 994, when he is said to have besieged London in company with Olaf Tryggvason, but there is evidence to suggest that he had been part of Olaf's force which had arrived in Essex in 991.[244] The confused historiography of the Scandinavian countries would have us believe that at this point in his career Swein was an exile from his own kingdom, recently expelled by Eirik, king of Sweden, as punishment for persecuting the Christians, though modern historians are loath to believe any of it.[245] At least it is clear that when Swein is next found attacking England, in 1003–4, he was doing so as king of Denmark, overlord of a large part of Norway and apparently as one who had recently embraced Christianity. He seems not to have been involved personally in the subsequent invasions in 1006 and 1009, though it is possible that he had some part or acquiesced in their organization. The Swein who arrived at Sandwich in the summer of 1013 was thus no stranger to England's shores, but neither was he by this time a mere raider out for a share of England's wealth. Adam of Bremen, whose information was derived from Swein Forkbeard's

---

[243] Keynes, 'Declining Reputation', p. 235 and n. 30.

[244] S 939 refers to the *unræd* that Swein should be received in Essex when 'first' he came there with a fleet, as if he had come more than once by the time the document was drawn up (995 × 9): he is known to have ravaged Essex in 994, but not on any subsequent occasion in the 990s. That his first arrival should have been in 991 is consistent with the statement in S 939 that Æthelric had lived for 'many years' after being accused of complicity in the *unræd*, since he was certainly dead when S 939 was drawn up (see Whitelock, *EHD*, p. 579).

[245] See Jones, *History of the Vikings*, pp. 135–6, and references.

grandson, asserts that Swein meant 'to avenge the outrages he had suffered long before, both the killing of his brother' (Hiring, allegedly betrayed and slain by the Northumbrians) 'and his own expulsion' (a reference to Æthelred's refusal to harbour Swein when an exile, and so apparently to Swein's attacks on England in the early 990s).[246] The author of the *Encomium Emmae*, on the other hand, writing about 1040, alleges that Swein's men had urged him to invade England in order to punish Thorkell for deserting to the English with forty ships when he should have returned with his army and given Swein the credit for his victory; Swein had himself been contemplating invasion for some time, but it was the exhortations of his men, reinforced by encouragement from his son Cnut, that aroused him to action.[247] Any one or all of these factors may have served as excuses for invasion, but it is not unlikely that Swein, described by his contemporary Thietmar as 'the fierce king of the Danes . . . not a ruler . . . but a destroyer',[248] was bent principally and unashamedly on conquest. He must have known about the chaos occasioned by Thorkell's invasion, for he was certainly quick to take advantage of it. In the words of the encomiast, the king 'ordered that a numerous fleet should be prepared, and that warning should be given on all sides to the entire military power of the Danes to be present under arms at a fixed date, and in obedience to the king's wish, to perform with the utmost devotion whatever they were commanded'; the Danes 'mustered without any objection' and once armed were presented troop by troop to the king.[249] We might dismiss the implied sophistication of Danish military organization as hyperbole, were it not for the existence of the extraordinary fortresses at Trelleborg, Fyrkat, Nonnebakken and Aggersborg: it is now known that these fortresses were built in the last quarter of the tenth century, and if they can therefore no longer be regarded principally as military garrisons (from which levies were co-ordinated and the attacks of the late tenth and early eleventh centuries launched), their suggested function as centres of royal authority in no way alters the impression that they symbolize the military

---

[246] Tschan, *History of the Archbishops*, p. 90.
[247] Campbell, *Encomium Emmae*, p. 10.
[248] Whitelock, *EHD*, p. 347.
[249] Campbell, *Encomium Emmae*, pp. 10–12.

resources of a powerful monarchy.[250] If all four camps were occupied simultaneously, their combined capacity would have approached 4,000 men;[251] and it is not impossible that there were others like them. It is important to emphasize at this point that the Viking forces, which under the leadership of Swein and subsequently of Cnut set out to achieve the conquest of the Anglo-Saxon kingdom between 1013 and 1016, were apparently considerably larger than any of the forces which had attacked the country previously. The fleets which descended on England's shores in the 990s seem to have numbered nearly a hundred ships,[252] and those which attacked in the following decade were still larger, to judge from the reference to the 'great fleet' of 1006 and from the choice of Psalm 3 ('O Lord how they are multiplied') in the penitential code as applied to the 'immense raiding army' of 1009; the fact that this army dispersed in 1012 'as widely as it had been collected', even so leaving forty-five ships which came over to the English, gives some indication of its original size. There is every reason to believe that the invasions of 1013 and 1015 brought further escalation in the size of the attacking forces, now that they represented the military might at the disposal of the Danish kings as organized for conquest rather than merely for plunder; and if the progressive increase in the amounts of tribute paid to the Vikings between 991 and 1018 can be assumed to be in some way proportional to an increase in the numbers of men involved who were entitled to a share of the spoils (besides reflecting their escalating demands), the payment to Cnut in 1018 of a sum over half as large again as the sum paid to Thorkell in 1012 may be roughly indicative of the relative sizes of their respective armies. Swein's fleet of 1013 was said to be numerous and his soldiers innumerable,[253] and the company of sixty ships was regarded as a

---

[250] For full discussion of the camps, see Olsen and Schmidt, *Fyrkat*, pp. 217–22, and Roesdahl, *Fyrkat*, pp. 198–207. A Swedish rune stone records that a certain Sven 'died in Jutland when he was on his way to England', and it is conceivable that he was a mercenary who had got no further than one of the assembly-garrisons (see Jansson, *Swedish Vikings in England*, pp. 10–11).

[251] Olsen, 'Viking Fortresses', p. 105; cf. Sawyer, *Age of the Vikings*, p. 136. The legends recited in the *Jómsvíkingasaga* may well have arisen from memories of the military discipline which the camps appear to represent.

[252] *ASC* MS 'A' records that the fleet which arrived in 991 comprised 93 ships, and MSS 'C', 'D', 'E' record that the fleet which arrived in 994 comprised 94 ships; as Loyn, *Vikings in Britain*, p. 85, remarks, these figures may indicate levies for a round 100 ships.

[253] Campbell, *Encomium Emmae*, pp. 10–12.

small proportion of the total force;[254] Cnut's fleet of 1015 probably comprised between 150 and 200 ships,[255] though in the imagination of certain contemporary authorities it numbered as many as 340 or an unbelievable 1,000 ships.[256] The ships themselves may well have been of different types and sizes, but there is evidence which tends to suggest that some and perhaps many of those in service in the first half of the eleventh century had sixty or sixty-four oars.[257] If the fleets gathered by Swein and Cnut comprised (for the sake of argument) 175 ships of this size, they would have been able to disembark forces of anything approaching 10,000 men. It would assuredly be hazardous to fasten on a particular approximate figure, given the uncertainty about the number of ships in the fleets and their average capacity, but at least it is clear that the campaigns conducted by Swein and Cnut easily surpassed in scale those conducted by the Viking leaders in the ninth century and may have been comparable with that conducted by William the Conqueror in 1066.[258]

Still reeling (one imagines) from the effects of Thorkell's invasion, King Æthelred and the English stood little chance when confronted by such a man as Swein Forkbeard, intent on conquest and at the

---

[254] Campbell, *Encomium Emmae*, p. 16.

[255] The encomiast states that Cnut had 200 ships (*ibid.* p. 18), and implies that he had 'inside' help from Thorkell with about 40 ships (*ibid.* pp. 18–20); in *ASC* MSS 'E', 'F' *s.a.* 1016, Cnut's force is numbered at 160 ships, supplemented (thanks to Eadric Streona) by 40 ships which may have been Thorkell's.

[256] Thietmar of Merseburg gives Cnut 340 ships each holding 80 men (Whitelock, *EHD*, p. 348), while Adam of Bremen gives him 'a thousand large ships' (Tschan, *History of the Archbishops*, p. 91).

[257] 11,048 pounds were paid as *heregeld* for 32 ships in 1041 (*ASC* MSS 'E', 'F'), and since the tax was distributed at 8 marks per rowlock (*ASC* MSS 'C', 'D' 'E', 'F' for 1040) this implies that the ships had on average about 64 oars. (To judge from literary sources, however, ships of this size were the famous exceptions: see Brøgger and Shetelig, *Viking Ships*, pp. 146–59. The largest Viking ship yet discovered is the wreck designated Skulde-lev 2, recovered from the Roskilde Fjord, which is believed to have been designed to carry up to 60 soldiers: see Olsen and Crumlin–Pedersen, 'Skuldelev Ships', pp. 111–18.) Note also that Archbishop Ælfric bequeathed his 'best ship' and its tackle to King Æthelred, with 60 helmets and 60 coats of mail which may have been intended to equip the crew (S 1488); cf. *ASC* MSS 'C', 'D', 'E', *s.a.* 1008 (an annal which may itself be taken to imply that the ships built in that year were rather smaller, with crews of about 40 men); Ælfwold, bishop of Crediton, bequeathed a 64-oared ship to King Æthelred (S 1492); Earl Godwine is said to have given King Harthacnut a ship manned with 80 soldiers (Florence of Worcester, in Thorpe, *Chronicon* I, 195).

[258] On the scale of these campaigns, see Sawyer, *Age of the Vikings*, pp. 123–31 and 215–16, and Stenton, *Anglo-Saxon England*, p. 593; but for an upward revision of estimates for the scale of the ninth-century campaigns, see Brooks, 'Crucible of Defeat'.

head of an army of several thousand men trained in the régime which had produced the Viking camps. And though Swein arrived at Sandwich, in the words of the chronicler 'he went very quickly round East Anglia into the mouth of the Humber, and so up along the Trent until he reached Gainsborough'. Evidently he expected that the men of the Danelaw, remembering their parentage, would prefer to submit to a Danish army under a Danish king rather than resist so powerful a force, and he was not disappointed. Thereafter, he was able to make almost uninterrupted progress, receiving the submission of the areas through which he passed until the whole nation regarded him as 'full king'. Æthelred was left only with Thorkell's fleet, lying at Greenwich on the Thames: as Freeman put it, 'the monarchy of Cerdic was now confined to the decks of forty-five Scandinavian war-ships'.[259] After spending Christmas on the Isle of Wight, Æthelred crossed the Channel to join Queen Emma and the athelings Edward and Alfred in Normandy, though he did not remain there for long. Following the death of King Swein in February 1014, the fleet elected Cnut king, but those *witan* who had remained in England 'determined to send for King Æthelred, and they said that no lord was dearer to them than their natural lord if he would govern them more justly (*gif he hi rihtlicor healdan wolde*) than he did before'. The last remark provides the best evidence for the dissatisfaction of Æthelred's subjects with his rule, at least in the strained conditions of the closing years of the reign when, perhaps, the interests of the country and of the individual would not necessarily have coincided. His return was conditional for his part on the making of certain unspecified reforms and on forgiving things that had been said and done against him, and for his subjects' part on their resolute and loyal support; when he did arrive home, during the spring of 1014, he was received *glædlice* by them all. Æthelred's 'eighth' code of laws, dated 1014, is said to have been 'one of the ordinances which the king of the English composed with the advice of his councillors',[260] suggesting that more than one code was promulgated in that year, perhaps as part of the promised reform: the extant code largely concerns ecclesiastical matters, and it may be that another was intended to make good the

[259] Freeman, *Norman Conquest* I, 359.
[260] Liebermann, *Gesetze* I, 263.

secular abuses which had troubled the English people.[261] The two years that remained of Æthelred's reign were passed in further struggles against the Danish army, now led by Cnut, and it is possible that at least initially Æthelred had the support of Olaf Haraldsson of Norway, no friend of the Danes: for a scaldic verse attributed to Óttar the Black appears to imply that Olaf had accompanied Æthelred to England on his return and had participated in fierce fighting.[262] Unfortunately, the efforts of the English were severely handicapped by dissension amongst their leaders, and particularly by the treacherous behaviour of Ealdorman Eadric. One should stress that in his account of the final years the chronicler does not level criticism at the king personally. Indeed, it seems that when resistance was planned or offered, Æthelred himself was always in some way involved. The citizens of London alone had withstood Swein in 1013, 'because King Æthelred was inside and Thorkell with him'; Æthelred ravaged Lindsey in 1014 'with his full force', apparently managing to drive Cnut away; the army gathered by Edmund during the Christmas season in 1015–16 demanded the king's presence, and did so again when summoned after the festival, presumably in the opening weeks of 1016. There even seems to be a note of sympathy behind the record of the king's death: 'Then it happened that King Æthelred died before the ships arrived. He ended his days on St George's Day, and he had held his kingdom with great toil and difficulties as long as his life lasted.'[263] Florence of Worcester adds that his body was buried in the church of St Paul, *honorifice*.[264] Further acts of treachery perpetrated by Eadric Streona undermined Edmund Ironside's strenuous attempts to resist Cnut after his father's death,[265] and in particular it was

---

[261] Wormald, 'Æthelred the Lawmaker', p. 59, raises the possibility that the secular measures are 'buried without trace in the code of Cnut'; but perhaps there is a trace, in II Cnut 69–83. For the abuses themselves, cf. Pope, *Homilies* II, 500 lines 67–71.

[262] Campbell, *Skaldic Verse*, pp. 11–12.

[263] See also Keynes, 'Declining Reputation', p. 236.

[264] Thorpe, *Chronicon* I, 173; also Campbell, *Encomium Emmae*, p. 22.

[265] According to Florence of Worcester (Thorpe, *Chronicon* I, 175), Eadric was joined on the Danish side at the battle of Sherston in 1016 by 'Ælfgar son of Meaw': the Ælfgar prominent in the witness lists between 1007 and 1014 can be identified as Ælfgar Mæw on the basis of S 896 and on the basis of his association with Æthelmær son of Æthelwold; he does appear to have inherited his nickname (which means 'gull') from his father (cf. Robertson, *Charters*, p. 387, and Tengvik, *Bynames*, p. 10), for documents relating to the endowment of Cranborne Abbey in the early eleventh century (Hart, *Charters of Eastern*

Eadric's desertion that precipitated the final defeat of the English at the battle of *Assandun* on 18 October 1016.[266] Edmund and Cnut came to terms at Alney and partitioned the kingdom between them, the one taking Wessex and the other Mercia, but it was not long thereafter that Edmund died and Cnut succeeded to the whole kingdom of England.

CONCLUSION

The account of Æthelred's reign in the *Anglo-Saxon Chronicle* took shape during the final years of military collapse, and it is no wonder therefore that the chronicler chose to focus his attention on Æthelred's struggle against the Vikings, presenting the broken series of coastal raids, more sustained incursions and then large-scale invasions as if they had formed part of a continuous progression leading inexorably and inevitably towards the defeat of the English at *Assandun* and the entry of Cnut's army into London in the winter of 1016. He allows his account of the struggle to eclipse any other developments which may have taken place during Æthelred's reign, affording us only the faintest and most disconnected glimpses of domestic affairs. The agonized tirade on the moral and concomitant political state of the nation given by Archbishop Wulfstan in his *Sermo ad Anglos* was similarly a product of the unhappy years of Danish conquest. Yet it was primarily the account of the reign in the *Anglo-Saxon Chronicle* that determined Æthelred's posthumous reputation, and it is largely on that account and on the *Sermo ad Anglos* that modern historians have depended for making their own assessments of the reign. It is not difficult to appreciate how the personal intrusion of the chronicler into his narrative renders it at the same time the more appealing to read and the more hazardous to use, and it is not difficult to appreciate the limitations of an elegantly rhetorical harangue as an historical source; but nor is it easy to judge how to make compensation in consequence. It is,

England, pp. 253–4) refer to the founder Ailward Meaw and to his son Ælfgar. Another of those on the Danish side at Sherston was 'Ælmer Darling', perhaps the 'Ælmær *minister*' who attested between 1004 and 1012 and who may be the 'Ælfmær' of S 890 (994) and 933 (1014).

[266] On the date of the battle, see Hart, 'Site of Assandun', p. 3; Hart prefers Ashdon to Ashingdon as the battle-site, *ibid.* p. 12.

however, possible to effect at least a partial escape from the pervading influence of Wulfstan and the chronicler. The royal diplomas issued in the name of King Æthelred may as a rule be less openly communicative than these authorities about matters regarding the progress of internal and external affairs, but there are notable exceptions (as it has long been realized) which illuminate particular aspects of the period, and examination of the diplomas collectively reveals that they too have an important contribution to make to the connected history of the reign. In the first place, diplomatic analysis demonstrates that a substantial proportion of the diplomas were the product of a writing office that acted on the occasion of the *witenagemot* where the transactions were completed, and thus they can be adduced to substantiate a case for the existence of a royal secretariat in the late tenth and early eleventh centuries; it was presumably the same secretariat that was responsible also for drawing up the administrative communications known to have been directed by the king to his subjects, and its members may have been employed for other purposes as well. It is apparent, therefore, that Æthelred had at his disposal an office competent to perform the written business of royal government, and – if he deserves no particular credit for thus maintaining a service inherited from his predecessors – it is important at least to register that it did not collapse during his reign and that he did not relinquish control over the production of royal diplomas; for had it and had he done so, it would have been paradoxical that the reign witnessed impressive achievements in other areas of royal government – for example, in legislation and in the organization of the coinage. In the second place, analysis of the witness lists attached to the diplomas reveals how the composition of the king's council changed during the course of a long reign, and in particular how it was modified in some respects not so much naturally by the passage of time but in such a way as to imply that the king was associated during successive periods with different groups of advisers who may be presumed to reflect and to have affected his attitudes and policies in their different ways; in so far as they can be identified, the sympathies of the prevailing group of advisers are found to accord well with other evidence on the general direction of affairs during the period of the group's ascendancy. The diplomas enable one in this way to establish a framework for

Æthelred's reign in which internal as well as external developments have a part to play, and in which the disastrous events of the closing years appear in their proper perspective. It emerges that the reign of Æthelred was not a period of such steady deterioration or uniform degeneracy as the principal literary sources, written during the closing years, would seem to imply, and that there was far more behind certain aspects of the reign than the alleged personal incompetence and bad character of the ruler himself: the course of events between 978 and 1016 took different turns at different times and was effected not only by the external pressure from the Vikings but also by the rise and fall of those in a position to influence the king; of course it comes as no surprise in so long a reign that this should have been so. There were, it is true, always some who were both prepared and able to exploit a situation in their own interests, whether by persuading the king in his youth to appropriate property from religious houses, or latterly by perpetrating cowardly and treacherous acts for self-preservation at critical times, when the security of the country was seriously threatened and when the outcome of events was in the balance; and there can be no doubt that the closing years witnessed a military collapse that is as damning as it is understandable. But none of this should be allowed to detract from or overshadow the positive and enduring achievements of Æthelred's government, particularly in the last decade of the tenth and early years of the eleventh century, and it should not be forgotten that favourable conditions were created in this period for a remarkable flowering of intellectual activity and material culture. The framework set out above is, however, no substitute for a properly balanced survey of the Anglo-Saxon kingdom in Æthelred's reign. It is intended primarily to pick out the salient developments in domestic affairs and to suggest where appropriate their relation to the course of the struggle against the Vikings, but it may also provide a convenient political back-drop as further work on the period progresses: for it remains to characterize fully the institutions of royal and local government and to set in their historical context Æthelred's coinage and the extensive legislation in his name; to clarify the developments in the fortunes of the Church during the reign and to assess the significance of the achievements in learning and material culture; to understand the complex but highly important prosopography of the period; to examine the web linking together all of the kingdoms of Northern Europe and the British Isles,[267] and to discover how their respective histories interacted on one another; and to consider Æthelred's own position in relation to these different aspects of his reign, with a view to establishing his influence on and responsibility for the various developments.[268]

According to William of Malmesbury, the course of Æthelred's life was said to have been cruel in the beginning, in the murder to which he gave his concurrence; wretched in the middle, in his outrageous flight and weakness; and disgraceful in the end, in the miserable circumstances of his death. We have at least come some way from this tripartite division of Æthelred's career, and for the moment we may in summary offer another, albeit less rhetorical: the course of Æthelred's life was beyond his own control in the beginning, in the murder of Edward at the hands of disaffected thegns and in the abuse of certain churches for the benefit of some unscrupulous men who were in a position to manipulate the young king; it was well conducted in the middle, when the domestic affairs of the kingdom appear in many respects to have prospered under good management; and it was certainly out of hand in the end, as the king and his subjects were undermined from within by the treachery of Eadric Streona, and overwhelmed from without by their powerful and highly organized adversaries, the Danes.

---

[267] Campbell, 'England, France, Flanders and Germany', makes an important start in this direction.

[268] I intend to cover these aspects of Æthelred's reign in a biographical study which I have in hand.

THE DIPLOMAS OF KING ÆTHELRED: DATING
AND WITNESS LISTS

A. THE DATING OF KING ÆTHELRED'S DIPLOMAS

The diplomas of King Æthelred are generally dated by the year of grace without specification of day or month, so that it rarely seems possible to place a text more precisely than within a twelve-month period from the beginning of January until the end of December.[1] About two-thirds of the documents add the appropriate indiction. Were the indictional system employed properly, one would expect to find some variation of indiction within a series of diplomas dated to the same year, distinguishing those issued after 1 or 24 September[2] from those issued before. However, diplomas (apparently) produced after September have the same indiction as diplomas (apparently) produced earlier in the year,[3] and such variation as does occur seems to be accidental rather than significant.[4] So one has to accept that the indiction was supplied merely as a chronological conceit – that it was not calculated independently each time, but was instead established probably by reference to current Easter tables:[5] consequently it changed in synchronization with the years of grace. Occasionally a regnal year was supplied, calculated either from a point in

---

[1] It seems reasonable to assume that the year was at this time calculated from 1 January: Ælfric, writing in the period 990–4, states that 'our reckoning' (*ure gerim*) began on this day in accordance with Roman usage (see Thorpe, *Homilies* I, 98), and the Old English *Menologium* places the beginning of the year on 1 January (see Dobbie, *Minor Poems*, p. 49 lines 5–10); Byrhtferth, writing *c.* 1011, is more confused, but he implies that the year began in January (see Crawford, *Manual*, p. 62).

[2] The beginning of the Greek and 'Bedan' indictions respectively; see further Harrison, *Framework*, pp. 38–42.

[3] S 872 (? November/December 988) has the same indiction (1) as S 869 (16 April 988); S 899 (post 7 October 1001) has the same indiction (14) as S 898 (ante 7 October); S 909 (7 December 1004) has the same indiction (2) as the other diplomas produced in the same year (S 906 and 907).

[4] S 852 (984) has indiction 13, whereas the other diplomas of 984 have 12 (S 855 and 853): but S 852 was certainly produced before 1 August. S 888 (996) has indiction 8, whereas the other diplomas of 996 have 9 (S 878, 887 and 877): the occurrence of Bishop Wulfstan (consecrated in 996) militates against a date late in 995 (with year calculated from September and with indiction for 995 as a whole). S 902 (1002) has indiction 14, whereas the other diplomas of 1002 have 15 (S 901, 903 and 905): but S 902 is certainly later than the others, since Wulfstan appears as archbishop of York. In S 882 it is the year of grace that requires correction, and in S 883 the indictional value 'XIIII' occurs in error for 'VIII'.

[5] Note the exceptionally detailed clause in S 1522 (15 April 998), very probably derived directly from successive columns in an Easter table. Harrison, *Framework*, pp. 113–19, studying material from the eighth and ninth centuries, reaches the same conclusion for the ninth century, so there was clearly nothing new in this practice in the tenth century.

978 (S 865, 876 and 891; also S 1817) or from a point in 979 (S 842, 869, 873, 875 and 886; also S 1348):[6] the only conceivable explanation is that the earlier point represents the king's accession (therefore 18 March 978) and the later one his coronation (therefore 4 May 979).[7] In four instances the provision of a regnal year may enable one to refine the date of the diploma concerned.[8]

It is often possible to compensate for the imprecision of the chronological data given in the documents themselves by analysing the attached witness lists. I have argued in Chapter 2 that one can sometimes detect between different lists similarities strong enough to suggest that the diplomas in question may have been produced on the same occasion.[9] One has to remember, however, that within a single year or over a short period the composition of the groups of witnesses subscribing royal diplomas may not have changed noticeably, so that the same memorandum of witnesses' names might have been used for two or more diplomas, even though they were certainly produced on separate occasions.[10] A strong case for suggesting that two diplomas emanated from a single *witenagemot* only arises when the similarities between the witness lists extend to all the groups of witnesses, and when the order in which the names are given implies an additional textual

[6] The regnal years in S 877, 903 and 1796 could have been calculated from 978 or from 979. The regnal years given in S 876 (dating clause), 904 and 909 are impossible by any calculation.

[7] The dates of Æthelred's accession and coronation have been the subject of much confusion in pre-Conquest sources and amongst modern authorities alike, but the regnal years appear to settle the issue. Evidence for the accession (i.e. for the murder of Edward) in 978 comes from *ASC* MSS 'A' and 'C', and for the coronation (on 4 May) in 979 from MS 'C' (and see also S 835); support for the occurrence of these events in successive years comes from MS 'F'. Note also that Edward's death is dated 978 in the Easter tables in B.L. Cotton Titus D xxvii (Birch, *Liber Vitae*, p. 276); it is dated 979 in the Easter tables in the Leofric Missal (Warren, *Leofric Missal*, p. 50), but the same source gives 976 for Edgar's death and 985 for Bishop Æthelwold's death. *ASC* MSS 'D' and 'E', representing a common source, place both the death of Edward and Æthelred's coronation in 979, but it seems likely that parts of two separate annals (as in MS 'F') were conflated in the process of transmission; the comment that Æthelred was crowned 'swiðe hrædlice' after his accession probably arose at this stage. The annal for 978 in MS 'C' implies that Æthelred was crowned in the same year as Edward was murdered, contradicting the annal for 979; annals from different sources may have been conflated, and the author of the 978 entry may simply have believed that Æthelred's coronation was a natural corollary of his accession. Versions of the West Saxon regnal table in the New Minster *Liber Vitae* and in the *Textus Roffensis* assign to Edward a reign of three years and eight months, but they are not independent of each other at this point and so do not corroborate one another; the length may have been calculated from a date for Edward's coronation in 975 to an estimated date for his death based on the assumption that it occurred shortly before the coronation of his successor in 979. Edward is assigned a reign of three years in the table in B.L. Cotton Tiberius B v (see Dumville, 'Anglian Collection', pp. 27 and 43 n. 1), probably representing simply the difference between 975 and 978.

[8] See below under S 842, 865, 875 and 886. In the same way, a Worcester lease (S 1348) can be dated 984, before 4 May.

[9] See above, pp. 41–2.

[10] See S 844 and 851 (both dated 983), and S 861 (dated 986), 864 and 867 (both dated 987). The common denominator might be the original memorandum itself, or a diploma into which it had been incorporated (see under S 924, dated 1011).

relationship between the diplomas, preferably supported by common elements of overall formulation which would further increase the possibility that a single agency underlies their production.[11] Alternatively, a series of diplomas assigned to a particular year might be arranged in a relative sequence in accordance with details of succession to bishoprics, abbacies and ealdormanries: such details might emerge either from the lists themselves, or there might be a record of a new appointment or an obit in an annalistic source – for example, the *Anglo-Saxon Chronicle*.[12] Other more unusual circumstances (exile, absence abroad, capture etc.) described in such sources, which would prevent the attendance of the person in question at a *witenagemot*, should also find reflection in the witness lists. Occasionally the sources attach a close date within the year to the event, but one can often supplement them, or the lists themselves, by searching calendars and martyrologies for the obits of prominent ecclesiastics and laymen: in this way it is possible to establish fixed points which serve to separate the diplomas affected and in many cases to narrow down their period of issue by several months. Where it is possible thus to refine the date of a given diploma, the grounds for so doing are explained in section D. It should be emphasized that within each year the relative order of the diplomas is often only partly established: the diplomas which remain unaffected by any criteria could have been issued before or after those more closely dated.

B. THE TRANSMISSION OF THE WITNESS LISTS

Of all the constituent parts of an Anglo-Saxon royal diploma, the witness list was perhaps the most prone to alteration or corruption during the process of transmission. Some cartulary copyists of the medieval period seemed not to regard the list as a particularly relevant or useful part of the title-deed, and were therefore content to record an abbreviated version. Thus the greater part of each list attached to the diplomas of King Æthelred preserved in the Burton archives was not copied by the compiler of National Library of Wales, Peniarth 390, and thus also the compiler of the Abingdon chronicle–cartulary in B.L. Cotton Claudius C ix abbreviated lists which are now known only because the later compiler of Claudius B vi took the trouble to turn back to the original documents when revising and expanding the collection. The compiler of the main part of the *Codex Wintoniensis* provided what appear to be full transcriptions of the lists, but he was evidently prepared to alter the status of some of the witnesses in order to present them in more homogeneous and well-balanced blocks: for his tendency to accord the

[11] One is fortunate to have more than two or three diplomas from any single year of Æthelred's reign, and since there might have been four or five occasions during a year when diplomas were issued, the initial probability that those that survive emanate from the same *witenagemot* is slight. For examples, however, see below under the years 985, 987 and 988.

[12] There are also some useful annals entered in the margins of Easter tables: B.L. Cotton Titus D xxvii, B.L. Cotton Caligula A xv, B.L. Cotton Tiberius C i; Oxford, Bodleian Library, Bodley 579 (Leofric Missal).

status proper to the names in one group to the leading names in the following group is so pronounced in such a carefully-written manuscript that it cannot be dismissed as mechanical scribal error.[13] Other types of corruption arose when the medieval copyists misread the unfamiliar names written in an unfamiliar script on their exemplars,[14] or when, for example, they muddled the distinction between forms in 'Æðel-' and forms in 'Ælf-'.[15] But as often as not, the garbling of a witness list can be attributed to those who by printing the texts effected the final stage in their transmission. There are instances where simply the collation of a different and textually superior manuscript would have produced a more accurate version of the document;[16] and there are instances where the discrete vertical columns of the original were obscured by a more ambiguous arrangement in the copy, to be interpreted in one way and then printed by a modern editor producing an order only indirectly related to that intended by the scribe of the original diploma.[17] It follows that it is often necessary to unscramble or to emend the texts of particular witness lists before accurate and instructive tables of all the lists attached to Æthelred's diplomas can be compiled; I indicate in section D where the manuscripts require emendation and where the printed editions are misleading.

C. THE COMPILATION OF TABLES 1-8

The diplomas occur in the relative order established in section D; note, however, that the positioning of those diplomas with witness lists that are clearly incompatible

---

[13] See comments below on S 860-1 and 867-8; in S 840 the cause might be mechanica scribal error. S 836 and 889 show the same tendency in the additions to the *Codex Wintoniensis*. See also under S 865 from the New Minster Winchester, S 902 from Abingdon, S 907 from Ely, and S 916 from St Albans.

[14] The commonest type of error is confusion between the elements '-ric' and '-sige': e.g. in S 862, 907 and 911-12. For other types of corruption, see S 882, 899, 900, 904 and 910.

[15] For instances, see under S 840, 850, 904 and 907 (where 'Ælf-' forms occur for 'Æðel-'); S 867, 872, ?874 and 882 (where 'Æðel-' forms occur for 'Ælf-'); in S 840 'Ælnoð' and 'Eþelnod' occur for the same name in two versions of the diploma, but whether 'Ælf-' or 'Æðel-' is correct is uncertain. The confusion of the elements can be traced back to the reign of Æthelred in S 890, where 'Ælfstan' occurs for 'Æðelstan' in an apparent original, and in S 877 and 891 (produced in 996 and 997 respectively), since a common denominator probably underlies the odd form 'Æðelfric' (for Ælfric, archbishop of Canterbury) in both. Etymologically and visually the elements 'Æðel-' and 'Ælf-' are quite distinct, so I can only imagine that the interchange arose phonologically, when the names were transmitted through their common reduced forms in 'Æl-' or 'Al-'. Interconsonantal *f* and intervocalic *ð* are sometimes lost already before the Conquest, and generally thereafter (see von Feilitzen, *Personal Names*, pp. 92, 102-3, 142), and the pronunciation of the names in 'Æðel-' and 'Ælf-' would in such cases have been ambiguous; yet the scribe of the original memorandum, on hearing the name, would still apparently choose to commit himself to one form or the other; alternatively, a copyist reading his exemplar might memorize the name in an ambiguous form and then return to the wrong form when writing his own text.

[16] E.g. S 838, 841, 862, 865, 880 and 904.

[17] E.g. S 834, 837, 850, 863, 872 and 942.

Appendix 1

with the purported date of the text or that are internally inconsistent, varies, since different elements of such lists sometimes seem to belong to different periods; note also that since all or part of the lists in many diplomas were omitted by the copyists, certain diplomas do not occur in certain tables. Each subscription is represented by a number which indicates the position of the witness in his group. The orthography of the personal names has to a necessary extent been normalized.

Some of the tables present particular problems which require comment:

Tables 2 and 3

An asterisk against a subscription indicates that the bishop's see is explicitly identified in the witness list. Where there are known to have been contemporary namesakes, and where none is explicitly identified in a list, or where his identification cannot reasonably be inferred from his position, it has been necessary to adopt the following convention: If two namesakes occur in the same diploma, an entry in the form ' " ?4' would indicate that it is not in doubt that the bishop concerned attested, but that the position in which he was listed is uncertain; the column for his namesake supplies the alternative position. If only one of the namesakes attested the diploma, an entry in the form ' ? 4' would mean that it is uncertain whether the bishop concerned attested, but that if he did he is fourth in the list; the column for his namesake has a duplicate entry.

Tables 4 and 5

In only two diplomas (S 876 and 891) are the abbeys of all the abbots explicitly identified, though in two others (S 877 and 896) two namesakes are distinguished by identification. It is remarkable, however, that good sense can be made of the material, for it is possible to identify the great majority of the abbots witnessing Æthelred's diplomas,[18] though obviously with varying degrees of certainty. The subscriptions accord well with the local histories that give some account of abbatial succession, and they also accord neatly with the subscriptions of the bishops where it is known or can be conjectured that an abbot was promoted to the episcopacy. But as in the case of the bishops, the requirements of a tabular arrangement involve committing oneself to identifications that are not always as secure as the tables imply. Thus there can be no guarantee that a series of subscriptions in a particular name belongs to one and the same person: in some cases it is known that there were two or more contemporary namesakes, though they may never occur together in the same list. So when only one of the namesakes occurs, it is necessary to decide which abbot is intended: the decision can sometimes be made by reference to the position of the witness in the list, but often it has to be arbitrary. In the tables, contemporary namesakes are grouped together in order to make the options clear, and the abbots who subscribe consistently are grouped above the rest.

---

[18] The process has been greatly facilitated by Knowles *et al.*, *Heads of Houses*.

Tables 7 and 8

These tables present obvious difficulties of identification. When the name is common, when the occurrences are sporadic and when the positioning fluctuates, it would clearly be rash to assume that a series of subscriptions in one name belongs to a single man. So the tables inevitably imply identifications which may not be dependable. When, on the other hand, a series of subscriptions is clearly delimited in time, when the occurrences are consistent and generally in the same company, and when their relative position does not fluctuate too much, then one has greater cause to assume that the subscriptions represent one and the same man. The tables have been designed to pick out the patterns that do quite clearly emerge when the witness lists are put together. In Table 7, the more prominent and consistent witnesses of the 980s are grouped at the top (Ælfric–Leofric); they are followed by the group that was to dominate the lists in the period *c.* 993–1006 (Æthelmær–Wulfgeat), so that one can see how and when it coalesced; there remain the more sporadic witnesses, given in the order in which they first appear in Æthelred's diplomas so that the apparently 'new' element in each list can be seen at a glance. In Table 8, the first group (Ælfsige–Leofwine) represents the possible survival into the 990s of the prominent witnesses of the 980s: one has little confidence that the recorded subscriptions of Leofric and Leofwine belong to only two men, but it would be impossible to draw any dividing lines. The second group (Æthelmær–Wulfgeat) comprises those who dominated the lists between *c.* 993 and 1006; they are followed by a group which may represent Eadric Streona, his father Æthelric and his brothers, and in turn by other consistent or identifiable witnesses of the latter part of Æthelred's reign. The more sporadic witnesses are given as in Table 7, though of course there would be an element of continuity from one period to the next which is to some extent obscured by this arrangement.

D. CHRONOLOGICAL LIST OF THE DIPLOMAS OF KING ÆTHELRED[19]

Besides supplying comments, where necessary, on the date and witness list of the particular diploma, each entry specifies where a printed text is to be found and in which archive the diploma was preserved. References to manuscripts follow the notation in Sawyer, *Anglo-Saxon Charters* (S). I have taken advantage of the form of presentation to hazard opinions on the authenticity or otherwise of Æthelred's diplomas, expressed by the following symbols:

¶ Apparently authentic: the document satisfies the available tests of authenticity and accords in form with contemporary diplomas.

‖ Authenticity uncertain: no conclusive objections can be raised, but the document is in some respects anomalous or suspicious.

§ Spurious as it stands: elements of the document were apparently or evidently

---

[19] A few texts which contain witness lists (entered in the tables) but which are not themselves royal diplomas are here included for the sake of comparison: see under S 877 (first entry) and 1379–80.

derived from pre-Conquest diplomas, but the whole is internally inconsistent, or there are other grounds for doubting its authenticity.

† Preserved on a single sheet which is probably contemporary with the given date.

‡ Preserved on a single sheet which may not be (strictly) contemporary with the given date.

979

¶ S 834 (KCD 621): 979

King Æthelred to Ælfhere, *comes* and kinsman: grant of 10 *mansae* at Olney in Buckinghamshire

(Peterborough)

Witness list: In MS 1 the bishops from Ælfstan to Theodred are arranged in two parallel columns, printed in KCD by reading left to right, line by line. But it is clear that the columns should be read vertically, each in turn, since verbs of attestation occur after all the names in the first column but after none in the second: this reflects a common arrangement on the extant originals.

¶ S 835 (KCD 622): 979, after 4 May

King Æthelred to Æthelwold, bishop of Winchester, for the Church of St Peter and St Paul, Winchester: grant of 5 *cassati* at Long Sutton in Hampshire

(Old Minster Winchester)

Date: The estate is said to be the first 'quod post nostram regalem dedicationem domino nostro Ihesu Christo quasi donorum primitias largitus sim'. The king's coronation took place on 4 May 979.[20]

980

¶ S 836 (KCD 626): 980, before 2 May

King Æthelred to the Old Minster Winchester: grant of $1\frac{1}{2}$ *mansae* at Calshot in Hampshire

(Old Minster Winchester)

Date: If Æthelgar attested as abbot (see below), the diploma was issued before his consecration as bishop of Selsey on 2 May (*ASC* MS 'C').

Witness list: The list of bishops ends with Osgar and Æthelgar: Osgar, abbot of Abingdon, was never a bishop, and so it is likely that the copyist has inadvertently 'promoted' two abbots.

¶ S 837 (KCD 624): 980

King Æthelred to the Old Minster Winchester: grant of the reversion of 7 *cassati* at Havant in Hampshire

(Old Minster Winchester)

Date: Æthelgar does not attest the diploma, so one cannot tell whether it was issued before or after 2 May.

---

[20] See above, p. 233. King Eadred is known to have issued diplomas on the occasion of his coronation: see S 520. See also S 186.

Witness list: The position of Queen Ælfthryth, in the middle of a group of ten bishops arranged in a single column, is irregular: perhaps she was above a second column of five bishops on the original, on the same line as the archbishop of York, in which case her intended position may have been between the archbishops and bishops. The two columns of witnesses of MS fo. 99r end thus:

EGO Goduuine abb.   Ego Wlfric min.

Ego Ælfric min.   Ego Goduuine min.

Kemble printed Ælfric *minister* among the abbots, who extend from the bottom of column one to the top of column two. But the *Codex Wintoniensis* copyist probably miscounted the number of witnesses when determining how long the first column should be in order to ensure that the second column would be of the same length: consequently he found that he had to add a *minister* to the end of the first column.[21] I regard Ælfric as the penultimate *minister*, though it is possible that he should follow Godwine. Amongst the abbots, a second 'Siric' cannot be identified and probably arose by inadvertent repetition of 'Siric' (Sigeric) of St Augustine's Canterbury.

981

§ S 838 (Finberg, *Tavistock*, pp. 278–83): 981, before 12 February
King Æthelred to Tavistock Abbey: grant of privileges and confirmation of lands
(Tavistock)
Date: The witness list includes the subscription of Ælfstan, bishop of Ramsbury (formerly abbot of Glastonbury), who died in 981 and was buried at Abingdon (*ASC* MS 'C'). His obit is given as 12 February in an eleventh-century Abingdon source,[22] and a similar obit occurs in a Glastonbury source.[23]

---

[21] This is supported by his use of a lower-case *g* in Ælfric's subscription: he generally changed from the upper-case G to the lower-case *g* in *Ego* during the course of a witness list, and the change invariably coincides with a change in the class of witness.

[22] Cambridge, Corpus Christi College MS 57: the manuscript was written in the late tenth or early eleventh century, and contains the Rule of St Benedict, a martyrology and Smaragdus' *Diadema monachorum*. During the eleventh century, nearly ninety obits accumulated in the margins of the martyrology; they have been printed by James, *Catalogue of MSS in Corpus Christi Coll.* I, 115–18. Most were probably inserted at one time by a s. xi¹ hand: since they refer largely to the first seven months of the year we may infer that the scribe was extracting them from an existing calendar and eventually tired of his task. The obit in question was damaged by a binder's plough: it appears as '. .lfstani ep.' under 2 Id. Feb.

[23] William of Malmesbury, *De Antiquitate Glastoniensis Ecclesiae*: William apparently extracted a collection of obits of bishops who had been members of the Glastonbury community from a calendar he found at the abbey; printed by Hearne, *Domerham* I, 93–4, from Cambridge, Trinity College MS R. 5. 33. William probably simplified some of the obits, for more than one would otherwise expect fell on the exact Ides or Nones of a month. The obit in question occurs as 'Idus Februarii obiit Ælfstanus episc. monachus Glaston.': Ælfstan had in fact been a monk of Abingdon and Winchester before becoming abbot of Glastonbury.

Appendix 1

¶ S 839 (Stevenson, *Chronicon* I, 384–5): 982, before 18 April

King Æthelred to Ælfgar, his *minister*: grant of 5 *cassati* at Charlton in Berkshire

(Abingdon)

Date: The diploma was attested by Ealdorman Æthelmær of Hampshire, who died in 982 (*ASC* MS 'C'), on 18 April, according to an obit in an eleventh-century calendar from the New Minster Winchester.[24]

¶ S 841 (Brewer, *Registrum*, pp. 318–19): 982, before 18 April

King Æthelred to Malmesbury Abbey: grant of 10 *manentes* at Rodbourne in Wiltshire

(Malmesbury)

Date: As for S 839.

Witness list: The list as printed by Kemble (KCD 632) is corrupt, but he used an inferior manuscript, B.L. Lansdowne 417 (MS 1), where the arrangement of the witnesses is both confused and confusing. Brewer's text, from MS 2, is rather better, though 'Aeldrich minister præfati regis concessi' after the king's subscription is obviously a corruption of 'Ælfðryð m[ate]r ...'. For the tables, I have used the version of the diploma in the Bodleian cartulary (MS 3): this shows that the ealdormen were in fact listed in the normal order (as in Brewer but not in KCD), and that Ælfric *minister* occurred at the head of the appropriate group (again as in Brewer but not KCD).[25] A second Abbot Æthelweard (unidentified if real) occurs in MS 1, but his absence from the other two versions suggests that he owes his existence to scribal inadvertence; but compare S 840.

¶ S 840 (KCD 633): 982, probably after 18 April and before the death of Ealdorman Eadwine

King Æthelred to Leofric: grant of 3 *mansae* and 30 *iugera* at Longstock in Hampshire

(Old Minster Winchester)

Date: Probably after the death of Ealdorman Æthelmær (see under S 839), but still before the death of Ealdorman Eadwine of Sussex on an unknown date in 982 (*ASC* MS 'C').

Witness list: Two texts of the diploma are entered consecutively in the *Codex Wintoniensis*, with some minor differences between the witness lists; the text in KCD is a conflation of both. In the first version, an impossible Ealdorman Ælfwine occurs in place of Æthelwine, and an improbable Ealdorman Godwine is likely to owe his existence to the duplication and promotion of Abbot Godwine. In the second version Ealdorman 'Ælfwine' occurs between Ælfhere and Æthelwine,

---

[24] B.L. Cotton Titus D xxvii. An extensive collection of obits accumulated in the margins of a s. xi[1] calendar from the New Minster: printed by Birch, *Liber Vitae*, pp. 269–73. The obit in question occurs as 'Obitus Æðelmæri ducis'. Ealdorman Æthelmær was a benefactor of the abbey: see S 842 and 1498.

[25] Hart, *Charters of Northern England*, p. 29 n., considered this 'a very doubtful text', but when the witness list is restored to its proper form there is no conclusive objection to the diploma on internal grounds.

and Godwine occurs only at the head of the list of abbots; a second Abbot Æthelweard occurs only in this version, at the end of the list of abbots. In the tables, I
have omitted Ealdorman 'Ælfwine' altogether, admitting Æthelwine on the
basis of the second list; I regard Godwine as the first abbot, on the basis of the
second list, and reject him as an ealdorman; I also reject the second Abbot Æthelweard, though this involves attributing a similar duplication in S 841 to coincidence. Kemble's 'Æðelnoð *minister*' is 'Ælnoð' in the first list and 'Eþelnod' in the
second: he occurs in Table 7 as 'Ælfnoth', though 'Æthelnoth' is no less likely.
¶ S 842 (Edwards, *Liber de Hyda*, pp. 217–27): 982, after 18 April (and after
3 May?) and before the death of Ealdorman Eadwine
    King Æthelred to the New Minster Winchester: confirmation of various
    estates amounting to 13 *mansae* in the Isle of Wight and Hampshire, bequeathed
    to the abbey by Ealdorman Æthelmær
    (New Minster Winchester)
Date: The text refers to the death of Ealdorman Æthelmær and to his burial at
the New Minster; see further under S 839 and 840. The dating clause incorporates
a regnal year, calculated from the king's coronation: the fourth such year ran
from 4 May 982 to 3 May 983.

983

¶ S 848 (KCD 636): 983, before the death of Ealdorman Ælfhere
    King Æthelred to Æthelwine, his *minister*: grant of 10 *mansae* at Clyffe Pypard
    in Wiltshire
    (Old Minster Winchester)
Date: The diploma was attested by Ealdorman Ælfhere of Mercia, who died in
983 (*ASC* MSS 'C', 'D', 'E').
Witness list: Compare S 846 (KCD 638) with an identical list derived from this
diploma. The apparent absence of Archbishop Oswald from the lists in S 848 and
846 may have originated as a copyist's error in the common exemplar: the expression 'sancte crucis taumate confirmavi' after Dunstan's subscription is characteristic
of Oswald's subscriptions, so the scribe may have jumped from 'archiepiscopus'
in Dunstan's subscription to the same point in Oswald's subscription.
§ S 846 (KCD 638): 983
    King Æthelred to Æthelmær, *dux*: grant of 10 *mansae* at Clyffe Pypard in
    Wiltshire
    (Old Minster Winchester)
Date: The given date is incompatible with the diploma's beneficiary, Ealdorman
Æthelmær, who died in 982 (see under S 839).
Witness list: The list is identical with that in S 848, from which it was probably
derived.[26] It is not entered in the tables.

---

[26] The estate concerned is not mentioned in the will of Ealdorman Æthelmær (S 1498).
S 846 may have been fabricated in order to associate the estate more directly with Ealdorman Æthelmær, one of the abbey's benefactors, but it is also possible that its date and witness
list were given in error from the text of S 848 (in *Codex Wintoniensis*, fo. 77v) when the

‖ S 849 (KCD 640): 983, before the death of Ealdorman Ælfhere
King Æthelred to Æthelwold, bishop of Winchester: grant of a fishery at
Ginanhecce on the Darent in Kent
(Old Minster Winchester)
Date: As for S 848.

¶ S 844 (KCD 639): 983, before the death of Ealdorman Ælfhere
King Æthelred to Ælfnoth, his *minister*: grant of 2½ *mansae* at *Westwuda*
(Old Minster Winchester)
Date: As for S 848.
Witness list: Compare S 851, issued later on in 983.

¶ S 851 (Stevenson, *Chronicon* I, 386–8): 983, after the death of Ealdorman Ælfhere
King Æthelred to Wulfgar, his man: grant of 3 *mansae* at Drayton and 1½
mansae at Sutton in Berkshire
(Abingdon)
Date: The diploma was attested by Ealdorman Ælfric, who succeeded Ælfhere
in 983 (*ASC* MSS 'C', 'D', 'E').
Witness list: The lists attached to S 844 and 851 are remarkably similar, though
the ealdormen recorded demonstrate conclusively that the diplomas were produced
at different times in the year.

¶ S 843 (Stevenson, *Chronicon* I, 370–2): 983, after the death of Ealdorman Ælfhere
King Æthelred to Abingdon Abbey: grant of 2 *manentes* at Arncot in Oxford-
shire
(Abingdon)
Date: As for S 851.

¶ S 845 (Edwards, *Liber de Hyda*, pp. 228–31): 983, after the death of Ealdorman
Ælfhere
King Æthelred to Æthelgar, bishop of Selsey: grant of a meadow in the
northern part of Winchester
(New Minster Winchester)
Date: As for S 851.

¶ S 847 (Hart, *Charters of Eastern England*, pp. 186–7): 983
King Æthelred to Æthelmær, *minister*: grant of 9 *cassati* at Thames Ditton
in Surrey
(Thorney)

984[27]

¶ S 855 (Stevenson, *Chronicon* I, 397–400): 984, before 1 August
King Æthelred to Brihtric, his *minister*: grant of 8 *mansae* near the River Kennet

copyist, transcribing S 846 on fos. 77v–78r, noticed the identity of formulation and decided
to repeat what he had just written. Note that the rubric (i.e. the endorsement) to S 846
describes Æthelmær as the king's thegn, though he is *dux* in the text. Note also that the
only difference between the formulation of the two diplomas is the expression 'quamdiu
vita comes fuerit' (see also S 123, 125, 1614, 177 and 440; cf. the normal expression 'vita
comite') in S 848, and 'quamdiu vita dux fuerit' in S 846.

[27] For a reference to a (lost) diploma dated 984 and in favour of Glastonbury Abbey, see
S 1774.

(Leverton in Hungerford, Berkshire)

(Abingdon)

Date: The diploma was attested by Æthelwold, bishop of Winchester, who died in 984 (*ASC* MSS 'A', 'C', 'D', 'E') on 1 August.[28]

¶ S 850 (KCD 641): 984, before 1 August

King Æthelred to Shaftesbury Abbey: confirmation of 20 *mansae* at Tisbury in Wiltshire and restoration of a wood called *Sfgcnyllebar*

(Shaftesbury)

Date: As for S 855. The diploma may have been produced on the same occasion as S 852.

Witness list: In MS 1, the witnesses are arranged in two columns: the first ends with the *ministri* Ordulf and Godwine, after Ealdorman Ælfric, and the second begins with the other Ealdorman Ælfric. As in the case of S 837, it is possible that the scribe had to insert the two *ministri* (Ordulf and Godwine) at the bottom of the first column in order to balance the second, thus separating one Ealdorman Ælfric from the other. This would mean that the list of *ministri* did begin with Ælfweard and Ælfsige, in accordance with other lists of the period. Moreover, on the basis of other diplomas which include the subscriptions of a Godwine (S 837, 838, 861, 862, 864 and 867) one would have to regard his apparent second position in S 850 as anomalous; Ordulf's apparently high position could be supported by S 840, but he was otherwise not prominent until the 990s. In Table 7 I therefore transfer Ordulf and Godwine to the end of the list of *ministri*: they could be fourteenth and sixteenth (as in the table), or sixteenth and seventeenth. Note that Ealdorman Æthelwine occurs as 'Ælwine' (KCD: Ælfwine).

¶ S 852 (Stevenson, *Chronicon* I, 392–4): 984, before 1 August

King Æthelred to Ælfheah, his *minister*: grant of 2 *cassati* at Osanlea

(Abingdon)

Date: As for S 855. For the indiction, see above, p. 232 n. 4. The diploma may have been produced on the same occasion as S 850.

¶ S 853 (Sawyer, *Charters of Burton*, pp. 39–41): 984, after 1 August and probably before 19 October

King Æthelred to Ælfwine *minister*, his *scriptor*: grant of 3 *cassati* at Brighthampton, 2 at Aston Bampton and 1 at Lew, in Oxfordshire

(Burton)

Date: The absence of a bishop of Winchester suggests that the diploma was produced after Æthelwold's death on 1 August (see under S 855) and before 19 October, when his successor Ælfheah was consecrated (*ASC* MS 'A'; Birch, *Liber Vitae*, p. 23).

Witness list: The list is abbreviated: after the bishops, the copyist indicates that there were 6 ealdormen, 4 abbots, 4 *disciferi*, 4 *pincernae* and 11 *ministri*.

§ S 854 (KCD 643): 984

King Æthelred to Bath Abbey: grant of 3½ *mansae* at Radstock in Somerset

(Bath)

[28] *ASC* MS 'C'; Cambridge, Corpus Christi College MS 57; B.L. Cotton Titus D xxvii; William of Malmesbury, *De Antiquitate Glastoniensis Ecclesiae*.

243

Date: The diploma itself is dated 984, but this is not compatible with the witness list.

Witness list: The archbishops and bishops belong to the period 1006×7 (Æthelwold of Winchester) – 1007×9 (Ordbriht of Selsey), and the athelings, abbots, ealdormen and *milites* are compatible with this date; all the witnesses occur in S 916 (1007). The athelings and ealdormen are not entered in the tables, because they appear to have become muddled in transmission. The former occur in the order Æthelstan, Edgar, Edmund, Edward, Edward (for Eadred) and Eadwig: but the formulae of attestation fit together better (compare S 922) if one supposes that the athelings were originally listed in their normal order as seen in Table 1. Since the athelings are disordered, the irregular order for the ealdormen (Leofwine, Ælfric) may well not be original.

985

¶ S 856 (KCD 648): 985, after the expulsion of Ealdorman Ælfric

King Æthelred to Æthelric, *minister*: grant of 17 *cassati* at Harwell in Berkshire
(Old Minster Winchester)

Date: The diploma was attested by only one Ealdorman Ælfric, very probably the ealdorman of Hampshire. According to *ASC* MSS 'C', 'D', 'E', Ealdorman Ælfric of Mercia was driven out of the land in 985, and it seems that this took place before any of the extant diplomas of 985 were issued. The diploma was probably produced on the same occasion as S 858 and 860.

¶ S 858 (Stevenson, *Chronicon* I, 400–3): 985, after the expulsion of Ealdorman Ælfric

King Æthelred to Leofwine, *minister*: grant of 10 *cassati* at Wootton in Berkshire
(Abingdon)

Date: As for S 856. The diploma was probably produced on the same occasion as S 856 and 860.

Witness list: The last abbot, Æthelweard, could be the abbot of Malmesbury, who occurs consistently between 980 and 984; but he is not found in either of the two lists closely related to this one, in S 856 and 860, and his relative position in S 858 could be anomalous in terms of his earlier subscriptions. Moreover, both S 856 and 860 show Ælfweard at the top of the list of *ministri* (though given as 'abbot' in S 860), but he is conspicuously absent from S 858. So it is possible that 'Æthelweard abbas' is an error for 'Ælfweard minister';[29] one should also record the alternative possibility that the copyist inadvertently omitted Ælfweard *minister*, having caught the last element of his name when he looked for the name which followed Æthelweard *abbas*.

¶ S 860 (KCD 650): 985, after the expulsion of Ealdorman Ælfric

King Æthelred to Wulfrun: grant of 10 *cassati* at Wolverhampton and Trescott in Staffordshire
(Old Minster Winchester)

[29] For confusion between the elements 'Æðel-' and 'Ælf-' in witness lists, see above, p. 235 n. 15.

Date: As for S 856. The diploma was probably produced on the same occasion as S 856 and 858.

Witness list: Abbots Ordbriht, Sigeric and Leofric are given incorrectly as ealdormen, and it is likely that 'Ælfweard abbas' is a further error for 'Ælfweard minister'. The main *Codex Wintoniensis* copyist had a preference for homogeneous blocks of witnesses, and having turned three abbots into ealdormen to create one substantial block, he may have detached the top *minister* to serve as a companion for the remaining abbot, Ælfhere. The manuscript is so fine and carefully written that such 'errors' are likely to be deliberate: it is improbable that the same error would be repeated three times.

¶ S 857 (KCD 652): 985

King Æthelred to Alfred, his *amicus*: grant of 11 *mansae* at Michelmersh in Hampshire

(Old Minster Winchester)

¶ S 859 (KCD 647): 985

King Æthelred to Wulfric, his *sacerdos*: grant of 1 *mansa* at *Borstealle*, *Hæsten dic* and *Cnollam*

(Christchurch / Twynham)

986

‖ S 1796 (Gibbs, *Church of St Paul*, p. 1): 986, at London

King Æthelred to   ?   :

(London, St Paul's)

Date: If the regnal year in the dating clause was calculated from the king's accession, the diploma was produced before 18 March in 986; if it was calculated from the king's coronation, the diploma was produced after 3 May in 986.

¶ S 862 (Brewer, *Registrum*, pp. 320–1): 986

King Æthelred to Wenoth, his *minister*: grant of 5 *mansiunculae* at Littleton on Severn in Gloucestershire

(Malmesbury)

Witness list: The witness list as printed by Kemble (KCD 654) is corrupt, but he used an inferior manuscript, B.L. Lansdowne 417 (MS 2), where the arrangement of the witnesses is both confused and confusing. Brewer's text, from MS 4, serves also for the version in the best Malmesbury cartulary, that in the Bodleian Library (MS 5). These two manuscripts show that Ealdorman Ælfric occurred in his proper place with the other ealdormen, not displaced amongst the *ministri* as in KCD: he appears as 'Alfrig' or 'Ælfrig' in all three manuscripts, and Kemble (or his amanuensis) was clearly mistaken to emend this to 'Ælfsige'. The lists in MSS 4 and 5 also provide six additional *ministri*: Leofwine, Wulfric, Thureferth, 'Wulfrig', Wulfnoth and Wulfgeat. On the analogy of the 'Alfrig'–Ælfric error, I emend 'Wulfrig' to Wulfric; I also emend 'Æþelrig' and 'Leofrig' in all versions to Æthelric and Leofric, for Kemble's Æthelsige and Leofsige. In each case, however, one could not discount the possibility that '-rig' stands for '-sige'.

‖ S 1450 (*O.S. Facs.* III, 34): 986

King Æthelred to Westminster Abbey: grant of 5 *mansiunculae* at Hampstead in Middlesex
(Westminster)
¶ S 861 (KCD 655): 986
King Æthelred to Ælfgar, *minister*: grant of 5 *manentes* at Ebbesborne in Wiltshire
(Old Minster Winchester)
Witness list: Ordbriht occurs as the last of the ealdormen, though he was certainly an abbot: as in the case of S 860, it is difficult to believe that the error was simply mechanical, for it seems that Ordbriht was 'promoted' to balance the column of ealdormen against the parallel column of bishops; the remaining three abbots occur in a separate group, lower down on the opposite side of the leaf from the ealdormen. The list is very similar to those in S 864 and 867 (both dated 987).

987

† ¶ S 864 (Campbell, *Charters of Rochester*, pp. 37–9): 987
King Æthelred to Æthelsige, *minister*: grant of 10 *aratra* at Bromley in Kent
(Rochester)
Date: The diploma was probably produced on the same occasion as S 867, 863 and 866.
Witness list: The list is very similar to those in S 861 and 867 (dated 986 and 987 respectively).
¶ S 867 (KCD 658): 987
King Æthelred to Leofwine, his *venator*: grant of 3 *mansae* at Westwood in Wiltshire and 3 *perticae* at Farleigh Hungerford in Somerset
(Old Minster Winchester)
Date: The diploma was probably produced on the same occasion as S 864, 863 and 866.
Witness list: There are two parallel columns of witnesses at the foot of MS fo. 106r: the left-hand one comprises eight bishops, and the right-hand one comprises eight 'ealdormen'. Again it seems that the abbots, and in this case all four of them, have been 'promoted' to balance the columns. Amongst the *ministri*, the first 'Æðelric' is probably an error for 'Ælfric': see S 864. The list is very similar to those in S 861 and 864 (dated 986 and 987 respectively).
¶ S 863 (Sawyer, *Charters of Burton*, pp. 41–2): 987
King Æthelred to Æthelsige, his *minister*: grant of 12 *mansae* at *Æsce*
(Burton)
Date: The diploma was probably produced on the same occasion as S 864, 867 and 866.
Witness list: The list is abbreviated: only the names of the bishops are given, and the rest are covered by the statement that there were twenty-one ealdormen, abbots and *ministri*. The copyist divided the bishops into three columns of two names each, and inserted Ælfwold in an available space after Archbishop Oswald's subscription. Hart, *Charters of Northern England*, p. 194, places Ælfwold in third

place, after Oswald, and then reads the other subscriptions across the line. This is the first subscription of Bishop Ælfwold, and third place would be remarkably high; moreover, his style is 'conclusi', which for obvious reasons is used more frequently for the last episcopal witness[30] than in all other positions combined.[31] After the archbishops I read each column in turn, and add Ælfwold at the end: the resulting order is strongly supported by contemporary diplomas (for example S 864 and 867).

¶ S 866 (Watkin, *Great Chartulary* III, 651): 987
  King Æthelred to Glastonbury Abbey: grant of 40 *mansae* at Kington in Wiltshire
  (Glastonbury)
Date: The diploma was probably produced on the same occasion as S 864, 867 and 863.

¶ S 865 (Edwards, *Liber de Hyda*, pp. 231–6): 987, ? after 17 March
  King Æthelred to Æthelwold: grant of 10 *manentia*[32] at Manningford Abbots in Wiltshire
  (New Minster Winchester)
Date: If, as is likely, the regnal year in the dating clause was calculated from the moment of the king's accession in 978, and not from 978 generally, the diploma was produced after 17 March in 987.
Witness list: The printed text of the diploma is from MS 3. The witness list in the earlier cartulary (MS 1, whence MS 2) of the abbey seems preferable: it shows Æthelwine and Brihtnoth at the head of the list of ealdormen, instead of Brihtnoth and Ælfric. In both versions (MSS 1 and 3) the first four *ministri* are given mistakenly as ealdormen; MS 1, however, has 'Ælfgar' for MS 3's 'Ælfgius'.

‡ ¶ S 1863 (Finberg, 'Supplement', pp. 33–5): ?987
  [King Æthelred] to Ordulf: grant of 2½ *perticae* by the Dart in Devon
  (archive uncertain)
Date: Only a fragment has been preserved, and the date is conjectural; but the two columns of *ministri* suggest an association with the diplomas of 987.

988

§ S 873 (KCD 662): 23 March 988
  King Æthelred to Northman, his *minister*: grant of 5 *manentes* at Hampton in Worcestershire
  (Evesham)
Date: The diploma itself is dated 23 March 988 (with a regnal year calculated from the king's coronation), but this is not compatible with the witness list.
Witness list: For 'Alfredus episcopus' in KCD, read 'Ælfegus episcopus' (MS). The

---

[30] E.g. S 839–40, 853, 861, 864, 868, 871, 870, 881, 886, 884, 888–9, 893, 896, 914, 905 and 916; cf. S 885.
[31] E.g. S 851, 855, 850, 860, 858, 872, 891, 899–900, 902, 906, 909–11, 920 and 930.
[32] Here and in S 869 *manens* is declined in the plural as a neuter noun. Cf. S 892 and 922.

list comprises only the king, two archbishops and four bishops, and the inclusion of Wulfstan, bishop of London, provides the limits 996 × 1002.

¶ S 869 (Edwards, *Liber de Hyda*, pp. 238–42): 16 April 988
   King Æthelred to Æthelgar, bishop of Selsey: grant of 7 *manentia*[33] at South Heighton in Sussex
   (New Minster Winchester)

Date: Note that the dating clause incorporates a regnal year, calculated from the king's coronation: the ninth such year ran from 4 May 987 to 3 May 988.

¶ S 868 (KCD 664): 988, before 19 May
   King Æthelred to Ælfgar, his *minister*: grant of 5 *mansae* at Wylye in Wiltshire
   (Old Minster Winchester)

Date: The diploma was attested by Archbishop Dunstan, who died in 988 (*ASC*, all MSS), on 19 May.[34]

Witness list: Again the *Codex Wintoniensis* copyist seems deliberately to have changed the status of some of the witnesses simply to balance his arrangement of the list. The first three *ministri* (Ælfsige, Æthelsige and Wulfsige) are given at the bottom of the first column with the – and as – abbots. All three names could be acceptable as abbots, but to regard them as such would be to incur the conspicuous absence of three of the consistently prominent *ministri* of the 980s.

¶ S 870 (KCD 665): 988, after 19 May and before ? November/December
   King Æthelred to Æthelnoth, his *minister*: grant of 1 *curtis* in Wilton
   (Wilton)

Date: The see of Canterbury is not represented, and Dunstan's successor Æthelgar occurs as bishop of Selsey: therefore the diploma was produced during a vacancy at Canterbury following Dunstan's death (see under S 868). According to *ASC* MSS 'C', 'D', 'E', Æthelgar lived for one year and three months after his translation to Canterbury. He died on 13 February[35] or on 12 February[36] in 990:[37] therefore he must have been translated to Canterbury in November/December 988.[38] In

[33] See above, p. 247 n. 32.
[34] Wharton, *Anglia Sacra* I, 54; Florence of Worcester. Wharton's details concerning obits, ordinations and translations of archbishops of Canterbury are said to be extracted from a manuscript in Lambeth Palace Library.
[35] B.L. Cotton Titus D xxvii. The obit is also in B.L. Cotton Vitellius C xii, as an addition to an eleventh-century martyrology from St Augustine's Canterbury. Æthelgar had been abbot of New Minster Winchester, and hence the obit of 'Algarus abbas' under 13 February in the Hyde Abbey breviary (Tolhurst, *Hyde Breviary, s.d.*).
[36] Cambridge, Corpus Christi College MS 57; B.L. Cotton Nero C ix, fo. 5v. Nero, fos. 3r–18v contain a fragment of a s. xiii obituary of Christ Church Canterbury, printed by Dart, *Canterbury*, pp. xxxii–xli; fos. 19–21 contain a fragment of a s. xii *in.* obituary of Christ Church, printed *ibid.* pp. xli–xlii; another fragment from the latter obituary is in London, Lambeth Palace MS 430, fly-leaves, printed by James and Jenkins, *Catalogue of MSS in Lambeth Palace*, pp. 593–4. Æthelgar's obit is also entered at 13 February in B.L. Egerton 2867.
[37] Leofric Missal (Oxford, Bodleian Library, Bodley 579): additions to a s. x² Anglo-Saxon calendar and Easter tables, printed by Warren, *Leofric Missal*, pp. l–li and 50 respectively.
[38] It is possible that the 'obit', 3 December, for Æthelgar given in Wharton, *Anglia Sacra* I, 54, in fact refers to his ordination as archbishop. But though entered by Wharton under Æthelgar, the entry reads: 'Obiit piæ memoriæ Lotarius Archiepiscopus.'

ASC MS 'F' (Old English and Latin) it is said that Æthelgar lived for one year and eight months after his translation: but the 'eight' is an alteration from 'three' and may have been suggested by the knowledge that Dunstan died in May and Æthelgar in the next February but one following. The diploma was probably produced on the same occasion as S 871.

¶ S 871 (Watkin, *Great Chartulary* III, 704): 988, after 19 May and before ? November/December
> King Æthelred to Æthelsige, bishop of Sherborne, and Æthelmær, his *miles*: grant of 1 *curtis* in Winchester
> (Glastonbury)

Date: As for S 870, which was probably produced on the same occasion.

¶ S 872 (Barker, 'Sussex Charters', pp. 103–5): 988, ? November/December
> King Æthelred to Leofstan, his *minister*: grant of 4 *mansae* at Colworth in Sussex
> (Chichester)

Date: After the translation of Æthelgar from Selsey to Canterbury, probably in November/December 988: see under S 870.

Witness list: Amongst the bishops, 'Ædelstanus' represents Ælfstan and 'Ædelwoldus' represents Ælfwold. The abbots are listed after the *ministri*, and are given as the third and last line of four parallel columns; one abbot occurs on the second line in the fourth column. Kemble (KCD 663) reads the columns vertically in turn, thus mixing the abbots with the *ministri*: but Barker is doubtless correct in reading horizontally, thus preserving the integrity of the groups of witnesses.

988 × 90

S 877 (Edwards, *Liber de Hyda*, pp. 242–53): ? November/December 988 × 13 February 990, at London
> List of those present at a synod of London, incorporated in S 877 (dated 996)
> (New Minster Winchester)

Date: The synod was held during the archiepiscopate of Æthelgar: see under S 870. It took place after the production of S 872, since Ordbriht occurs as bishop (of Selsey) and no longer as abbot (of Chertsey). The list of thegns present includes Ælfhelm Polga, and if Hart's suggestion ('Eadnoth', p. 65) that Ælfhelm died on 31 October 989 is accepted, it would take several weeks off the later limit.

Witness list: The Old English version of the list should be read in conjunction with the Middle English version, which has some additional names among the bishops: see Robertson, *Charters*, pp. 372–7.

990

‖ S 942 (KCD 712): 990, after 13 February and before 17 April
> King Æthelred to the Church of St Peter and All Saints, South Stoneham in Hampshire: grant of 10 *mansae* at Hinton Ampner in Hampshire
> (Old Minster Winchester)

Date: The diploma is not dated, but the list is fixed to the given period in 990 by the occurrence of Archbishop Sigeric (who succeeded after Æthelgar's death on 12/13 February 990: see under S 870) and Eadwine, abbot of Abingdon, who died in 990 (*ASC* MS 'C'), on 17 April (Cambridge, Corpus Christi College MS 57). *Witness list:* Apart from the king and Sigeric, the witnesses are arranged in two columns on MS fo. 85r. The *ministri* Ordulf and Brihtwold occur as the last two names in the first column, after the first five abbots; the remaining nine abbots are grouped together at the top of the second column, followed by the ealdormen and the other *ministri*. Kemble printed Ordulf and Brihtwold as the third and fourth *ministri*, but in Table 7 Brihtwold is given as the fifth, after rather than before Æthelmær:

EGO Ealdulf abb.	Ego Ælfsige min.
EGO Ælfun abb.	Ego Ordlaf min.
Ego Orddulf min.	Ego Æþelmer min.
Ego Byrhtwold min.	Ego Ælfgar min.

Ordlaf *minister* does not otherwise occur in Æthelred's diplomas; he is not included in the closely-related list in S 944.

§ S 944 (KCD 713): 990, after 13 February and before 17 April

King Æthelred to ? : grant of 8 *mansae* at Weston in South Stoneham in Hampshire

(Old Minster Winchester)

Date: As for S 942.

‖ S 875 (KCD 1285): 990, before 4 May

King Æthelred to Sigered, his *minister*: grant of 2 *cassati* at Sibertswold in Kent

(St Augustine's Canterbury)

Date: The text is dated 990, in the eleventh year of the king's reign. The eleventh regnal year can only coincide with the year of grace if it is calculated from the king's coronation: it would extend from 4 May 989 to 3 May 990.

¶ S 874 (KCD 673): 990, after 13 February (? and before 14 May)

King Æthelred to Æthelweard, *minister*: grant of 15 *tributaria* at Wootton St Lawrence in Hampshire, with 9 *hagan* in Winchester, a meadow at Basingstoke and a mill at *Hines clifæ*

(Old Minster Winchester)

Date: The diploma was attested by Archbishop Sigeric: see under S 942. The second Bishop Æthelsige in the witness list cannot be identified: it may be an error for Ælfsige, bishop of Chester-le-Street, making his only recorded subscription in Æthelred's reign in the last year of his life. Bishop Ælfsige died in 990 (Florence of Worcester, in Thorpe, *Chronicon* I, 149; Simeon of Durham, in Arnold, *Symeonis Monachi Opera* I, 78), and seems to be the only candidate for the obit of 'ælfsini ep' entered at 14 May in Cambridge, Corpus Christi College MS 57. *Witness list:* For the second Bishop Æthelsige, see above.

993

† ¶ S 876 (Stevenson, *Chronicon* I, 358–66): Pentecost, i.e. 4 June (at Winchester), and 17 July (at Gillingham) 993

King Æthelred to Abingdon Abbey: confirmation and grant of privileges
(Abingdon)

Date: The regnal year (17) given for the Winchester meeting is impossible by any calculation. In the same diploma, Bishop Æthelwold's death (1 August 984) is placed in the seventh regnal year, calculated from the king's accession. By the same calculation 4 June 993 would fall in the sixteenth regnal year.

Witness list: When the list was drawn up, the see of Sherborne was vacant, and its next incumbent, Wulfsige, was still abbot of Westminster. Wulfsige's name was subsequently inserted in a space left blank for the bishop of Sherborne's subscription, and Ælfwig, his successor at Westminster, was added at the end of the list of *ministri*. These additions probably guarantee and reflect the contemporaneity of the Cotton charter (MS 1).[39] The copy in MS 3 differs slightly from MS 1 and from the copy in MS 2: it gives 'Oswig' as bishop of Dorchester, 'Elsie' as bishop of Sherborne and 'Ælfsie' as abbot of Westminster in place of Wulfsige.

994

† ¶ S 880 (*O.S. Facs.* II, Exeter 8): 994, before 28 October
King Æthelred to Ealdred, bishop of Cornwall: grant of privileges
(Exeter)

Date: The diploma was attested by Archbishop Sigeric, who died in 994 (*ASC* MS 'A'; Leofric Missal; B.L. Cotton Titus D xxvii[40]) on 28 October.[41]

Witness list: Note that the texts given by Kemble (KCD 686) and Thorpe, *Diplomatarium*, pp. 285–7, are based on inferior manuscripts and contain several variations from the extant original diploma (MS 1) in the lower reach of the witness list.

¶ S 881 (KCD 687): 994, before 28 October
King Æthelred to Wilton Abbey: grant of 10 *cassati* at Fovant in Wiltshire
(Wilton)

Date: As for S 880.

¶ S 882 (KCD 689): 994, after 8 September and before 28 October
King Æthelred to Æscwig, bishop of Dorchester: confirmation of 30 *mansiunculae* at Monks Risborough in Buckinghamshire, granted to him by Archbishop Sigeric
(Christ Church Canterbury)

Date: The diploma is dated 995, but the subscription of Archbishop Sigeric and the given indiction show that this is a scribal error for 994; see further under S 880. In the text, reference is made to the Viking devastation of Kent, so the diploma

---

[39] For analogous alterations and additions to witness lists, see S 795 (in which the name of one bishop was erased, perhaps because he was found not to have been present) and 901 (with a second bishop of Dorchester added at the end).

[40] Sigeric's death, entered opposite 994 in the Easter tables in B.L. Cotton Titus D xxvii, was unaccountably omitted by Birch, *Liber Vitae*, p. 276.

[41] Wharton, *Anglia Sacra* I, 54; B.L. Arundel 68; B.L. Cotton Nero C ix, fo. 14r; B.L. Cotton Nero C ix, fo. 20r, but erased and transferred to 31 October. Arundel 68 contains a martyrology of Christ Church Canterbury (fos. 12r–52v), copied in London, Lambeth Palace MS 20, fos. 157r–248v. Amongst the many obits of Anglo-Saxon kings, bishops and abbots are several others which refer to the pre-Conquest benefactors of Christ Church.

is presumably later than 8 September, when Olaf and Swein arrived in the area: *ASC* MSS 'C', 'D', 'E' *s.a.* 994.

Witness list: Ælfstan, bishop of London, and Ælfstan, bishop of Rochester, both occur as 'Æðelstanus'. The list is intimately related to that in S 1379, extant as an original and from a different archive: the correct form 'Ælfstanus' is given for each Bishop 'Æðelstanus', and 'Wulfgeat' and 'Wulfheah' occur for the unaccountable forms 'Wolfryð' and 'Wolfeby' of S 882, which I emend accordingly.

† ¶ S 1379 (KCD 691): 994, after 8 September and before 28 October
Æscwig, bishop of Dorchester, to Ælfstan, his man: grant of 5 *mansae* at Cuxham in Oxfordshire
(archive uncertain)

Date: The diploma is dated 995, but the subscription of Archbishop Sigeric places the witness list before 28 October 994: see further under S 882, for which the same memorandum of witnesses' names was used.

§ S 1380 (Dugdale, *Monasticon*, pp. 988–92): 994?
Sigeric, archbishop of Canterbury, for Wulfrun and Wolverhampton: confirmation of privileges and of lands in Staffordshire
(Wolverhampton)

Date: The dating information given in the text is confused, but 994, the seventh indiction, seems to have been intended.

Witness list: Elements of the list are incompatible with the period of Archbishop Sigeric's office (post 12/13 February 990–28 October 994), though this privilege is in his name and bears his subscription. Ælfstan, bishop of Rochester, last occurs in 994, so his successor Godwine, who occurs in S 1380, could have been contemporary with Sigeric, though he does not otherwise occur until 995. But the subscription of Ealdulf, archbishop of York, is certainly incompatible both with the subscription of Sigeric and with the subscription of Ælfric as bishop of Ramsbury: S 885 and 886 demonstrate that he was only archbishop-*elect* after Sigeric's death and while Ælfric was himself archbishop-elect. I suspect that a witness list from a royal diploma of 995 × 6,[42] with the subscriptions of Archbishops Ælfric and Ealdulf, was used by the forger of the privilege, and that for his own purposes he had to replace Ælfric with Sigeric, transferring Ælfric to the list of bishops and thereby creating the anachronism. The other witnesses are compatible with the period 994 × 6. In Table 3, I enter the bishops without Sigeric and Ælfric; in Table 5, I enter the abbots as they stand; and in Table 7, I enter the *ministri* as they stand (though note that Æthelmær is styled *comes*). The document also contains the subscriptions of Ealdormen Leofwine, Æthelweard, Ælfric, Leofsige and Ælfhelm ('dux Transhumbranae gentis') – the correct combination for the period, but in a jumbled order; two deacons, Wulfsige and Ælfweard, occur between Æthelweard and Ælfric.[43]

---

[42] The occurrence amongst the bishops of Ælfstan of London and Sigar of Wells shows that the list could not be later than 996, and the occurrence of Archbishop Ealdulf shows that it could not be earlier than 995.

[43] There is a detailed account of the Wolverhampton privilege in Keynes, 'Studies' II, 595–629.

995

¶ S 883 (Stevenson, *Chronicon* I, 394–7): 995, before 21 April
King Æthelred to Æthelwig, his *miles*: grant of 5 *mansi*[44] at Ardley in Oxford-shire
(Abingdon)
Date: The diploma was attested by Ælfric as bishop of Ramsbury, and in the light of S 885 and 886 we may infer that it was produced before his election as arch-bishop of Canterbury on Easter Day 995 (*ASC* MS 'F'). For the indiction, see above, p. 232 n. 4.
Witness list: The name of Archbishop Sigeric was probably inserted in a space left blank during the vacancy at Canterbury created by his death in October 994. There was still a vacancy at York, so without the name of Sigeric the list would have had no archbishops.
¶ S 885 (Campbell, *Charters of Rochester*, pp. 39–42): 995, after 21 April
King Æthelred to the see of Rochester: restoration of 6 *mansae* (or *sulunga*) at Wouldham and 1 *mansa* at Littlebrook in Kent
(Rochester)
Date: Ælfric attests the diploma as 'Doruernensis ecclesie electus episcopus', so it was produced after, perhaps shortly after, his election on Easter Day 995 (*ASC* MS 'F'). Ealdulf similarly attests as 'Eboracensis ecclesie electus episcopus'.
¶ S 886 (Stevenson, *Chronicon* I, 388–92): 995, after 21 April (and after 3 May?)
King Æthelred to Wulfric, *minister*: grant of 2½ *mansae* at Dumbleton in Gloucestershire
(Abingdon)
Date: Archbishop Ælfric attests the diploma as 'electus ad archiepiscopatum Dorobernensis ecclesiæ': see under S 885. Ealdulf attests as 'electus in episcopatum Eboracensis ecclesiæ'. The dating clause incorporates a regnal year, calculated from the king's coronation: the seventeenth such year ran from 4 May 995 to 3 May 996. The original diploma was probably misdated DCCCCLXCV: this is the reading of MS I, and also of MS 3 (with the L erased).
† ¶ S 884 (Bates, *Muchelney*, pp. 43–5): 995, after 21 April (at Canterbury?)
King Æthelred to Muchelney Abbey: confirmation of lands, including estates at Ilminster and Camel in Somerset
(Muchelney)
Date: Ælfric attested the diploma as 'bishop' of Canterbury, so it was produced after Easter (see under S 885) and perhaps before Ælfric had received his pallium. For the evidence that the diploma was produced at Canterbury, see above, p. 120.

996

† ¶ S 878 (Sawyer, *Charters of Burton*, pp. 45–7): 996, perhaps before 5 May, certainly before 28 June (in Kent?)

---

[44] Here (as in S 897–8, 915, 918 and 943) the draftsman apparently believed that the word for 'hide' was a second-declension masculine noun. For other instances before and after Æthelred's reign, see S 586–7, 786–7, 1003, 1321 and 1407.

King Æthelred to Wulfric, his *minister*: grant of 3 *cassati* at Abbots Bromley in Staffordshire

(Burton)

Date: The diploma was attested by Sigar, bishop of Wells, and was therefore produced before his death on 28 June (William of Malmesbury, *De Antiquitate Glastoniensis Ecclesiae*) 996 (because his successor Ælfwine attested S 891, issued at Easter-time 997). It is possible that the diploma was produced before 5 May, for it was also attested by Brihtnoth, abbot of Ely, who died on 5 May (Cambridge, Trinity College MS O. 2. 1⁴⁵) in ?996 (to judge only from his non-appearance in S 891, which has a long list of abbots). For the evidence that the diploma may have been produced in Kent, see above, pp. 132–4. All of the extant diplomas of 996 were produced after the consecration of Wulfstan as bishop of London in that year (*ASC* MS 'F').

‡ § S 879 (Sawyer, *Charters of Burton*, pp. 43–4): 996

King Æthelred to Wulfric, his *minister*: grant of land at Pillaton in Staffordshire

(Burton)

Witness list: The list is an abbreviated version of that in S 878, from which it was derived, and it is not therefore entered in the tables.

¶ S 887 (Stevenson, *Chronicon* I, 404–6): 996, perhaps before 5 May

King Æthelred to Eadric, Eadwig and Ealdred, brothers: grant of 2 *mansae* at *Bynsingtun land* in Oxfordshire

(Abingdon)

Date: The diploma was attested by Brihtnoth, abbot of Ely, and so may have been produced before 5 May (see under S 878).

¶ S 877 (Edwards, *Liber de Hyda*, pp. 242–53): 996, perhaps before 5 May

King Æthelred to Queen Ælfthryth: grant of 3½ *sulunga* at Bradbourne, 3½ at Evegate, 2 at *Burhwarefelda*, 3 at Nackington, 3 at Chalk and 1 at ?Perry, all in Kent

(New Minster Winchester)

Date: As for S 887. The given date DCCCCXCIII is a misreading of DCCCCXCVI (confirmed by indiction). The dating clause incorporates a regnal year (18): if calculated from the king's accession, it would run from 18 March 995 to 17 March 996, and so it would follow that the diploma was produced before 18 March in 996; but one could not exclude the possibility that it was calculated from the king's coronation, whether counting 996 generally, or the period between 4 May 996 and 3 May 997, as the eighteenth.

Witness list: For 'Ulfsige abbas' read 'Ælfsige abbas', and for 'Grumus abbas' read 'Germanus abbas'. Archbishop Ælfric occurs as 'Æthelfricus'; compare S 891, produced in the following year.

¶ S 888 (KCD 696): 996, perhaps before 5 May

King Æthelred to St Albans Abbey: grant of 4 *mansae* at Burston (in St Albans),

---

⁴⁵ The manuscript contains an extensive collection of obits of Ely monks, abbots and bene-factors, as well as of other prominent laymen and ecclesiastics, added to a s. xii² calendar: the identifiable obits have been printed and discussed by Dickins, 'Byrhtnoth's Death'.

Dating and witness lists

4 at *Wincelfelda* (in St Albans), 9 *hagan* in St Albans and 8 *iugera* at Westwick (in St Albans)
(St Albans)
Date: As for S 887. For the indiction, see above, p. 232 n. 4. In Kemble's text, the diploma is said to have been written at a synod at Chelsea, but it is clear from the manuscript that the operative sentence belongs with the preceding document in it (S 150).
Witness list: In MS 3, Ealdorman Ælfric occurs before Ealdorman Æthelweard.
¶ S 889 (KCD 1291): 996
King Æthelred to the Old Minster Winchester: restoration of a *haga* in Winchester
(Old Minster Winchester)
Witness list: The witnesses are arranged in two columns, the first of bishops and the second of ealdormen: but the last three 'ealdormen' are properly *ministri*.

997

¶ S 891 (KCD 698): late March–early April 997, at Calne and then at Wantage
King Æthelred to the Old Minster Winchester: restoration of 55 *mansae* at Downton and 45 at Ebbesborne in Wiltshire
(Old Minster Winchester)
Date: The diploma is said to have been produced at Wantage, a few days after Easter (28 March) had been celebrated at Calne. The dating clause incorporates a regnal year, calculated from the king's accession.
Witness list: The abbots are identified by their abbeys (as in S 876)[46] and the ealdormen by their respective provinces. Note that Archbishop Ælfric occurs as 'Æðelfric', and compare S 877. Note also that the diploma is attested by Ælfric, abbot of Malmesbury: his successor Brihtwold attests S 890 (25 July 997).
‡ ¶ S 890 (*O.S. Facs.* III, 35): 25 July 997
King Æthelred to Ælfwold, bishop of Crediton: grant of 2 *cassati* at Sandford in Devon
(Crediton)
Witness list: The last bishop is 'ælfstan', presumably for Æthelstan of Elmham. Note that the diploma is attested by Brihtwold, abbot of Malmesbury, whose predecessor attested S 891, produced earlier in the same year.

998

¶ S 893 (Campbell, *Charters of Rochester*, pp. 42–4): *c.* 17 April 998
King Æthelred to the see of Rochester: restoration of 6 *sulunga* at Bromley in Kent, with the use of appurtenant woodland in the Weald
(Rochester)

---

[46] The names of the abbeys are written out in full, but this may be the work of the *Codex Wintoniensis* copyist: they are abbreviated in S 876, and the last one in S 891 occurs as 'Ego ælfric Eof'   abbas', as if the copyist was unable to expand the contraction in his exemplar. (Kemble prints 'Ego Ælfric Eofeshamensis aecclesiae abbas'.)

Appendix 1

Date: The dating clause states that the diploma was produced at Easter-time.

† ¶ S 892 (Napier and Stevenson, *Crawford Charters*, pp. 19–22): 998

    King Æthelred to Leofwine, his *dux*: grant of 7½ *tributaria*, comprising 3 *mansae* at Southam and 4 *manentes* with ½ *mansa* at Ladbroke and Radbourne, all in Warwickshire

    (?Coventry)

¶ S 895 (KCD 701): 998

    King Æthelred to Bishop Wulfsige and Sherborne Abbey: permission to convert the community to the Benedictine Rule, and confirmation of various estates in Devon and Dorset

    (Sherborne)

Date: The diploma was attested by Ælfwine, bishop of Wells, whose successor Lyfing occurs for the first time in 999 (S 896). An entry in the Leofric Missal reveals that a Bishop Ælfwine died on 29 August, but this may refer to Ælfwine, bishop of Winchester, who died on that day in 1047 (*ASC* MSS 'C', 'E'); moreover, one cannot be sure whether Ælfwine of Wells died in 998 or 999. Therefore there is only an outside chance that S 895 can be dated before 29 August 998.

§ S 894 (Thorpe, *Diplomatarium*, pp. 296–8): 998

    King Æthelred to Westminster Abbey: confirmation of privileges and of various estates in Middlesex, Hertfordshire and Sussex

    (Westminster)

999

¶ S 896 (Stevenson, *Chronicon* I, 373–7): 999

    King Æthelred to Abingdon Abbey: grant of 15 *cassati* at South Cerney in Gloucestershire

    (Abingdon)

Witness list: Note that MS 1 supplies a second atheling, Eadred, and distinguishes between the two Abbots Ælfsige: one is 'ceas abb' (New Minster Win*chester*)[47] and the other is 'elig abb' (Ely); Abbot Kenulf follows the second Ælfsige (compare MS 2). MS 1 does not have 'gaudens dictavi' in the subscription of Abbot Wulfgar. It provides the names of six *ministri* not in MS 2, though it omits one other. The original relative order of Wulfheah, Wulfric, Wulfgeat and Æthelric is uncertain.

‖ S 937 (Stevenson, *Chronicon* I, 367–70): ?999

    King Æthelred to Abingdon Abbey: explanation of grant of land at Farnborough in Berkshire or Warwickshire, Wormleighton in Warwickshire, South Cerney in Gloucestershire and Perry (in Oxfordshire?)

    (Abingdon)

Date: The document is undated, but can probably be assigned to 999 on the basis of its connection with S 896.

---

[47] The designation of Winchester as the 'chester' might reflect the provenance of the text: to the draftsman, 'chester' was naturally Winchester, rather than, e.g., Dorchester or Cirencester. On the other hand, it may be only the simplest way of distinguishing between the two abbots. Hart, *Charters of Northern England*, pp. 267–8, suggests that *ceas* stands for Chertsey.

1000[48]

§ S 897 (Stevenson, *Chronicon* I, 406–8): 1000

King Æthelred to Abingdon Abbey: grant of 3 *mansorum culturae*[49] at Drayton and 2 at Sutton in Berkshire

(Abingdon)

Date: The diploma itself is dated 1000, but this is not compatible with the list of bishops.

Witness list: The archbishops and bishops belong to the period 1002 × 5, with Wulfstan as archbishop of York, Ælfhun as bishop of London and Ælfric as archbishop of Canterbury. The athelings, abbots and *ministri* are compatible with the given date and also with the archbishops and bishops; the ealdormen are compatible with the given date, but the occurrence of Leofsige renders them incompatible with the archbishops and bishops: see under S 904 and 914.

1001

† ¶ S 898 (KCD 705): 1001, before 7 October

King Æthelred to Clofig: grant of 25 *mansi*[50] at Long Itchington (including 1 hide at Arley) in Warwickshire

(?Coventry)

Date: The diploma was attested by Æthelstan, bishop of Elmham, who died in 1001 (because his successor Ælfgar attested S 899, issued in 1001), on 7 October (Cambridge, Trinity College MS O. 2. 1).

Witness list: On the original diploma, the athelings Æthelstan and Edmund are crammed in between a column of bishops and a column of bishops with ealdormen: compare S 899?

¶ S 899 (KCD 706): 1001, after 7 October (in Kent?)

King Æthelred to Shaftesbury Abbey: grant of the *cenobium* at Bradford-on-Avon in Wiltshire, with land in the vicinity

(Shaftesbury)

Date: See under S 898.

Witness list: Six athelings are given in two columns between Wulfsige, bishop of Sherborne, and Athulf, bishop of Hereford: it would be hazardous to speculate how this irregular arrangement arose, but compare S 898 for a possible analogue. For 'Ælfstan', bishop of Winchester, read 'Ælfheah'; for 'Liefwine', bishop of Wells, read 'Lyfing'; for 'Alwoto', bishop of Crediton, read 'Ælfwold'; for 'Atheldred' (*sic* MS: not 'Æðelred' as in KCD), bishop of Cornwall, read 'Ealdred'.[51] For the evidence that the diploma may have been produced in Kent, see above, pp. 132–4.

48 For a reference to a (lost) diploma dated 1000 in favour of Glastonbury Abbey, see S 1775; see also Hart, *Charters of Eastern England*, p. 253, for a reference to a (lost) diploma dated 1000 in favour of Cranborne Abbey.

49 See above, p. 253 n. 44.   50 See p. 253 n. 44.

51 'Æðelred' occurs in Powicke and Fryde, *Handbook*, p. 218, as bishop of Cornwall in 1001, on the basis of this erroneous form; but Ealdred had occurred in 998 (S 893) and is found again in 1002 (S 900, 901).

1002

¶ S 904 (KCD 707): 1002, after 8 January and before 23 April (in Kent?)
King Æthelred to Wherwell Abbey: grant of privileges, and confirmation of 70 *mansae* in various places in the vicinity of the abbey; grant of 60 *cassati* at Dean in Sussex; additional note to the effect that 29 *praedia* in Winchester belong to the abbey, and grant, dated 1008, of 10 *mansae* at Bullington in Hampshire (Wherwell)

Date: The diploma is attested by Æthelric, bishop of Sherborne, whose predecessor Wulfsige died on 8 January[52] 1002 (because Wulfsige attested S 899, issued after 7 October in 1001, and because his successor attested S 904 etc.); it was also attested by Æscwig, bishop of Dorchester, who died on 23 April (Cambridge, Trinity College MS O. 2. 1) in 1002 (because his successor Ælfhelm attested S 902 in 1002; see also under S 901). It seems that all the extant diplomas of 1002 were produced after the banishment of Ealdorman Leofsige in the early part of the year (*ASC* MSS 'C', 'D', 'E': the context suggests that he was banished before the arrival of Emma in the spring); but see comments on S 914 below.

Witness list: The list in KCD, from a Charter Roll via the *Monasticon*, is hopelessly corrupt; the version in MS 1 resolves all the problems raised by Kemble's text. For Bishops 'Brihtric', 'Saxulf' and 'Egwine' in KCD read 'Æscwis' (Æscwig), 'Aþulf' and 'Lyuuncs' (Lyfing); for Bishop 'Ælfstan' read 'Aelfgar'; for Abbot 'Wulfstan' read 'Wulfgar'; in place of Abbot 'Ælfuric' read 'Ælfuere' and 'Ælfsige'; for Abbot 'Godwin' read 'Godman'; for Abbot 'Willnoð' read 'Æþelnod'; for 'Ælfric' *minister* read 'Æþelric', and for 'Egwin' *minister* read 'Lyuuincg' (and compare Bishop Egwine-Lyfing above). For the evidence that the diploma may have been produced in Kent, see above, pp. 132–4.

¶ S 900 (KCD 1297): 1002, after 8 January and before 23 April
  King Æthelred to Ælfhelm, his *fidelis minister*: grant of 5 *mansae* at Codicote in Hertfordshire
  (St Albans)

Date: As for S 904.
Witness list: MS 2 has Bishop Athulf twice in succession. The atheling 'Eadweardus' between Edmund and Eadwig is an error for 'Eadred'.

¶ S 901 (Stevenson, *Chronicon* I, 411–15): 1002, after 8 January and before 23 April
  King Æthelred to Ælfric, archbishop of Canterbury: grant of 24 *mansae* at Dumbleton in Gloucestershire (the estate comprising 17 *mansae* on the west side of the River Isbourne, 2 on the east side at Aston Somerville, and 5 in wooded land on both sides of the River Piddle at Flyford Flavell in Worcestershire)
  (Abingdon)

Date: As for S 904, and see further below.

---

[52] His feast is recorded in an eleventh-century Sherborne calendar (Cambridge, Corpus Christi College MS 422) and in Flete's *History of Westminster Abbey* (Robinson, *Flete*, p. 79). William of Malmesbury, in *De Antiquitate Glastoniensis Ecclesiae*, gives 'Id. Jan.', probably simplifying the obit from 'VI. Id. Jan.'

Witness list: The list includes the subscription of Æscwig, bishop of Dorchester, and the name of his successor Ælfhelm occurs at the end of the group of bishops. It is possible that the diploma was produced at about the time of Æscwig's death, so that it was felt desirable to add the name of his successor to the original: compare S 876, with similar duplication for the abbey of Westminster.

¶ S 903 (Robinson, *Crispin*, pp. 167–8): 1002, after 8 January
King Æthelred to Westminster Abbey: grant of 2 *mansae* at *Berewican* (near Tyburn in Middlesex)
(Westminster)

Date: The diploma was attested by Æthelric, bishop of Sherborne: see under S 904. Ealdulf, archbishop of York, died on 4 June[53] in 1002 (see S 904 and 902), and his absence from S 900, 901 and 903 may reflect his engagement in the translation of Oswald's bones to Worcester in mid-April 1002.[54] If the regnal year in the dating clause was calculated from the king's accession, the diploma was produced before 18 March in 1002; if it was calculated from his coronation, the diploma was produced after 3 May in 1002.

Witness list: Lyfing, bishop of Wells, uses his second name, Ælfstan, as in S 909.

‡¶ S 905 (*O.S. Facs.* III, 36): 11 July 1002, at Canterbury
King Æthelred to Æthelred, his *fidelis homo*: lease of land in Canterbury, with reversion to Christ Church
(Christ Church Canterbury)

Date: The year of grace is given as 1003, but the witness list and the detailed chronological information in the dating clause leave no doubt that the diploma was produced in 1002.

¶ S 902 (Stevenson, *Chronicon* I, 408–11): 1002, after 11 July
King Æthelred to Godwine, *fidelis minister*: grant of 10 *mansae* at Little Haseley in Oxfordshire
(Abingdon)

Date: Wulfstan attested as archbishop of York, whereas he had occurred in S 905 as bishop of London. For the indiction, see above, p. 232 n. 4.

Witness list: Æthelmær occurs as the fourth and last ealdorman; he should probably be regarded as the first *minister*.

1003

¶ S 1664 (KCD 1299): 1003
King Æthelred to ? : grant of land at Bengeworth in Worcestershire
(Evesham)

---

[53] According to Florence of Worcester, Ealdulf died on 6 May (secundo nonas Maii) 1002 (Thorpe, *Chronicon* I, 156), and this date has been followed by Searle, Stubbs and Hart. But 'Maii' is clearly an error for 'Junii': according to *ASC* MSS 'C', 'D', 'E', he died in the summer of 1002, and his obit is given as 4 June (II Non. Jun.) in Oxford, Bodleian Library, Hatton 113, an eleventh-century manuscript from Worcester which has considerable authority.

[54] Florence of Worcester, in Thorpe, *Chronicon* I, 156; it is said that bishops, abbots, priests, monks and religious men had gathered for the occasion.

Appendix 1

1004

‡ ¶ S 906 (Sawyer, *Charters of Burton*, pp. 48–53): 1004
King Æthelred to Burton Abbey: confirmation of privileges and of lands granted by Wulfric in his will
(Burton)

§ S 907 (Blake, *Liber Eliensis*, pp. 129–30): 1004
King Æthelred to Ely Abbey: grant of 20 *mansae* at Littlebury in Essex
(Ely)

Witness list: The atheling Æthelstan occurs as Ælfstan in MS 2, but the correct form is in MS 4. Æthelmær occurs as an ealdorman instead of as a *minister*, and Abbot Ælfsige occurs for Abbot Ælfric, in MS 6.

¶ S 909 (Wigram, *St. Frideswide* I, 2–6): 7 December 1004, at Headington
King Æthelred to St Frideswide's Abbey: confirmation of 10 hides at Winchendon in Buckinghamshire, and 3 hides at Whitehill, 3 hides at Cowley and 2 hides at Cutslow in Oxfordshire
(St Frideswide's)

Date: The dating clause incorporates a regnal year (25): but if calculated from the king's accession the year would be 27, and if calculated from his coronation it would be 26.

Witness list: As in S 903, Lyfing, bishop of Wells, attests as Ælfstan.

1005

¶ S 910 (KCD 1301): 1005, before 16 November
King Æthelred to Eadsige, his *minister*: grant of 1 *mansa* at Seaton in Devon
(Horton/Sherborne)

Date: The diploma was attested by Archbishop Ælfric, who died in 1005 (*ASC* MS 'A'; B.L. Cotton Tiberius C i; S 912), on 16 November.[55]

Witness list: 'Eadric' amongst the athelings is in error for 'Eadred'.

¶ S 911 (Salter, *Eynsham* I, 19–28): 1005, before 16 November
King Æthelred to Eynsham Abbey: confirmation of foundation and endowment
(Eynsham)

Date: As for S 910.

Witness list: KCD 714 has two Abbots Ælfric, but they should both be read as 'Ælfsige' (MS 11: Ælfrie).

¶ S 912 (KCD 672): 1005, after 16 November
King Æthelred to St Albans Abbey: grant of privileges and of 1 *cassata*[56] at Flamstead and 5 at St Albans in Hertfordshire

---

[55] Wharton, *Anglia Sacra* I, 54; B.L. Cotton Nero C ix, fo. 21r; B.L. Cotton Vitellius C xii. The obit occurs also in Cambridge, University Library, Kk. i. 22, as an addition to a s. xiii *ex.* Abingdon calendar, and in Förster, 'Glossenhandschrift', p. 154, incorporated in an elegaic verse commemorating the archbishop, which was added in s. xi¹ to a manuscript (Ker, *Catalogue*, no. 2) almost certainly from Abingdon.

[56] Here, and also in S 923, the accusative plural is *cassatas* and the word is clearly regarded as a first-declension feminine noun. The word is properly a second-declension masculine noun, but in S 842 it is declined as a neuter noun with the nominative plural *cassata*.

(St Albans)

Date: The diploma was clearly produced after the death of Archbishop Ælfric, since it implements provisions in his will and was not attested by him; see under S 910.

Witness list: In MS 2, the atheling Edward is wrongly placed between Edmund and Eadred; MS 3 is correct. Bishop 'Æðelsie' in KCD is 'æthelsie' in MS 2 and 'æþelrie' in MS 3: presumably Æthelric of Sherborne is intended. The two Abbots 'Ælfric' in KCD are 'ælfrie' or 'alfrie' in MSS 2 and 3: on the analogy of contemporary diplomas, the name should be read as 'Ælfsige' in each case: compare S 911 for the same confusion between the elements '-sige' and '-ric'. Among the *ministri*, 'Æðelric' in KCD is guaranteed by the forms 'Æthelric' and 'Æþelricus' (MS 2, duplicating the name) and 'Æþelric' (MS 3); 'Bryhtric' in KCD is 'Bryhtrie' in MSS 2 and 3, and so could be 'Brihtsige': I settle for 'Brihtric', on the analogy of S 910 and 912, which show a Brihtric in the same relative position.

|| S 913 (Ker, 'Hemming's Cartulary', p. 73): 1005
 King Æthelred to the see of St David's: grant of ? *manentes* at Over in Almondsbury, Gloucestershire
 (Worcester)

1006

§ S 914 (KCD 715): 1006
 King Æthelred to Christ Church Canterbury: confirmation of privileges and of various lands
 (Christ Church Canterbury)

Date: The diploma itself is dated 1006, but this is not compatible with the witness list.

Witness list: Amongst the bishops, the occurrence of Wulfstan (of London) indicates a date before his translation to York in 1002, while the occurrence of Æthelric of Sherborne indicates a date after the death of Wulfsige in 1002: therefore the bishops are firmly dated to 1002. The abbots could be compatible with the given date and with the bishops, and the *ministri* could be compatible with the bishops, though not perhaps with the given date (Æthelmær and Ordulf probably retired in 1005). The ealdormen belong to the period $998 \times 9 - 1001 \times 2$, with the subscription of Leofsige providing the *terminus ante quem*. If the list is authentic, it would have to belong to the early days of 1002, before any of the extant diplomas of that year were produced: see above under S 904. The Old English version of the list omits the second Abbot Ælfsige, and designates Æthelmær 'mines hlafordes discðen', Leofric 'hrægelðen' and Sired 'Siwardes broðor'; the last five names in the Old English list were mistakenly printed as part of S 1090 in KCD.

1006 × 11

¶ S 943 (Hart, *Charters of Eastern England*, pp. 190–1): 16 November 1006 × c. 8 September 1011

King Æthelred to Toti, a Dane: grant of 1 *mansus*[57] at Beckley and 5 at Horton in Oxfordshire

(Thorney)

Date: No date is given in the text, but the attestation of Archbishop Ælfheah places the diploma within the period 16 November 1006–September 1011. Wharton, *Anglia Sacra* I, 54, gives 16 November for his ordination, evidently as archbishop of Canterbury: it cannot refer to the year 984 (cf. Powicke and Fryde, *Handbook*, p. 210) when he became bishop of Winchester, since *ASC* MS 'A' indicates that he was consecrated then on 19 October and installed on 28 October. But given his appearance in S 912 as bishop of Winchester, it cannot refer to 1005 either, which year would of course be unlikely enough anyway. I infer, therefore, that Ælfheah was not ordained until 16 November 1006, being the first anniversary of Archbishop Ælfric's death. The interval of a year would explain the confusion in *ASC* MSS 'C', 'D', 'E', which give Ælfric's death and Ælfheah's succession under 1006; it accords with the Canterbury entries in MS 'A' that Ælfheah was consecrated archbishop in 1006, following the death of Ælfric in 1005. Ælfheah was captured by the Danes at Canterbury between 8 and 29 September 1011, and he was stoned to death seven months later, on 19 April 1012 (*ASC* MSS 'C', 'D', 'E').

§ S 940 (KCD 718): 16 November 1006 × *c.* 8 September 1011

King Æthelred to Chertsey Abbey: grant of privileges at a wharf in London

(Chertsey)

Date: As for S 943.

1007

‡¶ S 916 (Napier and Stevenson, *Crawford Charters*, pp. 24–7): 1007, before 25 August

King Æthelred to St Albans Abbey: grant of land at Norton, 1 *mansa* at *Rodanhangra* and land at Oxhey in Hertfordshire

(St Albans)

Date: The diploma was attested by Ælfsige, abbot of New Minster Winchester, who died on 25 August 1007.[58] Eadric (Streona) occurs as the first *minister*.

Witness list: I follow the list in the original diploma (MS 1). But it is worth noting that one of the Abbots Ælfsige is omitted in MS 2, though he occurs in MS 3; moreover, in both MSS 2 and 3, Eadric *minister* appears as the last ealdorman.

¶ S 915 (Stevenson, *Chronicon* I, 419–22): 1007, after 25 August, at *Beorchore*

King Æthelred to Ælfgar, his *præpositus*: grant of 8 *mansi*[59] at Waltham St Lawrence in Berkshire

(Abingdon)

Date: The diploma was attested by Brihtwold, Ælfsige's successor as abbot of the New Minster Winchester: see further under S 916. Eadric (Streona) occurs

[57] See p. 253 n. 44.

[58] 'OBITUS ÆLFSINI ABBATIS' against the day in the calendar, and the same opposite the year in the Easter tables, in B.L. Cotton Titus D xxvii: Birch, *Liber Vitae*, pp. 271, 276.

[59] See p. 253 n. 44.

second amongst the ealdormen, having been appointed in 1007 (*ASC* MSS 'C', 'D', 'E').

§ S 917 (Sawyer, *Charters of Burton*, pp. 56–7): 1007
  King Æthelred to ? , his *minister*: grant of land at ?
  (Burton)

Date: Perhaps after the appointment of Eadric as ealdorman, since the diploma was attested by three *comites* (see Table 6).

Witness list: The list is abbreviated: after the bishops, the copyist indicates that there were 6 *clitones*, 4 abbots, 3 *comites*, 1 *patricius*[60] and 16 *ministri*. A monk called Winsye claims to have written the diploma.

1008

§ S 918 (Stevenson, *Chronicon* I, 377–82): 1008
  King Æthelred to Abingdon Abbey: restoration of 20 *mansi*[61] at Moredon and grant of a *prædiolum* at Cricklade in Wiltshire
  (Abingdon)

Date: The diploma itself is dated 1008, but the witness list seems to have been derived from a diploma of the preceding year.

Witness list: The occurrence of Eadric first amongst the *ministri* cannot be reconciled with his appointment as ealdorman of Mercia in 1007 (see *ASC* MSS 'C', 'D', 'E', and S 915; compare S 916). The list as a whole is closely related to that in S 915, dated 1007.

¶ S 919 (Blake, *Liber Eliensis*, pp. 145–6): 1008
  King Æthelred to Ely Abbey: grant of 19 *cassati*, comprising 2 *mansae* at Hadstock and 10 at Stretley Green in Essex, and 7 at Linton in Cambridgeshire
  (Ely)

¶ S 920 (Sawyer, *Charters of Burton*, pp. 58–60): 1008
  King Æthelred to Wulfgeat, abbot of Burton: grant of 2½ *cassati* at Rolleston in Staffordshire
  (Burton)

Witness list: The list is abbreviated: after the bishops, the copyist indicates that there were 10 abbots, 3 ealdormen and 7 *ministri*. See also under S 930 below.

1009

¶ S 921 (KCD 1306): 1009, before the death of Ælfweard, abbot of Glastonbury
  King Æthelred to Athelney Abbey: grant of 3 *perticae* at Hamp in Somerset
  (Athelney)

Date: The diploma was attested by Ælfweard, abbot of Glastonbury,[62] whose successor occurs in S 922.

[60] On the use elsewhere of the term *patricius*, see Barker, 'Æthelweard', pp. 86–7.

[61] See p. 253 n. 44.

[62] There is an obit for an Abbot Ælfweard in B.L. Add. 29436, fo. 44r (fragment of a calendar from the Old Minster Winchester), under 20 December, but it is difficult to identify him securely.

Appendix 1

† ¶ S 922 (Sawyer, *Charters of Burton*, pp. 60–3): 1009, after the death of Ælfweard, abbot of Glastonbury

King Æthelred to Morcar, his *minister*: grant of 8 *manentes* at Weston-upon-
Trent, 1 *manens* at Morley, 1 at Smalley and Kidsley, 1 at Crich and 1 at Ingleby,
in Derbyshire

(Burton)

Date: The diploma was attested by Brihtræd, abbot of Glastonbury, whose
predecessor occurs in S 921.

Witness list: The list of bishops contains sixteen names, but the well-established
identifications leave two of them (Æthelsige and Ælfstan) and three sees (Selsey,
Cornwall and Lindsey) unaccounted for. Ordbriht of Selsey attested diplomas in
1007, and his successor Ælfmær appears in 1011: any intermediate bishop would
have had a brief period of office, and his existence would contradict the available
episcopal lists for the see.[63] So it would appear that Selsey was vacant in 1009,
leaving Cornwall and Lindsey for Æthelsige and Ælfstan. Bishop Æthelsige
attested between Æthelric of Sherborne and Ælfwold of Crediton in S 922 and in
S 924 (1011), and can probably be identified as the Bishop Æthelsige who witnessed
a local Sherborne document (S 1422) in company with Bishop Æthelric and Lyfing
of Wells: he would thus seem to belong in the south-west, and I therefore identify
him as the bishop of Cornwall.[64] It follows that Ælfstan was probably the bishop
of Lindsey, an identification supported by the fact that he attested between the
bishops of Elmham and Durham.[65]

1011

¶ S 923 (Sawyer, *Charters of Burton*, pp. 64–5): 1011, before *c.* 8 September

[63] The original transcriber of *ASC* MS 'A', in the burnt B.L. Cotton Otho B xi (*ASC* MS
'G'), reproduced the episcopal lists in 'A' (representing a situation during the period 985 × 6
–988) without continuation; but in the early eleventh century they were continued in
another hand to represent a situation *c.* 1013: after Æthelgar of Selsey were added the
names of Ordbriht and Ælfmær. See Whelock, *Historiæ Ecclesiasticæ Gentis Anglorum Libri
V*, p. 569, and Ker, *Catalogue*, pp. 231–2. The only other lists for Selsey which extend
beyond Ordbriht are those given by Florence of Worcester (Thorpe, *Chronicon* 1, 234)
and William of Malmesbury (Hamilton, *De Gestis Pontificum*, p. 205): in both, Ælfmær is
Ordbriht's immediate successor.

[64] Unfortunately there are no episcopal lists for Cornwall, but there is a gap between the
last known attestation of Ealdred in 1002 (S 901) and the first certain attestation of Buruhwold in 1012 (S 929). Barlow, *Edward the Confessor*, p. 30 n. 3, appears to regard the Bishop
Æthelsige of S 924 as Ælfsige of Winchester (and similarly Hart, *Charters of Northern
England*, p. 269), though this is quite impossible: see Table 3. Robertson, *Charters*, p. 393,
regards the Bishop Æthelsige of S 1422 as an error for Ælfsige of Winchester: S 922 and
924 may not be independent, but S 922 and 1422 show that 'Æthelsige' is more than a
scribal error. There is no reason to regard Æthelsige as Æthelric's successor at Sherborne,
attesting S 922 and 924 with his predecessor in error, or as a *chorepiscopus* (Hart, *Charters
of Northern England*, pp. 223, 234, 290). It is possible, on the other hand, that Æthelsige of
Cornwall was translated to Sherborne after Æthelric's death.

[65] There are no episcopal lists for Lindsey at this period. The last recorded attestation of
Sigeferth was in 1004 (S 906), and it is not otherwise known that he had a successor.

King Æthelred to Elemod, *minister*: grant of 2 *cassatae*[66] at Hallam in Derbyshire
(Burton)

Date: The diploma was attested by Archbishop Ælfheah, who was captured by
the Danes between 8 and 29 September 1011 (*ASC* MSS 'C', 'D', 'E').

Witness list: The list is abbreviated: after the athelings and bishops, the copyist
indicates that there were 6 abbots, 4 ealdormen and 23 *ministri*.

¶ S 924 (Sawyer, *Charters of Burton*, pp. 66–7): 1011, before *c*. 8 September
King Æthelred to Morcar, his *minister*: grant of 5 *mansae* at *Ufre*
(Burton)

Date: As for S 923.

Witness list: The list is abbreviated: after the athelings, bishops and one abbot, the
copyist indicates that there were 7 abbots, 4 ealdormen and 30 *ministri*. The list of
bishops closely resembles that in S 922.

1012

¶ S 926 (Campbell, *Charters of Rochester*, pp. 45–7): 1012, after 17 March
King Æthelred to Godwine, bishop of Rochester: grant of 15 *mansae* at Fen
Stanton and Hilton in Huntingdonshire
(Rochester)

Date: The diploma was attested by Brihtmær, abbot of the New Minster Winchester, whose predecessor Brihtwold died on 17 March 1012.[67]

§ S 927 (Stevenson, *Chronicon* I, 422–5): June or July 1012
King Æthelred to Leofric, his *minister*: grant of 10 *cassati* at Whitchurch in
Oxfordshire
(Abingdon)

Date: The diploma itself is dated June (MS 1) or July (MSS 2, 3) 1012, but the
witness list is not compatible with others of the period (especially S 926).

Witness list: The bishops belong to *c*. 1013, with Lyfing (representing Canterbury)
immediately after Archbishop Wulfstan and with Æthelstan as bishop of Hereford
(his predecessor Athulf having attested S 926 and 929 in 1012 and S 931 in 1013).
The abbots belong to a period before the production of S 926: the list includes the
subscription of Brihtwold, abbot of the New Minster Winchester, or of Malmesbury, and S 926 includes the subscription of Brihtmær, Brihtwold's successor at
Winchester, and Eadric, the other Brihtwold's successor at Malmesbury.

¶ S 929 (Sawyer, *Charters of Burton*, pp. 70–1): 1012
King Æthelred to Theodulf, his man: grant of 5 *cassati* at *Burtune*
(Burton)

Witness list: The list is abbreviated: after the bishops, the copyist indicates that
there were 6 abbots, 4 ealdormen and 16 *ministri*.

‖ S 925 (KCD 720): 1012
King Æthelred to Ælfgifu, his wife: grant of a *praedium* in Winchester

---

[66] See p. 260 n. 56.

[67] 'Obitus Byrhtwoldi abbatis' against the day in the calendar, and the same opposite the
year in the Easter tables, in B.L. Cotton Titus D xxvii: Birch, *Liber Vitae*, pp. 270, 276.

Appendix 1

(Old Minster Winchester)

|| S 928 (Sawyer, *Charters of Burton*, pp. 71–2): 1012

King Æthelred to Morcar, his *minister*: grant of 2 *mansae* at Eckington in Derbyshire

(Burton)

Witness list: The list is abbreviated: after two athelings and the archbishop of York, the copyist indicates that there were 10 bishops, 7 abbots, 4 ealdormen and 17 *ministri*.

§ S 930 (Sawyer, *Charters of Burton*, pp. 67–9): 1012

King Æthelred to Wulfgeat, abbot of Burton: grant of *unum mansem*[68] *et dimidium* at Wetmore in Staffordshire

(Burton)

Date: The diploma itself is dated 1012, but this is incompatible with some of the witnesses.

Witness list: The list of archbishops and bishops was apparently derived from S 920 (1008), creating an anachronism by retaining Archbishop Ælfheah (captured in September 1011) in a list purportedly of 1012; the draftsman added the impossible names Æscwig (Dorchester, *c.* 979–23 April 1002) and Sigar (Wells, (975 × 8) × 979–28 June 996). The names of 5 abbots, 5 ealdormen and 5 *ministri* were present on the diploma but are not given by the copyist. The list, which otherwise has the subscriptions of the king and the atheling Æthelstan, is not entered in the tables.

1013

¶ S 931 (Hart, *Charters of Eastern England*, pp. 193–4): 1013, ? before late summer

King Æthelred to Northman, *miles*: grant of 3½ *cassati* at Twywell in Northamptonshire

(Thorney)

Date: The diploma was attested by Ealdorman Uhtred, and so was presumably produced before his submission to the Danes in the late summer (*ASC* MSS 'C', 'D', 'E').

1014

¶ S 932 (Finberg, *Charters of West Midlands*, pp. 143–5): 1014, during or after the spring

King Æthelred to Leofwine, *dux*: grant of 4 *mansae* at Mathon in Herefordshire

(Pershore)

Date: The king returned from Normandy in the spring of 1014 (*ASC* MSS 'C', 'D', 'E').

|| – (Gibson, *Reliquiæ*, pp. 19–20): 1014, during or after the spring

King Æthelred to Sealwyne, his thegn: grant of 5 *cassati* at Raddon in Dorset

(Abbotsbury)

Date: As for S 932.

[68] Note that *mansa* is here declined as if it were a masculine noun, *mansis*.

|| S 933 (KCD 1309): 1014, during or after the spring; perhaps after 25 June
 King Æthelred to Sherborne Abbey: grant of 13 *mansiunculae* at Corscombe
 in Dorset
 (Sherborne)

Date: As for S 932. The non-appearance of the atheling Æthelstan may indicate
that the diploma was produced after his death, for the long series of his subscriptions comes to an end with S 931 (1013): see Table 1. The obit of Æthelstan was
kept at Christ Church Canterbury, on 25 June.[69] The will of Æthelstan (S 1503)
refers to Ælfsige, bishop of Winchester (1012×13 – 1032), and to Morcar and
Siferth (who were killed in 1015, apparently in the summer); it also refers to the
answer which the king sent by one Ælfgar on the Friday after the mass-day of
Midsummer (24 June, being the feast of St John the Baptist). In 1013, this Friday
was 26 June, and in 1015 it was 1 July: so if the obit can be trusted, Æthelstan
could not have died in either year. In 1014, the Friday in question was 25 June:
thus it seems that Æthelstan received the confirmation of his will and died on
25 June 1014.[70] This would accord with an eleventh-century note in B.L. Cotton
Claudius A iii, fo. 3v: 'Adhuc ego rex ÆÐELREDUS filium meum superuiuens
ÆÐELSTANUM ut ultimus dies statuit eius aecclesiae predicte christi HOLINGA-
BURNAN cum suis appendiciis animo libenti æternaliter contradidi.'
Witness list: Kemble omitted the subscription of 'Sigeferth *minister*' between
Ulfcetel and Godwine.

1015

¶ S 934 (Stevenson, *Chronicon* I, 425–8): 1015
 King Æthelred to Brihtwold, bishop of Ramsbury: grant of 5 *mansiunculae* at
 Chilton in Berkshire
 (Abingdon)

Witness list: According to *ASC* MS 'D', Ælfwig was consecrated bishop of
London (in succession to Ælfhun, who had accompanied the athelings to Normandy in 1013) at York in February 1014,[71] before the return of King Æthelred:
but Ælfhun attested S 934, revealing that he had returned by 1015 and had
apparently been reinstated as bishop of London.

1016

§ S 935 (KCD 723): before 23 April 1016
 King Æthelred to Evesham Abbey: restoration of 1 *mansa* at Maugersbury in
 Gloucestershire
 (Evesham)

---

[69] B.L. Arundel 68, fo. 32r: 'Athelstanus qui dedit holyngborne ecclesie christi cantuar'.'
[70] As Professor Whitelock observes, illness probably precipitated the drawing up of the will:
 see Whitelock, *Wills*, p. 168. Barlow, *Edward the Confessor*, p. 30 n. 3, dates the will 1012.
[71] Presumably at York because Lyfing of Canterbury had not yet received his pallium.
 Ælfwig's consecration may indicate that Ælfhun was not expected to return, and that
 London was too important a see to be left vacant.

Appendix 1

Date: King Æthelred died on 23 April 1016 (*ASC* MSS 'C', 'D', 'E'). But elements of the witness list are not compatible with the date.

Witness list: The subscriptions of Archbishop Dunstan (died 19 May 988) and the atheling Æthelstan (died 25 June 1014: see under S 933) are not compatible with each other or with the given date. The remaining witnesses are compatible with the closing years of Æthelred's reign, though perhaps not with 1016 in particular: Ealdorman Eadric was then on Cnut's side.

Undated[72]

§ S 938 (KCD 1284):

  King Æthelred to Atsere, *minister*: grant of land at Wyke Regis in Dorset
  (Old Minster Winchester)

Witness list: The subscriptions of Archbishops Dunstan and Oswald and Bishop Æthelwold suggest a date before 1 August 984 (see under S 855); but the subscriptions of Bishop Lyfing (of Wells: 998×9 – 1013) and Ulfcetel *minister* (only known in Æthelred's diplomas between 1002 and 1016), as well as that of Æthelmær at the head of the list of *ministri*, suggest a date in the latter part of the reign. The other witnesses are Bishop Hirwold (non-existent, but perhaps a corruption of Buruhwold) and Leofric *minister*. The list is not entered in the tables.

§ S 941 (KCD 1311):

  King Æthelred to St Paul's: confirmation of lands
  (St Paul's)

Date: The document is in the form of a letter. The addressee, Ælfstan, bishop of London (959×64 – 995×6), is not compatible with the co-addressor, Queen Emma (who arrived in England in 1002).

§ S 908 (KCD 1300):

  King Æthelred for St Paul's: confirmation of 4 *mansae* at Laver in Essex and 2 *mansae* at Cockhampstead in Hertfordshire, given by Æthelflæd
  (St Paul's)

Witness list: The witnesses could not have assembled at any one time, and the list must be imaginary. But a genuine element certainly underlies S 1495, of which S 908 apparently purports to be a confirmation. In MS 3 the archbishops are Æthelnoth (Canterbury, 1020–38) and Wulfstan (York, 1002–23); the only bishop is Ælfhun of London (1002×4 – 1015×18); the only abbot is Ælfric, though S 1495 adds Wighard (compare S 914 and 905) and Ælfsige of 'Cowwaford'; the ealdormen are Alfred (S 1495: Ælfhere), Brihtnoth and Eadric; there are three king's thegns: Ælfsige, Ufegeat (S 1495: styled sheriff) and Fræna, as well as two priests and a deacon. See also Gibbs, *Church of St Paul*, p. 3.

[72] For references to 'lost' and undated diplomas of King Æthelred, see S 1776–81 (from Glastonbury), S 1818 (from the Old Minster Winchester), Hart, *Charters of Northern England*, p. 384 (from Bath), Finberg, *Charters of Wessex*, pp. 103–4 (from Amesbury, perhaps *c.* 1002) and Mellows, *Hugh Candidus*, pp. 37 n., 39 and 40 n. And for miscellaneous spurious documents in Æthelred's name, see S 833, 936, 1212 and 1636.

MEETING PLACES OF THE KING'S COUNCILLORS DURING THE TENTH AND ELEVENTH CENTURIES

This Appendix is intended to provide the primary evidence (derived largely from royal diplomas, law-codes and the *Anglo-Saxon Chronicle*) upon which Fig. 1 is based.[1] The list aims to be exhaustive;[2] it includes references to coronations on the assumption that the councillors would have gathered on such occasions. Diplomas and other sources marked with asterisks are of dubious authority. County boundaries are those recognized up to 1974, and county abbreviations are those used by the English Place-Name Society.

Abingdon, Berks: S 1208 (*c.* 930); see also *William of Malmesbury, in Stubbs, *De Gestis Regum Anglorum* I, 150 (926).

Amesbury, W: S 418–19 (24 December 932); Florence of Worcester, in Thorpe, *Chronicon* I, 145 (977); *ASC* MS 'F', *s.a.* 995.

Andover, Ha: II Edgar and III Edgar (959 × 63; see IV Edgar 1.4); Wulfstan *Cantor*, 'Narratio de Sancto Swithuno', lines 75–80 (980; see Campbell, *Breuiloquium*, p. 67).

Axminster, D: S 364 (901).

Bath, So: coronation of Edgar on 11 May 973 (*ASC* MSS 'A', 'G', *s.a.* 973; MSS 'B', 'C', *s.a.* 974; MSS 'D', 'E', 'F', *s.a.* 972; see also *S 799 and *808); VII Æthelred (1009).

Beorchore (unidentified):[3] S 915 (1007).

Bicanleag (identification uncertain, but probably Bickleigh near Exeter or Bickleigh near Plymouth, D): S 372–4 and 1286 (904).

Bradford (location uncertain): *Vita Dunstani*, c. 25 (*c.* 959; Stubbs, *Memorials*, p. 36).

Britford, W: Barlow, *Life of Edward*, p. 52 (1065; cf. *ASC*).

Bromdun (identification uncertain): law-code of Æthelred (978× ?97; see I Æthelred 1.2 and III Æthelred 4).

---

[1] It may be compared with the similar lists in Kemble, *Saxons in England* II, 252–60; Liebermann, *National Assembly*, pp. 45–7; and Oleson, *Witenagemot*, pp. 70–4. See also Stenton, *Anglo-Saxon England*, map on p. 350.

[2] I exclude meetings which were evidently convened exclusively for the purposes of local administration (see, e.g., S 1211, 1216, 1454, 1456, 1460, 1462, 1473 and 1474); it is possible or apparent that the king was not himself present at a few of the meetings included in the list. Should any omissions be noticed, I would welcome information.

[3] See above, p. 127 n. 139.

Buckingham, Bk: S 426 (12 September 934).

Calne, W: *ASC* MSS 'D', 'E', 'F', *s.a.* 978 (for 977); S 891 (Easter (28 March) 997).

Canterbury, K: S 905 (11 July 1002); ? S 1465 (1032); ? S 1471 (*c.* 1045).[4]

Cheddar, So: *S 511 (24 July ?941); S 611 (29 November 956); *S 806 (Easter ?968).

Chippenham, W: S 405 (29 April 930); S 422-3 (26 January 933); S 473 (940); see also S 1445 (899 × 924).

Cirencester, Gl: S 1792 (935); S 633 (956); S 896 and 937 (985);[5] *ASC* MSS 'C', 'D', 'E', *s.a.* 1020.

Colchester, Ess: S 412 (23 March 931); S 472 (940).

Colyton, D: III Edmund (939 × 46).

Cookham, Berks: S 939 (*c.* 997); see also Thorpe, *Chronicon* I, 158 (1006).

Dorchester, Do: *S 391 (? 7 April 934); S 434-6 (21 December ?935).

Edington, W: S 646 (9 May 957).

Enham, ?King's, Ha: (? V and) VI Æthelred (1006 × 11, perhaps 1008); see also X Æthelred.

Exeter, D: II Edward (? 920 × 24); S 399-400 (16 April 928); V Æthelstan (Christmas 924 × 38); S 1021 (1050).

Faversham, K: III Æthelstan (924 × 39).

Frome, So: *S 427 (16 December 934).

Gadshill, K: *S 537 (?948); see also S 1457.

Gillingham, probably Do: S 876 (17 July 993); election of Edward the Confessor in 1042 (William of Malmesbury, in Stubbs, *De Gestis Regum Anglorum* I, 238; cf. below under London).

Glastonbury, So: *S 571 (953 × 5); *S 670 (?959); S 802 (975); *S 966 (1032).

Gloucester, Gl: *S 731 (28 December 964); *ASC* MS 'D', *s.a.* 1052, MS 'E', *s.a.* 1048, MS 'F', *s.a.* 1050 (for 1051, September; see also Barlow, *Life of Edward*, p. 21).

Grately, Ha: II Æthelstan (924 × 39).

Hamsey, Sx: S 1211 (924 × 39).

Headington, O: S 909 (7 December 1004).

Hursteshevet (unidentified): *Quadripartitus* Arg. 9 (?1041; see Liebermann, *Gesetze* I, 533).

Kingston upon Thames, Sr:[6] ? coronation of Edward the Elder on Pentecost (8 June) in 900 (for date, see Campbell, *Chronicle of Æthelweard*, p. 51; for location, see *Ralph de Diceto, in Stubbs, *Opera Historica* I, 140);[7] coronation of

---

[4] For the possibility of identifying other meetings in Kent, see above, pp. 132-4. According to the *Vita Ædwardi Regis*, Edward the Confessor was crowned at Christ Church Canterbury (Barlow, *Life of Edward*, pp. 9-10); but cf. below under Winchester.

[5] See above, p. 128 n. 146.

[6] The references to the coronations of Æthelstan, Eadred and Æthelred suffice to establish that kings were *often* crowned at Kingston in the tenth century, but one suspects that post-Conquest historians tended to assume that *all* tenth-century kings were crowned there (unless otherwise stated, as it were); thus, e.g., Ralph de Diceto's statements may be no more than assumptions.

[7] Liebermann, *National Assembly*, p. 47, places Edward's coronation at Winchester.

Æthelstan on 4 September 925 (for date, see S 394;[8] for location, see ASC MSS 'B', 'C', 'D', s.a. 924); *S 420 (16 December 933); *S 450 (6 October, 924 × 39); ? coronation of Edmund, perhaps c. 29 November 939 (for date, see Whitelock et al., *Anglo-Saxon Chronicle*, p. 4 n. 13, and Nelson, 'Inauguration Rituals', p. 66 n. 99; for location, see *Ralph de Diceto, in Stubbs, *Opera Historica* I, 146); coronation of Eadred, c. 16 August 946 (for date and location, see Florence of Worcester, in Thorpe, *Chronicon* I, 134; cf. Whitelock et al., *Anglo-Saxon Chronicle*, p. 4 n. 14; year and location given also by S 520); ? coronation of Eadwig on 27 January 956 (for date, see Nelson, 'Inauguration Rituals', p. 66 n. 99; for location, see *Florence of Worcester, in Thorpe, *Chronicon* I, 136); S 1451 (972); ? coronation of Edward the Martyr in 975 (for location, see *Ralph de Diceto, in Stubbs, *Opera Historica* I, 153);[9] Blake, *Liber Eliensis*, p. 116 (?975, after Edgar's death); coronation of Æthelred on 4 May 979 (for date and location, see ASC MS 'C'; for location, see ASC MSS 'D', 'E', s.a. 979, and MS 'F', s.a. 980);[10] *S 981 (Pentecost, '1032'); see also S 1461 (1016 × 20).

Kirtlington, O: S 1497 (943 × 6); ASC MSS 'B', 'C', s.a. 977, after Easter (8 April).

Lifton, D: S 416 (12 November 931).

Lincoln, L: S 1478 (1053 × 5).

London: *S 428 (7 June 930 or 934; but see below under Nottingham); see VI Æthelstan (924 × 39); I Edmund (942 × 6); *S 1294 (Octave of Pentecost (3 June) 966, in St Paul's Church); *S 783 (971); S 1328 (973); Blake, *Liber Eliensis*, p. 110 (974 × 5); S 1457 (963 × 75); Blake, *Liber Eliensis*, p. 85 (977 × 84); S 877 (a 'great meeting' in the 980s); S 1796 (986); S 877 (a 'great synod' in 988 × 90); *S 1382 (998); ASC MSS 'C', 'D', 'E', 'F', s.a. 1012, over Easter; election (? and coronation) of Edmund Ironside in 1016 (ASC MSS 'C', 'D', 'E', 'F'; for coronation, see *Ralph de Diceto, in Stubbs, *Opera Historica* I, 169); Florence of Worcester, in Thorpe, *Chronicon* I, 179 (1016); ? coronation of Cnut in 1017 (see *Ralph de Diceto, in Stubbs, *Opera Historica* I, 169); S 1463 (1020 × 23); *S 965 (1032); ? coronation of Harthacnut in 1040 (see *Ralph de Diceto, ibid. I, 186); election of Edward the Confessor in 1042 (ASC MSS 'E', 'F', s.a. 1041); Florence of Worcester, in Thorpe, *Chronicon* I, 199 (1044); *S 1011 (1 August '1045'); ASC MS 'E', s.a. 1047 (for 1050, mid-Lent); MS 'C', s.a. 1050 (for 1051, mid-Lent); ASC MS 'D', s.a. 1052, MS 'E', s.a. 1048, MS 'F', s.a. 1050 (for 1051, at the autumnal equinox; see also Barlow, *Life of Edward*, pp. 21–2); ASC MSS 'C', 'D', 'E', s.a. 1052, MS 'F', s.a. 1051 (for 1052, held outside London; see also Barlow, *Life of Edward*, pp. 27–8); ASC MS 'C' for 1055 (giving location) and ASC MS 'E', s.a. 1055 (giving

---

[8] See also Whitelock et al., *Anglo-Saxon Chronicle*, p. 4 n. 12.

[9] The reference in Raine, *Historians of York* II, 341, given by Plummer, *Chronicles* II, 163, is to Æthelred's coronation.

[10] For the coronation oath probably administered on this occasion, see Stubbs, *Memorials*, p. 355.

time, a week before mid-Lent); ? Florence of Worcester, in Thorpe, *Chronicon* I, 224 (Christmas 1065).

Lyminster, Sx: S 403 (5 April 930).

Milton, ?K: S 368 (903); S 417 (30 August 932).

Northampton, Nth: *ASC* MS 'C', *s.a.* 1065, in October.

Nottingham, Nt: S 407 (7 June 934); see also S 1453 (972 × ?75).

Oxford, O: *ASC* MSS 'C', 'D', 'E', 'F', *s.a.* 1015; *ASC* MSS 'C', 'D', 'E', 'F', *s.a.* 1018, and Whitelock, *EHD*, p. 452; *ASC* MS 'E', *s.a.* 1036 (for 1035, in November); *ASC* MS 'C', *s.a.* 1065, on 28 October (see also Barlow, *Life of Edward*, p. 52).

Penkridge, St: S 667 (958).

Perrott, So: S 1116 (1061 × 6).

Puddletown, Do: S 830 (976).

Shrewsbury, Sa: S 221 (901).

Slaughter, Lower and Upper, Gl: Blake, *Liber Eliensis*, p. 80 (975 × 83).

Somerton, So: S 549 (Easter 949).

Southampton, Ha: *S 360 (900 for 901) and *S 366 (901); S 369–70 (903); Florence of Worcester, in Thorpe, *Chronicon* I, 173 (1016).

Sutton, ?Berks: S 993 (1042).

Thunderfield, Sr: IV Æthelstan (924 × 39).

Wantage, Berks: III Æthelred (978 × 1008, perhaps 997); S 891 (a few days after Easter (28 March) 997).

Warminster, W: see S 1445 (899 × 924).

Weardburg (unidentified): S 225 (9 September 878, for 916).

Wellow, ?East, Ha: S 1604 (931).

Westminster, Mx: *S 894 (998); *S 1041 and *S 1043 (28 December 1066 = 1065); see *S 1110; coronation of Harold on 6 January 1066 (*ASC* MS 'E', *s.a.* 1066).[11]

Whittlebury, Nth: see VI Æthelstan 12.1 (924 × 39).

Wihtbordesstan (unidentified): IV Edgar (962 × 3).

Wilton, ?W: *S 379 (11 January 921, for 931).

Winchcombe, Gl: S 479 (942).

Winchester, Ha: *S 359 and *S 1284 (900);[12] S 385 (*c.* 909); S 425 (28 May 934);[13] S 876 (Pentecost (4 June) 993); I Cnut (1020 × 23, Christmas); coronation of Edward the Confessor on Easter Day (3 April) 1043 (*ASC* MSS 'C', 'D', *s.a.* 1043; MSS 'E', 'F', *s.a.* 1042);[14] S 1018 (1049); *KCD 815 (31 December 1065 = 1064?).

Windsor, Berks: S 1042 (24 May 1065); see also *S 1109.

[11] The *Chronicle* is not explicit about the place of Harold's coronation, but see Stenton, *Bayeux Tapestry*, p. 18.

[12] See also above, p. 270 n. 7.

[13] King Edgar commanded that a 'synodal council' be held at Winchester, probably in the closing years of his reign: see Symons, *Regularis Concordia*, pp. 2–3. S 1376 shows Edward the Martyr at Winchester, but not necessarily with any of his councillors. For a gathering at Winchester on the occasion of the rededication of the Old Minster (20 October 980), see Winterbottom, *Three Lives*, pp. 58–9.

[14] See also above, p. 270 n. 4.

Woodstock, O: I Æthelred (978 × 1008, perhaps *c.* 997); IX Æthelred (? 1008 × 16).

Woolmer, Ha: S 776 and 779 (Easter (27 March) 970); see also S 1454 (990 × 93).

Worthy, King's, Ha: S 413 (21 June 931).

York: *'John of Wallingford', in Vaughan, *John of Wallingford*, p. 54 (966); see also *William of Malmesbury, in Stubbs, *De Gestis Regum Anglorum* I, 149 (924 × 39), and Whitelock, *EHD*, p. 344 n. 5 (936).

ABBREVIATIONS AND BIBLIOGRAPHY OF
WORKS CITED

Adams, H., et al., Essays in Anglo-Saxon Law (Boston, 1905)

Arnold, T., ed., Henrici Archidiaconi Huntendunensis Historia Anglorum, Rolls Series (London, 1879)

ed., Symeonis Monachi Opera Omnia, 2 vols., Rolls Series (London, 1882–5)

Ashdown, M., English and Norse Documents Relating to the Reign of Ethelred the Unready (Cambridge, 1930)

Barker, E. E., 'Sussex Anglo-Saxon Charters', Sussex Archaeological Collections 88 (1949), 51–113

'The Anglo-Saxon Chronicle used by Æthelweard', Bulletin of the Institute of Historical Research 40 (1967), 74–91

'Two Lost Documents of King Athelstan', Anglo-Saxon England 6 (1977), 137–43

'The Bromley Charters', Archæologia Cantiana 93 (1978 for 1977), 179–85

Barlow, F., ed., The Life of King Edward (London, 1962)

Edward the Confessor (London, 1970)

The English Church 1000–1066, 2nd edn (London, 1979)

Barraclough, G., 'The Anglo-Saxon Writ', History 39 (1954), 193–215

Bates, the Rev. E. H., ed., Two Cartularies of the Benedictine Abbeys of Muchelney and Athelney in the County of Somerset, Somerset Record Society 14 (1899)

BCS: Birch, W. de G., Cartularium Saxonicum, 3 vols. (London, 1885–93)

Beckwith, J., Ivory Carvings in Early Medieval England (London, 1972)

Bethurum [Loomis], D., The Homilies of Wulfstan (Oxford, 1957)

'Wulfstan', Continuations and Beginnings, ed. E. G. Stanley (London, 1966), 210–46

'Regnum and Sacerdotium in the Early Eleventh Century', England before the Conquest, ed. P. Clemoes and K. Hughes (Cambridge, 1971), 129–45

Biddle, M., ed., Winchester in the Early Middle Ages, Winchester Studies 1 (Oxford, 1976)

Birch, W. de G., ed., Liber Vitae: Register and Martyrology of New Minster and Hyde Abbey, Winchester (Hampshire Record Society, 1892)

Birkeli, F., 'The Earliest Missionary Activities from England to Norway', Nottingham Mediaeval Studies 15 (1971), 27–37

Bishop, T.A.M., 'A Charter of King Edwy', Bodleian Library Record 6 (1957), 369–73

'Notes on Cambridge Manuscripts, Part IV: MSS. Connected with St. Aug-

Bibliography

ustine's Canterbury', *Transactions of the Cambridge Bibliographical Society* 2 (1957), 323–36

'Notes on Cambridge Manuscripts, Part VII: The Early Minuscule of Christ Church Canterbury', *Transactions of the Cambridge Bibliographical Society* 3 (1963), 413–23

'The Copenhagen Gospel Book', *Nordisk Tidskrift för Bok- och Biblioteksväsen* 54 (1967), 33–41

English Caroline Minuscule (Oxford, 1971)

Bishop, T.A.M., and P. Chaplais, ed., *Facsimiles of English Royal Writs to A.D. 1100* (Oxford, 1957)

Blake, E.O., ed., *Liber Eliensis*, Camden Third Series 92 (London, 1962)

Blake, N.F., *The Saga of the Jomsvikings* (London, 1962)

Blunt, C.E., 'The Coinage of Athelstan, 924–939', *British Numismatic Journal* 42 (1974), 35–160

Braekman, W., 'Wyrdwriteras: an Unpublished Ælfrician Text in Manuscript Hatton 115', *Revue belge de philologie et d'histoire* 44 (1966), 959–70

Brewer, J.S., ed., *Registrum Malmesburiense* I, Rolls Series (London, 1879)

Britton, J., ed., *Aubrey's Natural History of Wiltshire* (London, 1847)

Brøgger, A.W., and H. Shetelig, *The Viking Ships. Their Ancestry and Evolution* (repr. London, 1971)

Brooke, C., *The Saxon and Norman Kings* (London, 1963)

Brooks, N., 'Anglo-Saxon Charters: the Work of the Last Twenty Years', *Anglo-Saxon England* 3 (1974), 211–31

'England in the Ninth Century: The Crucible of Defeat', *Transactions of the Royal Historical Society* 5th ser. 29 (1979), 1–20

Bruckner, A., and R. Marichal, *Chartae Latinae Antiquiores* III–IV (Olten and Lausanne, 1963–7)

Buckalew, R.E., 'Leland's Transcript of Ælfric's *Glossary*', *Anglo-Saxon England* 7 (1978), 149–64

Bullough, D.A., 'The Educational Tradition in England from Alfred to Ælfric: Teaching *Utriusque Linguae*', *Settimane di Studio del Centro Italiano di Studi sull'Alto Medioevo* 19 (1972), 453–94

Butler, V.J., 'The Metrology of the Late Anglo-Saxon Penny: the Reigns of Æthelræd II and Cnut', *Anglo-Saxon Coins*, ed. R.H.M. Dolley (London, 1961), 195–214

Cameron, K., *The Place-Names of Derbyshire*, 3 vols., English Place-Name Society 27–9 (Cambridge, 1959)

Campbell, A., ed., *Encomium Emmae Reginae*, Camden Third Series 72 (London, 1949)

ed., *Frithegodi Monachi Breuiloquium Vitæ Beati Wilfredi et Wulfstani Cantoris Narratio Metrica de Sancto Swithuno* (Zürich, 1950)

ed., *The Chronicle of Æthelweard* (London, 1962)

Skaldic Verse and Anglo-Saxon History, Dorothea Coke Memorial Lecture (London, 1971)

ed., *Charters of Rochester*, Anglo-Saxon Charters I (London, 1973)

Bibliography

Campbell, J., 'England, France and Germany: Some Comparisons and Connections', *Ethelred the Unready: Papers from the Millenary Conference*, ed. D. Hill, British Archaeological Reports, British Series 59 (1978), 255–70

Carnicelli, T.A., ed., *King Alfred's Version of St Augustine's* Soliloquies (Harvard, 1969)

Chaney, W.A., *The Cult of Kingship in Anglo-Saxon England* (Manchester, 1970)

Chaplais, P., 'The Authenticity of the Royal Anglo-Saxon Diplomas of Exeter', *Bulletin of the Institute of Historical Research* 39 (1966), 1–34

  'The Origin and Authenticity of the Royal Anglo-Saxon Diploma', repr. in *Prisca Munimenta*, ed. F. Ranger (London, 1973), 28–42

  'The Anglo-Saxon Chancery: from the Diploma to the Writ', repr. in *Prisca Munimenta*, ed. F. Ranger (London, 1973), 43–62

  'Some Early Anglo-Saxon Diplomas on Single Sheets: Originals or Copies?', repr. in *Prisca Munimenta*, ed. F. Ranger (London, 1973), 63–87

Cheney, C.R., *Medieval Texts and Studies* (Oxford, 1973)

Chrimes, S.B., *An Introduction to the Administrative History of Mediaeval England*, 3rd edn (Oxford, 1966)

Clanchy, M.T., *From Memory to Written Record. England 1066–1307* (London, 1979)

Clemoes, P.A.M., 'The Chronology of Ælfric's Works', *The Anglo-Saxons*, ed. P. Clemoes (London, 1959), 212–47

  'Ælfric', *Continuations and Beginnings*, ed. E.G. Stanley (London, 1966), 176–209

Cramp, R., 'Anglo-Saxon Sculpture of the Reform Period', *Tenth-Century Studies*, ed. D. Parsons (Chichester, 1975), 184–99

Crawford, S.J., ed., *Byrhtferth's Manual (A.D. 1011)*, Early English Text Society, o.s. 177 (Oxford, 1929)

Dart, J., *The History and Antiquities of the Cathedral Church of Canterbury* (London, 1726)

Davis, H.W.C., *Regesta Regum Anglo-Normannorum* I (Oxford, 1913)

Day, V., 'The Influence of the Catechetical *Narratio* on Old English and some other Medieval Literature', *Anglo-Saxon England* 3 (1974), 51–61

DB: *Domesday Book*, ed. Abraham Farley, 2 vols. (London, 1783)

Dickins, B., 'The Day of Byrhtnoth's Death and other Obits from a Twelfth-Century Ely Kalendar', *Leeds Studies in English* 6 (1937), 14–24

  'The Day of the Battle of Æthelingadene (ASC 1001 A)', *Leeds Studies in English* 6 (1937), 25–7

Dobbie, E. van K., ed., *The Anglo-Saxon Minor Poems*, Anglo-Saxon Poetic Records 6 (New York, 1942)

Dodwell, B., ed., *The Charters of Norwich Cathedral Priory* I, Pipe Roll Society, n.s. 40 (London, 1974)

Dolley, R.H.M., 'The Shaftesbury Hoard of Pence of Æthelræd II', *Numismatic Chronicle* 6th ser. 16 (1956), 267–80

  'Some Reflections on Hildebrand Type A of Æthelræd II', *Antikvariskt Arkiv* 9 (1958), 1–41

  The Hiberno-Norse Coins in the British Museum, Sylloge of Coins of the British Isles 8 (London, 1966)

Bibliography

'Æthelræd's Rochester Ravaging of 986 – an Intriguing Numismatic Sidelight', *Spink's Numismatic Circular* 75 (1967), 33–4

'The Nummular Brooch from Sulgrave', *England before the Conquest*, ed. P. Clemoes and K. Hughes (Cambridge, 1971), 333–49

'The Coins', *The Archaeology of Anglo-Saxon England*, ed. D.M. Wilson (London, 1976), 349–72

'An Introduction to the Coinage of Æthelræd II', *Ethelred the Unready: Papers from the Millenary Conference*, ed. D. Hill, British Archaeological Reports, British Series 59 (1978), 115–33

Dolley, R.H.M., and D.M. Metcalf, 'The Reform of the English Coinage under Eadgar', *Anglo-Saxon Coins*, ed. R.H.M. Dolley (London, 1961), 136–68

Dolley, R.H.M., and T. Talvio, 'The Twelfth of the Agnus Dei Pennies of Æthelræd II', *British Numismatic Journal* 47 (1977), 131–3

Douglas, D.C., *William the Conqueror* (London, 1964)

Downer, L.J., ed., *Leges Henrici Primi* (Oxford, 1972)

Drögereit, R. 'Gab es eine angelsächsische Königskanzlei?', *Archiv für Urkundenforschung* 13 (1935), 335–436

Dugdale, W., and R. Dodsworth, *Monasticon Anglicanum* 1 (London, 1655)

Dumville, D.N., 'The Anglian Collection of Royal Genealogies and Regnal Lists', *Anglo-Saxon England* 5 (1976), 23–50

'The Ætheling: a Study in Anglo-Saxon Constitutional History', *Anglo-Saxon England* 8 (1979), 1–33

Edwards, E., ed., *Liber Monasterii de Hyda*, Rolls Series (London, 1866)

Farmer, D.H., 'Two Biographies by William of Malmesbury', *Latin Biography*, ed. T.A. Dorey (London, 1967), 157–76

Fell, C.E., *Edward King and Martyr*, Leeds Texts and Monographs, N.S. (Leeds, 1971)

'Edward King and Martyr and the Anglo-Saxon Hagiographic Tradition', *Ethelred the Unready: Papers from the Millenary Conference*, ed. D. Hill, British Archaeological Reports, British Series 59 (1978), 1–13

Fifoot, C.H.S., ed., *The Letters of Frederic William Maitland* (Cambridge, 1965)

Finberg, H.P.R., *Tavistock Abbey* (Cambridge, 1951)

'Supplement to *The Early Charters of Devon and Cornwall*', in W.G. Hoskins, *The Westward Expansion of Wessex* (Leicester, 1960), 23–35

Lucerna (London, 1964)

The Early Charters of Wessex (Leicester, 1964)

West-Country Historical Studies (Newton Abbot, 1969)

The Early Charters of the West Midlands, 2nd edn (Leicester, 1972)

Fisher, D.J.V., 'The Anti-Monastic Reaction in the Reign of Edward the Martyr', *Cambridge Historical Journal* 10 (1950–2), 254–70

Fleckenstein, J., *Die Hofkapelle der deutschen Könige I: Grundlegung. Die karolingische Hofkapelle*, Schriften der Monumenta Germaniae Historica 16, 1 (Stuttgart, 1959)

Flower, R., 'The Text of the Burghal Hidage', *London Mediæval Studies* 1 (1937), 60–4

Bibliography

Förster, M., 'Die altenglische Glossenhandschrift Plantinus 32 (Antwerpen) und Additional 32246 (London)', *Anglia* 41 (1917), 94–161

Freeman, E.A., *The History of the Norman Conquest of England, its Causes and its Results* I–II, 2nd edn (Oxford, 1870)

Galbraith, V.H., 'Monastic Foundation Charters of the Eleventh and Twelfth Centuries', *Cambridge Historical Journal* 4 (1934), 205–22, 296–8
Studies in the Public Records (London, 1948)

Gelling, M., *The Place-Names of Berkshire*, 3 vols., English Place-Name Society 49–51 (Cambridge, 1973–6)

Gem, R., 'A Recession in English Architecture during the Early Eleventh Century, and its Effect on the Development of the Romanesque Style', *Journal of the British Archaeological Association* 38 (1975), 28–49

Gibbs, M., ed., *Early Charters of the Cathedral Church of St. Paul, London*, Camden Third Series 48 (London, 1939)

Gibson, E., *Reliquiæ Spelmannianæ. The Posthumous Works of Sir Henry Spelman Kt. Relating to the Laws and Antiquities of England* (Oxford, 1698)

Giry, A., *Manuel de diplomatique* (Paris, 1894)

Gjerløw, L., *Adoratio Crucis. The Regularis Concordia and the Decreta Lanfranci. Manuscript Studies in the Early Medieval Church of Norway* (Oslo, 1961)

Gordon, E.V., 'The Date of Æthelred's Treaty with the Vikings: Olaf Tryggvason and the Battle of Maldon', *Modern Language Review* 32 (1937), 24–32

Gover, J.E.B., A. Mawer and F.M. Stenton, *The Place-Names of Wiltshire*, English Place-Name Society 16 (Cambridge, 1939)

Gransden, A., *Historical Writing in England c. 550 to c. 1307* (London, 1974)

Haddan, A.W., and W. Stubbs, ed., *Councils and Ecclesiastical Documents*, 3 vols. (Oxford, 1869–71)

Hall, H., *Studies in English Official Historical Documents* (Cambridge, 1908)

Hamilton, N.E.S.A., ed., *Willelmi Malmesbiriensis Monachi De Gestis Pontificum Anglorum Libri Quinque*, Rolls Series (London, 1870)

Hardwick, C., ed., *Historia Monasterii S. Augustini Cantuariensis, by Thomas of Elmham*, Rolls Series (London, 1858)

Harmer, F.E., ed., *Select English Historical Documents of the Ninth and Tenth Centuries* (Cambridge, 1914)
Anglo-Saxon Writs (Manchester, 1952)

Harrison, K., *The Framework of Anglo-Saxon History to A.D. 900* (Cambridge, 1976)

Hart, C.R., 'Eadnoth, First Abbot of Ramsey, and the Foundation of Chatteris and St Ives', *Proceedings of the Cambridge Antiquarian Society* 56–7 (1964), 61–7
The Early Charters of Eastern England (Leicester, 1966)
'The Site of Assandun', *History Studies* I (1968), 1–12
The Hidation of Northamptonshire (Leicester, 1970)
'The *Codex Wintoniensis* and the King's *Haligdom*', *Land, Church, and People*, ed. J. Thirsk (Reading, 1970), 7–38
'Danelaw Charters and the Glastonbury Scriptorium', *Downside Review* 90 (1972), 125–32
'Athelstan "Half King" and his Family', *Anglo-Saxon England* 2 (1973), 115–44

Bibliography

The Early Charters of Northern England and the North Midlands (Leicester, 1975)
'Two Queens of England', *Ampleforth Journal* 82 (1977), 10–15, 54
Harvey, B., *Westminster Abbey and its Estates in the Middle Ages* (Oxford, 1977)
Hearne, T., ed., *Hemingi Chartularium Ecclesiæ Wigorniensis* (Oxford, 1723)
    ed., *Adami de Domerham Historia de Rebus Gestis Glastoniensibus*, 2 vols. (Oxford, 1727)
Hollister, C.W., *Anglo-Saxon Military Institutions on the Eve of the Norman Conquest* (Oxford, 1962)
Hurt, J., *Ælfric* (New York, 1972)
Indrebø, G., ed., *Sverris Saga* (Kristiania, 1920)
James, M.R., *A Descriptive Catalogue of the Manuscripts in the Library of Corpus Christi College Cambridge*, 2 vols. (Cambridge, 1912)
James, M.R., and C. Jenkins, *Descriptive Catalogue of the MSS. in the Library of Lambeth Palace* (Cambridge, 1955)
Jansson, S.B.F., *Swedish Vikings in England. The Evidence of the Rune Stones*, Dorothea Coke Memorial Lecture (London, 1966)
John, E., *Land Tenure in Early England* (Leicester, 1960)
    Orbis Britanniae (Leicester, 1966)
    'War and Society in the Tenth Century: the Maldon Campaign', *Transactions of the Royal Historical Society* 5th ser. 27 (1977), 173–95
Johnson, C., ed. and trans., *Dialogus de Scaccario* (London, 1950)
Jones, G., *A History of the Vikings* (Oxford, 1968)
Jost, K., *Wulfstanstudien*, Swiss Studies in English 23 (Bern, 1950)
KCD: Kemble, J.M., *Codex Diplomaticus Aevi Saxonici*, 6 vols. (London, 1839–48)
Kemble, J.M., *The Saxons in England*, 2 vols. (London, 1849)
Ker, N.R., 'Hemming's Cartulary: a Description of the Two Worcester Cartularies in Cotton Tiberius A xiii', *Studies in Medieval History presented to Frederick Maurice Powicke*, ed. R.W. Hunt, W.A. Pantin and R.W. Southern (Oxford, 1948), 49–75
    Catalogue of Manuscripts Containing Anglo-Saxon (Oxford, 1957)
Keynes, S.D., 'Studies on Anglo-Saxon Royal Diplomas', 2 vols., unpublished Fellowship thesis, Trinity College, Cambridge (1976)
    'An Interpretation of the *Pacx*, *Pax* and *Paxs* Pennies', *Anglo-Saxon England* 7 (1978), 165–73
    'The Declining Reputation of King Æthelred the Unready', *Ethelred the Unready: Papers from the Millenary Conference*, ed. D. Hill, British Archaeological Reports, British Series 59 (1978), 227–53
King, E., *Peterborough Abbey 1086–1310* (Cambridge, 1973)
Kirby, D.P., *The Making of Early England* (London, 1967)
Klewitz, H. W., 'Cancellaria. Ein Beitrag zur Geschichte des geistlichen Hofdienstes', repr. in *Ausgewählte Aufsätze zur Kirchen- und Geistesgeschichte des Mittelalters* (Aalen, 1971), 13–48
Kluge, F., 'Angelsächsische Glossen', *Anglia* 8 (1885), 448–52
Knowles, Dom D., *The Monastic Order in England*, 2nd edn (Cambridge, 1963)

Bibliography

Knowles, Dom D., C.N.L. Brooke and V.C.M. London, *The Heads of Religious Houses. England and Wales. 940–1216* (Cambridge, 1972)

Korhammer, P.M., 'The Origin of the Bosworth Psalter', *Anglo-Saxon England* 2 (1973), 173–87

Ladd, C.A., 'The "Rubens" Manuscript and *Archbishop Ælfric's Vocabulary*', *Review of English Studies* N.S. 11 (1960), 353–64

Lapidge, M., 'Some Remnants of Bede's Lost "Liber Epigrammatum" ', *English Historical Review* 90 (1975), 798–820

'The Hermeneutic Style in Tenth-Century Anglo-Latin Literature', *Anglo-Saxon England* 4 (1975), 67–111

Larson, L.M., *The King's Household in England before the Norman Conquest* (Madison, 1904)

Le Patourel, J., *The Norman Empire* (Oxford, 1976)

Levison, W., *England and the Continent in the Eighth Century* (Oxford, 1946)

Liebermann, F., *Die Gesetze der Angelsachsen*, 3 vols. (Halle, 1903–16)

The National Assembly in the Anglo-Saxon Period (Halle, 1913)

Loyn, H.R., *Anglo-Saxon England and the Norman Conquest* (London, 1962)

'Church and State in England in the Tenth and Eleventh Centuries', *Tenth-Century Studies*, ed. D. Parsons (Chichester, 1975), 94–102

The Vikings in Britain (London, 1977)

Luard, H.R., ed., *Annales Monastici*, 5 vols., Rolls Series (London, 1864–9)

Lund, N., 'King Edgar and the Danelaw', *Medieval Scandinavia* 9 (1976), 181–95

Lyon, S., 'Some Problems in Interpreting Anglo-Saxon Coinage', *Anglo-Saxon England* 5 (1976), 173–224

Macray, W.D., ed., *Chronicon Abbatiæ de Evesham*, Rolls Series (London, 1863)

Maitland, F.W., *Domesday Book and Beyond* (Cambridge, 1897)

Mawer, A., and F.M. Stenton, *The Place-Names of Sussex*, 2 vols., English Place-Name Society 6–7 (Cambridge, 1929–30)

Mellows, W.T., ed., *The Chronicle of Hugh Candidus* (Oxford, 1949)

Metcalf, D.M., 'The Ranking of Boroughs: Numismatic Evidence from the Reign of Æthelred II', *Ethelred the Unready: Papers from the Millenary Conference*, ed. D. Hill, British Archaeological Reports, British Series 59 (1978), 159–212

Meyer, M.A., 'Women and the Tenth Century English Monastic Reform', *Revue Bénédictine* 87 (1977), 34–61

Migne, J.P., ed., *Patrologiæ Cursus Completus. Series (Latina) Prima*, 221 vols. (Paris, 1844–64)

Miller, E., *The Abbey and Bishopric of Ely* (Cambridge, 1951)

Morris, W.A., *The Medieval English Sheriff to 1300* (Manchester, 1927)

Napier, A.S., and W.H. Stevenson, ed., *The Crawford Collection of Early Charters and Documents* (Oxford, 1895)

Nelson, J.L., 'Inauguration Rituals', *Early Medieval Kingship*, ed. P.H. Sawyer and I.N. Wood (Leeds, 1977), 50–71

O'Donovan, M.A., 'An Interim Revision of Episcopal Dates for the Province of Canterbury, 850–950: Part I', *Anglo-Saxon England* 1 (1972), 23–44

Bibliography

'An Interim Revision of Episcopal Dates for the Province of Canterbury, 850–950: Part II', *Anglo-Saxon England* 2 (1973), 91–113

Okasha, E., *Hand-List of Anglo-Saxon Non-Runic Inscriptions* (Cambridge, 1971)

Oleson, T.J., *The Witenagemot in the Reign of Edward the Confessor* (Toronto, 1955)

Olsen, O., 'Viking Fortresses in Denmark', *Recent Archaeological Excavations in Europe*, ed. R. Bruce-Mitford (London, 1975), 90–110

Olsen, O., and O. Crumlin-Pedersen, 'The Skuldelev Ships (II)', *Acta Archaeologica* 38 (Copenhagen, 1967), 73–174

Olsen, O., and H. Schmidt, *Fyrkat. En jysk Vikingeborg I: Borgen og bebyggelsen* (Copenhagen, 1977)

O.S. Facs.: Sanders, W.B., *Facsimiles of Anglo-Saxon Manuscripts*, 3 vols., Ordnance Survey (Southampton, 1878–84)

Owst, G.R., *Preaching in Medieval England* (Cambridge, 1926)

Parkes, M.B., 'The Palaeography of the Parker Manuscript of the *Chronicle*, Laws and Sedulius, and Historiography at Winchester in the Late Ninth and Tenth Centuries', *Anglo-Saxon England* 5 (1976), 149–71

Parsons, M.P., 'Some Scribal Memoranda for Anglo-Saxon Charters of the 8th and 9th Centuries', *Mitteilungen des Österreichischen Instituts für Geschichtsforschung*, 14 Erg. Bd. (1939), 13–32

Petersson, H.B.A., *Anglo-Saxon Currency: King Edgar's Reform to the Norman Conquest*, Bibliotheca Historica Lundensis 22 (Lund, 1969)

Plummer, C., ed., *Two of the Saxon Chronicles Parallel*, 2 vols. (Oxford, 1892–9)

Poole, R.L., *Lectures on the History of the Papal Chancery down to the Time of Innocent III* (Cambridge, 1915)

Pope, J.C., ed., *Homilies of Ælfric: a Supplementary Collection*, 2 vols., Early English Text Society, o.s. 259–60 (London, 1967–8)

Powicke, Sir F.M., and E.B. Fryde, ed., *Handbook of British Chronology*, Royal Historical Society Guides and Handbooks 2, 2nd edn (London, 1961)

Raban, S., *The Estates of Thorney and Crowland* (University of Cambridge, Department of Land Economy, 1977)

Raftis, J.A., *The Estates of Ramsey Abbey* (Toronto, 1957)

Raine, J., ed., *The Historians of the Church of York and its Archbishops*, 3 vols., Rolls Series (London, 1879–94)

Richardson, H.G., and G.O. Sayles, *Law and Legislation from Æthelberht to Magna Carta* (Edinburgh, 1966)

Riley, H.T., ed., *Gesta Abbatum Monasterii Sancti Albani*, 3 vols., Rolls Series (London, 1867–9)

Robertson, A.J., ed., *Anglo-Saxon Charters* (Cambridge, 1939)

Robinson, J.A., ed., *John Flete's History of Westminster Abbey* (Cambridge, 1909)
Gilbert Crispin, Abbot of Westminster (Cambridge, 1911)
Somerset Historical Essays (London, 1921)
The Times of Saint Dunstan (Oxford, 1923)

Roesdahl, E., *Fyrkat. En jysk Vikingeborg II: Oldsagerne og gravpladsen* (Copenhagen, 1977)

Round, J.H., *Feudal England* (London, 1909)

Bibliography

Salter, H E., ed., *The Cartulary of the Abbey of Eynsham*, 2 vols., Oxford Historical Society 49, 51 (Oxford, 1907–8)

Sawyer, P.H., *Anglo-Saxon Charters. An Annotated List and Bibliography*, Royal Historical Society Guides and Handbooks 8 (London, 1968)

The Age of the Vikings, 2nd edn (London, 1971)

'Charters of the Reform Movement: the Worcester Archive', *Tenth-Century Studies*, ed. D. Parsons (Chichester, 1975), 84–93

From Roman Britain to Norman England (London, 1978)

ed., *Charters of Burton Abbey*, Anglo-Saxon Charters II (London, 1979)

Scholz, B.W., 'Sulcard of Westminster: "Prologus de Construccione West-monasterii" ', *Traditio* 20 (1964), 59–91

Sheerin, D.J., 'The Dedication of the Old Minster, Winchester, in 980', *Revue Bénédictine* 88 (1978), 261–73

Sisam, K., *Studies in the History of Old English Literature* (Oxford, 1953)

Skeat, W.W., ed., *Ælfric's Lives of Saints*, 4 vols., Early English Text Society, o.s. 76, 82, 94, 114 (Oxford, 1881–1900)

Smith, A.H., *English Place-Name Elements*, 2 vols., English Place-Name Society 25–6 (Cambridge, 1956)

Stafford, P., 'Sons and Mothers: Family Politics in the Early Middle Ages', *Medieval Women*, ed. D. Baker, Studies in Church History, Subsidia I (Oxford, 1978), 79–100

'The Reign of Æthelred II, A Study in the Limitations on Royal Policy and Action', *Ethelred the Unready: Papers from the Millenary Conference*, ed. D. Hill, British Archaeological Reports, British Series 59 (1978), 15–46

Stenton, F.M., *The Early History of the Abbey of Abingdon* (Reading, 1913)

The Latin Charters of the Anglo-Saxon Period (Oxford, 1955)

ed., *The Bayeux Tapestry* (London, 1957)

'The Danes in England', *Preparatory to Anglo-Saxon England*, ed. D.M. Stenton (Oxford, 1970), 136–65

'St. Frideswide and her Times', *Preparatory to Anglo-Saxon England*, ed. D.M. Stenton (Oxford, 1970), 224–33

Anglo-Saxon England, 3rd edn (Oxford, 1971)

Stephens, W.R.W., and F.T. Madge, ed., *Documents Relating to the History of the Cathedral Church of Winchester, A.D. 1636–83* (Hampshire Record Society, 1897)

Stevenson, J., ed., *Chronicon Monasterii de Abingdon*, 2 vols., Rolls Series (London, 1858)

Stevenson, W.H., 'An Old English Charter of William the Conqueror in Favour of St Martin's-Le-Grand, London, A.D. 1068', *English Historical Review* 11 (1896), 731–44

ed., *Asser's Life of King Alfred* (Oxford, 1904)

Stowell, T.E.A., 'The Bones of Edward the Martyr', *Criminologist* 5 (1970), 97–119

Stubbs, W., ed., *Memorials of Saint Dunstan*, Rolls Series (London, 1874)

ed., *Radulfi de Diceto Decani Lundoniensis Opera Historica*, 2 vols., Rolls Series (London, 1876)

Bibliography

ed., *Willelmi Malmesbiriensis Monachi De Gestis Regum Anglorum Libri Quinque*, 2 vols., Rolls Series (London, 1887-9)

Symons, Dom T., ed., *The Regularis Concordia* (London, 1953)

Taylor, C.S., 'The Origin of the Mercian Shires', *Gloucestershire Studies*, ed. H.P.R. Finberg (Leicester, 1957), 17-45

Temple, E., *Anglo-Saxon Manuscripts 900-1066*, Survey of Manuscripts Illuminated in the British Isles 2 (London, 1976)

Tengvik, G., *Old English Bynames*, Nomina Germanica 4 (Uppsala, 1938)

Tessier, G., *Diplomatique royale française* (Paris, 1962)

Thompson, E.M., 'Ælfric's Vocabulary', *Journal of the British Archaeological Association* 41 (1885), 144-52

Thorpe, B., *The Homilies of the Anglo-Saxon Church*, 2 vols. (London, 1844-6)

ed., *Florentii Wigorniensis Monachi Chronicon ex Chronicis*, 2 vols. (London, 1848-9)

Diplomatarium Anglicum Ævi Saxonici (London, 1865)

Tolhurst, J.B.L., ed., *The Monastic Breviary of Hyde Abbey, Winchester* v, Henry Bradshaw Society (London, 1934)

Toller, T.N., *An Anglo-Saxon Dictionary. Supplement* (Oxford, 1921)

Tonnochy, A.B., *Catalogue of British Seal Dies in the British Museum* (London, 1952)

Tschan, F.J., *Adam of Bremen. History of the Archbishops of Hamburg-Bremen* (New York, 1959)

Vaughan, R., ed., *The Chronicle Attributed to John of Wallingford*, Camden Third Series 90 (London, 1958)

von Feilitzen, O., *The Pre-Conquest Personal Names of Domesday Book* (Uppsala, 1937)

Ward, G., 'The Witan Meets at Canterbury', *Archæologia Cantiana* 69 (1955), 41-61

Warren, F.E., ed., *The Leofric Missal* (Oxford, 1883)

Watkin, Dom A., ed., *The Great Chartulary of Glastonbury*, 3 vols., Somerset Record Society 59, 63-4 (1947-56)

Wharton, H., *Anglia Sacra*, 2 vols. (London, 1691)

Whelock, A., ed., *Historiæ Ecclesiasticæ Gentis Anglorum Libri V* (Cambridge, 1643)

Whitelock, D., ed., *Anglo-Saxon Wills* (Cambridge, 1930)

'Two Notes on Ælfric and Wulfstan', *Modern Language Review* 38 (1943), 122-6

'The Dealings of the Kings of England with Northumbria in the Tenth and Eleventh Centuries', *The Anglo-Saxons*, ed. P. Clemoes (London, 1959), 70-88

ed., *Sermo Lupi ad Anglos*, 3rd edn (London, 1963)

'Archbishop Wulfstan, Homilist and Statesman', repr. in *Essays in Medieval History*, ed. R.W. Southern (London, 1968), 42-60

The Will of Æthelgifu (Oxford, 1968)

'The Authorship of the Account of King Edgar's Establishment of Monasteries', *Philological Essays in Honour of Herbert Dean Meritt*, ed. J. L. Rosier (The Hague, 1970), 125-36

Bibliography

'The Appointment of Dunstan as Archbishop of Canterbury', *Otium et Negotium*, ed. F. Sandgren (Stockholm, 1973), 232–47

Some Anglo-Saxon Bishops of London, Chambers Memorial Lecture 1974 (London, 1975)

ed., *English Historical Documents c. 500–1042*, 2nd edn (London, 1979)

'Some Charters in the Name of King Alfred', *Saints Scholars and Heroes. Studies in Medieval Culture in Honour of Charles W. Jones*, ed. Margot H. King and Wesley M. Stevens, 2 vols. (Minnesota, 1979), I, 77–98

Whitelock, D., D.C. Douglas and S.I. Tucker, ed., *The Anglo-Saxon Chronicle. A Revised Translation*, 2nd imp. (London, 1965)

Wigram, S.R., ed., *The Cartulary of the Monastery of St. Frideswide at Oxford*, 2 vols., Oxford Historical Society 28, 31 (Oxford, 1895–6)

Wilson, D.M., *Anglo-Saxon Ornamental Metalwork 700–1100 in the British Museum*, Catalogue of Antiquities of the Later Saxon Period I (London, 1964)

Wilson, H.A., ed., *The Missal of Robert of Jumièges*, Henry Bradshaw Society (London, 1896)

Wilson, R.M., *The Lost Literature of Medieval England*, 2nd edn (London, 1970)

Winterbottom, M., 'The Style of Aethelweard', *Medium Ævum* 36 (1967), 109–18

ed., *Three Lives of English Saints* (Toronto, 1972)

Wormald, F., 'The Sherborne "Chartulary"', *Knowledge and Learning*, ed. D.J. Gordon (London, 1957), 101–19

Wormald, P., 'The Uses of Literacy in Anglo-Saxon England and its Neighbours', *Transactions of the Royal Historical Society* 5th ser. 27 (1977), 95–114

'Æthelred the Lawmaker', *Ethelred the Unready: Papers from the Millenary Conference*, ed. D. Hill, British Archaeological Reports, British Series 59 (1978), 47–80

Wright, T., *Anglo-Saxon and Old English Vocabularies*, 2nd edn, ed. and collated by R.P. Wülcker, 2 vols. (London, 1884)

Zupitza, J., *Ælfrics Grammatik und Glossar* (Berlin, 1880)

INDEX TO CITATIONS OF
THE DIPLOMAS OF KING ÆTHELRED

Index

GENERAL INDEX

abbots: appointment of, 157 n. 9; as witnesses to royal diplomas, 49 n. 93, 90 n. 24, 91, 94, 101, 115 n. 108, 118, 152 n. 240, 156–7, 182, 236

Abbotsbury Abbey: diplomas from (cited from lost cartulary), 9, 34 n. 58, 69 n. 135, 94, 141, 142 n. 208

Abingdon Abbey: cartularies of, 67 n. 127, (B.L. Cotton Claudius B vi) 10–13, 96 n. 42, 234, (B.L. Cotton Claudius C ix) 6 n. 5, 10–12, 96 n. 42, 234, (eleventh-century diplomas in) 140–1, (writs in) 143; diplomas from, (classification of) 10–13, (drawn up at Abingdon) 22, (suspicious groups of) 74 n. 149, 75 n. 152, 98–100, 107 n. 68, 199 n. 167, (a type of formulation in) 114 n. 99, (use of *dictavi* in) 27; land appropriated from, 177–8; manuscripts from, (glossary) 145–7, 149, 152, (with obits) 239 n. 22, 260 n. 55; scribe assigned to scriptorium of, 68 n. 132, *see also* 'Edgar A'

Ælfgar, king's reeve (*fl.* 980s), 183–4

Ælfgar, king's reeve (*fl.* 1007), 127, 183 n. 110

Ælfgar, *minister*, 180, 183–4, 186, 188

Ælfgar, son of Ealdorman Ælfric, 184

Ælfgar Mæw, 209, 227 n. 265

Ælfgifu, first wife of King Æthelred, 187

Ælfheah, bishop of Winchester (died 951), 17

Ælfheah, bishop of Winchester, archbishop of Canterbury, 102, 131 n. 161, 182, 221, 262

Ælfhelm, ealdorman of Northumbria: appointment of, 197; subscriptions of, 132 n. 165, 158 n. 11, 189, 210, 213; murder of, 211, 213, 214

Ælfhelm Polga, 249

Ælfhere, ealdorman of Mercia: his alleged complicity in King Edward the Martyr's murder, 169, 172–3; subscriptions of, 50, 87, 157, 175 n. 84; translated King Edward the Martyr's remains, 166, 170, 172–3, 214 n. 216

Ælfhun, bishop of London, 156 n. 8, 267

Ælfric, seal of, 139, 140 n. 199

Ælfric, abbot of Eynsham, homilist: and Archbishop Sigeric, 190; on beginning of year, 232 n. 1; correspondents of, 193 n. 143; and Ealdorman Æthelweard, 192; glossary by, 146, 159; on king's *gewrit*, 136–7; on king's household, 158; on royal consecration, 174; *Life* of St Æthelwold by, 200; *Wyrdwriteras* attributed to, 206–8

Ælfric, abbot of St Albans, bishop of Ramsbury, archbishop of Canterbury, 137, 138; as archbishop, 119 n. 115, 120 n. 119, 128; as '*cancellarius*' of King Æthelred, 136; elegaic verse on, 260 n. 55; subscriptions of, 120, 131 n. 161, 235 n. 15, 252, 253, 260; will of, 109 n. 75, 124 n. 132, 225 n. 257, 261

Ælfric, brother of Eadric Streona, 212

Ælfric, ealdorman of Hampshire, 197; and Abingdon Abbey, 177; and Glastonbury Abbey?, 182 n. 104; and payments of tribute, 202 n. 182; subscriptions of, 157, 213–14; treachery of, 184, 205–6

Ælfric, ealdorman of Mercia, 177 n. 91, 182 n. 104, 197 n. 163; subscriptions of, 87, 131 n. 160, (as *minister*) 182 n. 104; banishment of, 128 n. 146, 244

Ælfsige, abbot of New Minster Winchester, 191, 262

Ælfsige, bishop of Chester-le-Street, 250

Ælfsige, *minister*, 183, 188

Ælfstan, bishop of London, 179 n. 99, 252 n. 42

Ælfstan, bishop of Ramsbury, 239

Ælfstan, bishop of Rochester, 132 n. 163, 178–9, 182, 252

Ælfthryth, queen, wife of King Edgar, mother of King Æthelred, 104, 138, 174; and the disputed succession in 975, 164–6; her alleged complicity in King Edward the Martyr's murder, 167–74; sub-

288

Index